AN AWAKENED MINORITY:

THE [partially obscured] ANS

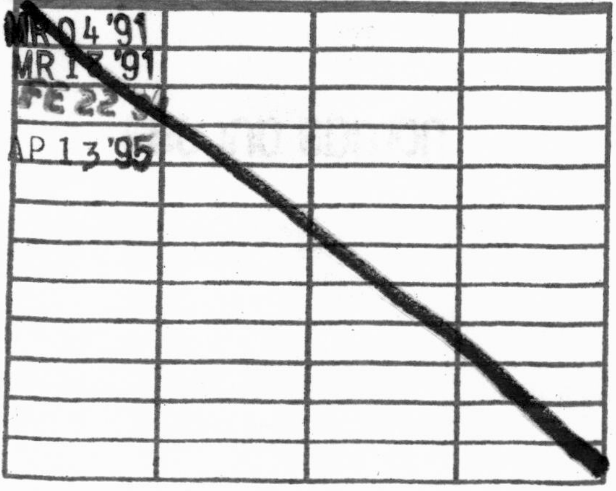

AN AWAKENED MINORITY:

THE MEXICAN-AMERICANS

SECOND EDITION

Manuel P. Servín

Professor of Southwest and Mexican History
and
Co-ordinator, American Studies Program
Arizona State University

GLENCOE PRESS

A division of Benziger Bruce & Glencoe, Inc.
Beverly Hills

Printed in the United States of America.

Earlier edition entitled The Mexican-Americans: An Awakening Minority.

Glencoe Press
A division of Benziger Bruce & Glencoe, Inc.
8701 Wilshire Boulevard
Beverly Hills, California 90211
Collier-Macmillan Canada, Ltd.

Library of Congress catalog card number: 73-8357

First Printing, 1974

Contents

Preface

In 1969 when I wrote the preface for *The Mexican-Americans: An Awakening Minority,* I noted that Mexican-Americans were "the most historically neglected and ignored group of all the peoples who make up our great nation," that we possessed "not one embracing historical survey," and that there were "only one or two scholarly articles in historical journals." Now, four years later, as I write the preface to this new edition I realize—as the title indicates—how much progress has been accomplished in this brief period.

Since that date, historical literature on the Mexican-American has appeared in substantial volume. Two fine historical surveys, *The Chicanos: A History of Mexican-Americans* by Matt S. Meier and Feliciano Rivera and *Occupied America: The Chicano's Struggle Toward Liberation* by Rodolfo Acuña, were both published in 1972, filling a most important role in the literature of United States history. Excellent articles have also appeared since then in such solid, scholarly periodicals as *The Journal of Mexican-American History, Aztlán: Chicano Journal of Social Sciences,* and the *Pacific Historical Review.* Consequently, insofar as historical research and writing is concerned, the Mexican-American has awakened despite the hesitance of Anglo-American historians to incorporate these new contributions into their lectures and writings.

Mexican-Americans have awakened also in the historical academic field. A new generation of Mexican-American historians has appeared upon the scene. Scholarly historians such as Rodolfo Acuña, Feliciano Rivera, Juan Goméz-Quiñones, Carlos Cortés, Enrique Cortés, Raoul Isáis, Guillermo Lux, Enrique Orozco, Féliz D. Almaraz, Jr., Frank Cruz, Salomé Hernández, Joseph P. Sánchez, and Joseph Peter Navarro

—to mention but a few—are now making their presence felt in institutions of higher education.

Of course the Mexican-American has also matured and awakened in fields other than that of history. Their leaders in such areas as labor, social action, and politics have gained experience and are nationally recognized. Undoubtedly the most distinguished and famous is César Chávez of the United Farm Workers Organizing Committee. Not as well known but almost as influential are the crusaders Reies López Tijerina of New Mexico and Rodolfo "Corky" Gonzales of Colorado, and the politicians José Angel Gutiérrez of the Raza Unida political party in Texas and Raúl Hector Castro of the Democratic party in Arizona.

In addition, Mexican-Americans have demanded their place in the American scene by organizing student organizations on college campuses and parent groups for the public schools; by being instrumental in the establishment of departments and classes in Mexican-American studies, both in college and high school lines; and by forcing the establishment to open up job opportunities in areas previously closed to persons of Mexican descent.

This anthology, which traces and analyzes various aspects of the Mexican-American's life as he has matured, then demanded, and finally started receiving his proper position in our nation, is unique. It is not a collection of previously published articles or excerpts. Rather, it is preponderantly a collection of original unpublished explorations of topics heretofore unresearched. These new articles, as well as those previously published, have been arranged chronologically so that the reader sees the history of the awakening Mexican-American unfold in the total American historical scene.

Manuel P. Servín

Arizona State University
Tempe, Arizona
January 1974

AN AWAKENED MINORITY:

THE MEXICAN-AMERICANS

SECOND EDITION

Chapter One

Background of Discrimination

The prejudice against the Mexican-Americans, who in the overwhelming majority are mixed-bloods, antedates that against any other minority group in North America. Long before the English colonists settled and prospered in America, the Mexican mixed-bloods of Indian, Spanish, and Negro stock were discriminated against in New Spain, or colonial Mexico. The Mexican mixed-bloods, unless they were of royal Aztec descent, were disdainfully treated. They were not generally acceptable to either their European or their Indian parents. Unable to attain positions in the Spanish world and unwilling to submit to the Indian life, they were relegated, with few exceptions, to laboring in the mines, haciendas, and ranchos by the European-descended ruling class. In seeking to rise from their dubious position—an actuality that they did not achieve until after Mexico's independence in 1821—the mixed-bloods acquired an unsavory, stereotyped reputation: they were manipulators and law breakers who were immoral, irreligious, disrespectful, and, of course, lazy.

The first selection in this chapter, "The Beginnings of California's Anti-Mexican Prejudice," attempts to demonstrate that discrimination against the stereotyped mixed-bloods in California originated before the Anglo-Americans arrived in the Golden State. The second selection, "Stereotyping of Mexico's Far Northern Frontier," by distinguished historian David J. Weber, presents the Anglo-American Anti-Mexican attitudes that prevailed among the English-speaking Americans in the borderlands and even in Mexico before the United States conquest of the Southwest. The reading of both selections should give the student of Mexican-American history a concrete idea of the prejudice that the later Mexican immigrant to the United States, especially to the Southwest, would encounter in migrating "North of Mexico."

The Beginnings of California's Anti-Mexican Prejudice*

Manuel P. Servín

Anti-Mexican prejudice in the Golden State, despite the fashionable views of militants, did not incubate and fester when the Anglo-American settlers arrived in Spanish and Mexican California. Actually, when the gringos arrived California already possessed a strong but not virulent anti-Mexican (anti-mixed-blood) attitude. This attitude, which disdained both Mexican mixed-bloods and things Mexican, appears to have originated in the Spanish period as real and alleged Spaniards attributed a position of inferiority to the racially impure Mexican-Californians. Paradoxically, this anti-Mexican attitude continued and even intensified during the subsequent Mexican period when Mexican mixed-bloods, passing as Spaniards, ruled the political and economic destiny of the province. Finally, this prejudice against Mexicans and Mexico was further inflamed by the arrival of the post-1830s American and European settlers whose disdain for nonwhites and mixed-bloods was notorious.

As prejudiced as the Americans may have been against the Mexicans in the first half of the nineteenth century, they do not merit the credit of beginning California's anti-Mexican attitude. This distinction, as will be seen, primarily belongs to the officials of the Spanish government and the missionaries of the College of San Fernando of Mexico.

GOVERNOR FERNANDO DE RIVERA'S TREATMENT

Prejudice against Mexicans made its appearance early in Spanish California. In fact, if the selection of the commander of the Alta California colonizing expedition is considered, it may be said that anti-Mexican prejudice seems to have appeared simultaneously with the founding of the province when the commander of the colonizing expedition was selected.

Judging by standards of achievement and experience in the New World, especially in Baja California, the most prepared person for leading Alta California's founding expedition was the Mexican-born frontier captain, Don Fernando de Rivera y Moncada. Rivera, so maligned by early California historians,[1] had started his military

---

*This essay was delivered originally at the Annual Conference of the Rocky Mountain Social Science Association in April 1972, at Salt Lake City, Utah.

career at Loreto, Baja California, in 1742 at the age of seventeen. "Few men in Spanish colonial history," states the distinguished Jesuit scholar, Ernest J. Burrus, "devoted more years to serving their country than Don Fernando. . . . His sense of duty, diligence, endurance, and exceptional ability are attested to by numerous rugged frontiersmen who were not easily satisfied, among them Consag, Barco, Linck, and Ceballos."[2]

Despite his distinguished service in Baja California, where he served as captain from 1752 to 1767, Rivera was passed over for the post of commander of the Alta California expedition. José de Gálvez, the Andalucían-born visitor general, instead selected Catalán-born Gaspar de Portolá. Although Portolá's record of military service was unblemished,[3] neither his experience nor his activities in New Spain appear to have warranted his nomination as commander of the colonizing expedition by Visitor General Gálvez. Had Portolá's appointment been the only time that Rivera had been slighted by Spaniards, it could be argued that perhaps his close connections with the Baja California Jesuits had influenced the bigotedly anti-Jesuit Gálvez against him. But such is not the case.

In addition to being strongly criticized by Junípero Serra,[4] who along with Gaspar de Portolá followed his footsteps from Baja to Alta California, Rivera suffered slights at the hands of the Spaniards. On July 9, 1770, after being in California for just over a year, Portolá departed. As military commander he left Lieutenant Pedro Fages, a Catalán who had arrived in New Spain in 1767. Thus Captain Rivera, who outranked Fages, was once again passed over.

It was not until 1773 that Rivera was appointed military commander of Alta California. But even as military commander he was unable to escape slights from the Catalán- and Mallorquín-born Spaniards. In 1776 Rivera was unwarrantedly excommunicated by the San Diego Franciscans for removing an "Indian culprit, Carlos, from the San Diego warehouse serving as temporary chapel."[5] Rivera, the first and only Mexican military commander of Spanish Alta California, thus became the only governor of Alta California to be excommunicated.

ATTITUDE TOWARD MIXED-BLOODS

Actually, Rivera's treatment is only a reflection of the anti-Mexican attitude that prevailed in Spanish California. A more direct and distinct picture of anti-Mexican prejudice, especially the anti-mixed-blood type, can be found in the words and actions of the Alta California Franciscan friars whose home base was the Apostolic

College of San Fernando of Mexico. The friars from this college—known as Fernandinos—possessed a great zeal for converting the Indians and also a reputation of being inflexible and of clashing with local government officials.[6] In addition, unlike the Franciscan missionaries from other colleges, the Fernandinos were unique in their opposition to the establishment of pueblos and settlements of Mexican mixed-bloods who in California were euphemistically called *gente de razón*.[7]

Although Alta California's first true settlers were the Mexican mixed-bloods who had arrived with the founding land and sea expeditions,[8] their contributions and presence do not appear to have been appreciated by the Fernandino friars. Whether the friars were still suffering from a peninsular attitude of racial superiority or whether they were influenced by the behavior or ambitions of some of the mixed-bloods is difficult to ascertain. But in either case the friars' general attitude is one of unappreciation and even hostility toward the Mexican-born persons, especially the mixed-bloods of Indian, African, and Spanish stock.

Actually there seems to be little documentary indication that the friars considered the mixed-bloods inferior simply because they were non-Europeans. Fermín Francisco Lasuén, the second father-president, appears to show such a prejudice when he stated in the Biennial Report of 1799–1800 that "In the remaining missions there is no lack of diligence as all the missionaries are Europeans."[9] Junípero Serra, whose opposition to mixed-blood *poblanos* (town dwellers) and *rancheros* (ranch owners) is well known, at least in his voluminous correspondence, does not seem to be tainted with any spirit of superiority simply because he was a pure-born European. His unappreciation and perhaps disdain of the mixed-bloods seems to be based upon problems that they *might* pose to the conversion of the Indians and also to the control of the province by the missionaries.[10]

ATTITUDE TOWARD *POBLANOS*

The Fernandinos, beginning with Serra, demonstrated an opposition to the settlement of *gente de razón* in Alta California. The establishment of pueblos, where the mixed-bloods would be congregated, was vehemently opposed.[11] So adamant was Serra in avoiding the presence of mixed-bloods that even the instructions of Viceroy Antonio María Bucareli,[12] the *Reglamento* (regulations) of Governor Felipe de Neve,[13] and the recommendations of the distinguished Miguel Costansó[14]—all of whom called for the erection of settlements—were opposed. Thus, writing to Viceroy Bucareli in mid-1778 after the establishment of the pueblo of San José, Serra gradually expressed his opposition to the establishment of pueblos and his guarded opinion of the mixed-blood settlers when he stated that

> Only on the subject of pueblos of Spaniards,[15] and the way they have begun to establish them, I have in private conversations expressed my opinion that it did not appear to me the best thing to do; and that even the purpose they claimed for the pueblos . . . would be better obtained by increasing and helping the Missions than by means of such pueblos, . . .
>
> The position I upheld was that the settlers who suitably fit into such a scheme—and at the present their numbers are few—should be distributed until more promising times among the missions. But all of this discussion was no more than to express my feelings on the subject without there being the least trace of antagonism.[16]

Insofar as Serra and the Fernandinos were concerned, more promising times for the missions and consequently for the establishment of mixed-blood pueblos never came. Franciscan opposition to San José, California's first pueblo, continued after its founding in 1777. Both Serra and the other missionaries, according to Governor Neve, opposed not only San José but any other pueblos that might be established.[17]

Serra's and the Franciscans' opposition to *gente de razón* pueblos did not, however, deter the strong-minded, pro-mixed-blood, California governor, Felipe de Neve. After establishing and maintaining San José, despite the clerical opposition, Neve was instrumental in the founding of the Pueblo de los Angeles in 1781. Regarding Los Angeles—whose inhabitants California historian Charles Edward Chapman characterized as "mongrel racial types" with "far more Indian and Negro blood than white" and "By all accounts . . . a dissolute, immoral, lazy, gambling lot"[18]—there is little documentation extant for the period prior to 1801.[19]

Although the correspondence of Father-Presidents Junípero Serra (1769–84) and Fermín Francisco de Lasuén (1785–1803) does not harp on the poor caliber of the town settlers, this does not mean that these mixed-blood *poblanos* were appreciated by the Fernandinos. Correspondence in the early and late 1810s—after Lasuén's death—shows that the Angeleños were neglected by the Fernandinos either because the missionaries lacked the necessary manpower or because they did not make the effort. Specifically, the correspondence between Father-President Esteban Tapis (1803–12) and Father-Ministers José de Miguel and José María de Zalvidea reveals the complaints that friars were denying spiritual aid to the *poblanos* of Los Angeles.[20] According to Franciscan historian Zephyrin Engelhardt, who accepted the missionaries' explanation that the priests were too occupied with their Indian charges to make two sick calls, the Fernandinos were justly meeting their obligation and acting appropriately.[21]

Whether the Angeleños' complaint against the friars was just or trumped up, the Fernandinos, continuing their well-earned tradition and reputation of being legalistic and inflexible, failed to heed the entreaties of the mixed-bloods. On August 21, 1816, Governor Vicente Solá wrote to the Viceroy of New Spain and noted that

> These and other duties with which the missionaries are burdened do not permit them the complete execution of all they desire, because various Fathers find themselves worn out through age or infirmities; in such cases they are content to do in their mission what they can and is necessary. Hence it is the people [the *gente de razón*], in the presidios, pueblos, ranchos, etc., [who] lack the necessary spiritual aid. From the pueblo of Our Lady of Los Angeles, for instance, with more than five hundred souls, scarcely twenty go every Sunday and holy-day of obligation to the neighboring mission of San Gabriel, three leagues distant for the purpose of assisting at holy Mass.[22]

Father-President Mariano Payeras (1815–19) also expressed the same sentiments of the impossibility of ministering to the *poblanos* in a letter to Governor Solá on October 22, 1816.[23]

Yet one wonders whether the impossibility of friars' finding time to minister to the Angeleños arose from overwork or dislike of the *gente de razón*. Writing in November 6, 1819, Payeras caustically remarked that "It seems as if around here the plan is taking shape of having the missions supply all the troops with everything and, as a natural consequence, the whole province, thus enslaving the priests and their neophytes, while all of those of *razón* live in absolute idleness and inactivity."[24] In 1820 Payeras again demonstrated an antagonism to the *gente de razón* as he expressed the thought that "the poor Indian of California and the poor priest of California sweat and toil to maintain themselves and in vain maintain all the people of *razón* whether they be troops or not, . . . If there is anything in the mission warehouses . . ., they take it from us and accompany it with insults."[25] That Father-President Payeras may have been overly critical of all the Angeleño mixed-bloods is plausible from his 1820 suggestion "that if the citizens would give their attention to other products of industry than wine and brandy, it would be better for both province and pueblo."[26]

Although the Franciscan criticism of the Angeleños may have been warranted by the actions of some of the settlers, it certainly does not appear applicable to all the mixed-blood settlers of Los Angeles. This is especially true when one learns that its "agricultural products exceeded the average of the missions" and that "Los Angeles, in 1790, yielded more grain than any mission, San Gabriel only excepted."[27]

The padres' criticism of the Angeleños was, however, mild when compared with that of the citizens of the Villa de Branciforte, the third Spanish town, founded just south of Santa Cruz Mission in 1797. Even before it was established, the future Mexican mixed-blood settlers ran into prejudice—they simply were not wanted as colonizers. Instead of mixed-bloods, the government wanted pure-bloods. Therefore, "The intendancies of Guadalajara, Zacatecas, Potosí, Guanajuato, and Valladolid were searched for families, poor, honorable, and of pure blood, who might be sent to California to increase the population, and who, far from corrupting the Christian Indians, would give them a good example. Thirteen voluminous notebooks were filled with lists of families, plans, questionnaires, answers, and conclusions. Results were almost nil."[28] Consequently, Branciforte had to be established by mixed-bloods. And to make the situation worse, the mixed-bloods were not from poor and honorable families but were from dubious backgrounds. The two colonist groups, organized in Guadalajara and in Guanajuato, consisted of men condemned for petty crimes.[29] However, they were more Spanish, as "they differed from the first settlers of other pueblos in being for the most part so-called Spaniards."[30]

In addition to suffering from the disadvantage of not being either pure-bloods or clean-living, the colonists also felt the opposition of the friars to the founding of a pueblo too close to the mission of Santa Cruz. As in the case of San José where the Pueblo had been founded nearer the mission than the Laws of the Indies allowed, the Fernandinos protested strongly against the villa's establishment. But, as in the case of San José, the friars lost and the pueblo remained.[31] There also remained, however, the hostility of the friars.

Undoubtedly, no group of settlers was more closely watched and perhaps deserved it more than those of Branciforte. Father-President Lasuén, who so greatly opposed the establishment of Branciforte, made this clear as he wrote to Interim Governor José Joaquín de Arrillaga in December 1801 that "It is common knowledge that the establishment of Villa Branciforte was watched with great attention as to its people and their progress; . . .[32] As the result of the close scrutiny of the unappreciated and unwanted settlers of Branciforte it was learned—as Franciscan historian Florian Guest wrote—that

> The trouble the convicts caused the government was more than legal in character. Their reputation for good conduct was not an enviable one. Their immorality and disorderly behavior were a scandal to the

> troops, the settlers, and the Indians. Sometimes their offenses were more than minor. José Barboza, one of the citizens of Branciforte, made an attempt on the life of Hermenegildo Sal, the commander of the presidio of Monterey. Another convict made various attempts to assassinate Governor Borica himself. In another letter to the viceroy, Arrillaga describes the convicts as insolent, vicious, brutal, and immoral and asks that the sending of any more be suspended. . . .[33]

It was also observed that they "never showed a disposition for hard work." Consequently "In 1798 Governor Borica requested Moraga to stir them up against their natural laziness. Indeed, they were not only lazy, but vicious, and the governor pronounced them a curse to the country for their dishonesty and immorality."[34]

Another Spanish officer, José de la Guerra y Noriega, while commandant of Monterey, wrote to Governor Arrillaga that the settlers of Branciforte "are not so bad as other colonists sent to California; yet to take a charitable view of the matter, their absence for a couple of centuries at a distance of a million leagues, would prove most beneficial to the province and redound to the service of God and King."[35] Such an absence or disappearance of Branciforte's settlers, although not as the one desired by the "Gran Capitán José de Guerra," almost did take place. By 1805, almost a decade after its founding, the villa had only five settlers.[36] Branciforte, as Bancroft states, "was of no advantage whatever to its inhabitants or the country."[37] Yet, to place all the responsibility and blame upon the *mestizo* settlers of the villa for the failure of the settlement does not seem just. This is especially so when it is remembered that friars controlled all the good lands adjacent to Branciforte and that the mixed-blood settlers could not aspire even to a dream of success.[38]

ATTITUDE TOWARD RANCHEROS

If the Fernandinos had demonstrated a general distrust and neglect of only the *poblanos* of the mixed-blood towns, San José, Los Angeles, and Branciforte, it might be argued that they were merely being realistic and not prejudiced. The friars, however, were not too fond of either the mixed-blood rancheros or the soldiers. Whether they were mainly seeking to protect the Indians from the supposedly deleterious contact with the mixed-bloods or whether they were particularly interested in maintaining control over the gargantuan "mission lands" of Alta California, in either case the Fernandinos bitterly opposed the granting of ranchos to *gente de razón* settlers.

Aside from the land granted to such Franciscan favorites as the Santa Barbara Ortegas,[39] who accompanied Father Serra in the founding expedition of 1768, few grants were made without meeting Fernandino opposition. Among such grants, however, was the small one made to Manuel Butrón, California's first land grantee. A settler of San José and husband of an Indian neophyte from San Carlos Mission, Butrón formally petitioned Governor Rivera in 1775 that he be permitted to retire from military service and "be assigned a parcel of land of one hundred and forty varas square, the acreage where he had already planted his corn, not to be alienated from him or his descendants."[40] Rivera, despite his problems with the Franciscans, forwarded the request to the father-president for clearance. Serra, apparently acting on behalf of the Indians, approved the request, writing, "We the ministers of this mission of San Carlos in the name of the natives who constitute it, assign to said [Butrón] in virtue of his wife Margarita who is one of them 140 varas square where he had his planting of corn so that the said family and its descendants may possess it in conformity with royal orders and that they may not sell, give away, or alienate it from the mission should they lack children or heirs."[41]

Consequently, Butrón received the grant in virtue of his marriage to a mission Indian woman; Rivera originated the policy of submitting proposed grants to the approval of the missionaries; and Serra seized the opportunity to determine whether the grants to colonists should be made or denied. In brief, the missionaries acquired great power in determining the extent of mixed-blood colonization and development.

By basing the initial California private rancho upon the grantee's marriage to a neophyte, the missionaries automatically limited the number of grants and the amount of land that on that basis could be given to mixed-blood colonists. The grants would indeed be few, since the marriages between neophytes and mixed-bloods were few. In fact, only twenty-four neophyte women married *gente de razón* in the first thirty-year period between 1769 and 1800.[42] By being the arbitrators between the petitioners and the governors, the missionaries augmented their influence in controlling the activities and ambitions of the mixed-blood colonists. Thus the missionaries could approve the individual requests of palatable petitioners, deny those of independent or hostile ones, seek to reclaim granted areas, and, in general, prevent the *gente de razón* from obtaining grants, rising in status, and becoming influential in the province.

Historical evidence leaves slight doubt of the missionaries' antagonism toward aspiring mixed-blood grantees. As early as 1790, when Corporal Francisco Cayuelas, the husband of a San Luis Obispo Indian neophyte, petitioned for land, "the grant was opposed, probably with success, by the friars, on the ground that the land was needed for the community, to which the neophyte in question had rendered no service."[43] In 1803 Mariano Castro returned from Mexico City with a license to establish a settlement in La Brea, but "The friars protested against the grant, refused to remove their cattle, and so successfully urged their claims that before the end of the decade Castro had to give up for years all hope of possessing La Brea."[44] A year later the missionaries at San Buenaventura opposed the establishment of Rancho Camulus because it would be too far from the mission to attend Mass and it would be detrimental to the mission.[45] That same year of 1804 the missionaries at San Gabriel objected to Francisco Avila's petition for a land grant, basing their objection on the family's manner of living and on the Indian ownership of the land.[46]

The Fernandinos' opposition to land grants for *gente de razón* continued unabated throughout the Spanish period, which ended in 1821. Bancroft presents a good picture of Franciscan attitude toward would-be rancheros in 1820 when he writes that "in this last decade of Spanish control the changes were few, and the system remained monotonously in status quo. The padres still opposed the granting of private ranchos, and kept here and there a minor quarrel with the occupants."[47] The padres, it should be noted, so greatly and successfully opposed the rancho system during Spanish period—the period of their power and influence—that only some thirty or fewer ranchos were granted during it.[48] This, it must be stressed, is in sharp contrast to the some eight hundred which were granted during the twenty-five-year Mexican period when the mixed-blood *Californio* reigned supreme.[49]

Not content with limiting the colonists to some thirty grants during their period of ascendancy, the Fernandinos also battled to regain some of the lands given to the rancheros. Thus in 1796 a portion of the grant made by Governor Pedro Fages to Manuel Nieto "was taken from him on the claim of San Gabriel missionaries that it was needed by the natives. In 1797 the Encino Ranch, held by Francisco Reyes, was taken from him, and both land and buildings were appropriated by the new mission of San Fernando."[50] The Franciscan opposition to allowing the mixed-bloods to receive grants from the huge lands surrounding each mission reached its pinnacle with the reclamation of rancho lands. In fact, so great was the Franciscan opposition that pueblo life was extolled and even encouraged. Consequently, future Father-President José Señán, writing to Viceroy Branciforte in 1796, stated that

> Towns cannot exist without people; as the number of inhabitants increases, so do the opportunities for their well-being. I therefore believe that under no circumstances should retired soldiers or others with special credentials who wish to settle in the Province be permitted to establish themselves separately in remote areas or villages outside the towns, a practice that I have tolerated these past few years. Such persons should rather be required to reside in towns, . . . otherwise we shall never have towns. The consequences to be expected from scattered and isolated colonization are distressing to contemplate. Colonists thus openly exposed are likely to suffer mischief at the hands of gentiles [pagan Indians], . . . In short, they will live in those remote regions without King to rule or Pope to excommunicate them; . . .[51]

Actually, it was not the need of pueblos and the welfare of the *gente de razón* that prompted Señán to write such a letter to the viceroy. As in the case of pueblos, the friars simply had very little use for the mixed-bloods, and, as Bancroft wrote, they

> express very freely their ideas respecting rancheros in general. Their presence was detrimental to the success of missionary effort; they [the rancheros] led an idle, vagabond life, often left their farms and lives in charge of gentiles, and set a bad example, rarely coming to hear mass or missing a fandango. The Indians found it hard to understand why they should be flogged for not attending religious services neglected with impunity by the Spaniards; therefore Indians who were brought up among Christians were always hardest to convert. The rancheros, the friars claimed, did not accumulate property, nor add in any respect to the prosperity of the country.[52]

ATTITUDE TOWARD THE SOLDIERY

Despite the friars' attitude toward the mixed-bloods in both the ranchos and the pueblos, their feelings could to a degree be excused because of their blind zeal for saving their beloved Indians. Their anti-mixed-blood attitude, however, extended even to the presidial soldiers—individuals somewhat removed from immediate and continual contact with the neophytes.

The friars' attitude toward the mixed-blood, presidial soldiers was demonstrated not so much by hostility but by neglect. This neglect—amazingly for men of God—was manifested either by ignoring or by refusing to celebrate Mass in the presidios for the spiritual benefit of the troops. The friars' neglect of the presidial soldiers appears quite early in the annals of the province. As early as 1775 Serra opposed stationing Lasuén, who was not assigned to any mission, in the presidio of Monterey. According to Serra, he finally permitted Lasuén to serve as presidial chaplain because "Don

Fernando Rivera interposed, offering to keep him [Lasuén] with him at the presidio until a new mission should be given him. Although I explained my objections to this arrangement both to the said Father and to the Captain, I had to give in although with little pleasure. So there Father Fray Fermín is, and I hope his good example will be an edification for those gentlemen in whose midst he is living."[53] Although Lasuén, as Father Maynard Geiger writes, "enjoyed his presidio chaplaincy" and "believed that he was serving a useful purpose as chaplain," Serra remained inflexible, at least during Rivera's administration, to stationing a friar at the presidio. According to Geiger, "Serra was always opposed to a Franciscan residing at the presidio though he reiterated the need of a chaplain for the establishment to serve it from Mission San Carlos. According to Serra, a diocesan priest should have been appointed to that position; if a friar held it, then he should live at San Carlos."[54]

Serra's opposition to stationing a Franciscan as chaplain at Monterey Presidio continued after Father Lasuén moved from Monterey to found Mission San Juan Capistrano.[55] His opposition was so determined that on October 26, 1775, Rivera, who was angry at Serra, openly accused the latter of neglecting the presidial settlers. Notwithstanding the friars' Sunday and holy-day ministering at the presidios, Rivera felt that "a regular presidio chaplain who could say daily Mass, instruct the children during the week, etc." was needed; therefore he vented his spleen on Serra as he wrote to him:

> May God forgive Your Reverence for the Christian doctrine which the children [at the presidio] are not learning and for the education they are not receiving. May God forgive you for the sermons and Masses which both the adults and the children are not hearing; may God forgive you for the confessions which perhaps the people are not making because you have taken away from us Father Fermín [Lasuén]; these things indeed are reason to cause worry because they refer to the salvation of the neighbor and God knows if all this is not due to his [Lasuén's] removal. There is not the least excuse for it because there is no dearth of padres; rather there are supernumeraries. Of this no account will be given in the tribunal of Mexico [but rather to Heaven] as on one occasion Your Reverence wrote to me. Less noise and more fruitful cooperation so that esteem and confidence will be increased, and I believe that the words *dilectísimo* and *carísimo* ["my dearly beloved"] mean something and suppose not a little. May Our Lord guard Your Reverence for many years.[56]

Rivera's words may not have gone unheeded by Serra. When the Spaniard Neve was appointed governor, Serra graciously offered the Spanish officer "the services of Lasuén or any other Father who could be spared from the missions."[57] However, Neve declined the offer. Serra, on the other hand, was never again to be so charitably inclined, although Sunday and holy-day services were performed in the presidios (except Santa Barbara) rather regularly between 1769 and 1783.[58]

After 1783 the friars, who considered the services at the presidios an act of charity and not of justice, halted saying Mass in the presidio of San Francisco in 1783. Such a drastic act, which affected the mixed-blood troops and their families so drastically, occurred "When Governor Fages and his soldiers began to say that missionaries were obliged to serve them as chaplains." Father Serra gives a picture of the touchiness of the Fernandinos and of their lack of regard of the presidial *gente de razón* population when he wrote to his superior in Mexico City:

> There is something else that I forgot to tell you. I must let you know about it before it reaches your ears from some other party. The missions which have presidios in their immediate vicinity have been accustomed to provide Mass and other religious services every Sunday and feast day of obligation in the chapels attached to the presidios without being in any way obliged to do so, and without receiving any recompense for the service rendered. We put an end to this practice—in San Francisco, since the first of January of the present year; in Monterey, since the month of March. . . .
>
> In San Diego Mass was not stopped completely (although they would miss saying quite often, which formerly did not happen). . . .
>
> In Monterey the provocation was even greater. We had to put up with the ridicule of the Lieutenant, who knew our obligation better than we ourselves. Señor Fages said the custom had the force of law, and since we had gone ten years without being paid for it, we [were] obliged to do so now. And more than this, although they had wine to drink—and good wine too—they never wanted us to sample any of it, not even for Mass, and we were compelled to bring the wine with us in our sleeve from the mission in order to provide them with Mass. . .[59]

This withdrawal of religious service to presidial population, the vast majority of whom were mixed-bloods, lasted for about two and a half years. Despite the supplications of the people affected,[60] religious services were not resumed until after Serra's death and Lasuén's rise to the presidency of the mission. But even Lasuén cannot alone be credited with the resumption of religious services. Ultimate credit must be divided among the government authorities in both California and Chihuahua and Father-President Lasuén.[61]

The resumption of services at the presidios did not, however, put an end to the problem. In July 1806 Governor José Joaquín de Arrillaga found it necessary to complain to the viceroy about the lack of religious instruction for the troops and the *gente de razón.* Judging from Arrillaga's letter of this date, the neglect of the presidial population extended back for more than a dozen years.[62] In 1820, some fourteen years later, the problem of services to the presidial population remained unsolved. José María Estudillo, the commandant at Monterey Presidio, in hope of securing "the services of a friar on fixed days, and not according to convenience" as Father-President Vicente Francisco Sarria insisted, wrote to Governor Pablo de Solá and gave a historical account of chaplain service at Monterey since 1796.[63]

Since Estudillo's letter came just as the Spanish period of California was coming to an end, it must be acknowledged that the neglect of the presidial population, which was overwhelmingly mixed-blood, existed intermittently throughout the entire period. It should also be noted that this neglect was not lost on either the soldiers or the *poblanos*. Consequently, the 1816 remark of the visiting Russian navigator, Otto von Kotzebue, that "The soldiers seem as dissatisfied with the government as with the Mission," accurately portrays the attitude of the *gente de razón* toward Spanish Fernandino friars who had neglected them for almost five decades.

CONCLUSION

Regardless of the reasons and excuses that the Franciscans and the pro-Franciscan historians have proffered, the fact remains that the Fernandinos' neglect and at times dislike of the mixed-blood Mexicans was not isolated. The mixed-blood, whether he was a townsman, a ranchero, a soldier, or a settler of any type, was not welcomed or appreciated by the Fernandinos. Almost whenever he appeared on the California horizon he was considered a menace to the Indians, to society, to missionization, and to Christianity. Consequently it may be concluded that Franciscans were prejudiced against the Mexican-bloods and that this prejudice has not been made known by historians of California.

Notes

1. See Hubert Howe Bancroft, *History of California*, 7 vols. (San Francisco, 1884), 1: 269–73, 361–63, for an example of the anti-Rivera historical attitude.
2. Ernest J. Burrus, "Rivera y Moncada, Explorer and Military Commander of Both Californias, in the Light of His Diary and Other Contemporary Documents," *Hispanic American Historical Review* 50 (November 1970): 683.
3. Donald A. Nuttall, "Gaspar de Portolá: Disenchanted Conquistador of Spanish Upper California," *Southern California Quarterly* 53 (September 1971): 185–86, presents a fine overview of Portolá's European service.
4. Junípero Serra was not only very critical of Rivera but apparently was embittered by Rivera's actions and attitude. See Antonine Tibesar, ed., *Writings of Junípero Serra*, 4 vols. (Washington, 1955–66), 1: xvii–xviii. For random examples of Serra's criticism of Rivera, a truly devout Catholic layman, see the correspondence of Junípero Serra to Francisco Pangua, Monterey, April 17, 1776, in Tibesar, *Writings*

of Serra, 3: 3–7; Serra to Pangua, Monterey, July 18, 1774, in Tibesar, *Writings of Serra,* 2: 95–119; Serra to Rivera, Monterey, July 24, 1775, in Tibesar, *Writings of Serra,* 2: 285–87; and Serra to Pangua, Monterey, October 29, 1775, in Tibesar, *Writings of Serra,* 2: 379–97. California's distinguished Franciscan history authority, Maynard Geiger, O.F.M., presents an objective and complete account of the Serra-Rivera encounters in *The Life and Times of Fray Junípero Serra, O.F.M.,* 2 vols. (Washington, 1959). See chaps. 59, 60.

5. Burrus, "Rivera y Moncada," 692, indicates that excommunication was not warranted when he states that "Canon lawyers today will endorse Rivera's action in removing the Indian culprit Carlos . . . and agree with the commander that he did not incur any ecclesiastical excommunication." Also see Geiger, *Life and Times of Serra,* 2: 88–98, for a complete narration of the excommunication.

6. Manuel P. Servín, "The Secularization of the California Missions: A Reappraisal," *Southern California Quarterly* 47 (June 1965): 135.

7. See John W. Caughey, *California: A Remarkable State's Life History* (Englewood Cliffs, N.J., 1970), p. 76; Servín, "Secularization of the California Missions," p. 137. Father Maynard Geiger states that *gente de razón* are "all non-mission people of whatever racial strain or mixture." See Maynard Geiger, "Mission San Gabriel," *Southern California Quarterly* 52 (September 1971): 249, n. 3.

In accordance with usage of the truly Spanish settlers, I define *gente de razón* as Hispanicized non-Spaniards who were generally a mixture of Indian, African, and Spanish stock. Spanish settlers referred to themselves as "Spaniards" and not as *gente de razón*—a term that would equate them with mixed-bloods.

8. The number of *gente de razón* or Mexican mixed-blood settlers who arrived in Alta California with the founding expedition was about sixty. The number of Spaniards who arrived and remained in Alta California after the initial settlements of San Diego and Monterey were made was only five. See Manuel P. Servín, "California's Hispanic Heritage: A View into the Spanish Myth," MS, Arizona State University, 1972.

9. Finbar Kenneally, *Writings of Fermín Francisco de Lasuén,* 2 vols. (Washington, 1965), 2: 389.

10. Serra made exceedingly few references to the mixed-bloods. In a letter to Fray Francisco Pangua, Monterey, December 8, 1782, he does however show some hostility toward the mixed-bloods. Referring to the establishment of the pueblo of San José, he states that "The Governor . . . made up his mind to start a pueblo . . . to be composed of people, as they say *de razón*—just as if the Indians did not have the use of reason too." See Tibesar, *Writings of Serra,* 4: 167–75. For understanding the friars' desire to control the province, see Servín, "Secularization of the California Missions," pp. 133–49.

11. Geiger, *Life and Times of Serra,* 2: 194.

12. "Instrucción, que debe observar, el Comandante nombrado para los nuevos Establecimientos de San Diego y Monterrey," M-M 281, Bancroft Library, University of California, Berkeley.

13. "Reglamento e Ynstrucc.^{n} para los Presidios de la Peninsula de California, crec.^{n} de nuevas Mis.^{nes} y fomento del pueblo y estension de establecimientos de Monterrey," C-A 52, Bancroft Library.

14. Manuel P. Servín, "Costansó's 1794 Report of Strengthening New California's Presidios," *California Historical Quarterly* 49 (September 1970): 227. Spanish copies of Costansó's recommendations are located in the Biblioteca Nacional in Madrid and in the Bancroft Library.

15. By "Spaniards" Serra was referring to Hispanicized mixed-bloods and not to pure-bloods.

16. Junípero Serra to Viceroy Antonio María Bucareli, Monterey, June 30, 1778, in Tibesar, *Writings of Serra,* 3: 195–201.

17. Felipe de Neve to the Comandante General, Monterey, August 10, 1778, C-A 22, Bancroft Library; see also Geiger, *Life and Times of Serra,* 2: 194, and Junípero Serra to Francisco Pangua, Monterey, December 8, 1782, in Tibesar, *Writings of Serra,* 4: 167–75.

18. Charles E. Chapman, *California! The American Period* (New York, 1951), pp. 391–92.

19. Bancroft, *History of California*, 1: 659.

20. Esteban Tapis to José de Miguel and José María de Zalvidea, San Luis Obispo, March 6, 1810, C-C 15, Bancroft Library; Tapis to Miguel and Zalvidea (confidential letter), San Luis Obispo, March 6, 1810, C-C 15, Bancroft Library; Miguel and Zalvidea to Tapis, San Gabriel, March 17, 1810, C-C 15, Bancroft Library; Miguel and Zalvidea to Tapis (confidential), San Gabriel, March 17, 1810, C-C 15, Bancroft Library; and Miguel and Zalvidea to Tapis, San Gabriel, May 24, 1810, C-C 15, Bancroft Library.

21. Zephyrin Engelhardt, *San Gabriel Mission and the Beginnings of Los Angeles* (San Gabriel, 1927), p. 81.

22. Vicente Solá to the Viceroy of New Spain, Monterey, August 21, 1816, in Engelhardt, *Missions and Missionaries of California*, 3: 48–51. Original Letter in the Santa Barbara Mission Archives, Document 679.

23. Mariano Payeras to Vicente Solá, La Purísima Concepción, October 22, 1816, C-C 1, Bancroft Library.

24. Mariano Payeras to Baldomero López, San Gabriel, November 6, 1819, Academy of American Franciscan History.

25. Payeras to López, "La Purísima," July 26, 1820, Academy of American Franciscan History.

26. Bancroft, *History of California*, 2: 559, n. 3; Payeras to Solá, La Purísima, January 17, 1820, C-C 2, Bancroft Library.

27. Hubert Howe Bancroft, *California Pastoral* (San Francisco, 1888), p. 252.

28. Florian Guest, "The Establishment of the Villa de Branciforte," *California Historical Quarterly* 41 (March 1962): 37.

29. *Ibid.*, pp. 37–40.

30. Bancroft, *History of California*, 1: 569, n. 44. Bancroft's statement of so-called Spaniards is confirmed by the Lists of Settlers found in the "Provincial State Papers," C-A 10, Bancroft Library; and in the "State Papers: Missions and Colonization," C-A 52, Bancroft Library.

31. Guest, "Establishment of the Villa de Branciforte," pp. 41–43; Lasuén to Diego de Borica, San Carlos, May 5, 1797, in Kenneally, *Writings of Lasuén*, 2: 26–28; Lasuén to Pedro Callejas, San Buenaventura, February 1, 1798, in Kenneally, *Writings of Lasuén*, 2: 69; Lasuén to Callejas, San Buenaventura, March 1, 1798, in Kenneally, *Writings of Lasuén*, 2: 72–74; Lasuén to Callejas, San Diego, November 2, 1797, in Kenneally, *Writings of Lasuén*, 2: 55–57; Lasuén to Callejas, San Carlos, May 28, 1797, in Kenneally, *Writings of Lasuén*, 2: 29–30.

32. Lasuén to José Joaquín de Arrillaga, San Francisco, December 27, 1801, in Kenneally, *Writings of Lasuén*, 2: 255–56.

33. Guest, "Establishment of the Villa de Branciforte," p. 40. Diego de Borica, a Spanish colonel, was governor of California from October 1794 to January 1800. José Joaquín de Arrillaga, a Spanish lieutenant colonel and a model administrator, was interim governor in 1793–94 and in 1800–04 and governor from 1804 to 1814.

34. Bancroft, *California Pastoral*, pp. 254–55. For Borica's original words, which were truly harsh, see Borica to the Comisionado de Branciforte, Monterey, January 28, 1798, C-A 74, Bancroft Library. Gabriel Moraga, son of José Joaquín who came with Juan Bautista de Anza in 1776, served as enlisted man, noncommissioned officer, and as lieutenant of the San Francisco, Monterey, and Santa Barbara companies.

35. Quoted in Joseph A. Thompson, *El Grán Capitán José de la Guerra* (Los Angeles, 1961), p. 10. See also Guest, "Establishment of the Villa de Branciforte," p. 41; Kenneally, *Writings of Lasuén*, 2: 256; Bancroft, *History of California*, 2: 155.

36. José Joaquín de Arrillaga, Loreto, May 18, 1805, C-A 50, Bancroft Library.

37. Bancroft, *History of California*, 2: 156.

38. Felipe Goycoechea, "Medios para el Fomento de Californias," 1805, C-A 12, Bancroft Library.

39. José Francisco Ortega was the sergeant whom Serra recommended to Viceroy Bucareli for the office of military commander of Alta California. For Ortega's grant of 1794 and later disputes see Bancroft *History of California,* 1: 663, 670–72; Maynard Geiger, "History of Mission Santa Barbara California (1786–1961)," vol. 1, part 1—The Spanish and Mexican Periods (1786–1846), MS, Santa Barbara Mission Archives; Zephyrin Engelhardt, *Santa Barbara Mission* (San Francisco, 1923), pp. 105–106; José de Ortega to the governor of California, Presidio de Santa Bárbara, February 28, 1804, Doc. 468, Santa Barbara Mission Archives; Esteban Tapis and Juan Cortés to the governor of California, Mission Santa Barbara, June 1, 1804, Taylor Collection, vol. 2, Doc. 279, Archives of the Archdiocese of San Francisco.

40. Geiger, *Life and Times of Serra,* 2: 56; see also Bancroft, *History of California,* 1: 608. A *vara,* sometimes called a Spanish yard, is equivalent to thirty-three inches.

41. Serra to Rivera, San Carlos Mission, November 22, 1775, as quoted in Geiger, *Life and Times of Serra,* 2: 56; W. W. Robinson, *Land in California* (Berkeley, 1948), p. 46.

42. "Representación hecha por Fr. Fermín Frn.[co] de Lasuén . . . San Carlos de Monterrey y Noviembre 12 de 1800," C-C 8, Bancroft Library.

43. Bancroft, *History of California,* 1: 610. For original correspondence on Cayuelas, see "Archivo de la Misión de Santa Bárbara," 11, C-C 17, Bancroft Library.

44. Bancroft, *History of California,* 2: 171.

45. Vicente de Santa María and José Señán to the governor of California, April 27, 1804, Taylor Collection, vol. 2, Doc. 269, Archives of the Archdiocese of San Francisco.

46. Francisco Dumetz and Francisco Javier Uría to the governor of California, May 4, 1802, Taylor Collection, vol. 2, Doc. 270, Archives of the Archdiocese of San Francisco.

47. Bancroft, *History of California,* 2: 414.

48. Caughey, *California,* p. 89; Bancroft, *History of California,* 2: 414, n. 3.

49. Caughey, *California,* p. 114.

50. Bancroft, *History of California,* 1: 612.

51. José Señán to the Marqués de Branciforte, Mexico, May 14, 1796, *The Letters of José Señán, O.F.M., Mission San Buenaventura, 1796–1823,* trans. by Paul D. Nathan, ed. by Lesley B. Simpson (San Francisco, 1962), p. 88.

52. Bancroft, *History of California,* 2: 172.

53. Serra to Francisco Pangua, San Carlos Mission, July 24, 1775, in Tibesar, *Writings of Serra,* 2: 288–97. For a complete and unbiased presentation of the chaplaincy problem between Serra and Rivera, see Geiger, *Life and Times of Serra,* 2: 31–34.

54. Geiger, *Life and Times of Serra,* 2: 32.

55. Lázaro Lamadrid Jiménez, *El Alavés Fray Fermín Francisco de Lasuén, O.F.M. (1736–1803): Fundador de Misiones en California* (Alva, 1963), 2: 169.

56. Rivera to Serra, October 26, 1875, as quoted in Geiger, *Life and Times of Serra,* 2: 53–54.

57. Geiger, *Life and Times of Serra,* 2: 148–49.

58. Geiger, *Life and Times of Serra,* 2: 261.

59. Serra to Juan Sancho, San Gabriel Mission, October 29, 1873, in Tibesar, *Writings of Serra,* 4: 199–207.

60. Francisco Palou and Pedro Benito Cambón to Fages, San Francisco Mission, January 8, 1783, Californias 12, Archivo General de la Nación, Bancroft Library.

61. Geiger, *Life and Times of Serra,* 2: 265.

62. Arrillaga to the viceroy, Monterey, July 15, 1806, C-A 25, Bancroft Library.

63. Estudillo to Solá, Monterey, August 21, 1816, C-A 13, Bancroft Library; see also Bancroft, *History of California,* 2: 411–12.

Stereotyping of Mexico's Far Northern Frontier*

David J. Weber

Many nineteenth-century Anglo-American visitors to what is today's Southwest (which can be defined for present purposes as the four border states of California, Arizona, New Mexico and Texas) depicted the Mexican residents of that area in the most unflattering terms. Mexicans were described as lazy, ignorant, bigoted, superstitious, cheating, thieving, gambling, cruel, sinister, cowardly half-breeds. As a consequence of their supposed innate depravity, Mexicans were seen as incapable of developing republican institutions or achieving material progress.[1] These opinions of Mexicans, some of which endure to the present day, are familiar to most southwesterners and can be found in the writings of many early Anglo-American writers. One example will suffice. Thomas Jefferson Farnham, a New England attorney who toured California in the early 1840s, described the Californians thus:

> There never was a doubt among Californians that they were at the head of the human race. In cowardice, ignorance, pretension, and dastardly tyranny, the reader has learned that this pretension is well founded.
>
> Thus much for the Spanish population of the Californias; in every way a poor apology of European extraction; as a general thing, incapable of reading or writing, and knowing nothing of science or literature, nothing of government but its brutal force, nothing of virtue but the sanction of the Church, nothing of religion but ceremonies of the national ritual. Destitute of industry themselves, they compel the poor Indian to labor for them, affording him a bare savage existence for his toil, upon their plantations and the fields of the Missions. In a word, the Californians are an imbecile, pusillanimous, race of men, and unfit to control the destinies of that beautiful country. . . .
>
> No one acquainted with the indolent, mixed race of California, will ever believe that they will populate, much less, for any length of time, govern the country. The law of Nature which curses the mulatto here with a constitution less robust than that of either race from which he sprang, lays a similar penalty upon the mingling of the Indian and white races in California and Mexico. They must fade away. . . .[2]

If Anglo-Americans had portrayed individual Mexicans in such a negative fashion, we should think little of it, for surely there were

*This essay was originally read at the annual meeting of the Texas State Historical Association in Austin, March 1973. Brief portions are excerpted from *Foreigners in Their Native Land: Historical Roots of the Mexican-Americans* (1973), edited by David J. Weber, and reprinted here with permission of the University of New Mexico Press.

Mexicans, just as there were Anglo-Americans, who fitted the description. When such characterizations are applied to an entire people, however, they clearly are no longer based on empirical evidence and cannot be regarded as valid generalizations. Sweeping generalizations, which either have no basis in fact or are based on "overgeneralizations of facts," are known as stereotypes.[3] Negative stereotypes are, of course, an obstacle to communication and understanding for they are usually expressions of prejudice which, as Walter Lippmann once put it, "precede the use of reason."[4]

Stereotypes need not always be negative, of course. In describing Mexicans as a peculiarly depraved people, early Anglo-American writers, who were usually males, frequently took pains to exempt attractive Mexican women from most of their disparaging remarks. In the view of one American writer, whose male hormones seem to have influenced his judgment, "women is women the whole world over, no matter where she is found." That, of course, is a stereotype too.[5]

How did a negative stereotype of Mexican males develop? There are many approaches to that question which cannot be explored in a brief paper. As a historian, I would like to suggest simply that the answer has larger dimensions than are usually suggested by writers about the Southwest. One popular explanation, which is implied more often than it is stated, is that a negative stereotype of Mexicans developed as a result of contacts between Americans and Mexicans here in the Southwest.[6]

It is generally agreed that Americans, who entered far northern Mexico to trap, trade, or settle, made the first significant contact with Mexicans, especially after Mexican independence was achieved in 1821 and restrictions against foreigners were relaxed. Most of the foreigners came to frontier areas such as California, New Mexico and Texas—areas, so the argument goes, which were politically, economically, and culturally backward when compared with central Mexico. Thus, it has been suggested, Anglo-Americans formed a mistaken notion of what *all* Mexicans were like on the basis of contact with relatively *few* Mexicans on the far northern frontier.

Writers who have taken this position have found support from a contemporary Mexican visitor to the frontier, General Manuel Mier y Terán, who, after inspecting Texas in 1828, reported to President Guadalupe Victoria:

> It would cause you the same chagrin that it has caused me to see the opinion that is held of our nation by these foreign colonists [i.e., Anglo-Americans], since, with the exception of some few who have journeyed

to our capital, they know no other Mexicans than the inhabitants about here, and excepting the authorities . . . the said inhabitants are the most ignorant of negroes and Indians.[7]

As literary historian Cecil Robinson summed up the situation, "Early American writers and chroniclers in dealing with Mexico generally mistook a part for the whole thing."[8]

I would like to suggest that no such mistake occurred. On the contrary, many Anglo-American writers held a contemptuous view of Mexican males wherever they encountered them. General Mier y Terán, for example, would have been more chagrined had he known the views that Stephen Austin expressed about Mexicans in 1822, during a visit to Mexico City. Austin wrote that "the people are bigoted and superstitious to an extreem [*sic*], and indolence appears to be the general order of the day—in fact the City Magnificent [Mexico City] . . . is at least one century behind many other places in point of intelligence and improvement 'in the arts' and the nation generally is in the same situation."[9]

It could be said that Austin's previous experience in Texas had predisposed him to dislike Mexicans wherever he found them. This was not the case with Joel Roberts Poinsett, who never set foot in what is today the Southwest. In 1822 Poinsett visited Mexico for the first time,[10] traveling to Mexico City by way of Vera Cruz. In his well-known *Notes on Mexico,* Poinsett pronounced Mexicans in general to be lazy.[11] The Indians and mixed-bloods were "indolent," he said, and the "lazy" creoles "are not remarkable for their attainments, or for the strictness of their morals." He described the upper class as a complacent, self-satisfied group. The clergy, Poinsett said, had too great an influence in society, and the people were superstitious.[12] Just as visitors to the frontier would note, Mexicans practiced the terrible vices of gambling and smoking and gave little thought to the future. Poinsett found the people to be generally ugly, and one can only wonder if this was because he had also discovered them to be "swarthy."[13] Compared with those of most of his contemporaries, Poinsett's observations tended to be sophisticated. The well-traveled Poinsett showed some awareness of his prejudices and tried, but often failed, to avoid overgeneralizing.[14]

More typical was another visitor to Mexico in 1822 whose notes, describing a journey from Tampico to Mexico City, appeared in the appendix to Poinsett's work. This anonymous traveler dismissed all Mexicans with the characteristic stereotype: "Their occupation seems to consist, principally, in removing fleas and lice from each other, drinking pulque, smoking cigars, when they can, and sleeping."[15]

On a return visit to Mexico in 1825, Joel Poinsett brought with him a young secretary, Edward Thornton Tayloe, another person who had no previous contact with Mexicans. Tayloe quickly judged the residents of Mexico City, including the upper class, to be superstitious and lazy. Not as gallant as some of his contemporaries, Tayloe singled out upper-class women, especially, as "idle and useless." "They can do naught but eat, sleep, smoke or talk, or visit the theatre." The Mexicans, Tayloe wrote, were ignorant, vicious, thieving, and incapable of governing themselves as republicans. In fact, Mexicans had no virtues whatsoever. "Should I attempt to find them out," Tayloe wrote, "I fear I shall fail."[16]

These remarks by a necessarily small sample[17] of Anglo-American visitors to Mexico City in the early 1820s seem to indicate that Anglo-Americans did not, as Cecil Robinson said, mistake "a part" of Mexico "for the whole thing." A negative stereotype of Mexicans was articulated very early, almost as soon as foreigners began to get a good look at Mexico City after 1821.[18] The relative uniformity of the stereotype suggests the possibility that the observers were making valid generalizations—that Mexicans were lazy, ignorant, bigoted, superstitious, cheating, thieving, gambling, cruel, sinister, cowardly half-breeds, incapable of self-government or material progress. Yet, a closer look at American thought suggests that the stereotype was not so much based on direct observation or experience with Mexicans but was in large part an extension of negative attitudes toward Catholic Spaniards which Anglo-Americans had inherited from their Protestant English forefathers.

During the colonial period, English colonists on the Atlantic coast had almost no contact with Mexicans or other Latin-Americans. Nonetheless, seventeenth-century New Englanders, such as Samuel Sewall and Cotton Mather, took a jaundiced view of Catholic Latin America, based largely on what they had read in literature from England. Sewall believed that Mexican culture was doomed to fall before a triumphant Protestantism and hoped that Mexico would hasten the process by revolting against Spain. Mather took the trouble to learn Spanish in order to write a missionary tract for Spaniards in the New World which was designed "to open their eyes and be converted . . . away from Satan to God."[19]

Anti-Spanish views inherited from England were far more complex than simple anti-Catholicism, however. The English colonists also believed that Spanish government was authoritarian, corrupt, and decadent, and that Spaniards were bigoted, cruel, greedy, tyrannical, fanatical, treacherous, and lazy. In attempting to respond to these charges, Spanish historians have found it convenient to give them a pejorative label: the Black Legend. Not surprisingly, in defending themselves against the "blackening" effect of this "legend," Spaniards have often gone to the other extreme of whitewashing Spain of all faults, giving rise to what Spain's detractors called a White Legend.

The origins of the Black Legend are complex. Some of its roots lie in the New World where Spanish conquistadores have been viewed as the apotheosis of evil. Interestingly, Spain's enemies drew much of their inspiration from the self-critical writings of Spaniards, most notably Bartolomé de las Casas, who was widely read in England and in her American colonies. In this literature, Spaniards were depicted as grasping adventurers who came to the New World not to seek better homes for their families as did the English but to search for treasure and to live in idleness on the sweat of aborigines. For our purposes, it is sufficient to say that Mexicans, the descendants of the Spanish conquistadores, inherited the reputation of their forefathers. As Phillip Wayne Powell recently put it: "We [Anglo-Americans] transferred some of our ingrained antipathy toward Catholic Spain to her American heirs."[20]

Powell is one of the few historians to take note of this connection between the Black Legend and anti-Mexicanism,[21] but one does not need to read too carefully in the writings of Anglo-American visitors to the Mexican frontier to find evidences of the Black Legend. One of the most explicit statements comes from young Lewis Garrard, who visited New Mexico during the Mexican War. After briefly characterizing the New Mexican males as alternatively "servile" and "villainous," he explained the reason for their depravity in terms that show clearly the influence of the Black Legend. "The extreme degradation into which they are fallen," Garrard observed, "seems a fearful retribution on the destroyers of [the] Aztec Empire."[22]

In addition to the Black Legend, Anglo-Americans found one other element to despise in Mexicans—racial mixture. Color-conscious Anglo-Americans were nearly unanimous in commenting on the dark skin of the "swarthy" Mexican *mestizos* who, it was generally agreed, had inherited the worst qualities of Spaniards and Indians, resulting in a "race" still more despicable than that of either parent group.[23] In suggesting that Anglo-Americans were racists, I am not trying to ignore the racist nature of Mexican society. It is not within the scope of this essay to elaborate on this matter, and for present purposes I simply want to suggest that a belief in the Black Legend, combined with a belief in the inferiority of mixed-bloods, enabled Anglo-Americans to erroneously predict what Mexicans would be like (that is, to construct a stereotype) even before coming into significant contact with them. Not surprisingly, the Anglo-Americans' expectations were fulfilled.

Let us look briefly now at this stereotype by examining the functioning of its components—that is, the frequent charge that frontier Mexicans were lazy. Some historians have taken that charge at face value.[24] Yet it is possible to argue not only that Mexicans in general were not indolent but also that there is reason to suppose that Mexicans on the frontier were energetic pioneers who worked harder than did their compatriots in more "civilized" areas of Mexico. First, on the frontier it was more difficult to exploit Indian labor, and the colonists had to work with their own hands. For example, the *encomienda* (a system of distributing Indian labor) was unsuccessful and short-lived in the borderlands, operating only in seventeenth-century New Mexico.[25] Hard work by colonists from Mexico was necessary in some areas of the frontier to provide defense against hostile Indians. Moreover, hard work was probably rewarded on the frontier, where there seems to have been greater social mobility than there was in central Mexico.

The idea that Mexican frontiersmen were industrious has been suggested by historians such as Silvio Zavala and France Scholes.[26] It was also mentioned by contemporaries such as Miguel Ramos de Arizpe in Texas, Pedro Bautista Pino in New Mexico, Alexander von Humboldt, the German savant and traveler, and Zebulon Montgomery Pike, the "lost pathfinder."[27] Pike, for example, termed the inhabitants of New Mexico "the bravest and most hardy subjects in New Spain," because of "their continual wars with the savage nations who surround them," because of their isolation from the rest of New Spain, and because they lacked gold and silver, sources of easy wealth.[28]

It is possible, then, that Mexicans on the frontier were not lazy and were perhaps even harder working than were their countrymen to the south.[29] Nevertheless, Anglo-American visitors generally described frontier Mexicans as lazy. How can this be explained? The Black Legend, which identifies Spaniards as lazy, offers part of the explanation. An understanding of Anglo-American attitudes toward racial mixture also adds to the explanation, for Anglo-Americans generally regarded persons of mixed blood as lazy. In 1884, for example, Thomas Jefferson Farnham described the complexion of upper-class Californians as "a light clear bronze; not white . . . not remarkably pure in any way; a lazy color."[30] Still a third explanation needs to be considered. Psychologists tell us that we stereotype ethnic groups in part because "in them we may perceive our own shortcomings."[31] According to Maurice Janowitz and Bruno Bettelheim, "ethnic hostility is a projection of unacceptable inner strivings onto a minority group."[32] The ethnic group, in other words, becomes our alter ego. Examined in this context, the Anglo-American observation that Mexicans were lazy may tell us more about the rigorous work-ethic of nineteenth-century Americans than it does about Mexican culture.[33]

The fact that many Anglo-Americans blamed the economic and cultural underdevelopment of Mexico's far northern frontier on the "indolent" character of the Mexican colonists not only is simplistic but also reveals a bias. Better explanations for underdevelopment could have been found by looking into historical and geographical circumstances that contributed to the relative backwardness of this region. Yet, for most Anglo-American observers, the stereotype itself seems to have constituted a sufficient explanation.

What I am suggesting here is, of course, unprovable. But to argue that a generation of Anglo-American observers did not see what they said they saw does not seem unreasonable. A stereotype, psychologist Gordon Allport tells us, "may interfere with even the simplest rational judgments."[34]

Notes

1. This is the picture that emerges from such studies as Cecil Robinson, *With the Ears of Strangers: The Mexican in American Literature* (Tucson, 1963), and David T. Leary, "The Attitudes of Certain United States Citizens toward Mexico, 1821–1846" (Ph.D. diss., University of Southern California, 1970).

2. Thomas Jefferson Farnham, *Travels in California* (Oakland, Calif., 1947 [first published in 1844]), pp. 161–62.

3. In this paper I am following Gordon Allport's widely accepted distinction between a stereotype and a valid generalization. *The Nature of Prejudice* (Cambridge, Mass., 1954), pp. 190–91.

4. Quoted in Rosemary Gordon, *Stereotype of Imagery and Belief as an Ego Defence* (Cambridge, Mass., 1962), p. 5. Psychologists give Walter Lippmann considerable credit for popularizing the term *stereotype.*

5. Lewis H. Garrard, *Wah-To-Yah and the Taos Trail* (Palo Alto, Calif., 1968), p. 194. Anglo views of Mexican women are discussed in James H. Lacy, "New Mexico Women in Early American Writings," *New Mexico Historical Review* 34 (January 1959): 41–51.

6. This argument was put forth by Cecil Robinson, *With the Ears of Strangers,* pp. 29–30, and Samuel H. Lowrie, *Culture Conflict in Texas, 1821–35* (New York, 1935), pp. 82, 88. Herbert E. Bolton, in a more generalized essay, advanced a similar thesis; see Bolton, "Defensive Spanish Exploration and the Significance of the Borderlands," in John Francis Bannon, ed., *Bolton and the Spanish Borderlands* (Norman, Okla., 1964), pp 33–34.

7. Mier y Terán to Guadalupe Victoria, Nacogdoches, June 30, 1828, in Allaine

Howren, "Causes and Origin of the Decree of April 6, 1830," *Southwestern Historical Quarterly* 16 (April 1913): 395.

8. Robinson, *With the Ears of Strangers*, p. 29.

9. Austin to J. E. B. Austin, July 8, 1822, Austin Papers, quoted in Lowrie, *Culture Conflict*, p. 89.

10. See J. Fred Rippy, *Joel R. Poinsett, Versatile American* (Durham, N.C., 1935).

11. J. R. Poinsett, *Notes on Mexico, Made in the Autumn of 1822 . . .* (London, 1825), p. 37. At one point Poinsett departs from his generalization to indicate that the "labouring class" in cities, towns and countryside is "industrious" (p. 163).

12. *Ibid.*, pp. 161, 162, 112.

13. *Ibid.*, pp. 160, 100, 174, 51.

14. See, for example, *ibid.*, p. 88.

15. *Ibid.*, Appendix, p. 7.

16. C. Harvey Gardiner, ed., *Mexico, 1825–1828. The Journal and Correspondence of Edward Thornton Tayloe* (Chapel Hill, N.C., 1959), pp. 54, 69, 116, 55.

17. The writings of Poinsett and Tayloe are the only book-length descriptions of Mexico by Anglo-Americans to be published in the 1820s. See C. Harvey Gardiner, "Foreign Travelers' Accounts of Mexico, 1810–1910," *The Americas* 8 (January 1952): 321–51.

18. Such views continued to be articulated by visitors to Mexico City in the 1830s and 1840s, as Leary's dissertation, "Attitudes of Certain United States Citizens," suggests. By that time, of course, these views could have been influenced by reports about Mexicans on the frontier.

19. Harry Bernstein, *Making an Inter-American Mind* (Gainesville, Fla., 1961), pp. 6–10. See also Stanley T. Williams, *The Spanish Background of American Literature*, 2 vols. (New Haven, Conn., 1955), 1: 9, 18.

20. Phillip Wayne Powell, *Tree of Hate: Propaganda and Prejudices Affecting United States Relations with the Hispanic World* (New York, 1971), p. 118. Powell's work is the best history of the Black Legend in English. Charles Gibson, ed., *The Black Legend: Anti-Spanish Attitudes in the Old World and the New* (New York, 1971), contains well-chosen selections of anti-Spanish writing.

21. The only other writers whom I am aware of who have made this connection are Robinson, in discussing the notion that Mexicans are unusually cruel in *With the Ears of Strangers*, p. 190, and Bernstein, who says that the Black Legend "became Americanized under the name of Manifest Destiny." See Bernstein, *Making an Inter-American Mind*, p. 4. Powell and Bernstein were both trained in Latin-American history. Historians of Manifest Destiny, such as Frederick Merk and Albert K. Weinberg, who were trained in United States history, seem to be unaware of the depth of anti-Latin feeling in the United States, or else believe it unimportant.

22. Garrard, *Wah-To-Yah and the Taos Trail*, p. 194.

23. For a discussion of this theme see Robinson, *With the Ears of Strangers*, pp. 67–74. In addition to those writers cited by Robinson, explicit statements about the evils of miscegenation are found in the writings of men like Rufus B. Sage, Thomas James, and Thomas J. Farnham.

24. See, for example, Odie B. Faulk, *Land of Many Frontiers. A History of the American Southwest* (New York: Oxford University Press, 1968), p. 79.

25. Charles Gibson, *Spain in America* (New York: Harper and Row, 1966), p. 190.

26. Silvio Zavala, "The Frontiers of Hispanic America," in Walker D. Wyman and Clifton B. Kroeber, eds., *The Frontier in Perspective* (Madison: University of Wisconsin Press, 1965), pp. 36–58. France Scholes, "Civil Government and Society in New Mexico in the Seventeenth Century," *New Mexico Historical Review* 10 (April 1935): 98. Not all historians, of course, would agree with Scholes and Zavala. Two recent works that suggest opposite conclusions are C. Alan Hutchinson, *Frontier Settlement in Mexican California* (New Haven: Yale University Press, 1969), p. 399; and Lynn I. Perrigo, *The American Southwest: Its Peoples and Cultures* (New York: Holt, Rinehart and Winston, 1971), pp. 416–17.

27. For Ramos de Arizpe and Von Humboldt see Zavala, "The Frontiers of Hispanic America," pp. 48–49. For Pino, see his comments about paupers in Mexico in H. Bailey Carroll and J. Villasana Haggard, eds., *Three New Mexico Chronicles* (Albuquerque: Quivira Society, 1942), pp. 27–28.

28. "Pike's Observations on New Spain," in Donald Jackson, ed., *The Journals of Zebulon Montgomery Pike with Letters and Related Documents*, 2 vols. (Norman: University of Oklahoma Press, 1966), 2: 58. Among the few Americans who agreed with Pike's analysis in later years was John Fox Hammond, who thought the New Mexicans indolent, but nonetheless more industrious than "the inhabitants of lower Mexico." See Hammond, *A Surgeon's Report on Socorro New Mexico, 1852* (Santa Fe: Stagecoach Press, 1966), pp. 26–27.

29. Poinsett and Tayloe suggest this possibility in their observations on Mexico. Poinsett found rural Mexicans generally more virtuous than city-dwellers (*Notes on Mexico*, pp. 266–67; 163; 175). Both men offered something of a "reverse frontier thesis." As Poinsett put it, "where nature has done much, man is indolent," and he added: "To no part of the world has nature been more bountiful, and in no part of it is there so little of comfort among people" (p. 181). This environmental explanation for indolence was popular through much of the nineteenth century in describing Anglo-American residents of Texas, too. See Marilyn McAdams Sibley, *Travelers in Texas, 1761–1860* (Austin: University of Texas Press, 1967), p. 100. A more detailed analysis of the question of indolence on Mexico's far northern frontier would need to distinguish between regions of the frontier. See, for example, how Pike's description of Texas differed from his description of New York (Jackson, *Journals*, 2: 58, 80).

30. Farnham, *Travels*, p. 163.

31. Allport, *Nature of Prejudice*, p. 200.

32. Quoted in *ibid.*, p. 199. See also their fine brief discussion of this question in Joan W. Moore and Alfredo Cuéllar's *Mexican Americans* (Englewood Cliffs, N.J.: Prentice-Hall, 1970), p. 5.

33. Some Mexican visitors to the borderlands also viewed the residents there as lazy. An explanation for their reasons for doing so would require another paper. A good explanation in the case of the Franciscans in California is provided by Manuel P. Servín in "California's Hispanic Heritage: A View into the Spanish Myth," *Journal of San Diego History* 19 (Winter 1973): 1–9.

34. Allport, *Nature of Prejudice*, p. 190.

Chapter Two

Mexican Immigration

Mexican emigration to the United States is generally believed to have originated with the beginning of the bloody Mexican Revolution that overthrew the achieving, but despotic, Don Porfirio Díaz. Furthermore, it is generally believed by Chicanos and also by romantic Anglos that the Mexicans emigrated from areas formerly populated by the Aztecs; that the Mexican-Americans were of Spanish and Aztec descent; and, consequently, that they are sons of Aztlán, the mythical home of the Aztecs.

In reality, the Mexican emigration to the United States first took place after the Gadsden Purchase of 1853. The Mexicans, who were the often maligned Sonorans from less cultured northern Mexico, crossed the border into Arizona. Here these unrecognized pioneers worked as miners and railroad workers. But, as Manuel Servín shows in his article, "The Role of the Mexican-Americans in the Development of Early Arizona," they were also builders and leaders of the Copper State. And, to a great degree, they were an awakened minority who achieved more than the post-Revolution Mexican emigrants.

The post-Revolution emigration that lasted roughly from the fall of Díaz to the Great Depression is the one from which most Mexican-Americans are descended. It is the emigration from central Mexico that has led many Chicanos and Anglos to believe in the myth of Aztec descendancy and of Aztlán. Manuel Gamio, the distinguished Mexican anthropologist, presents a penetrating characterization of these Mexican emigrants from the central plateau in his "Culture Backgrounds and Culture Contacts."

The Role of Mexican-Americans in the Development of Early Arizona

Manuel P. Servín

The Mexican and Mexican-American impact on the development of Arizona truly begins after the Gadsden Purchase of 1853. Although Mexico possessed the former Spanish-settled area of the south from 1821 to 1853, Mexican influence in developing the territory failed to materialize. Apache raids, mission secularization policies, and national political chaos, as well as disregard for the frontier settlements, affected the establishments so drastically that

> When the United States acquired the strip of land below the Gila River, it was nearly deserted.... Ranchos and missions had been abandoned, rich mines containing gold and silver lay idle.... Tubac had been completely abandoned, while the population of Tucson,... had dwindled to about three hundred inhabitants. The adobe houses of these two towns were dilapidated and falling in ruins. The fertile bottom lands of the Santa Cruz River,... were now neglected.[1]

This sad picture of a declining Arizona did not change until after the United States took possession of the purchased territory and began the pacification of Indian hostilities. When the American reopening of mining areas was made possible by such prominent persons as Charles D. Poston, Herman Erhenberg, S. P. Heintzelman, and Sylvester Mowry, Mexican miners and settlers began immigrating in proportionately large numbers. By 1860 the population of Arizona was approximately 2,775, with some 963 Mexicans and 752 Mexican-Americans.[2] A decade later the territory's population increased to 9,659, having about 4,364 Mexicans and 871 Mexican-Americans.[3] Consequently it is evident that the impact of Mexicans and Mexican-Americans upon Arizona occurred and continued after annexation by the United States.

The Mexican and Mexican-American impact, whether it is praised or condemned, provided at least the needed manpower for starting anew the region's economic development and for enriching unscrupulous Anglo-American mining entrepreneurs. "The silver mine operators of Arizona," as W. Clement Eaton wrote,

> recruited their rough manual laborers almost wholly from the Mexican poor class. The Mexican peons, Phocian Way observed, were treated no better than slaves in the South. The peon was given fifty cents a day paid chiefly in merchandise at a high profit.... In addition to being lazy and stupid and not being able to speak English, they were treacherous and dangerous laborers, many of them criminals who fled from Sonora....[4]

Whether the poorly paid Mexicans were lazy, stupid, treacherous, and criminal appears debatable. Sylvester Mowry, Arizona's foremost Lothario and pioneer mine owner, presented a less critical view as he wrote that

> The question of labor is one which commends itself to the attention on the capitalist: cheap, and, under proper management, efficient and permanent. My own experience has taught me that the lower class of Mexicans, with the Opata and Yaqui Indians, are docile, faithful, good servants, capable of strong attachments when firmly and kindly treated. They have been peons . . . for generations. They will always remain so, as it is their natural condition.[5]

Apparently Mowry was not the only American mine owner who appreciated Mexican miners. Mexicans not only worked in Patagonia, Tubac, Cerro Colorado, the Santa Rita Mountains, the Santa Cruz Valley, and Ajo, but they also helped open the copper-mining areas of Morenci in the 1870s.[6]

Mexican miners, whether in the Tubac area or in Morenci, did much more than just rough manual work. Possessing a long mining tradition Mexican miners furnished the methods that proved successful in Arizona's pioneering mining industry. Joseph F. Park, writing on Tubac area mining, amply demonstrates this in his "History of Mexican Labor in Arizona During the Territorial Period" when he states that

> Even if other labor could have been obtained, the managers probably would have relied largely on Mexican workers during the early period. The Mexican people were adapted to this region and knew many practical applications of the resources in the Arizona-Sonora environment. There were always some hands who were familiar with the silver ores in southern Arizona and could prepare and extract them by simple methods where operators unaccustomed to this zone would have been at a loss without machinery and elaborate equipment.[7]

Park, however, is not the only Arizona historian who recognizes the Mexican contribution. Roberta Watt, in her "History of Morenci, Arizona," clearly shows the role played by Mexican miners in the opening of the Morenci copper mines by informing readers that

> The first smelter, known as the Stone House, was erected in Chase Creek. [Henry] Lesinsky, aware of the skill of the Mexicans in the craft of smelting, left them without interference to build and operate the first smelter in the district. The Mexicans in their native country for many generations had been engaged in mining and smelting copper ore. . . . For many years the Mexicans and Spanish had worked mines in what was later Arizona Territory. From 1855 the Ajo Mine was worked continuously, smelters were erected, and ore treated there. From this background came the first furnaces used in the Morenci district.[8]

In addition to furnishing labor and mining methods, the Mexicans—if one is to believe the Father of Arizona, Charles D. Poston—also contributed to civilizing the early mining frontier. According to the romantic, fun-loving Poston,

> Sonora has always been famous for the beauty and gracefulness of its señoritas. The civil wars in Mexico, and the exodus of the male population from Northern Mexico to California had disturbed the equilibrium of population. . . . Consequently, the señoritas and grass widows sought the American camp on the Santa Cruz River. . . .
>
> The Mexican señoritas really had a refining influence on the frontier population. Many of them had been educated at convents, and all of them were good Catholics. . . . They are exceedingly dainty in their underclothing—wear the finest linen they can afford; and spend their lives over the washing machine. The men of Northern Mexico are far inferior to the women in every respect.
>
> This accretion of female population added very much to the charms of frontier society. The Mexican women were not by any means useless appendages in camp. They could keep house, cook some dainty dishes, wash clothes, sew, dance and sing. Moreover, they were expert at cards. . . .[9]

Poston, incidentally, was not the only American who appreciated Mexican women and disdained the poorer Mexican men. According to Raphael Pumpelly, who published in 1870, "the men are mostly cut-throats and the women angels."[10]

Despite the racial or cultural antipathy demonstrated against poorer Mexican men by many Anglo-Americans—and especially by the *Weekly Arizonian* that warned "all 'gringos' who may have to pass through 'greaser' country, if they want to come out of it unscathed, to be always on the alert"[11]—a number of Mexicans and Mexican-Americans became eminently successful business, political, cultural, and community leaders. Outstanding among such achievers were Esteban Ochoa (1831–88), Mariano Guadalupe Samaniego (1844–1907), and Carlos C. Jácome (1870–1932) of Tucson; and Francisco Contreras (1795–?)[12] and José María Redondo of Yuma (1830–78).

Undoubtedly the best known of this Mexican-American elite was Esteban Ochoa, whose firm of Tully and Ochoa was "The king of the freighting industry in Arizona, prior to the arrival of the railroads."[13] Ochoa, however, was more than just the most successful businessman. He was one of Arizona's staunchest supporters of public education. As a member of the territorial legislature he introduced Governor A. P. K. Safford's bill for the establishment of Arizona's public schools. Later he donated ground for the first modern public school in Arizona and served as president of the Tucson School Board at the same time (1875) that he was mayor of the pueblo.[14]

Mariano Guadalupe Samaniego, who like Ochoa was born in Mexico, "belonged to that class of citizens of Spanish lineage who did so much for the establishment and development of the territory."[15] Becoming a United States citizen after the Gadsden Purchase, Samaniego lived at La Mesilla with his mother, attended and was graduated from Saint Louis University in 1862, and moved to Tucson in 1864. Samaniego achieved prominence as a freighter, cattle raiser, and public official.[16] Whereas Ochoa served three terms in the territorial legislature, Samaniego served four.[17] Like Ochoa, who promoted the public school system and served various terms on the Tucson School Board, Samaniego "was one of the first to espouse the cause of the State University and was one of the first members of its board of regents and for a time acted as treasurer of the institution."[18] Crowning Samaniego's cultural contributions to Arizonan life were his one term as president, five terms as a director, and seven terms as a vice-president of the renowned Arizona Pioneers' Historical Society.[19] Yet, despite the respect and honors bestowed upon him, Mariano G. Samaniego did not forget his people or reject his culture. Seeking to protect the Mexican-American in an area where the Anglo-American was arriving in large numbers, he became a founder and later president of the Alianza Hispano-Americana, the first successful Mexican-American organization in the entire Southwest.[20]

Carlos Corella Jácome, the third of the eminent Mexican-Americans of Tucson, also was born in Mexico.[21] Like Ochoa and Samaniego, Jácome was for that period a cultured person despite his lack of formal education. "He had been enrolled in Tucson's first public school and had been taught—for just three years—by the pioneer teacher, Ingeniero (Engineer) Ignacio Bonillas, a graduate of Massachusetts Institute of Technology who later became Mexican ambassador to the United States."[22] Bonillas greatly impressed Jácome who unfortunately had to leave school to support the family.[23] Beginning his career in the dry goods field by working for Isadore Mayer as cash boy and later as a clerk for I. Zeckendorf, Carlos Jácome, with his partner Loreto Carrillo, opened a dry goods store in 1896. Eventually Jácome obtained complete control, incorporated the company, and expanded the business into one of Tucson's leading stores.[24] Jácome, however, had interests other than just the development of his business. Like Mariano Samaniego, Jácome was deeply interested in the welfare of the Mexican-American. Consequently he belonged to the Alianza Hispano-Americana, in which he held the position of supreme treasurer for eighteen years.[25] In addition, and of greater importance to Arizona, he was a member of the Constitutional Convention of 1910.[26]

Ochoa, Samaniego, and Jácome, as well as the other, less-important Mexican-American pioneers of southern Arizona, definitely present proof that the Hispanic element in territorial Arizona was neither unprogressive nor irresponsible. Furthermore, the presence of these men proves the falsity of the repeated charge that "The Mexicans of the northern frontier [Sonora and Arizona] are the very lowest and poorest of their countrymen, living in hovels and sustaining themselves in some manner never yet determined or ascertained by any other people. They contaminate the region near them. They live in any manner except by hard work."[27]

It was not only the Mexican-American aristocracy of Tucson who worked hard and contributed to the territory's development and thereby disproved the above statement, but also the Contreras and Redondo families of Yuma. Francisco Contreras, a former California Sonoran miner and pioneer miner in the area of La Laguna near the Colorado River, became an early cattle raiser in that area.[28] He moved to Yuma shortly after its founding in 1867 and built an adobe with high and well-ventilated rooms,[29] just as Charles Trumbull Hayden had done in the Mexican-populated area of Tempe. Antonio Contreras, son of Francisco, became a teacher and merchant at La Laguna, then moved to Yuma where he constructed a family residence and a store.[30] In 1872 he served as a member of the United States Grand Jury. Jesús Contreras, another member of the family, also was appointed to the federal grand jury, in 1873.[31]

José María Redondo, who married Francisco's daughter Piedad, became more prominent in the history of Yuma than did Francisco Contreras.[32] Born in Altar, Sonora, José María accompanied his father to the California mines. He remained there until 1859 when he settled in La Laguna, becoming a placer miner, baker, and merchant.[33] By 1864 Redondo was classified by the *Federal Census* as the richest individual in the area of La Laguna.[34] In this same year he was elected to the council (upper house) of the First Legislative Assembly but was unable to serve because he was not a United States citizen. After receiving his naturalization papers, he was elected in 1873 to the house of representatives (lower house) where he became well known by voting against the celebrated divorce bill that would allow Governor Safford to marry Margarita Grijalva of Magdalena, Sonora.[35] A year later Redondo defeated his friend Michael Goldwater for a seat on the council and was instrumental in securing the territorial prison for Yuma.[36] His last political victory occurred in 1878 when he was elected mayor of Yuma, whose name he had helped change from Arizona City.[37]

José María Redondo was, however, more than just a political figure. In the North Gila Valley, lying between the Gila and the Colorado rivers, Redondo established the largest ranch—La Hacienda de San Isidro—in western Arizona.[38] As a pioneer of irrigation in Gila Valley, Redondo built "27 miles of canal, lateral and ditch costing $25,000. And he built them nearly 40 years before the Bureau of Reclamation existed or a government canal was started in the Yuma region."[39] According to Harold D. Weight, "With water on the land, orchards of peach, pear, apricot, pomegranate and date were set out. Vineyards were started. Two thousand acres were planted to corn, beans, wheat, barley, oats, alfalfa, melons, sugar cane, peanuts, garden vegetables. Cattle browsed in the bottomlands, horses and sheep in the pastures."[40] That cattle should browse in the hacienda's bottomlands was to be expected. José and his brother Jesús, who had a Spanish grant in Sonora, as early as 1854 had tried unsuccessfully to bring cattle from Mexico. "In 1874 they brought herds from California to their ranch near Yuma. Their cattle, the first large herd in Yuma County, ranged over an area of a hundred miles. The Redondos supplied the local market, and also had contracts with Uncle Sam. In the late 1870's they sold beef to the Southern Pacific, which was then building across southern Arizona."[41]

In addition to such prominent men as José María Redondo, Francisco Contreras, Carlos C. Jácome, Mariano G. Samaniego, and Esteban Ochoa, there were numerous less-distinguished Mexican-Americans who contributed to the development of Arizona in prestate days. Included in this group of less-distinguished Mexican-Americans are some of the delegates from the Gadsden Purchase area who, after seeing ten Arizona territorial bills fail, decided in 1860 "to create a government of their own without benefit of congressional sanction." On April 2, 1860, an unsanctioned constitutional convention began deliberations at Tucson. Among the thirty-one representatives who signed the illegal Provisional Constitution of the Territory of Arizona—a constitution that in fact governed the residents of the Gadsden Purchase for a brief period—were nine or ten Mexican-Americans. Four signers—Esteban Ochoa, Epifanio Aguirre, José María Chávez, and José María García—were living or later lived in present-day Arizona.[42] The other Mexican-Americans—including the lieutenant governor of the provisional territory, Ignacio Orrantia—were from New Mexico.[43]

Although the illegal provisional territorial government is considered by some authorities to be the precursor of the Confederate territory of Arizona (1861–62),[44] it is interesting to note that very few Mexican-Americans played any role during this Confederate period.[45] Esteban Ochoa, Tucson's most prominent citizen, preferred exile to swearing allegiance to the Confederate States.[46]

After the downfall of the Confederacy (1862) and the establishment of an organized Arizona Territory by Congress (1863), Mexican-Americans, both the elite and lesser lights, once again contributed actively in public life. Although the new officials of the territory "were mostly defeated 'lame-duck' politicians,"[47] legislative members of the council and the house of representatives were elected. In the First Legislative Assembly of the State of Arizona (1864)—which was composed of nine council members and eighteen representatives—two Mexican-American councillors (Francisco S. León of Tucson and José María Redondo of Arizona City) and one representative (Jesús M. Elías of Tucson) were elected.[48] After this initial showing, Mexican-Americans became visibly weaker in the political life of the territory. Between 1865 and 1909 the Mexican-American population of the territory was represented by Francisco León (1865 and 1871), Esteban Ochoa (1868, 1871, and 1877), Jesús Elías (1868 and 1875), Juan Elías (1871 and 1873), Ramón Romano (1871), José María Redondo (1873, 1875, and 1877), M. G. Samaniego (1877, 1881, 1891, and 1895), N. González (1899 and 1903), and Alfred Ruiz (1905).[49] Thus it is patent that as far as prestate Arizona was concerned Mexican-American representation and participation in the governmental administration of the territory greatly diminished after 1877. This was the turning point for Mexican-American political strength, as Jay J. Wagoner so cogently stated:

> That year [1877] may be counted as something of a turning point in Arizona's history. The Indians had in the main been pacified, although outbreaks occurred after this date; the Southern Pacific Railroad was coming in from the west; many rich mines were being discovered, and prospectors were swarming into the territory. Since there was relative safety from Indians, stockmen were bringing in herds of cattle and sheep to graze on fresh pastures, and the export and import trade was growing rapidly. Northern Arizona received the bulk of this new immigration. The change in balance of power from south to north was signalized . . . by the scarcity of Mexican-American representation after that date.[50]

It was to prevent their being overwhelmed by the hordes of Anglo-American and European immigrants—many of whom would demonstrate an anti-Mexican bias in the next few decades—that the Mexican-American elite of Arizona founded the Alianza Hispano-Americana. Through this organization they sought to maintain political representation as well as to continue the contribution of Mexican-Americans to the development of Arizona and the greater Southwest.[51]

The Alianza was founded in Tucson on January 14, 1894. Its founders and early members included such prominent individuals as Carlos Ignacio Velasco, Mariano Guadalupe Samaniego, Pedro C. Pellón, Enrique (Henry) Meyer, Carlos (Charles) Tully, Mateo Poe, Carlos Jácome, and José M. Elías.[52] Ostensibly founded to strive for and to preserve the unity and well-being of as well as give help and protection to the Hispanic-American residents of Tucson,[53] the organization was incorporated in 1907, becoming more than just a fraternal and mutual benefit society.[54] Under the articles of incorporation the Alianza could be classified as a financial Mexican-American organization.[55]

Expanding throughout Arizona, the West, and even Mexico, the organization by November 1932 claimed 11,176 members in Arizona, California, New Mexico, Texas, Colorado, Wyoming, and Mexico.[56] Furthermore, it had a balance of $26,318.97 in funeral funds and $796,757.34 in capital, real estate, loans, equipment, and stock.[57] Yet, the Alianza did not neglect its primary goals of "Protección, Moralidad, and Instrucción" (Protection, Morality, and Instruction). In 1931 the Alianza initiated in California a plan "for the establishment of classes in grammar, history, civics and English in addition to the regular ritualistic work required of juveniles by Alianza."[58] In 1955 the Alianza officially began working for civil rights when it established a Civil Rights Department "equipped with a means to defend the legal rights of the Mexican-American people within the framework of American Democracy."[59] A year later the organization embarked on an educational project "of making scholarships available to qualified students of Mexican-American descent having need for such financial assistance."[60]

Although the Alianza officially never participated in politics, there are persuasive indications that unofficially the organization, through its officers and members, was at various times politically involved by its support of candidates acceptable to Mexican-Americans.[61] Unfortunately, the Alianza, the first successful organization to influence Mexican-Americans and Anglo-Americans throughout the Southwest, had a devastating decline in the 1960s.

The work that the Alianza accomplished—despite its ignominious decline—is important to both Mexican-Americans and Anglo-Americans. It provided needed fraternal and insurance benefits to all classes of Spanish-speaking southwesterners. It guaranteed Mexican-Americans some representation and political power. It created a class of leaders at a time when Mexican-Americans were most neglected and even despised outside of southern Arizona and New Mexico. Finally, because of the aspirations of the leaders and membership, it bridged, depending on the leadership and the area, the gap or gulf existing between the Spanish- and English-speaking Americans.

Less known than the work of the Alianza Hispano-Americana is the role that Mexican miners played in instigating the development of the labor movement in the territory of Arizona. "The first local of the Western Federation of Mines [WFM] to survive was formed in Globe in 1896."[62] The issue that most unified and spurred the members of this white labor organization was their prejudice against Mexican workers who received less wages for the same type work. As the first miners' union to successfully strike, the Globe WFM local not only succeeded in protecting white wages but also helped "all those who wished to keep Globe a 'white man's town.' "[63]

A more positive contribution to the development of the labor movement and to social justice in Arizona was made in 1903 by the Mexican and central-European miners of the Clifton-Morenci area. Ignored by organized labor and discriminated against by management, Mexican and Italian and Slavonian workers—led by Abrán F. Salicido (Mexican), Frank Colombo (Italian), and W. H. "Mocho" Laustenneau (Rumanian)—closed down the Clifton-Morenci district as they sought wages equal to those paid native white Americans and northern Europeans.[64] Although the strike failed as the result of the activities of the sheriff, his civilian deputies, the Arizona Rangers, the National Guard, and federal troops, the Anglo-American populace become more anti-Mexican as a vast majority of the strikers were Mexicans and several newspapers vigorously denounced them.[65] Yet, not all the results of the strike were detrimental to the Spanish-speaking community of the territory. Joseph F. Park, the authority on Mexican labor in territorial Arizona, makes this clear when he describes the end of the strike:

> Arizona's first major strike came to a close. The strikers were disarmed, their houses searched, and arrests made, following which leaders were taken for trial and ultimate confinement in the territorial prison at Yuma. Though the companies won an easy victory, they had done so behind an array of troops larger than any witnessed in Arizona since the campaigns of General Crook during the closing years of the Apache wars. This fact brought even greater notoriety to the "Mexican Affair" at Clifton and may have exerted a sobering effect on the WFM in regard to Mexican workers, as well as illustrating the extent to which employers might go to prevent the spread of unionism in Arizona. In any event, the WFM was impressed to the point of making a statement which constituted the only tribute the strikers received for their efforts. On being questioned as to the position the union intended to take in regard to the strike and its outcome, WFM President, Charles Moyer, answered from their regional headquarters at Denver, "The men at Morenci have the full support of the Western Federation of Miners."[66]

Although the Mexican miners might have won the support of the white WFM and advanced the cause of labor, they did not win the sympathy of the Anglo-Arizonans whose sentiments were agitated by the antedeluvian newspapers.

The anti-Mexican feeling that was aggravated by the strikes of 1886 and 1903 in a tragic manner led to the most selfless contribution that the underpaid Mexican-American miners of Clifton-Morenci made, in their initiation of the children's adoption movement in territorial Arizona. In 1904, about a year after the Mexican-American miners had lost the battle to get equal pay for equal work in "Arizona's first major strike,"[67] Father Constant Mandin of Clifton-Morenci received two letters from the New York Foundling Hospital, informing him "of the availability of small children for placement in foster homes." Reading the second letter to his preponderantly Mexican-American parish, Father Mandin, recently arrived from France and unaware of the area's deep racial prejudice, recommended thirty-three families as foster parents for the orphans. The families, all perhaps but one, were those of Mexican-American miners earning one dollar and fifty cents to two dollars and fifty cents daily.[68] Somehow each family was able to save between thirty dollars and forty dollars to pay for part of the children's clothing and railroad fare. Consequently, a special railroad car from New York arrived at Clifton with some forty children, three Sisters of Charity, three nurses, and the agent of the Foundling Hospital.[69]

The children's arrival as well as the news that they were to be placed in "Mexican" homes precipitated a memorable scene at the station. Anglo-American women asked about the placement of the children from New York; "Noticing that some of the people were not as fair as she had hoped," Sister Anna Michaella Bowen was "purported to have asked if there were any 'half breeds' " among the future foster parents;[70] finally, "some of the [Anglo-American] ladies, so struck by the children's beauty, held them in arms longer than necessary, and some came right out and asked the agent and the priest if they could have a child to keep."[71]

When the Anglo-Americans learned that sixteen children had been placed in various Clifton Mexican-American homes, they became an excited crowd that counted among its leaders Deputy Sheriff Jeff Dunagan. After a second meeting at Clifton, the so-called Anglo-Americans formed a vigilante committee of twenty-five to take the children from the Mexican-American foster parents. Armed, and acting in a ruthless manner, the vigilantes quickly obtained the children and alleged that they were in a "filthy condition, covered with vermin, and with two or three exceptions, ill and nauseated from the effects of coarse Mexican beans, chiles, watermelons, and other 'improper' food which had been fed them. In some instances beer and whiskey had been given them to drink."[72]

Also at Morenci, where the remainder of the orphans had been taken, a small group of bigoted Anglo-Americans sought to recover children given to Mexican-American foster parents. Charles E. Mills, superintendent of the Detroit Copper Company, acted as leader of the Anglo-American group first in trying to persuade the Foundling Hospital agent, G. Whitney Swayne, to remove the children from the Mexican homes and then in demanding it.[73] After Swayne rejected Mills' first entreaty,

> Mills once again tried to explain the situation to him [Swayne] in calm measured words. He said that the families which got the children, at least in Morenci, were the lowest of the low Mexicans. Some of them did not even have a bed to sleep on, and those that were working got only two dollars a day. In some cases they would sleep five or six to a room. It was a disgrace to the American people to place white children with people like that.
>
> Swayne had heard enough, and he told the three men that sort of talk and attitude expressed was a disgrace and made him ashamed to be an American. . . .[74]

When asked if he would like to explain his feelings to the people of Morenci, Swayne refused on the grounds that he was not going to be dictated to. His words and attitude were related to the crowd, which became "fighting mad" and threatened to recover the children. Fearing action by the crowd, Mills accompanied by Deputy Dunagan and three other men again approached Swayne who was with Father Mandin.[75]

> Mills began to lecture to the two men. Besides being the most important man in town, Mills was a forceful and impressive personality, so Swayne listened as he was told that no matter what his sensibilities or the sentiments he had brought with him from New York, he was now in Morenci, Arizona Territory, and what he had done in placing the children violated some of the deepest feelings and strongest convictions of the Americans in the community. . . . Swayne could not have lit a faster fuse, he said, than by putting these white babies in low-class Mexican homes.[76]

Consequently Swayne ordered the children withdrawn from the Mexican-American homes at Morenci. At Clifton, however, the foundlings were taken from the foster parents by the Anglo-Saxons. Some children were redistributed by the crowd among Anglo-American or European-born persons. Wanting to adopt the children, the Anglo-Americans were frustrated as Agent Swayne continued to insist that the children belonged to the New York Foundling Hospital. Furthermore, County Probate Judge P. C. Little stated that he could not issue "adoption papers without the consent of the institution." The crowd became so angry that it shouted Judge Little down and took on the aspect of a "lynch mob." Father Mandin and Agent Swayne—after the people of Morenci also had decided to distribute the children among themselves—found it imperative to depart from Clifton and go to El Paso. The Sisters of Charity were pressured into departing. Mocked and reviled, they were forced to leave nineteen children in Anglo-American homes in territorial Arizona.[77]

After the departure of the Sisters of Charity and Agent Swayne, the press, especially the southwestern press, preponderantly defended the action of the vigilante mob, castigated Swayne and the Foundling Hospital, and degraded the Mexican-American families.[78] Such press activities, however, did not insure the illegal Anglo-American foster parents against legal action by the Foundling Hospital. Consequently, the foster parents, represented by John C. Gatti, a Clifton butcher, began proceedings for adoption by petitioning the probate court of Judge Little. Judge Little did his duty as he saw it, and ruled against the Foundling Hospital by awarding guardianship to the foster parents. The hospital reacted by having its attorneys in Arizona appeal Judge Little's decision to the Arizona Supreme Court. The hearings took one week—a week in which Mexicans were downgraded. On January 21, 1905, the supreme court ruled in favor of the Anglo-American foster parents.[79]

By its ruling the court not only awarded the children to the Anglo-American foster parents but also gave legal credence to rampant anti-Mexican prejudice. Yet, despite the prejudice, anguish, and debasement that the Mexicans and Mexican-Americans of Clifton-Morenci endured, their contribution to the adoption movement in territorial Arizona was positive. Although deprived of the foster children because of their Mexican background, the Mexican-Americans by their initial move to give a home to Celto- and Anglo-American children of dubious background aroused the English-speaking Arizonans to join the first adoption program, one that they had never conceived, planned, or even considered.

The prejudice fanned by the tragic Clifton-Morenci adoptions was intensified to a previously unreached height. In 1909 the Anglo-American majority took a serious step in forestalling whatever political impact Mexican-Arizonans might have had in the political life of the territory by passage of the Literacy Law. The Democrats, believing that the Mexican and Mexican-American element favored the Republican party, overrode Governor Joseph Kibbey's veto and passed the law.[80] The actual law sounded innocuous if not patriotic, since it stated that "no person shall be registered who not being prevented by physical disability from so doing is unable to read the Constitution in the English language in such a manner as to show he is neither prompted nor reciting from memory or unable to write his name."[81]

Whether acting from vested interest or from a sense of justice, Republican Governor Richard E. Sloan complained bitterly against this law. Writing to Michael G. Burns, the Irish-named Democratic Campaign Committee chairman on February 18, 1910, Governor Sloan denounced the law and the Democratic party:

> The territorial act disfranchising Spanish speaking citizens is in my judgment to be condemned because it is plainly partisan, unjust, discriminatory and instead of intending to purify and elevate the elector, it is so drawn as to be a ready instrument of fraud in hands of corrupt and unfair election officers and boards. . . .
>
> It is unjust and undemocratic to include in this discrimination a large number of intelligent, respectable, law-abiding and patriotic men, whose ancestors lived here long before any American visited the territory, . . . who have property and pay taxes, who are rearing children here, and who by every consideration are entitled to all rights and privileges of citizenship.
>
> It is a wholesale disfranchisement of the respectable element of our Mexican population who by all rights of birth, ancestry, identification with country and treaty rights as well, have a just claim to consideration in any scheme looking to the curtailment of the privileges of citizenship.[82]

Strong as Governor Sloan's protest was, it had little impact on either the leaders of the Democratic party or the captains of labor. Working in almost complete unity, like a family living out of wedlock, leading members of the Democratic party and of organized labor attempted to impose another legislative child during the Constitutional Convention of 1910. This bastard child would prohibit noncitizens from working on public works and exclude non-English-speaking persons from doing hazardous work,[83] and it would seriously curtail the right of Mexicans and Mexican-Americans to support their families and to contribute to the development of the area. The prohibition of noncitizens—except prisoners—from working on public works was approved and included in the Arizona State Constitution.[84] The move to exclude non-English-speaking persons from performance of hazardous work—a ruse to deprive Mexicans and Mexican-Americans of work in the mines and to prevent the mine operators from obtaining cheap labor—fortunately failed.[85]

Despite this important victory, allowing them to perform hazardous work, Mexicans and Mexican-Arizonans by the time Arizona became a state could not and were not allowed to play an essential role in the development of their state. Their previous role in which they had contributed to the territory's economic, social, and political growth was ignored. Unfortunately, this role, which is one of achievement, is still being ignored in Arizona.

Notes

1. W. Clement Eaton, "Frontier Life in Southern Arizona, 1858–1861," *The Southwestern Historical Quarterly*, 36 (January 1933): 173–174.
2. Joseph F. Park, "The History of Mexican Labor in Arizona during the Territorial Period" (M.A. thesis, University of Arizona, 1961), pp. 118, 119. Park estimates that in the Census of 1860 over 80 percent of the 941 Arizona-born population was of Mexican descent. To avoid overestimating the Mexican-American population, I have kept the estimate to a strict 80 percent.
3. *Ibid.*, pp. 137, 138. In this Census of 1870 Park estimates that over 70 percent of the Arizona-born inhabitants were Mexican-Americans. Again to avoid overestimating the Mexican-American population, I have kept the figure to a strict 70 percent.
4. Eaton, "Frontier Life in Southern Arizona," pp. 188–189. See also William A. Duffen, "Overland Via 'Jackass Mail' in 1858: The Diary of Phocian R. Way," *Arizona and the West* 2 (Autumn 1960): 288–289.
5. Sylvester Mowry, *Arizona and Sonora: The Geography, History, and Resources of the Silver Region of North America* (New York: Harper and Brothers, 1864), p. 94.
6. Roberta Watt, "History of Morenci, Arizona" (M.A. thesis, University of Arizona, 1956), pp. 13–14.
7. Park, "History of Mexican Labor," pp. 51–52.
8. Watt, "History of Morenci," pp. 13–14.
9. As quoted in Thomas Edwin Farish, *History of Arizona*, 8 vols. (Phoenix: State of Arizona, 1915–18), 1: 282.
10. Raphael Pumpelly, *Across America and Asia* (New York: Leypoldt and Holt, 1870), p. 44. For another example of the Anglo-Americans' attraction to Mexican women in Arizona in the early days, see Duffen, "Diary of Phocian R. Way," p. 162, where he writes "Among the native women here I believe that chastity is a virtue unknown. They are remarkable for the ease and grace of their movements and their brilliant black eyes. Some of them are very bold. They have a great fancy for Americans and a greaser stands no chance with a white man. They are generally tender-hearted and humane, and in sickness are noted for being good and faithful nurses. Nearly every man in our mail party seems to have a lover here, . . ."
11. *Weekly Arizonan*, October 6, 1859, Arizona Historical Foundation, Charles Trumbull Hayden Library, Arizona State University.
12. I have been unable to ascertain the date of Francisco Contreras's death.
13. Odie B. Faulk, *Arizona: A Short History* (Norman: University of Oklahoma Press, 1970), p. 151. See also Frank C. Lockwood, *Pioneer Portraits* (Tucson: University of Arizona Press, 1968), pp. 73–75; "Estevan Ochoa," Clip Books, Arizona Historical Society; Elizabeth Albrecht, "Estevan Ochoa, Mexican-American Businessman–Settler–and Union Supporter," Esteban Ochoa Collection, Arizona Historical Society.
14. Lockwood, *Pioneer Portraits*, p. 77; "Old Tucson News and Stories by Herbert Drachman," *Tucson Citizen*, October 22, 1924, Arizona Historical Society; John G. Bourke, *On the Border with Crook* (New York: Charles Scribner's Sons, 1891), pp. 76–77. For contemporary clippings on Ochoa's activities see "Estevan Ochoa,"

Clip Books, Arizona Historical Society and Esteban Ochoa Collection, Arizona Historical Society.

15. John C. McClintock, *Arizona: Prehistoric–Aboriginal–Pioneer–Modern: The Nation's Youngest Commonwealth within a Land of Ancient Culture: Biographical*, 3 vols. (Chicago: S. J. Clarke Publishing Co., 1916), 3: 543. See also Richard G. Schaus, "Mariano Samaniego, 1844–1907," *Arizona Cattlelog* 22 (April 1966): 42, 40.

16. *Arizona Daily Star*, August 9, 1907, Arizona Historical Society; Schaus, "Mariano G. Samaniego, pp. 42, 40; "Mariano G. Samaniego," Clip Books, Arizona Historical Society; Mariano G. Samaniego Collection, Arizona Historical Society.

17. Jay J. Wagoner, *Arizona Territory, 1863–1912: A Political History* (Tucson: University of Arizona Press, 1970), pp. 509, 510, 513, 515, 520, 522.

18. McClintock, *Arizona*, 3: 544. See also Douglas D. Martin, *The Lamp in the Desert: The Story of the University of Arizona* (Tucson: University of Arizona Press, 1960), pp. 24–25, 290; Tomás Serrano Cabo, *Crónicas: Alianza Hispano-Americana* (Tucson: [Alianza Hispano-Americana, 1929]), p. 287, Chicano Collection, Arizona State University.

19. "Officers of the Arizona Pioneers' Historical Society, 1884–1915," Arizona Historical Society; Serrano Cabo, *Crónicas*, pp. 19–20.

20. Serrano Cabo, *Crónicas*, pp. 19–20.

21. *Arizona Daily Star*, March 16, 1946, Arizona Historical Society.

22. "The Jácome Story by Alex G. Jácome: Part I—How It Began," *Arizona Daily Star*, August 11, 1957, Arizona Historical Society.

23. *Ibid.*

24. *Arizona Daily Star*, March 16, 1946, Arizona Historical Society; Alex G. Jácome, *1896-1946: The Story of Jácome's* (Tucson: n.p., 1946); Mose Drachman to Carlos Jácome (Tucson, n.d.), Alexander G. Jácome Collection, Arizona Historical Society.

25. Richard E. Sloan and Ward R. Adams, *History of Arizona*, 4 vols. (Phoenix: Record Publishing Co., 1930), 4: 306.

26. *Arizona Daily Star*, March 16, 1946, Arizona Historical Society.

27. *A Reprint of The History of Arizona Territory, Showing its Resources and Advantages* (Flagstaff: Northland Press, 1964), p. 150. See also Park, "History of Mexican Labor," pp. 1–45.

28. Paul Figueroa, "The Early Days of Yuma," *Arizona Quarterly*, 1 (Spring 1945): 44–46; Frank D. Robertson, "A History of Yuma Arizona, 1540–1920" (M.A. thesis, University of Arizona, 1942), pp. 58–59.

29. Figueroa, "The Early Days of Yuma," p. 46.

30. Robertson, "History of Yuma Arizona," p. 60; *Federal Census—Territory of New Mexico and Territory of Arizona*, Senate Doc. 13, 89th Cong., 1st Sess. (Washington, D.C.: Government Printing Office, 1965), pp. 95, 235.

31. Apparently Jesús Contreras also was the son of Francisco. See Genealogy in Francisco Contreras Collection, Arizona Historical Society, and *Federal Census—Territory of New Mexico and Territory of Arizona*, p. 95.

32. Genealogy in Francisco Contreras Collection, Arizona Historical Society; "Hon. José M. Redondo," *Arizona Sentinel*, June 22, 1878, Sacks Collection, Arizona State University.

33. William H. Westover, *Yuma Footprints* (Tucson: Arizona Pioneers' Historical Society, 1966), p. 81; "Hon. José M. Redondo," *Arizona Sentinel*.

34. *Federal Census—Territory of New Mexico and Territory of Arizona*, pp. 95–96.

35. Wagoner, *Arizona Territory*, pp. 114–115.

36. *Ibid.*

37. "Hon. José M. Redondo," *Arizona Sentinel*; Harold O. Weight, "Lost Rancho on the Gila," *Westways*, 48 (March 1956): 11; Westover, *Yuma Footprints*, p. 84. For a very complete list of Redondo's public service as school board trustee, county supervisor, mayor, and legislator see "José María Redondo," Hayden Bibliographical File, Charles Trumbull Hayden Library, Arizona State University.

38. "Hon. José M. Redondo," *Arizona Sentinel*; Westover, *Yuma Footprints*, p. 82; Weight, "Lost Rancho on the Gila," pp. 10–11.
39. Weight, "Lost Rancho on the Gila," p. 11.
40. *Ibid.*
41. Madaline Paré with the collaboration of Bert Fireman, *Arizona Pageant: A Short History of the 48th State* (Tempe: Arizona Historical Foundation, 1970), p. 186. Also see Bert Haskett, "Early History of the Cattle Industry," in "José María Redondo," Hayden Biographical File, Arizona State University.
42. B. Sacks, *Be It Enacted: The Creation of the Territory of Arizona* (Phoenix: Arizona Historical Foundation, 1964), pp. 35–36, 133–53; Will C. Barnes, *Arizona Place Names* (Tucson: University of Arizona Press, 1935), *passim*.
43. Sacks, *Be It Enacted*, pp. 35–36, 133, 153.
44. *Ibid.*, p. 40.
45. Mariano G. Samaniego is one of the rare exceptions. He was an interpreter for the Confederates during the occupation of Arizona. See Schaus, "Mariano G. Samaniego, 1844–1907," p. 42.
46. Bourke, *On the Border with Crook*, pp. 76–77.
47. Wagoner, *Arizona Territory*, pp. 30–31.
48. *Ibid.*, p. 43.
49. *Ibid.*, pp. 506–29.
50. *Ibid.*, p. 117.
51. Serrano Cabo, *Crónicas*, pp. 17–18.
52. *Ibid.*, pp. 18–19. See also "Acta de la Instalación de la Sociedad Alianza Hispano-Americana," copy of the original, March 11, 1906, in Alianza Hispano-Americana Collection, Arizona Historical Society.
53. "Estatutos de la Sociedad Hispano-Americana de Tucsón, Arizona, Aprobados el 18 de Febrero de 1893, Reformados el 10 de Marzo de 1895" in the Alianza Hispano-Americana Collection, Arizona Historical Society.
54. "Articles of Incorporation, Sociedad del Edificio de la Logia Fundadora de la A.H.A." in the Alianza Hispano-Americana Collection, Arizona Historical Society.
55. *Ibid.*
56. *Alianza*, 25 (Diciembre 1932–Enero 1933), p. 45.
57. *Ibid.*
58. Clipping, *Arizona Daily Star*, July 8, 1931, Alianza Hispano-Americana Collection, Arizona Historical Society.
59. *Alianza*, 48 (Marzo de 1955), pp. 12–13.
60. *Looking Across: Toward the Education of a People—Alianza Scholarship Foundation*, mimeographed pamphlet, March 9, 1956, p. 2.
61. See Kathleen Conrad, "Alianza Hispano-Americana: A Preliminary Study of the First Successful Mexican-American Organization" (Paper delivered at the Phi Alpha Theta Regional Conference, April 24, 1971, New Mexico State University, Las Cruces), "Alianza Hispano-Americana," MS, January 4, 1971, and "Motivation behind the Alianza Hispano-Americana," MS, March 19, 1971. See also Kaye Briegel, "The Development of Mexican-American Organizations," in Manuel P. Servín, ed., *The Mexican-Americans: An Awakening Minority* (Beverly Hills: Glencoe Press, 1970), pp. 163–64.
62. Edward H. Peplow, Jr., *History of Arizona*, 3 vols. (New York: Lewis Historical Publishing Co., 1958), 2: 56; Park, "History of Mexican Labor," pp. 248–49.
63. Park, "History of Mexican Labor," pp. 249–50; A. Blake Brophy, *Foundlings on the Frontier: Racial and Religious Conflict in Arizona Territory, 1904–1905* (Tucson: University of Arizona Press, 1972), p. 17.
64. Park, "History of Mexican Labor," pp. 253, 255–57; Brophy, *Foundlings on the Frontier*, pp. 17–19; Wagoner, *Arizona Territory*, pp. 384–86.
65. Wagoner, *Arizona Territory*, pp. 385–90; Park, "History of Mexican Labor," pp. 358–59; Brophy, *Foundlings on the Frontier*, pp. 18–19; McClintock, *Arizona*, 2: 527–28.

66. Park, "History of Mexican Labor," p. 259.
67. Brophy, *Foundlings on the Frontier,* pp. 18–19. Park, "History of Mexican Labor," p. 259, classifies this strike as "Arizona's first major strike."
68. Brophy, *Foundlings on the Frontier,* pp. 27–28.
69. Raymond A. Mulligan, "New York Foundlings at Clifton-Morenci: Social Justice in Arizona Territory, 1904–1905," in Servín, *Mexican-Americans,* pp. 57–59.
70. *Ibid.,* p. 58.
71. Brophy, *Foundlings on the Frontier,* p. 31.
72. Mulligan, "New York Foundlings at Clifton-Morenci," pp. 59–60.
73. Brophy, *Foundlings on the Frontier,* pp. 34–41.
74. *Ibid.,* p. 41.
75. *Ibid.,* pp. 41–43.
76. *Ibid.,* p. 43.
77. *Ibid.,* pp. 43–62.
78. *Ibid.,* pp. 67–76.
79. *Ibid.,* pp. 77–96; Mulligan, "New York Foundlings at Clifton-Morenci," pp. 62–65.
80. *Acts, Resolutions and Memorials of the Twenty-fifth Legislative Assembly of the Territory of Arizona* (Phoenix: H. H. McNeil Co., 1909), p. 13; Wagoner, *Arizona Territory,* p. 448; McClintock, Arizona, 2: 358.
81. *Acts, Resolutions and Memorials of the Twenty-fifth Legislative Assembly of the Territory of Arizona,* p. 13.
82. "Disfranchising the Spanish-American Pioneers," in *Statehood: The Paramount Issue* [Tucson: Citizen Print, 1910], GP-18, Arizona Collection, Arizona State University.
83. Park, "History of Mexican Labor," pp. 269–70; Calvin N. Brice, "The Constitutional Convention of Arizona" (M.A. thesis, Arizona State University, 1953), pp. 59–60. For the influence of white labor in the Constitutional Convention, see Tru Anthony McGinnis, "The Influence of Organized Labor on the Making of the Arizona Constitution" (M.A. thesis, University of Arizona, 1930).
84. Constitution of the State of Arizona (Phoenix: Department of Library and Archives, 1939), art. 18, sec. 10; Brice, "Constitutional Convention of Arizona," p. 60.
85. Park, "History of Mexican Labor," pp. 269–78; Brice, "Constitutional Convention of Arizona," p. 60.

Culture Backgrounds and Culture Contacts*

Manuel Gamio

In studying contact between American civilization and that of the Mexican immigrants, we must first consider the separate character of each. The first is a modern, integrated, and homogeneous civilization, with material and intellectual characteristics shared by all the people living within the borders of the country with some vari-

*From Manuel Gamio, *Mexican Immigration to the United States* (New York: Arno Press, 1969). Reprinted by permission of Arno Press, Inc.

ations between social levels, but always preserving its typical characteristics.

The Mexican immigrants, on the other hand, arrive in the United States with widely diverse cultural baggage, differing completely from that of the United States and also exhibiting marked differences within itself. Roughly divided, three cultural groups corresponding to racial elements can be described among the Mexican immigrants as follows:

1. Modern civilization derived from Europe or the United States, but developed within and modeled to Mexican environment. To this belong the social minorities of white Mexicans and mestizos. The proportion of immigrants of this type is very small, and therefore it is not necessary to consider them as a part of the general problem.

2. Ancient aboriginal civilization, different in type from the modern, and much simpler, that is, with fewer material and intellectual cultural elements. It represents the type of social groups still in relatively inferior stages of development. In Mexico the majority of Indians and a minority of mestizos are included in this cultural group. From this group comes a fairly large proportion of the immigrants, the number of which cannot be calculated but which direct observation indicates to be considerable.

3. *Mixed Civilization* This is between the two former groups. It characterizes a great proportion of mestizos, Indians, and fewer whites. Probably the majority of immigrants belongs to this mixed cultural type.

Let us consider, therefore, in detail, the indigenous and the mixed cultures, since they contribute practically all the Mexican immigration.

The Indigenous Civilization This is an indigenous development undisturbed until the Spanish Conquest. It was made up of various cultural subtypes differing among themselves, the differences due chiefly to the geographic and climatic variations of the country and the cultural influences of new migratory groups. In some places, such as Tenochtitlán (now Mexico City), this culture has disappeared completely, in others it has disappeared partly; but in general it has carried over to the present, though degenerated. This degeneration is due to the fact that the Indian has been losing ground continually, or has been forced to abandon his traditional expressions and at the same time has assimilated very slowly and most incompletely the habits and culture of the upper strata. . . .

This is in turn due not so much to unwillingness and apathy of the Indian as to the fact that the ruling classes have not wished or have not known how to substitute their culture for the aboriginal culture. Of these aboriginal groups not all provide immigrants; therefore we shall examine more fully only those to which immigrants belong.

Prehispanic Antecedents of the Indigenous Groups One of the principal characteristics of the prehispanic Indians of Mexico was their migratory tendency. We may cite as an example the Aztecs, who from unknown regions of the North or Northeast moved southward until they reached what is today Mexico City. The episodes of this famous peregrination are known through hieroglyphic characters in a codex, or native book, now in the National Museum of Mexico and well known to archaeologists; the Aztec emigrants even reached Central America and the Gulf and Pacific coasts.

The extent or intensity of the migrations would appear to be in a direct ratio to the grade of cultural evolution which characterized the various Indian groups. Indeed, the nature, the abundance, and the geographic distribution of archaeological remains prove that the most civilized groups, such as the Mayas, Aztecs, and Toltecs, covered in their migrations extensive areas, while the more primitive groups, such as the Tepehuanes, Yaquis, and Tarahumares, confined themselves to very limited areas. States of the *mesa central*—Michoacán, Guanajuato, Jalisco—those which in fact contribute the largest number of emigrants to the United States, were inhabited by Tarascans and Otomies, descendants of the archaic or subpedregalian peoples, who were apparently the earliest comers to Mexico. . . .

We have already shown that the geographic source of the greatest part of the Mexican immigration to the United States is the central plateau, in which are situated the states of Jalisco, Guanajuato, and Michoacán, and the northern mesa and northwestern coast, where are Lower California, Sonora, Coahuila, Sinaloa, Tamaulipas, Chihuahua, Durango, Zacatecas, and Nuevo León. Archaeological investigations established that, prior to the conquest, the regions now Jalisco, Michoacán, and Guanajuato were largely inhabited by groups of the Tarascan of Otomí or archaic type, a culture incomparably the inferior of the Toltec, Aztec, and Maya who inhabited the southern parts of the central plateau and the escarpments, and coast and peninsular regions in the south which do not contribute immigrants. In Guanajuato the archaic aboriginal culture remained always in a very primitive state. In Jalisco and Michoacán it developed farther, and the decoration and design of pottery and clay sculpture became highly conventionalized and stylized, indicating evolution beyond the primitive archaic type found in Mexico and

Guatemala. This region also furnishes architectural structures called *yácatas.* Social institutions and intellectual forms were inferior to those of the culture of the more southern groups already mentioned. As to the prehispanic antecedents of the aboriginal type of immigrants from the northern plateau, except for some cultural groups (pueblos in Chihuahua, the transition type like Chalchihuites in Zacatecas, and groups of Huastecan culture in Tamaulipas, cultures in stages of evolution analogous to that of the Tarascan or archaic of Michoacán and Jalisco), the rest were very primitive, in both material and nonmaterial feature. These groups were the Yaquis, Seris, Mayos, Papagos, Tepehuanes, and other related tribes.

Colonial Antecedents of Indigenous Groups The almost exclusively utilitarian character of the Spanish Conquest and domination kept a part of the primitive group of the northern mesa, as well as tribes in Sonora and California, in a state of almost animal slavery. Of Spanish civilization, these Indians adopted only scant rudiments in some instances, and continued their savage existence of prehispanic times. In Jalisco and Michoacán the conquest and colonization assumed an interesting and humanitarian aspect, in one sense, for here men of real genius like Archbishop Vasco de Quiroga observed and utilized the practical and beautiful elements of the native culture, fusing them harmoniously with analogous elements of the Spanish civilization, and developing new and important crafts and industries, often of an artistic character, such as lacquer, beautifully decorated pottery, leather tanning and carving, woodcarving and metal work. Yet the development of modern civilization along educational and scientific lines has not advanced in these regions, since illiteracy and fanaticism were important limiting factors during the colonial regime.

Present Characteristics of Indigenous Groups Little is known accurately about the present indigenous groups as a whole from the ethnographic viewpoint, as even less is known from the physical. Nevertheless, some investigation has been made, by both Mexican and foreign students, and this information has been compiled by the Department of Anthropology of Mexico. . . . The sudden contact of this simplest culture and of the mixed cultural type with modern civilization produces interesting results, commented on more fully in the section on mixed culture.

The Mixed Civilization This is a heterogeneous culture which began to form at the conquest, but which as yet is not fully integrated. So far the development has been very slow and gradual, a fusion of some elements of Spanish civilization and of the modern

European-American culture with elements of the Mexican Indigenous civilization, which is in turn made up of contributions from different cultural groups.

Colonial Antecedents of Mixed Culture Fusion between Spanish civilization and native occurred chiefly with respect to economic, legal, and administrative features. The system of taxation which the Spanish authorities first established was a combination of the fiscal administration of Spain and the old native system of tributes. The religion of the colonial period, as a result of the efforts of the missionaries, was a peculiar polytheism in which native gods disappeared but their personalities and attributes became attracted to saints. As to the legal fusion, the Laws of Indies can well be considered a union of Spanish codes with laws directly derived from the need of the natives and the prehispanic laws which had existed to meet them. In the cities the municipal governments were also a product of Indo-Hispanic interadjustment. The most important or most productive union occurred principally in art, architecture, and fine arts, producing works which breathed of both native and Spanish tradition, and were truly original, interesting, and unique.

Present Characteristics of Mixed Culture The development of the mixed civilization was more rapid and intense during the eighteenth century because after Mexico declared her independence from Spain, she threw wide her doors to the European cultural current. During the last thirty or forty years factors have appeared which confused the grouping into the culture types and have modified the mixed and even the Indian culture types. Railways and other means of communication which facilitated contact within the Mexican Republic and with the United States; the spread of popular education; the rapid industrial or agricultural development of some regions and the decadence of others; the social, economic, and cultural transformations and reversals produced by revolution; the return of hundreds of thousands of immigrants from the United States who brought new ideas and tendencies—these are some of the profoundly influential factors which, thrust suddenly into the slow evolution of the masses, have produced such strange and fantastic cultural fusions, substitutions, and juxtapositions that it is difficult to identify and classify without falling into serious error the characteristics of the immigrants belonging to the cultural groups in question.

For instance: Some groups characterized by the essentials of the civilization we classify as "mixed" have recently received sporadic injections of modern culture, the outgrowths of which are more visible than the original groundwork, and for this reason such groups are often classified as belonging to modern civilization when in reality they do not. The reverse also occurs. Civilization fundamentally modern, outgrowing certain characteristics of the mixed culture, since these are on the surface and therefore visible, often causes such groups to be classified erroneously as of mixed civilization. Then sometimes it happens that only the material civilization evolves to the level of the modern type, while the ideas and attitudes prevailing are still in those of the mixed group. Moreover, sometimes a single group exhibits material and non-material characteristics of both modern and mixed type, and finally, though more rarely, there are groups whose intellectual development is modern and whose material condition is properly of the "mixed" cultural type.

Contacts of Preceding Types of Civilization in the United States The change from the aboriginal and mixed cultures to the highly modern civilization of the United States is therefore exceedingly abrupt. The contact therefore results in substitutions and artificial integrations, even more intense and contradictory than in present-day Mexico. The abnormality of the situation is heightened by the geographic and climatic change.

The cultural contacts of the Mexican immigrants in the United States are complicated by the fact that besides the modern American civilization there is another and different Mexican-American culture, that of the Americans of Mexican origin. This civilization is American nominally, and exhibits the principal material aspects of modern American civilization, but intellectually and emotionally it lives in local Mexican traditions. This element can be said to constitute a peculiar nationality, within the United States. To the immigrant it is a sort of go-between, since these Mexican-Americans do not feel racial prejudice against him. Though a struggle occurs between the purely Mexican culture and this semi-Mexican, in the end it often absorbs the Mexican immigrant. With it there can occur a closer fusion than with the purely American culture, for with the latter it already shares many traits, while the great difference between the purely American and the purely Mexican, together with the factor of race prejudice, makes an intellectual, emotional, and traditional disparity too great to be bridged rapidly or perhaps never completely.

In later chapters [omitted here] the various cultural aspects of the Mexican immigrants and the nature of their contacts with the social elements of the American civilization will be treated in more detail, but it is thought proper at this point to give some general conclusions.

1. *Intellectual Culture* Among the Mexican immigrants in the United States may be noted a great persistency of cultural characteristics of Mexican origin, and as a result few such American features are acquired.

2. *Material Culture* Among the Mexican immigrants in the United States few features of Mexican material culture persist; as a result many American characteristics are taken over.

3. Among the Mexican-American elements, or Americans of Mexican origin, the Mexican type of intellectual culture exerts a great influence, while the Mexican type of material culture exerts much less.

4. Among the white American elements in contact with the large groups of Mexican immigrants in states such as California, Texas, and Arizona certain intellectual and material influence of Mexican cultural type may be noted; for example, in music, decorative arts, architectural style, and cookery.

We are aware that the value of these conclusions might be questioned, for although they are based on careful observation made by us and our assistants, and on information furnished us by other investigators, after all they can only be considered as personal opinions and interpretations. Furthermore, the American cultural influences exerted on the immigrant during his stay in the United States may be only temporary, because of restrictions imposed by the American environment. A group of Mexicans living, for example, in Minnesota, where they are unable to get foodstuffs, newspapers, and other articles from Mexico or from Mexican centers in the United States, might very naturally appear to have absorbed the American culture very thoroughly, especially in its material aspects. But if this group is transient, as is often the case, and goes back to Mexico, or to American localities where there are large numbers of Mexicans, it will probably lose many, or at least some, of the American influences, and Mexican characteristics will again reappear.

With these thoughts in mind, we attempted to study the cultural condition of Mexicans returned to their original homes after having lived for some time in the United States. This plan was not successful because at the time of this investigation (in 1927 and part of 1928) the return of immigrants had decreased greatly in the regions visited, namely, Guanajuato, Jalisco, and Michoacán; because of the religious conflicts in these regions nearly all the repatriates, instead of returning to their states, went to less disordered sections of the country. As far as we could ascertain, these people hid their cultural characteristics of American origin in order not to appear to their neighbors to have affected foreign customs.

The material obtained on cultural influence of an intellectual nature was not very abundant and did not permit us to reach really satisfactory conclusions. We therefore began an investigation of the influence of American material culture suggested to us by the observation of immigrants returning from the United States through the various frontier points.

These repatriates carried with them objects they had acquired and used in the United States. We noted that some groups crossing the frontier carried large numbers of objects, while others had but few. This was due, according to the custom officials, to the fact that the Secretaría de Relaciones issued Circular 202 of December 14, 1926, exempting from duty objects brought in by repatriates who intended to colonize lands. Each of these persons had to submit a list of the objects belonging to him so that custom inspectors could examine them and prevent contraband. In the controller's office we were able to examine and tabulate the list of objects belonging to 2,104 immigrants returning to Mexico from the United States during 1927 by way of Ciudad Juárez, Laredo, Agua Prieta, Piedras Negras, Matamoros, Reynosa, Naco, Ojinaga, Sasabe, and Ciudad Guerrero.

We believe that these quite objective data permit of more satisfactory conclusions than the purely personal interpretations and opinions previously referred to. An examination of the table summarizing [some of] these data enables us to reach the following conclusions:

Taking into consideration the generally miserable conditions of the great mass of immigrants that enter the United States, it is obvious that in the case of 2,104 individuals considered, new needs have been created during their stay in the United States. Most notable is the tendency to raise the standard of domestic comfort, as is indicated by the number of objects brought in which these immigrants either did not use in Mexico or which were there very rare among them.

Clothing of American origin is represented by a high ratio . . ., notwithstanding that simple clothing used by the common people is manufactured and sold at low prices in Mexico. In fact, the trunks, valises, and bundles which contained clothing alone numbered 3,653, a ratio of 173.51, so that the number of separate articles of clothing must have reached tens of thousands. The fact that part of this clothing was for sale does not prevent this from being a case of cultural influence, for they represent the collective taste as to clothing acquired by the Mexican immigrants in the American environment.

Article	*Ratio of number of objects of class indicated to every 100 immigrants listed*
Bathtubs	38.19
Wood or metal toilets	12.73
Refrigerators	3.80
Metal kitchen utensils	77.99
Washing machines	0.38
Stoves	27.58
Beds	82.88
Mattresses	70.53
Chairs	134.58
Sewing machines	16.57
Typewriters	1.42

The possession of automobiles is absolutely unheard of in the humble social class to which the immigrants generally belong. Nevertheless, 37.69 percent of the persons in question, or more than one out of every three, owned an automobile on his return to Mexico. Of these, 27.81 percent represented passenger cars and 9.88 trucks. According to information received, nearly all cheap cars had been acquired new, while the expensive ones were bought secondhand. The fact that the immigrant takes back to Mexico such a large number of automobiles is partly an advantage and partly a waste. Many sections of rural Mexico where the repatriated immigrant goes to colonize have no suitable automobile roads, and either there is no gasoline or else it is expensive or hard to get, with the result that automobiles are often useless. The good that results is that the possession of automobiles stimulates the owners to build roads, however poor these might be due to the humble circumstances of the owners. It would have been better had they brought in more buggies and carriages, actually represented only by the figures 1.14 and 6.41, respectively.

As for cattle, which would have been so useful for improving the native breeds, relatively few were brought in, [the ratio of] horses, burros, cows, goats, etc., being 25, of which 15.81 represented goats. The ratio of chickens reached 122.35 and of incubators 2.61. The number of agricultural and industrial tools was moderate, for the boxes containing these represented a ratio of 13.72, in addition to the tools that were separated. The proportion of plows was 8.64, cultivators 0.95, and planters 1.04.

Considering that the large majority of immigrants do not know how to read or write when they go to the United States, the intellectual progress made there might be expressed to a certain extent by the quantity of books brought back; the boxes in which these came numbered sixty-five, and represented a ratio of 3.08. Assuming that each box contained an average of forty books, or a total of two thousand six hundred, there was at least one book for each individual of the groups considered.

The musical and artistic tendencies of the immigrants are indicated by the figure as to phonographs, which is 21.82, and as to records, which is 118.00. The ratio of other musical instruments is 4.44, which is small. Perhaps the price of stringed instruments is generally high for the immigrants, and those manufactured in Mexico are much cheaper than the American ones. Nevertheless it is remarkable that player-pianos, which are probably the most expensive of musical instruments, have the highest [ratio], namely, 1.04.

Chapter Three

Life of the Mexican Immigrants and Mexican-Americans until World War II

The life of the Mexican immigrants and of the Mexican-Americans during the first four decades of the twentieth century was hard. Whether they lived in cities or in rural areas, the Mexicans and their American offspring suffered many indignities and injustices. Racially and socially, they were considered inferiors. Economically, they were relegated to the lowest-paying and hardest work. Legally, they were deprived not only of the right to unionize but also of due process of law.

To illustrate the life that the Mexicans and the Mexican-Americans lived during these decades of intensive discrimination and suffering, four important selections are presented to the reader in this chapter. The first two selections are contemporary studies dealing with their living conditions; the last two are current research articles treating their early labor conditions and unionization activities.

The first selection, "Social Conditions of Mexicans in the United States," by Victor S. Clark, presents a 1908 study of the Mexicans throughout the entire Southwest. Although this essay reflects the Anglo-American attitudes of that generation, it is nevertheless significant because despite this failing the study gives a more objective and understanding picture of the life of the early Mexican immigrants and Mexican-Americans than other writings of the period. Somewhat more detailed but less penetrating than Clarke's study is the second selection which was excerpted from the 1930 report to California's Governor C. C. Young. This excerpt, "Health, Relief, and Delinquency Conditions among the Mexicans of California," deals mainly with the living conditions of the growing Mexican population of Los Angeles in the late 1920s. It is important because the lot of the Mexicans and Mexican-Americans did not change greatly until World War II broke out.

The last two selections in this section study Mexican working conditions in the period before and just after World War II. In his article, "The First Steps: Chicano Labor Conflict and Organizing, 1900–20," Juan Gómez-Quiñones presents a vivid picture not only of the working conditions but also of the earliest unionizing efforts of Mexicans and Mexican-Americans. In the last article, Herbert B. Peterson, a former labor organizer, poignantly delineates the exploitation of Mexican labor in the Salt River Valley of Arizona.

Social Conditions of Mexicans in the United States in 1908*

Victor S. Clark

The Spanish-speaking population of the United States has not increased rapidly, and in localities where it is brought into close competition with other races appears to be decreasing. But the population of Mexico has more than doubled within one hundred years, without appreciable immigration. The number of inhabitants in the Republic at present probably exceeds fifteen million. The race has not been as prolific in Mexico as either the white or the black race in the United States. This has probably been due not so much to a lower birth rate as to a higher death rate, caused by poorer sanitary conditions and less-nourishing food. Mexicans are fatalists in case of epidemics, exposing themselves to contagion without regard to consequences. They are said to be susceptible to tuberculosis. While they do not impress one as able to resist the stress of modern urban life, they literally swarm in the crowded, unsanitary courts of the City of Mexico.

Physicians familiar with Mexican immigrants in the United States usually speak of them as poorly nourished, with less vigor

*From "Mexican Labor in the United States," by Victor S. Clark, in *Bulletin of the Bureau of Labor, Number 78, September 1908* (Washington: Department of Commerce, 1908).

and resistance to disease than Europeans, Negroes, or Americans. A mine physician said: "Mexicans in this country have fairly large families, but the population resident here increases but slowly, if at all, on account of the low resistance power of the race." Parasitic anaemia, or the "hookworm," is not the cause of this, apparently, since the disease is unknown in many parts of Mexico and not common among immigrants. There are a few cases in coal mines near the border, all popularly supposed to be brought from a single mining district of Mexico and to be due to the habit of earth-eating said to prevail in that locality. Speaking of Mexican communities in Colorado, a person familiar with them said: "New Mexicans have large families, but seem to be dying out; and the Mexican population of Pueblo and Trinidad appears to be decreasing, and would decrease more were it not for immigration from the south." There are no statistics to show whether or not this surmise is correct. The American population of these western towns and cities is growing so rapidly, and the country is filling up so fast with European immigrants, that the so-called Mexican population, while really growing, may by contrast appear to be lessening; also, the New Mexicans are more widely distributed than formerly, entering new occupations and old occupations in a country that was entirely without settlers a few years ago. Therefore a local decrease might accompany a general increase throughout the state or in neighboring states. At one place in Colorado an election official said that the poll books showed a decreasing Mexican population. But such evidence has no value for general purposes. In Los Angeles immigrant Mexicans are said to be more robust than natives of Mexican descent and to be displacing them. The impression of Americans here and in the territories accords with the opinions given from Colorado, that the American-born Mexicans are a decadent race, yielding before the physically more vigorous immigrants from Europe and the east. One cause given for the decline of the New Mexican population is inbreeding-intermarriage for generations among the few families of a village, said to result in [stunted growth] and deformities and in a general decrease of virility.

Los Angeles has probably the largest urban colony of immigrant Mexicans in the United States. The total Spanish-speaking population of the city is said not to be increasing, but natives are being supplanted by immigrants so that in a district in the old Spanish town, where there are still many hundreds of Mexicans, a social settlement worker knew of but four families that were born in this country. These people live in courts and in alleys, into which open one-story huts having one or two rooms, built of wood or brick and adobe, weatherproof, but ill-lighted, unclean, unwholesome, and hardly to be tolerated by the poorest except in the sunny and warm California climate. Not long ago a physician found twenty-three Mexicans sleeping in one small room in this district, and another was added to the number before he left. These courts harbor not only Mexicans but Negroes and Slavs as well. Families of different race and nationality occupy adjoining tenements. There is nothing to distinguish the house of one from the other, except that a box of flowers occasionally is seen in front of the Mexican quarters. Single-room huts rent for three dollars a month, and this rate per room is charged for larger tenements. On account of a recent tenement house ordinance in Los Angeles the condition of these courts had improved somewhat when they were visited, in the autumn of 1907. Outside water taps and closets—apparently serving an entire court—with sewer connection had been installed.

Austin and San Antonio, Texas, have large colonies of immigrant Mexicans, which are undoubtedly growing rapidly, and not, like that of Los Angeles, about stationary in total population. But housing conditions are better, partly because land values are lower and there is less necessity for crowding.

Los Angeles is a native American city, settled mostly by people from the eastern states. Of a total public school enrollment of 42,260, but 2,046 are foreign-born. Of these foreign-born children, 938 are natives of Mexico. The last census statistics are already too old to show the relative numbers of Mexicans and other foreigners in the city, but these figures are thought by the school authorities to indicate that the school attendance of Mexicans is relatively as large as that of other nationalities.

The Mexicans of San Antonio show an interest in the public schools and the attendance is rapidly increasing. In fact the authorities find it difficult to provide adequate accommodations in the Mexican quarter of the city. In one district, where seven eighths of the enrollment is Mexican, within five years an eight-room building has been increased to sixteen rooms and a seven-room building built in a different part of the district. Parents show great interest in the schools and a Mexican merchant presented a bell to one of the buildings at the time of its completion. There is usually a Mexican member—an American-born citizen of Mexican descent—on the school board to represent the Spanish-speaking people of the city. All instruction is in English and the children are taught to salute the flag. American parents send their children to the same schools with Mexican children. The attitude of the people of the city toward Mexican children in the schools was thus explicitly described by an educational officer:

> The citizens of San Antonio want the Mexican children to have the same advantages as their own in the public schools for four reasons: (1) From humanitarian considerations they want to raise the Mexican population and give it a better chance in life; (2) from political considerations they want to satisfy the Mexican voters; (3) many business men see a practical advantage in having their children—more especially boys—associate with Mexican children in school and learn their character, because they will have to deal with them in after life; (4) we all want to keep the Mexican population contented, so more Mexican labor will immigrate to this country.

In this city the testimony was that Mexican children were well behaved in school, and that they were bright in the primary grades and in the manual training departments, but that they entered later and left earlier than American children. It was pointed out that the adult Mexican population of Texas and of the territories had never enjoyed public school advantages, and so the present generation of children grows up in ignorant homes. But this will not be true of the next generation.

In Los Angeles few Mexican pupils remain longer than through the second grade, which gives them the mere elements of reading and writing; but it takes them longer than American children to advance this far, because they have to learn English. When placed in an ungraded room as an experiment some Mexican children made more progress. Of course there are exceptional cases where children pass beyond the primary grades; and three Mexicans of a better class were attending the polytechnic high school. The children are reported to be tractable and to like going to school. They give no trouble, and their only difficulty comes from the aggressions of a rougher class of white pupils. The girls are said to be moral—better safeguarded either by principle or by home discipline than the lower class of white girls. Mexican children are rather studious by nature, but those in Los Angeles are hampered by poor home surroundings. Partly from lack of home conveniences for washing, the children are apt to come to school dirty. After-school baths were installed in one building; there was much improvement in this respect. But Mexicans are prejudiced against water, believing that washing causes fever. After their children have been vaccinated Mexican parents will keep them away from water for weeks, though the parents have superstitious faith in the vaccination itself, as a sort of mystic rite. But it is easier for school authorities to enforce some sort of home hygiene for these pupils, because the Mexicans have much respect for authority and make an attempt to follow official directions.

Irregular attendance retards the progress of Mexican pupils. Boys are sent on errands, and usually have to provide the family with fuel, which they pick up in the streets and around new buildings. Children of both sexes are often absent on feast days and on holy days. Though children are sent to church on these occasions, Mexican parents usually patronize public rather than parochial schools. This does not seem to be from motives of economy; for they make sacrifices to provide their children with textbooks, and will not appeal to the authorities for free books, though these can be obtained where parents are themselves unable to provide them. In this matter Mexicans are in strong contrast with Italians, who try to get textbooks from the school board after they are well-to-do and taxpayers on city property. A Mexican family almost in distress prefers not to make this appeal, but manages in some way to obtain money for necessary school expenses.

Mexicans excel in design and in the manual arts. At the College Settlement, a social betterment center in a quarter of Los Angeles having many Mexican immigrants, children of that nationality show special skill in tile modeling and in carving blocks of original design for printing patterns on cloth. Teachers say their work is equal to or better than that of pupils in the technical high school.

Mexican boys are not fond of athletic sports, and as a race these people are not aggressive. At a rummage sale the Mexicans stood back while Italians and other Europeans crowded forward and got all the good bargains. Likewise, when a colony of Italians settles in a quarter formerly occupied by Mexicans, the latter quietly move out to a less crowded locality. Sometimes they buy cheap suburban lots on installments, and move their shacks to these places, or buy secondhand building materials where old tenements—frequently condemned—are being torn down, from which they erect rude shelters for their families. In this, as in other ways, the Mexican shows the retiring traits of the Indian and the countryman, even after several years' experience with city life.

Social workers with experience among different nationalities, in Los Angeles and elsewhere, think that there is less illiteracy among the Mexican immigrants than among the Slavs. Superficial observers commonly assume that a knowledge of reading and of writing is as rare among the former as a knowledge of English. This is not entirely true. Several payrolls of unskilled Mexican laborers were seen, which indicated that from one half to three fourths of these workers could at least sign their names. A Spanish-speaking American labor agent in El Paso estimated that 10 percent of the immigrants could read and write. One old laborer in Los Angeles, who was signing a payroll, said his children had taught him to write, adding in Spanish: "I'll never go back to Old Mexico, because I have five children in the public school." Wherever there are large Mexican labor camps postmasters report that a large number of letters are sent to Mexico. Though many of these are written by some local "patron," or headman, yet this is by no means always the case. In several instances immigrants passing through El Paso showed letters from a brother or other relative in the United States. A number of Mexican men attend night school in Los Angeles.

The Mexicans are sympathetic—generous not only to their own people, but to those of another nationality in time of trouble. For this reason they seldom become dependent upon public charity. Americans in parts of the country where Mexicans are numerous frequently observed: "There are no Mexican tramps." By this it is not meant that there are not many Mexican laborers traveling on foot from place to place, but these laborers are so in fact as well as name and seldom apply for assistance except among their own people. At the time of the San Francisco earthquake, according to settlement workers in Los Angeles, when there was a call for help in making clothing and furnishing other supplies, the Mexican mothers turned out, and in their small way gave more assistance than any other foreigners.

The professional criminal element among Mexicans in the United States appears to be small, but there is a considerable number of occasional criminals. Most arrests are caused by cheap whisky or mescal. The Mexican is not often a sot, but many Mexicans are inclined to short, sharp, periodic sprees. Along the frontier resides a number of parasitic Mexicans, who live off the vices of their more industrious countrymen and the lower class of Americans. This is a disagreeable and at times a dangerous element. Gambling is its main profession. There are so-called American towns within the frontier district where public opinion is as decidedly against Mexican immigration as it is against Negro immigration in some white sections of the South. Where there is this opposition to the Mexican, it is usually to the Mexican who becomes a resident rather than to the transient laborer. And it is this resident class that provides most of the criminals and semicriminals.

In 1906 the penal and charitable institutions of Arizona and of New Mexico, not counting county institutions, contained 773 American citizens, 382 Mexican citizens, and 456 persons of other foreign nationalities, while the nationalities of 19 were unknown. In county jails visited a large percent of the inmates were obviously of Mexican blood, on whichever side [of] the border they might have been born. But in these localities the same predominance of Mexican blood was also obvious outside the jail.

SENTIMENT AND RACE PREJUDICE

Organized labor, and white workers in general, do not appear to be opposed to Mexicans in the same way that they are to Orientals. There are two main reasons for this; the Mexican immigrant does not compete in occupations which the white worker greatly cares to enter, and he is regarded as something of an American, with more moral right in this country than the Asiatic. One labor editor said: "The Mexicans don't trouble us much, and are not likely to do so unless we have bad times. Then it may be a bad thing to have the country filled up with cheap labor. They can't do white man's work. Besides they were born in this country, or pretty nearly in this country, and have more right to be here than Japanese and Italians and Greeks." One candid American mechanic said: "They will never pay a Mexican what he's really worth compared with a white man. I know a Mexican that's the best blacksmith I ever knew. He has made some of the best tools I ever used. But they pay him one dollar and fifty cents a day as a helper, working under an American blacksmith who gets seven dollars a day." Another workingman said: "The Mexican is all right in his place, and he's not so likely to get out of his place as a Japanese or a Negro." The fact that the Mexican is not socially or industrially ambitious, like European and Asiatic immigrants, counts very much in his favor with white workers.

The race sentiment of Americans toward Mexicans is, like most race sentiment, peculiar and illogical. There is nothing of that stern race consciousness that marks the attitude of the white man in the South toward the Negro. There is more of the tolerance with which Americans have traditionally regarded the Indians. Yet a Mexican can fraternize with Negroes and not lose caste, as would a white man. Negro foremen are employed in Mexican coal mines, directing gangs of Mexican miners. The American Negro considers himself above the Mexican, and yet the latter receives more social recognition from the white man. Perhaps the existence of an upper class in Mexico, distinct from the laboring class and equal socially to Americans, gives even the laborer a better standing in this country. Mexican immigrants ride in white cars in Texas, and might eat at the same table with Americans. Practically there is little social intermingling. Intermarriage is rare, and when it occurs seems to be a subject for apology. This is true even of Europeans. A person familiar with a large mining district, where hundreds of Italians and Mexicans were employed, knew of but a single case where an Italian had married a Mexican. The Mexican does not put himself forward, or seek white society. He observes his own canons of reserve and dignity, which are never offensive.

In Colorado an American said: "There is less race prejudice against an Indian than against a Mexican, and less against a Mexican than against a Negro." This about expresses the situation in the West; but in Texas, where people are more familiar with Mexicans, and a larger proportion of them are residents of the better class, the Mexicans as a body socially far outrank Indians or Negroes. The gradation, from those who associate on terms of equality with Americans to the peon, is so gradual that a race distinction as such hardly exists; and though the preponderant Indian blood of most recent Mexican immigrants can not be dismissed from a consideration of the effect of this immigration, it has not as yet created a race question along our southern frontier.

The economic race contest is not so much between the Mexican and the Negro or the American as between the Mexican and the other nationalities mentioned previously—Italians, Greeks, and Japanese. Japanese compete with Negroes on the Pacific coast in what are called "easy jobs," such as hotel waiters and porters, bootblacks, and servants of different kinds. Mexicans have never entered these occupations, though a few are employed as coachmen. In Mexico it has sometimes been necessary to place Chinese laborers together in a mine entirely separate from the Mexicans.

The attitude of Americans of Mexican descent toward immigrants from Mexico seems to be friendly, except where there is direct competition between the two. In Colorado the former regard the latter as interlopers, though they are not actively hostile to them. New Mexicans complain that the immigrants can work cheaper, because they have no families with them. The New Mexican is different from the Old Mexican, in that he sometimes objects to working with Negroes. Another evidence of nascent social consciousness is that he considers himself very much above the immigrant, and does not want to be confounded with him in public opinion. This sentiment is observed in parts of New Mexico where labor is so scarce that there is no opposition by the natives to immigration from Mexico on economic grounds. In Texas, where there are labor organizations among resident Mexicans, the latter oppose an inflow of immigrants likely to lower wages; and in some cases they have lodged complaints of alleged violations of the contract labor law.

Health, Relief, and Delinquency Conditions among the Mexicans of California*

Report of Governor C. C. Young's Fact-Finding Committee

INTRODUCTION

In gathering material concerning social welfare problems among the Mexicans of California, the Department of Social Welfare has drawn upon records and reports of the State Departments of Public Health, Education, Institutions, and Social Welfare, city and county records from the localities where the Mexicans constitute a considerable proportion of the population, and records of private social agencies in those districts. Some of this material has been issued in published reports, much is compiled from unpublished but official records, and part was secured by these agencies for the present survey. The bulk of the data from sources other than the state departments is from Los Angeles County for the reasons that, on account of its size and organization, far more record material is available in that county than elsewhere in the state, and also far more Mexicans reside in that county than in any other. In the smaller counties much of the data sought were not obtainable, since the keeping of records is not well developed in the smaller counties nor was it found possible to segregate social data relating to Mexicans. All pertinent data secured, except fragmentary and disconnected items, have been included.

Estimates as to the Mexican population of California vary widely. For the first six months of 1929 the State Bureau of Vital Statistics records over one sixth of all births in the state as Mexicans. As the birth rate among Mexicans is undoubtedly higher than among the

*From *Mexicans in California: Report of Governor C. C. Young's Fact-Finding Committee* (San Francisco: California State Printing Office, 1930).

general population and as a large number of the Mexicans have come into the state in the child-bearing ages, the proportion of Mexican births to total births is doubtless far higher than the proportion of Mexicans in the population. Lack of recent census data as to the general population of California as well as to the Mexican population makes difficult any attempt to draw comparisons, but certain estimates of population will assist in arriving at a sense of the significance of the social data which follow.

The estimated Mexican population of Los Angeles County in 1928, as figured by the Los Angeles County Charities Department, the Mexican consul at Los Angeles, and others working directly with the Mexicans, was approximately two hundred and fifty thousand. The total population of the county at the same date was estimated as approximately two million, two hundred and seventy thousand which would indicate that the Mexicans represented about 11 percent of the county population. At the same date the population of the city of Los Angeles was estimated by the Los Angeles Police Department as one million, three hundred and forty-three thousand. Of this total Mexicans were estimated to represent slightly over 10 percent. The Los Angeles city school system in the school census of 1928 accounted for forty-eight thousand Mexican children, and according to a statement issued by the school department, Los Angeles has a larger population of Mexicans than any other city in the United States or even Mexico with exception of Mexico City.

HOUSING

The Mexican in California, like various other foreign-speaking immigrants in the United States, tends to live in colonies, retaining his traditions and a mode of life not always satisfactory to his American neighbors. How many or what proportion of the Mexicans live in distinctly Mexican districts can not be stated, but the existence of "Little Mexicos," both urban and rural, is a matter of common knowledge.

The tendency of the Mexican to live in a racial group is strengthened by several conditions. On arrival he seldom speaks English and consequently is dependent upon the Spanish-speaking group for adjustment to his new environment. The Mexican commonly performs unskilled and consequently low-paid work, so that his choice as to quarters is restricted. In Mexico the laboring classes have been used to very simple living with only the most primitive sanitation, and owners are naturally reluctant to rent their buildings to Mexican tenants if others can be found. In addition, there exists a prejudice against the Mexican which manifests itself in the common classification of the Mexican as "not white."[1]

From an inquiry sent to realty boards in various cities of the state,[2] forty-seven replies were received, of which number the following twenty-four reported segregated districts composed of Mexicans, or Mexicans and other foreigners:

Azusa	Monrovia	San Bernardino
Bakersfield	Montebello	San Fernando
Bell	Napa	Santa Barbara
Compton	Ontario	Santa Maria
Huntington Park	Pomona	Santa Monica
Lankershim	Porterville	Van Nuys
Madera	Redlands	Visalia
Modesto	Riverside	Whittier

In addition, other boards cited clauses inserted in deeds and sales contracts calculated to confine Orientals, Mexicans, and Negroes to certain districts. Although most of these clauses seek to restrict the occupants of the premises to "persons of Caucasian race," in some instances the Mexican was definitely specified as prohibited from occupancy.

Further evidence of the concentration of Mexicans in separate localities and districts is presented in the following list of counties having regular elementary schools with an enrollment of over 90 percent Mexican. A total of fifty-eight elementary public schools appear on the record for the school year 1927–28 as having from 90 to 100 percent enrollment of Mexicans. It should be noted that these schools are not separate schools in mixed districts to which Mexicans must send their children, but are regular public schools, the almost exclusive enrollment of Mexicans being due to the fact that the district is inhabited by virtually none but Mexicans.

County	*Number of schools having an enrollment 90 to 100% Mexican*
Imperial	8
Kern	8
Orange	14
Los Angeles	10
Riverside	2
San Bernardino	16
Santa Barbara	2
Ventura	4

The older section of Los Angeles, around and east of the Plaza, is a distinctly Mexican settlement. Spanish is the language commonly heard, the signs in the shops are in Spanish, the goods on sale are distinctly for Mexicans, and the moving picture theaters show only Spanish titles. In the old mission are celebrated colorful and picturesque festivals with all the traditional Mexican games of chance. In a study of the home conditions of the Mexican families made by the principal of the Macey Street School, and including all families whether or not they had children attending school, the fact was brought out that virtually none of these families owned their own homes. The explanation given was that property in that district was held for industrial developments at prices too high to permit the Mexicans to purchase, and that the developments within the city have forced many of the Mexicans to move to districts farther out. The largest of these is in the Belvedere district, just outside of Los Angeles, known as Maravilla Park. The Mexican population in this district numbers about forty-five thousand, and six large modern public schools have been built in which the enrollment is practically 100 percent Mexican. One of these schools is a "development school" for subnormal children.

This district is just beyond the city limits and was built up without regard to the proper requirements for sanitation in congested districts. Two, and sometimes three, shacks are built upon one very small lot, leaving little unoccupied ground space. The shacks are flimsy shells, usually constructed of scrap lumber, old boxes, or other salvage.

At various times the city and county health departments have made housing surveys of the Mexican districts. Summary findings of two housing surveys made recently by the Los Angeles County Health Department[3] give a fair picture of life in the Mexican districts.

One district covered by the survey consisted of eight city blocks in Maravilla Park, containing 317 houses having a population of 1,509 persons, or an average of practically 40 houses to the block and 4.8 persons to the house.

The average annual family income was seven hundred and ninety-five dollars, almost all of the workers being classed as unskilled laborers. Of the 317 houses, 199 were owned and 118 rented, of which number 211 were rated as mere shacks and the remaining 106 as bungalows or semibungalows. Light and ventilation were classed as reasonably good in 154 cases, and as poor in 163 cases. Sixty-two houses had good screens, and 255 had poor screens or none. Only 10 of the houses had cesspools connected up to flush toilets, 16 had cesspools not connected to flush toilets; 147 had privies in fair condition and 144 were classed as privies in poor condition. The attempt to maintain cleanliness under these difficult conditions was evidenced by the report that 227 of the houses were clean and 252 of the yards at least fairly clean.

A check on food supplies and diet showed 158 houses with sufficient food, 95 in which food was somewhat lacking, and 64 in which food was distinctly scant. For preserving food, only 9 had refrigerators, 128 had screened cupboards and coolers, and the balance of 180 had no provisions for keeping food in good condition.

On the home index score card,[4] with 25 as the standard, the district averages 8.3.[5]

A similar housing survey[6] made in a Mexican district in San Fernando covered 357 families, with a total of 1,668 persons—851 adults and 817 children. The income range of the families showed 79 having less than four hundred dollars per year; 112 from six hundred dollars to eight hundred dollars per year; 79 from eight hundred dollars to one thousand dollars per year; and 87, one thousand dollars or over. A special study was made of their diet and food supplies which indicated that 35 percent had plenty of meat in their diet, 56 percent very little, and 9 percent none at all. Of vegetables, 40 percent had plenty, and 60 percent very few. Milk was received daily by 45 percent, while 25 percent took milk occasionally and 30 percent never bought milk. Automobiles of some description were owned by 39 percent and 37 percent possessed musical instruments. On the home index card the San Fernando district, with 25 as the standard, averaged 9.5.

In addition to the large settlements of Mexicans, there are smaller camps located on the outskirts of Whittier, Montebello, and El Monte [; these] were inspected by representatives of the Department of Social Welfare, accompanied by Los Angeles County health, charities, and school officials. In camps of this character as the renter has no security of tenure he naturally wastes no money on lasting sanitary improvements. These settlements are sources of constant annoyance to the localities, and only by continual inspection and vigilance on the part of the health authorities can the menace of widespread disease be held in check. Patches of ground are rented as small as twenty by thirty feet. Ground rent varies from one, two, three, five, even ten dollars a month, and in several camps inspected by the department the annual rental would amount to over a thousand dollars an acre, in return for which the owner had made no investment whatever in sanitation or road improvements.

In his study of Mexican labor in the Imperial Valley, Paul S. Taylor discusses the housing of agricultural labor in that district:

> In the more permanent camps one finds rough lumber houses of a room or two, often screened, seldom painted. Sometimes the kitchen is in one

of the rooms, often [it] is in a separate shelter outside the house. A roof of brush or arrow weed may be built out across the front or rear for shade. The "ditch-bank camp" is the typical temporary camp for the seasonal labor forces which harvest the crops (of course many permanent camps also are located along ditch banks). This type of camp is usually located among the trees that line the irrigation ditches. Its shelters are commonly tents, which the Mexicans generally supply themselves, or pieces of canvas stretched across a pole, with boxes, brush, burlap or what-not across the end. Sometimes the shelters are nothing more than the typical arrow weed *ramada*, consisting of roof and from one to three sides, which provides shade and wind protection. . . . The impermanent types of shelter, tents, *ramadas*, etc., are, of course, not confined to the temporary camps, but may be found also accommodating the seasonal influx in the permanent camps. The inspectors of the State Housing Commission endeavor to enforce certain minimum standards. These include tents (floored during lettuce season, but not necessarily in the cantaloupe season), beds, screened cook houses and toilets, bathing facilities, and garbage disposal. Employers are held responsible for the cleanliness of the camps. Up to the present time (1927) inspectors have experienced considerable difficulty in enforcing these standards, which are by no means universally observed.

BIRTH STATISTICS OF MEXICANS IN CALIFORNIA

Beginning in 1926 the State Bureau of Vital Statistics began segregating Mexican births in their records. In that year Mexican births equaled one seventh of the total. Two years later they rose to one sixth, and the first six months of 1929 indicate a continued increase. The figures for these years are (shown below).

Total Births and Number of Mexican Births
in California, 1926–29

Year	*Total births*	*Mexican births*	*Percent Mexican*
1926	82,372	11,721	14.2
1927	84,334	12,688	15.0
1928	83,643	13,846	16.6
1929 (January–June)	39,221	6,959	17.7

Most of these births occur in the southern part of the state. In the rural districts of Imperial County, 52 percent of all births in 1928 were Mexican. In the rural districts of San Bernardino and Riverside counties, more than 40 percent of all births were Mexican. In some of the cities of Imperial County, the Mexican births in 1928 were between 60 and 70 percent of all births.

. . . This distribution of Mexican births [omitted here] indicates the migration of Mexican families into the San Joaquin Valley and certain counties of northern California. Santa Barbara and Ventura indicate the presence of a large proportion of Mexicans. In the San

Joaquin Valley, Madera [and] Kings [counties], and the rural districts of Fresno and Kern counties indicate over one fifth of all births to be Mexican; while an unexpectedly large proportion of Mexican births are found in Amador (26 percent), Contra Costa rural (19.8 percent), Lassen (18.2 percent), Placer (19.7 percent), San Benito (18 percent) and Tuolumne (16.4 percent) [counties]. . . .

Since 1916 the Los Angeles County Health Department has been segregating its statistics of Mexican births and deaths, in the unincorporated area of the county, and the rapid increase in the number of Mexican births and the proportion which they represent of the total indicate the increase of Mexican population in that district. It will be noted that in 1916 Mexican births represented one eighth of the total but the population has increased to nearly one third of the total in 1927.

Total Births in Los Angeles County (Unincorporated Area), Number of White and Mexican Births, and Percentage which White and Mexican Births Represent of Total, 1916–27.[7]

Year	*Total births*	*Number white births*	*Number Mexican births*	*Percent white of total*	*Percent Mexican of total*
1916	1,519	843	193	55.5	12.7
1917	1,571	830	196	52.8	12.5
1918	1,503	828	258	55.1	17.2
1919	1,474	776	276	52.6	18.7
1920	1,867	1,079	375	57.8	20.1
1921	2,300	1,374	458	59.7	19.9
1922	2,468	1,531	489	62.0	19.8
1923	3,229	1,999	806	61.9	25.0
1924	4,194	2,674	1,189	63.7	28.4
1925	4,044	2,461	1,222	60.8	30.2
1926	4,230	2,702	1,276	63.9	30.2
1927	4,435	2,827	1,406	63.7	31.7

Corresponding figures for Los Angeles City from 1918 to 1927 indicate a similar, rapid increase in the number of Mexican births and in the proportion from approximately one twelfth of the total in 1918 to nearly one fifth in 1927.

A tabulation of the white[8] and Mexican deaths in the unincorporated area of Los Angeles County from 1921 to the present time, and a comparison with the births for the same period, indicates a steadily increasing excess of births over deaths among the Mexicans from 247 in 1921 to 950 in 1927, but among the white population in three years out of the seven, the number of deaths exceeded the number of births and the total excess of births over deaths for

Total Number of Births and Mexican Births in Los Angeles City, 1918–27, with Percentage which Mexican Births Comprise of Total

Year	*Total births*	*Number Mexican births*	*Percent Mexican of total*
1918	8,581	733	8.5
1919	8,822	850	9.6
1920	10,439	1,313	12.6
1921	12,097	1,708	14.1
1922	13,473	1,869	13.9
1923	14,807	2,206	14.9
1924	18,425	3,140	17.0
1925	19,124	3,225	16.9
1926	18,207	2,976	16.3
1927	18,053	3,449	19.1

the seven years is only 241. The rapid increase in all classes of the population by migration overshadows the importance of the increase through excess of births over deaths, but the trend should be noted.

Corresponding figures of the excess of births over deaths, or of deaths over births, for the general population and for the Mexican population of Los Angeles City from 1918 to 1928, indicate that the Mexican share of this increase has grown from one sixteenth in 1918 to well over one third in 1927, and during the period of ten years almost one fourth of the natural increase in population has been Mexican. . . .

INFANT MORTALITY

As has been demonstrated by the elaborate studies made by the United States Children's Bureau,[9] infant mortality may be accepted as an index of the standard of living and intelligence of the group. A comparison of the infant mortality rate[10] among the Mexican and white population of Los Angeles County's unincorporated area is significant. With a foreign language group the tendency toward incompleteness in the reporting of vital statistics always exists, but under the present maternal and infant hygiene service conducted by the Los Angeles County Department of Health, every precaution is taken to insure completeness and accuracy. During all this period the district has been within the birth registration area, which implies repeated checks upon the completeness and accuracy of reporting.

Infant Mortality Rate of the White and Mexican Population of Los Angeles County (Unincorporated Area), 1916–29 Inclusive.[11]

Year	*Infant mortality rate*	
	White	*Mexican*
1916	70.0	285.0
1917	67.4	255.1
1918	71.3	348.1
1919	61.9	170.0
1920	60.2	186.7
1921	57.6	179.0
1922	78.4	243.4
1923	80.5	250.6
1924	61.3	163.2
1925	58.5	166.1
1926	41.9	124.6
1927	45.4	96.9
1928	51.7	116.8
1929	39.6	104.5

Comparison of the white and Mexican infant mortality rates indicates sharply the poverty and unintelligent mode of living of the Mexican group. In 1916 over one fourth of all Mexican babies born died within their first year of life, an extraordinarily high rate, and while the rate showed improvements in 1919, 1920, and 1921, it still stood at 250.6 in 1923. At that time the county established an intensive program of maternal and infant hygiene, which has served to reduce the death rate among Mexican infants to 104.5 in 1929, but this rate still remains over two and a half times as high as among the white population.

Comparison of the white and Mexican infant mortality by causes brings out the contrast still more sharply. In his analysis of the causes of infant deaths, Dr. John L. Pomeroy, director, Los Angeles County Health Department, states: "Premature birth is a general cause not related to mode of living, and for this cause little difference is to be noted between the white and Mexican rates. For the other causes, gastrointestinal, communicable, and respiratory diseases, are all controlled mainly by intelligent type[s] of living habits and precaution measures. For these causes the Mexican rate is from two to eight times higher than the white rate. . . ."[12]

COMMUNICABLE DISEASE

A study of communicable disease, the number of cases, number of deaths, and particularly the case fatality rate, serves as a general index of the mode of living, the care received, and the physical resistance of the individual.[13] From 1921 the Los Angeles County

Health Department has made a racial segregation in its records. This separation of figures as to the white and the Mexican population brings out the fact that one sixth of all communicable cases and one fourth of all such deaths are of Mexicans. Without accurate population statistics, which are not obtainable, the percentage of Mexicans in the population can not be computed, but according to estimates of population, the number of cases and deaths among the Mexicans is disproportionately high. The case fatality rate—the number of deaths per hundred cases—can, however, be computed and this serves as an index of care and resistance. In 1921, among the Mexican population, nearly one fourth of all cases of communicable disease (which includes all diseases reportable by law) terminated fatally. This rate was nearly twice as high as the fatality [rate] among the white population. Under an expanded service inaugurated by the County Health Department in 1921, the communicable diseases have been given care and treatment far more intensively than in former years; the general case fatality rate nearly cut in two, and the Mexican rate still more sharply reduced. The "white" rate was cut from 13.4 to 7.4 and the Mexican rate from 22.9 to 9.6. The greater decrease in the Mexican rate is credited to the fact that it was so much higher when the situation was taken in hand by the County Health Department, and for this reason the county had to assume a more complete measure of authority. But in spite of all their efforts the Mexican rate remains nearly a third higher than the white rate, and is considered by the health authorities as indicative of a fundamentally less sturdy stock.[!]

TUBERCULOSIS

The prevalence of tuberculosis among the Mexican population of California is one of the outstanding problems of health and relief agencies wherever Mexicans are found in large numbers. Statistics from the Los Angeles County Health Department for the unincorporated area of the county indicate this condition. In 1921 all deaths of Mexicans (211) represented 11.5 percent of the total deaths (1,835) in that area, while . . . Mexican deaths from tuberculosis amounted to 14.8 percent of the total due to that cause. In 1927 all deaths of Mexicans (459) represented 13.9 percent of the total deaths (3,303), while among the deaths due to tuberculosis Mexican deaths represented 19.6 percent, while in 1925 it will be noted that Mexican deaths from tuberculosis were almost one fourth (24.0 percent) of all deaths from that disease. The increasing proportion of all Mexican deaths in that area is probably due to the increasing proportion of Mexicans in the population; but the Mexican proportion of deaths from tuberculosis has increased much more rapidly than their proportion of all deaths. . . .

Comparable figures regarding the prevalence of tuberculosis among Mexicans in other sections of the state are not available, but the seriousness of the situation is borne out by a census taken of all cases under observation in the tuberculosis clinic maintained by the Los Angeles City Health Department, on June 1, 1928. Out of 1,516 patients, which included diagnosed cases, pretubercular cases, patients under observation, and contact cases, 413, or 27 percent of the total, were Mexican. As Mexicans are estimated to constitute about 10 percent of the city's population, the fact that he totals [*sic*] over one fourth of the clientele of the tuberculosis clinics is probably due in part to poverty and the necessity of seeking free treatment, but undoubtedly reflects also a high general tuberculosis rate among the Mexican population. . . .*

MEXICANS IN THE STATE HOSPITALS

The care of the insane and feeble-minded is one of the increasing burdens of public charity. At the present time all of the state institutions are overcrowded and only the cases most urgently in need of institutional care can be given treatment. Under these conditions, fewer admissions have been made in recent years than would have been made if facilities had permitted the admission of all cases where state care is desirable. The factor of deportation also affects analysis of these figures, since an alien who becomes insane within five years after entry may be deported. In the biennium, 1927–28, 218 Mexican patients were admitted to state hospitals, of which number 88 (40 percent) were deported by federal authorities. The policy of deportation accounts for the fact . . . that the proportion of Mexican inmates is much less than the proportion of Mexicans admitted to the hospitals. The possibility of deportation undoubtedly serves also as a deterrent to the reporting of milder cases. . . .

For the year 1922–23 Mexicans constituted 3 percent of the total admissions to hospitals for the insane and 2.7 percent of admissions

*Such conclusions are indicative of the conclusions which public officials consistently tried to draw about not only Mexican-Americans, but members of other minority groups as well. To blame "fundamentally less sturdy stock" or a "high general tuberculosis rate among the Mexican population" was to discount the effects of squalid living conditions and to absolve the dominant society of blame for those conditions and of responsibility for rectifying them.

to institutions for the feeble-minded. In 1927–28 Mexicans admitted to the hospitals for the insane had increased to 4.3 percent of the total, an increase of nearly 50 percent in five years, and in the institutions for the feeble-minded the number of Mexicans increased in the same period of five years from 2.7 percent to 6.9 percent of all persons admitted.

THE DEPENDENCE OF MEXICANS UPON CHARITY

Mexican Families Receiving State Aid

State aid is granted in California to orphans, half orphans, and certain classes of children whose fathers are tubercular or completely incapacitated. On January 1, 1928, aid was paid to 5,288 families, representing a total of 13,105 children. Of this total 515 families were Mexican, which represents 9.7 percent of the total number of families. Family groups among the Mexicans being larger than among the general population brought the total number of Mexican children receiving aid slightly above one tenth of the total.

Among the conditions of eligibility for aid is that of legal residence within the state for at least two years. Largely on account of this requirement the eight counties of southern California, because of the recent arrival of a large part of their population, received in 1928 only 30.8 percent of the total amount of the state aid, although their estimated population was about half that of the entire state. This residence condition renders many needy Mexican families ineligible to aid from the state, since many have resided in the state less than two years. Also, state aid may not be paid to a family which entered [the] state in a dependent condition, and this condition also renders many Mexican families ineligible. From the fact that one tenth of all state aid to children is now paid to Mexican families and that residence qualifications render many other needy Mexican families ineligible to aid, it becomes evident that poverty and need are proportionately more common among Mexicans than among the general population of the state. In Los Angeles County Mexicans represented one fourth of the families receiving state aid. As they are estimated to comprise about 11 percent of the population, their greater general poverty and need is indicated.

Dependent Children in Institutions

Information concerning the racial background of all children in all orphanages and other institutions for dependent children was secured by the Department of Social Welfare as of April 1, 1928. These institutions were caring for a total of 5,357 children, of which number 416, or 7.8 percent, were Mexican. Among the institutions in northern California only 85 Mexican children were being cared for out of a total of 3,019, but in the southern counties Mexican children numbered 331 out of 2,338, or 14.1 percent, and in the institutions in Los Angeles County practically one sixth (16.4 percent) of all the children were Mexican. As a number of the institutions accept no Mexicans, the proportion in the rest of the institutions becomes conspicuously high. . . .

County Relief in Los Angeles County

Financial relief to the needy in Los Angeles County is administered almost entirely by the Outdoor Relief Division of the County Charities Department, the Community Chest, and other private charities devoting their efforts and resources to family welfare, clinics and other health services, and other community projects. A statement of the funds given by the county charities in total and to Mexicans, therefore, covers the bulk of financial relief given in that area.

In the following table [omitted here, are] given the total number of cases and the number of Mexican cases on county relief for the five years, 1923/24 to 1927/28. In 1924/25 Mexican cases ran over one third of the total, but for the other years they have represented approximately one fourth. The total amount of money given in relief has risen from $938,167 in 1923/24 to $1,509,780 in 1927/28. The amounts paid to the Mexican families have not been segregated, so . . . it is not possible to state whether the amounts given to them are greater or less than their proportion of the toal number of cases. . . .

In addition to . . . the County Charities Department, the only agency administering a considerable relief budget is the Catholic Welfare Bureau. In the accompanying table [omitted here] are given the number of children cared for during 1924, 1926, 1927, and six months of 1928. Nearly half of all the children cared for are Mexican, but less than half of the funds expended were for their care. In family relief the bureau has cared for a far smaller proportion of Mexican families.

Public Care of Indigents at Los Angeles County Farm

For the care of the indigent aged the Los Angeles County Charities conducts a county farm at which institution the cost of care and treatment of inmates totals $913,156 in 1926/27. Comparatively few Mexicans are sent to the farm, their standard of living, racial clannishness, and national food habits making assistance to them in their own group a happier solution of their needs. . . .

Hospital Care of Mexicans, Los Angeles County Hospital

Aid in the form of free medical and hospital service has come to be a most important item of public charity. A survey made by the State Department of Public Health covering the service rendered to Mexicans by the Los Angeles General (County) Hospital for two years July 1, 1922, to June 30, 1924,[14] disclosed the fact that the care and treatment given to Mexicans during that period cost the county $2,358,088 or well over a million dollars a year. Since that time the number of Mexicans cared for in the hospital has increased over a third.

In 1919/20 the number of Mexican patients totaled 11.3 percent of the total, and this percentage increased irregularly to 18.4 in 1926/27, but dropped to 15.4 in 1927/28.

CRIME AND DELINQUENCY AMONG THE MEXICAN POPULATION

Statistics of crime and delinquency of the Mexican element in the state in comparison with corresponding figures for the general population serve as an index of racial or national characteristics and also as an index of the adjustment or lack of adjustment of the Mexicans to American customs and standards. . . .

From this table [omitted here] it will be noted that on June 30, 1909, there were 87 Mexicans in San Quentin out of a total prison population of 1,814, or 4.8 percent, and during that year the Mexicans committed to San Quentin represented 5 percent of the total. From 1909 the number and proportion of Mexicans increased fairly steadily until 1918; and since that time they have remained approximately one eighth of the total prisoners and the same proportion as to yearly commitments.

A comparison of the figures concerning the prisoners at Folsom indicates a much smaller percentage of Mexicans at that prison than among the first offenders at San Quentin—6.6 percent at Folsom, September 30, 1929, as against 12.7 percent at San Quentin, June 30, 1929. The fact that a large part of the Mexicans in California have been in the state only a few years probably explains at least in part the smaller percentage of recidivists.[!]

A comparison of the Mexicans with the total as to the nature of their crimes indicates that the offenses which proportionately they are most inclined to commit are violations of the State Poison Act, which relates to narcotics, and the carrying [of] and assault with deadly weapons. The crimes which they rarely commit are forgery, which is to be expected among a people having a high rate of illiteracy and little familiarity with banking, and violations of the Motor Vehicle Act. The crime for which the largest number of Mexicans are sent to Folsom is burglary, which is true of the total prison population also, but the Mexicans represent more than their proportion of persons committed for burglary; and at the same time they have a comparatively low rate of commitment for robbery. In other figures relating to crime among the Mexicans this tendency toward a high incidence of burglary as against a lower incidence of robbery, which latter crime includes personal encounter, is interesting to note. . . .

The 1910 census gives the population of California as 2,377,549, of which number 51,037 or 2.1 percent were native-born Mexicans. The 1920 census records 3,426,861 as the total population of the state, of which number 86,610 or 2.5 percent were native-born Mexicans. In the absence of a recent census, it is not possible to draw any close comparison with the general population. It [the Mexican crime rate] would appear to be very high but the comparison is affected by the fact that more men than women have entered the country, and the age distribution gives a larger proportion of Mexicans in the age groups most commonly found in prison. Police officials generally state a greater tendency among arrested Mexicans to plead guilty to charges and the common financial inability to extended defense and appeal of cases, both of which causes undoubtedly increase the apparent crime among the Mexicans.

Notes

1. In his study of Mexican labor in the Imperial Valley, Paul S. Taylor discusses this domiciliary isolation: "One of the most striking aspects of the Mexican labor situation in Imperial Valley is the concentration of Mexican town population in colonies geographically apart from the American community. . . . Most of the Mexicans outside of Calexico are poor, and poverty leaves them little choice of residence outside of the cheapest quarters. Furthermore, there is the natural tendency to gravitate toward the places where, in a strange land, others of one's language, class, and culture may be found. Finally, there is the social pressure from the American community, which generally does not desire Mexicans as neighbors. A symptom of this pressure is the race restriction sometimes included in the deeds to property. . . . The Mexicans in the valley are sensitive to the social ostracism which they face, and do not force themselves in where they feel the pressure against them. . . . The separation of rural Mexicans from American neighbors is as clear as the separation prevailing in the towns." *Mexican Labor in the United States: Imperial Valley* (Berkeley, 1928), pp. 79, 80, 82.

2. Inquiry sent out by Professor Elliott G. Mears of Stanford University in cooperation with the California Real Estate Association, February, 1927.

3. Los Angeles County Health Department, June 1928, "The Mexican as a Health Problem" (unpublished report).

4. Score card used in the inspection and rating of home conditions, numerical values being given in place of such rating as "excellent," "fair," or "poor." On such a card a rating of 25 would be given where all the itemized conditions were found "excellent." A score of 8.3 would be decidedly poor.

5. Concerning the mode of life of the Mexicans of this district the following statement is made by Los Angeles County Charities Department: "Virtually all of the Mexicans, regardless of age and physical inability, migrate 'to the fruit' in early summer and return when the seasonal work is over. In good years they bring back enough funds to carry them into, and sometimes through the winter, but in poor years they return with no money, their clothes worn out, and worse off than when they left." And again: "There are possibly not ten homes in Maravilla where income is really adequate for the family needs."

6. Figures from California State Department of Public Health, Bureau of Vital Statistics, 1928.

7. Figures [for Tables 3 and 4] from the Los Angeles County Health Department, 1929. The large number of Japanese births in the earlier years covered in this table accounts for most of the difference between the sum of the whites plus the Mexicans, and the total.

8. In addition to the white (Caucasian) and Mexican figures, the total includes Negroes and Orientals. To simplify the table, detail figures for these other groups are not here given, as not significant to the present study.

9. United States Department of Labor, Children's Bureau. "Causal Factors in Infant Mortality" (1925).

10. The infant mortality rate is the number of deaths, exclusive of stillbirths, under one year of age per 1,000 live births.

11. Figures from Los Angeles County Health Department, 1930.

12. Los Angeles County Health Department, "The Mexican as a Health Problem," 1928.

13. Figures, statements and analysis by Dr. John L. Pomeroy, director, Los Angeles County Health Department.

14. California State Department of Health, "Statistical Study of Sickness among the Mexicans in the Los Angeles County Hospital, 1922–1924" (Sacramento: State Department of Health, 1924).

The First Steps: Chicano Labor Conflict and Organizing, 1900–20*

Juan Gómez-Quiñones

". . . solo les cuento los hechos y bases con los que iniciaron los viejos obreros su lucha de clases"

corrido popular

From 1900 to 1920 the Chicano community initiated a new phase in the process to redress the balance upset by the lost battles of 1848. This paper discusses Chicano labor and organizing during the period 1900–20. It is based on published information and some

**Aztlán*, Chicano Journal of the Social Sciences and the Arts (Spring 1973), Vol. 3, No. 1 (Aztlán Publications, Chicano Studies Center, University of California, Los Angeles), pp. 13–49.

archival material; presented is a profile of Chicano labor, suggestions as to patterns of Chicano activity, and indications for possible future research. The intent is to provide a summary of the information available and a tentative analysis of it. Hopefully this historical review will stimulate young Chicano scholars to begin research contributing to a working-class history of their people.

The most important determining aspect for the Chicano community is its economic role and position. Thus, it is preeminently important to understand Chicano labor history. Labor history enlightens the following: the impact of economic changes on the community, the development of internal divisions and their political reflections in the community, the degree of tension between the Chicano and the larger society, the pattern of resistance, the degree of politicization and cohesion, the role of government agencies in regard to the community, the attitudes toward and possibility of interminority cooperation, the state of class-consciousness and how in given circumstances it transcends national antagonisms. In each of the preceding aspects meaningful questions can be asked. If the Chicano community is to change its present situation, it will be on the basis of economic-political power. For workers, the unions are the historic vehicles for the realization of self-determined change.

LABOR IN THE UNITED STATES

The Chicano worker was a part of the working class and the poor of the United States during the period 1900–20.[1] At the turn of the century, most people in the United States were native-born. By 1910, 46 percent lived in cities and in towns. Already by 1900, the United States had passed from artisan, semi-independent labor to mass labor, dependent for its wages, tenure, equipment, and working environment on large-scale capital. The average income of workers in 1900 was small, about four hundred dollars to five hundred dollars a year, at a time when six hundred dollars was considered the minimum for bare comfort. The average work schedule was ten hours per day, six days a week. Working conditions, health, and nutrition, as is known, were appalling. Work was often hazardous and the worker bore the consequences; one in every 26 railroad workers was injured, one in every 399 was killed. Over ten million lived in poverty. In contrast, wealth and power became progressively concentrated; 1 percent of the families owned seven eighths of the wealth. Generally, employers and government authorities were overtly hostile to labor and unions. Unionism was seen as "un-American" and the "independent" worker, the strike breaker, was the "American hero."

Not surprisingly, the unions and radical movements increased greatly between 1900 and World War I. The Socialist party at its peak had one hundred and twenty-six thousand members, won municipal elections in Milwaukee, Schenectady, and Berkeley, and garnered nearly a million votes in the 1912 election. Strikes were common and over the years the number of workers participating in strikes grew; 1894, a depression year, witnessed over seven hundred thousand on strike; in 1919 a wave of strikes swept the country, involving four million workers. The major strike issue was union recognition followed by disputes involving wages, hours, and conditions. The frequency rate of strikes from 1881 to 1935 paralleled the business cycle.[2] Union membership rose from eight hundred and sixty-eight thousand five hundred in 1900 to five million in 1919. Despite this union growth, in 1900 only 4 percent of the work force outside agriculture was organized, and in 1920 the mass of labor was still unorganized.

Labor unrest and the popularity of radical ideologies were factors in mobilizing government repression and government liberalism. Congress, in 1912, formed the Commission on Industrial Relations. It held public hearings "to discover the underlying causes of dissatisfaction in the industrial situation." It discovered the obvious, that working conditions were poor, wages were low, and that employers and local officials often used questionable methods to thwart workers' efforts to better their situation. The commission confessed that a basic cause of industrial unrest was the denial of the right to form effective labor organizations. The hearings contributed to inducing President Taft to establish the United States Department of Labor which was "to foster, promote and develop the welfare of the wage earners of the United States."

The major labor organizations which affected Chicanos were the American Federation of Labor (AFL),* its affiliates, and the International Workers of the World (IWW). Formed in 1881, the American Federation of Labor adopted its present name in 1886; by 1900 it was the largest federation in the United States. Membership was five hundred and forty-eight thousand in 1900 and two million by 1914. The federation was built on the basis of a limited constituency and narrow objectives. It organized skilled workers into national craft unions which enjoyed autonomy within the larger umbrella

---

*The AFL, properly speaking, is not a union. It is a federation in which the dominant power has always been held by the national officers of the large craft unions.

organization. The AFL rejected utopian goals and concentrated on wages, hours, working conditions, and union recognition for skilled labor. The AFL, like the railroad brotherhoods (engineers, conductors, firemen, and trainmen exclusively), was composed of skilled labor and generally excluded other workers. Temporarily it held a "neutral" political position. It later reconsidered this line and participated in the congressional campaigns of 1906, and supported the Democratic presidential candidate in 1908, 1912, and 1916. Originally, it sought, through political activity, to free labor from antitrust restraints by securing amendments to the Sherman Anti-Trust Acts. An unknown but probably small number of Chicano workers participated in AFL local and state action. Its affiliates also had some Chicano members. The AFL was *the* conservative alternative to more radical labor organizing such as the IWW and, therefore, had a limited appeal to those caught at the bottom of the laboring class.[3]

The national labor organization which had major impact upon the Chicano was the IWW, known as the Wobblies. The IWW was founded in 1905 by militant miners and lumbermen, many of whom were anarchists and socialists.[4] Its organizing focus was the semiskilled and unskilled workers, often immigrants. The IWW was, naturally, concerned with bread-and-butter issues, but its major objectives were the politicization of all workers and the formation of "one big union" including all labor, in order to be able to call a general strike, take over the government, and initiate a social revolution. It depended on spirit and commitment; membership and structure was loose, but not uncoordinated. Chicanos often came into contact with the IWW as a result of its organizing activities in mining, agricultural, and urban areas. The Western Federation of Miners (WFM), active in mining camps of the Southwest, was associated with the IWW from 1905 to 1908. As a whole, the WFM was less progressive than the IWW but more militant than the AFL. After 1908 it moved toward a moderate position. In the West, the WFM was of more influence than the United Mine Workers of America. Importantly, the IWW also tried to organize agricultural workers. In 1915 it set up the Agricultural Workers Organization (AWO). Often Wobblies worked with Chicano-Mexicano radical organizations such as the Partido Liberal Mexicano. It can be argued that the net effect of the IWW's rejection of bourgeois politics was to depoliticize workers and to reinforce the focus on the bread-and-butter issues, though with a more intense militancy. By 1920, the IWW had collapsed. This was due, in part, to management's decision to deal with more conservative unions, such as the AFL, thus determining for the workers their organization. Looking at the two major unions one can speculate that if forced to choose among labor organizations, a realistic government or business would choose the AFL, which was hostile to Mexican migration and the Chicano community.

"y el que niega su raza ni madre tiene"

corrido popular

POPULATION

The Chicano community during the period 1900–20, though seen as alien by most "Americans," was composed of both recent immigrants and native born.[5] Deplorably, precise census data on numbers are lacking. A rough estimate of the native-born of native parents in the Southwest is 200,000 in 1900.[6] These were concentrated in New Mexico, Texas, and California, respectively. The recorded immigrant population in 1900 is estimated at 103,393. By 1920 the native-born and immigrant Chicanos had grown to 486,418.[7] Recorded immigration from Mexico for the years 1900–09 is 24,000 and for 1910–19, 174,000.[8] However, the United States census in 1910 reported 162,959 citizens whose parents had been born in Mexico and for 1920, 253,176 citizens.[9] The following table provides a profile of geographic distribution of persons born in Mexico and of persons native-born of Mexican parents not born in the United States (excludes native-born of native-born).

Percentage distribution of persons born in Mexico and native-born of Mexican parents

Area	*1910*	*1920*
Arizona	13.4	12.6
California	13.4	17.6
Colorado	.9	2.0
New Mexico	5.7	4.7
Texas	61.0	54.6
Total Southwest	94.4	91.5
Other states	5.6	8.5
	100.0%	100.0%

Source: Adapted from Grebler, *The Mexican American People,* p. 111.

Mexican northward expansion, never stilled, in 1900 was on the increase again. The assumption that prior to 1915 Mexican migration was slight must be questioned as well as the assumption that

Mexican society was static prior to the Revolution.[10] Within Mexico the trend of migration to the northern states and to the towns is noticeable in the Mexican censuses of 1900 and 1910. At the border, observers noted the increase in crossings. In 1907, a United States Deputy Collector of Customs reported to Captain W. S. Scott that an "unusual number of Mexicans" were crossing around the Del Rio area of Texas en route to cotton districts in the interior.[11] The 1911 *Annual Report of the [United States] Commissioner General of Immigration* noted at least fifty thousand "non-statistical" aliens annually for "normal years."[12] Several articles appeared in the Mexico City press between 1900 and 1912 on the problem of immigrants in the United States indicating concern for the consequences.[13] Clearly, immigration was hardly slight before the Revolution.

MEXICAN FACTORS

A review of some facts concerning Mexico and Mexican labor provides a basis for understanding the migrant, his motives, and his labor relations in the United States. Mexico in 1900 was undergoing modernization and strain; it was also a society of limited opportunity, high cost of living, low wages, and political repression. Population increased from ten million to fifteen million between 1885 and 1910.[14] Agricultural production, especially export crops, increased by one hundred million pesos between 1877 and 1907. However, bean production dropped fifty thousand tons and corn dropped six hundred and three thousand tons.[15] In effect, in a time of increasing population and agricultural production, foodstuffs declined.

Indicative of the economic growth, the gross national product grew by 37 percent between 1900 and 1910.[16] However, while the average wage per day was thirty-two centavos in 1890, it was thirty centavos in 1911; and the price index, 85.0 in 1890, was 132.0 in 1908, a 47-point spread.[17] Though agriculture claimed three fifths of the work force, the industrial work force increased from 692,697 people in 1895 to 803,262 in 1910.[18] Mining employed 97,700 people in 1907; construction 75,000; and transportation 55,000.[19]

In addition to economic facts there are social ones which are important. Between 1890 and 1910, 70 percent of the population was [less than thirty-one] years of age.[20] National literacy only increased from 14 percent to 20 percent, but there was wide regional variation.[21] For example, in Mexico City full literacy was 50 percent, and in the states of Chihuahua, Nuevo León, Sonora, Coahuila, Zacatecas, and Jalisco, 50 percent at least knew how to read.[22] Thus, newspapers increased in number from 310 in 1893 to 1,571 in 1907, and circulation rose 400 percent.[23] Students enrolled at all levels of schooling numbered 246,267 in 1878, and 848,487, in 1907.[24] Thus, between 1890 and 1910, greater numbers of Mexicans were working in industrial tasks and were receiving education.

As the situation was one of social and economic change, so it was intellectually. There was a body of ideas and an organizational heritage pertinent to labor. Liberalism, as developed in Mexico, though critically questioned from a variety of viewpoints, was the strongest thread in popular political thought. Liberal-oriented newspapers in Mexico City such as *Diario del Hogar, El Monitor Republicano,* and *El Hijo del Ahuizote* noticeably increased their concern for labor's rights between 1890 and 1910 and supported the right to unionize, to better pay and working conditions, to accident compensation, and so forth.[25] Often the arguments had a nationalist overtone because in many situations labor was national and management foreign.

A minority element in the Church also took up problems of the workingman. Catholic clergy and laity between 1902 and 1909 organized four congresses which debated such topics as education, alcoholism, land reform, conditions on the haciendas, a living wage, and labor protection of women and children.[26] The impetus for the congresses was in large part due to the impact of the encyclical Rerum Novarum (1891). The first congress, held in Puebla in 1903, was important because it committed laity and clergy to undertake action on the social incorporation of the Indian, to increase and improve Catholic education, and to organize workers' clubs that would provide aid and support in securing material welfare as well as spiritual enrichment.

Mutualism, cooperativism, anarchism, and socialism, often in their most utopian forms, had their adherents and propagandists in Mexico from at least 1870, when the first workingman's *central* was founded, the Gran Círculo de Obreros.[27] In 1876, the Congreso Nacional de Obreros Mexicanos had fifty thousand members and it affiliated with the anarchist international in 1880. Marx, Bakunin, and Kropotkin, in low-cost editions, were circulating in 1900.[28]

Given these conditions, and the ideas available, as it is to be expected, Mexican labor was in turmoil; it is important to remember that this organizational heritage was part of the baggage carried by the migrants to the United States. From 1890 to 1910 various labor associations were formed, such as the Liga Obrera, Unión de Obreros, Unión de Mineros, La Confederacíon del Trabajo, Gran Liga Mexicana de Ferrocarrileros, and the largest, with eighty branches, Gran Círculo de Obreros Libres. The number of workers involved is difficult to calculate but these figures provide perspective:

in 1907, of twenty-one thousand Mexican railroad workers eleven thousand and five hundred were members of labor associations; the mutual aid societies in 1906 numbered 426 and had eighty thousand members.[29] From 1877 to 1910 there were two hundred and fifty strikes. Strike activity was particularly intense in 1881, 1884, 1889, 1890, 1891, and 1895; the peak of strike activity occurred between 1905 and 1907, thereafter declining up to the Revolution.[30] The conflict is even more impressive when one considers that to agitate for better wages, and to unionize was against the law, punishable by fines and imprisonment.[31] Repression by the army and the police was brutal, and as a matter of course workers involved were imprisoned and blackballed. The usual causes for strikes were wage cuts, speed-up practices, increase in hours, ill treatment of workers, demands for salary increase, special privileges of foreign technicians, and resentment of foreign ownership.[32]

Between 1906 and 1907, 128 strikes occurred. The best-known ones were those at Cananea, Sonora, and Orizaba, Veracruz. At Cananea on June 1, 1906, several hundred workers struck; marching with the Mexican and Red flags, they attacked the lumber store and killed two managers.[33] The government used national armed contingents and armed United States irregular volunteers to end the strike. In the South, a series of strikes occurred spreading principally over the states of Tlaxcala, Puebla, and Veracruz, involving over six thousand workers in some ninety textile mills.[34] Rejecting a one-sided compromise, the Orizaba workers, led by Lucrecia Toriz and other women, rioted, attacked a foreign-owned store, tried to burn the factory, set prisoners free from jails, distributed foodstuff, and armed themselves. Some of the militia sent to restore order went over to the workers' side. Eventually, order was imposed after two hundred workers were killed. Mexican labor was not apathetic, unorganized, or unpoliticized.

Recognition of this widespread strike activity forces us to change our view of Mexican workers in the United States. The standard assumption is that the Mexican migrant of the period 1900–20 was drawn from agriculture, thus rural, unskilled, and illiterate and was politicized, if at all, only through the beneficial contact with Anglos. This characterization makes gratuitously superfluous questions concerning social or political attitudes of the migrants. Though it has been observed that the migrants of the period 1915–18 were varied due to the pressures of the Revolution, diversity in social categories, motivation, or political experience has not been recognized for migrants of the late nineteenth and early twentieth centuries. Recognizing these factors is a step toward better understanding the events in the Chicano community during 1900–20. Agricultural production in Mexico was undergoing modernization. The mobility from this sector was limited, however, because of the harshness and degree of control in this area. Industrialization and the economic policy of the Porfiriato resulted in greater fluidity as well as economic frustration for the lower-middle class and the industrial labor sector. It was these two elements which had the economic means and the consciousness to entertain exit across the border for the sake of economic improvement. Political harassment existent in Mexico prior to 1911 must be considered as a stimulus to emigration. The Díaz regime, though not possessing the control of modern totalitarian regimes, was a dictatorship zealous in maintaining power. Generally, citizens, then as now, were secure in their persons or property provided their behavior stayed within the boundaries of what was politically acceptable to the regime and they avoided clashes with persons or interests of greater import to the regime; if not, they faced harassment, loss of employment, imprisonment, or worse. After 1899 there was a gradual increase in political dissent and labor unrest and concomitantly the regime responded. Thus there was a push operating selectively on persons active in politics and labor organizations to migrate north.

"Ya nos vamos reenganchados
A Trabajar al contado"

corrido popular

LABOR DISTRIBUTION

For Mexican migrants, El Paso, Laredo and Eagle Pass, Texas, were the major crossing places, although crossings occurred at numerous other points.[35] Migrants were drawn principally from the northern states of Mexico: Sonora, Chihuahua, Coahuila, and Nuevo León; and from the states of the central plateau such as Zacatecas, Aguas Calientes, Guanajuato, Jalisco, and Michoacán.[36] The Chicano at this time was employed in a wide range of activities—railroads, mining, industry, construction, and agriculture. Changes in production and technology, it should be observed, affected Chicano labor and its patterns.

During 1900 to 1920, railroads were the major employers of Chicano labor. Within the industry Chicanos were spread from the West Coast to the Midwest.[37] Most of the Chicano laborers worked at one time for the railroads. They substituted, not displaced, Italians, Greeks, Chinese, Japanese, and so forth. Chicano laborers worked as trackmen, in maintenance, construction, and yard gangs, cleaned cinder pits, iced cars, loaded stock, cleaned cars, and occasionally worked as boilermakers, machinists, and section bosses.[38] Chicanos comprised from 70 percent to 90 percent of the work force and were concentrated in low-status jobs.[39] Although many Chicanos had experience and high skills from working in the Mexican railroad system, they generally were relegated to lower-level jobs in the United States. Railroads directly recruited workers at major border towns like El Paso. They were usually hired on a six-month contract. In 1906 to 1907 wages were seventy-five cents to one dollar a day including living huts or bunk cars, but wages were not standard and tended to be higher as the worker went northward.[40] Railroads served as a dispersal vehicle for the Chicano because of their network organization and the mobility of much of the work, and also because once a particular construction was completed, crews were released on the spot. For instance, many barrios date their beginnings from these railroad camps. Chicano labor in the Chicago and Calumet region was at first introduced by the railroads.[41]

Chicano labor was a major component in the extractive industries, principally mining, but also lumber and oil. Chicanos who came to the United States fields most likely had experience in mining in Mexico. Chicanos were employed in the Arizona copper and smelting operations where they had been the original work force. Chicano labor was also present in the coal mines of Colorado and New Mexico and in the coke and ore production areas of northern New Mexico.[42] In Texas, Chicano miners worked in the coal mines at Thurber and the soft coal and lignite mines of Laredo and Eagle Pass.[43] Chicanos were more numerous in areas where the quality of the coal was poor, veins thin, and the climate arid and hot. Chicano labor was widespread in the silver and copper mines of New Mexico and Arizona.[44] For the most part, they had opened the mines, worked underground, done the surface work, and operated the smelters. In some instances they remained a majority of the work force but often they were gradually displaced by Anglos especially at the more-skilled, higher-paid positions. In Colorado, the best jobs went to Anglos while Chicanos were used for dangerous assignments, in odd jobs, and as a reserve labor force.[45]

Chicano laborers worked in a variety of heavy and light industries during 1900 to 1920: iron and auto works in the Midwest, building trades in Arizona, rail building in Southern California and parts of Texas, and slaughterhouse work in Kansas and Chicago.[46] In regard to the latter, Chicano labor moved from rail work in the Chicago and Calumet areas to the slaughterhouses in noticeable numbers around 1916. This was not only a result of the general need for more labor at the time but also was promoted by companies seeking to hamper union efforts.

Of all the industries, agriculture is the one most indelibly stamped by Chicano workers. In the period 1900–20, they were one of several ethnic and social groups consigned to the fields. Only gradually did they gain predominance.[47] With the construction of the Spreckles sugar beet operation in Watsonville, Monterey County, California, in 1899, and the organizing of the Sugar Trust in 1902, the sugar beet increased in importance and, with it, Chicano labor. For the sugar beet crop, labor was seasonal, employment was on a contract basis and mostly migratory. The labor force was approximately one fifth (1/5) Japanese, four fifths (4/5) Chicano. Cantaloupe, melon, cotton, pea, peach, tomato, asparagus, and lima bean workers in California were Chicanos. Citrus work for the Chicano also increased over the years. In Texas, Chicano labor was in the majority in the Bermuda onion, spinach, and cotton crops.[48] Here were both a stable labor force as a result of sharecropping and construction work, as well as transient imported labor. Chicanos were also active in Arizona and New Mexico agriculture, picking cotton and raising vegetables, alfalfa, and other forage crops.[49] In Colorado, Chicanos competed with Russians and Japanese in the locally important sugar beet and melon crops. Agricultural work was seasonal, migratory, and on a contract basis apparently from the beginning. Agriculture was a late development compared with railroads or mining, and agricultural labor reflected the changes effected by intensification of irrigation and the changeover in crops. In nearly all sectors where Chicanos worked there were attempts at labor organization.

"Abajo ese rico insano
que el pobre quiere moler
que vivan los Sindicatos
que nos han de defender"

corrido popular

EARLY LABOR CONFLICT

Among the first strikes of the twentieth century involving Chicanos were the ones in the Colorado mines. A major strike occurred in Telluride in 1901, one of a series of conflicts in this period.[50] A minority among the workers, Chicanos apparently were involved both as strikers and strikebreakers, a recurring circumstance throughout this period. This paradox is understandable, given their status and economic situation. The Western Federation of Miners was the most important and militant organization in the Colorado area. Almost every strike became a small-scale war. Management was ruthless; it readily recruited and used armed guards against strikers. Workers also were confronted by members of the local community who, instigated by the owners, formed "Citizen Alliances" to harass and beat strikers. They raised the banner of the sanctity of "private property" and the right of "individual freedom" as convenient catchalls to legitimize repressive action. Thus, management had at its disposal local authorities to control dissident workers; when this did not suffice, companies further used their political influence to send in the militia to impose "law and order." During the 1903–04 phase of Colorado strikes, Chicanos readily joined the union when urged and remained loyal to the labor cause as long as they received strike benefits. These benefits were particularly necessary for them because of their below-average wages and the presence and size of their families. In 1902, labor agitation was reported among Chicano workers in Arizona. Abraham Salcido, an organizer, was sentenced to the penitentiary for agitation.[51]

In California, Chicano agricultural workers joined other nationalities to strike at Fresno in 1901 and 1902, in the San Francisco Bay Area in 1902, and in Redlands during 1903. However, the most significant strike of 1903 occurred in Oxnard, a major sugar beet area.[52] The Oxnard strike involved an alliance of Chicanos and Japanese against a contracting agency and, less directly, the growers. The episode has classic colonial aspects and requires further explanation.

OXNARD, 1903

By 1897, when Oxnard was incorporated, the original Mexican settlers in the area had generally been displaced from land ownership but Chicano settlements persisted. The need for labor attracted more recently arrived Chicano migrants and also Japanese emigrants. Newspapers referred to them as "muttering half-drunk natives," "cholos" [mixed Indian and white], and "dusky skinned Japs and Mexicans."[53] By 1903, there were identifiable Chicano and Oriental neighborhoods; within these communities there was a middle sector. The growers, the major contractors, major businessmen, the judges, juries, sheriffs, and officials were Anglo.

The major grievances leading to the strike were the practices of the Western Agricultural Contracting Company. The company was the main supplier of labor to the growers, who generally did not directly hire laborers. Workers objected to the large cut taken from their wages by the contracting company, for what they deemed was an unnecessary service. They also resented being paid in script redeemable at the Japanese-American Mercantile Store. The store, for example, charged one dollar and twenty cents for a seventy-five-cent pair of overalls.[54]

It would seem from contemporary newspaper accounts that Chicano and Japanese *workers* came together to form the JMLA (Japanese-Mexican Labor Association) and, thus, to eliminate the Anglo contracting company, and deal directly with the grower.[55] However, an intriguing question is the involvement of Chicano and Japanese would-be contractors. Exactly when the JMLA organized is not known; however, it was holding meetings in Oxnard two weeks before the strike. The strike began on February 28, 1903, and lasted until April 1, 1903. It involved several hundred workers, perhaps five hundred to one thousand. The JMLA claimed one thousand and three hundred members and stated that most of them were citizens.[56] The president of the association was José Baba; J. M. Lizarraras was secretary of the Mexican branch and Y. Yamaguchi secretary of the Japanese branch.[57] The JMLA position was rather modest: elimination of the monopoly contractor, "some persons are trying to monopolize the beet work and . . . don't care how low their prices fall. No Japanese or Mexican is able to do good work for a small price. We want fair wages to insure a good job."[58] JMLA reassured the growers, "you will not have to pay any more than you have paid for your work before."[59]

Both sides, the growers and the JMLA, mobilized. The strikers distributed literature, held marches, and tried to block strikebreakers. A newspaper described them as "silent grim fellows most of them young belonging to the lower class of Japanese and Mexicans."[60] An AFL organizer, F. C. Wheeler, gave verbal support at a meeting.[61] The growers deployed institutional power. Two local newspapers, the *Ventura Daily Democrat* and the *Oxnard Courier,* castigated the workers as agitators, charged that they were incompetent to judge the economic issues, that they were prone to violence, and that in the final analysis the support should be for "reliable 'American' contractors." The growers also had law enforcement agencies as allies. JMLA spokesmen K. Obata and K. Yoshinari were arrested for trespassing on the Patterson Ranch on the complaint of Manager John Roupp.[62] Growers also had armed guards, such as Charles Arnold, sworn as deputy constables to give legal protection to nonunion crews transported to break the strike. This tactic led to *the* sensational event of the conflict.

On March 23, in the "Chinatown" section, a gunfight erupted between JMLA supporters and strikebreakers, injuring three Chicanos and two Japanese.[63] Agents of the Western Agricultural Contracting Company, aided by armed guards, transported two wagons filled with men and provisions when they were met by strikers who tried to dissuade the recruits from continuing. A non-JMLA Japanese rushed the wagon, shotgun in hand. Perfecto Ogas, a union man, went for the shotgun, was seized by two deputies, and in the scuffle was shot in the neck. Besides Ogas, Luis Vásquez, M. Ramírez, and two Japanese were hit. Union men believed Charles Arnold responsible. Chicanos went looking for him but Arnold stayed at the justice of the peace office, protected by armed Anglos.[64] A warrant was issued for Arnold, who was booked and then released. On March 25 Luis Vásquez died of his wounds. An inquest was held and despite the testimony by R. Salcido, J. Morales, José Guerrero, Manuel Ramírez, E. López, and S. Manricas charging Arnold as responsible for the incident, the verdict was death at the hands of an unknown party.[65] Perhaps this incident, which had incensed the strikers and their supporters, encouraged the growers to negotiate.

The first meeting between the opposing sides had been held on March 21 at Pioneer Hall, Oxnard, presided over by Colonel T. A. Driffill. It was inconclusive. On March 25, during the tension of the shoot-out, the growers and the contractors met. The strikers were represented by J. Espinsosa, M. Lizarras, Y. Yamaguchi, and José Baba and their counsel, W. E. Sheperd. George E. Herz, representing the Western Agricultural Contracting Company (WACC), offered two thousand of their seven thousand contracted acreage in return for ending the strike and ceasing pressure on non-JMLA men. As a counterproposal JMLA offered acreage in proportion to manpower: they had thirteen hundred men, WACC had sixty. The meeting ended. At the next meeting JMLA agreed not to approach hired workers. Meanwhile the contracting company (as a result of public attitudes toward it) was having problems recruiting alternative workers. On April 1, JMLA secured the agreement that the WACC would release seven thousand acres and retain only eighteen hundred.[66] The strike was over. From JMLA's point of view it was a victory.

> "La Compañía de Tranvías con su afán de lucro insano desprecia las energías del obrero Mexicano"
>
> corrido popular

FROM THE RAILS TO THE FIELDS

Urban workers in Los Angeles, battling during the same year, did not fare as well as those in Oxnard. In February 1903, about five hundred Chicano trackmen struck against the Pacific Electric

Railway and the Los Angeles Railway.[67] The strike was in conjunction with efforts by the Amalgamated Association of Street and Electric Railway Employees, primarily motormen and conductors. Lemuel Biddle of the Council of Labor was active in the strike. The Chicano workers organized the Mexican Federal Union and as a first demand called for a wage increase. Management responded by firing sixty-eight union sympathizers and broke the strike.

Chicano workers, though perhaps too trusting of the Amalgamated, did not lack tenacity or courage. They reorganized and, asking for higher wages, struck again in April, this time fourteen-hundred-strong.[68] The company, taken aback by the workers, at first acceded; later however, securing public support and strike-breakers, it rescinded the wage hike charging that the strike was the work of outside agitators. Poor blacks and Japanese willingly replaced the Chicanos and the strike failed despite the support of some local unions.

Again in 1904, some fifty of the remaining Chicano workers reorganized and struck when wages were cut from a dollar and seventy-five cents to a one dollar a day.[69] Management refused even to acknowledge the existence of a strike. It admitted only that some workers had quit because of work conditions. Other workers were hired. Ironically, prior to this series of conflicts AFL locals in Los Angeles had opposed Chicanos because they lowered wages and rejected unionization.

As Chicanos mobilized in Los Angeles, Chicanos in Thurber, Texas, alongside other workers, organized under the auspices of the United Mine Workers.[70] What sparked the 1903 Thurber strike was the anger aroused by the disappearance of a Chicano organizer (a body of a Mexican was later found). Sixteen hundred workers struck against the Texas and Pacific Coal Company asking for a wage increase, an eight-hour day, the removal of company fences around the town, and the removal of armed guards. The strike was settled by a compromise: increase in wages, an eight-hour day and two paydays per month. Eventually, Thurber became a strong union town partially as a result of Chicano dedication; but nonetheless, it also became a hostile town to Chicano labor. In the 1920's, one hundred and sixty-two Chicanos were deported with union acquiescence.

The years between 1905 and 1909 were apparently relatively quiet in labor relations involving Chicanos. This was due to economic circumstances and perhaps to the more politicized workers' interest in Mexico-oriented activity. This interest came as a result of the organizing carried on by Mexican revolutionaries. The Partido

Liberal Mexicano (PLM), headed by Ricardo Flores Magón, was dedicated to engineering a social revolution in Mexico and during the period 1905–09 was highly active among Chicanos.[71] The information pertinent to Chicano labor activity in this period is related to PLM organizing. Praxedis Guerrero, perhaps PLM's ablest organizer, moved into Morenci, Arizona, in 1907, and organized the Unión de Obreros Libres. The secretary was Manuel Vásquez and treasurer, Agustín Pacheco.[72] Following PLM patterns, Guerrero formed the union, directed it toward action in Mexico, and then left for other organizing fields. Manuel Sarabia and Lázaro Gutiérrez de Lara, then PLM members, were active among workers, especially miners, in Douglas and Bisbee, Arizona.[73] An indicator of circumstances and attitudes for the Chicano worker in 1907–08 was the repatriation of hundreds of Chicanos by the Santa Fe and Southern Pacific railroads.[74] PLM-IWW organizing among migrant Chicanos is evident at this time by the strong Fresno, California IWW local #66, composed mostly of Chicanos.[75] It also presented a tentative success in organizing a difficult sector, agricultural workers.

In Los Angeles during 1910–11, a number of labor developments took place. As in so many instances, the sketchy information currently available poses more questions than it answers. In what was now a tradition, the Chicano workers in March 1910 struck for higher wages against the Los Angeles Railway Company and the Los Angeles Pacific Railway.[76] The strike failed. Feelings were extremely bitter among all workers in Los Angeles. It was at this time that the *Los Angeles Times* building was bombed. The newspaper and the owner, the erstwhile Harrison Gray Otis, were rabid foes of workers and unions. The *Los Angeles Times* maintained this tradition for many years.

In August 1910, workers of the Los Angeles Gas Works struck for higher wages. Over ninety percent of the laborers involved were Chicano. Some were IWW members and the IWW was credited as being behind the strike. After two weeks the strike was settled in favor of the workers. Wages were raised to two dollars and twenty-five cents a day and the company agreed to hire union members. Some participants may have been members of a union formed in 1911 among Chicano workers.

The Unión de Jornaleros Unidos, número 13097, was established in 1911. It was among the first fairly stable community-based unions. Credit for it is usually awarded to Juan Ramírez, an organizer for the California State Federation of Labor.[77] What is more certain is that it had PML support and that its secretary was Amelio B. Velarde, a man of Magonista sympathies. It met on

Sunday mornings from 10 to 12 A.M. at the Templo del Trabajo, 538 Maple Ave., Los Angeles, and it announced: "se invita a los obreros mexicanos."

Meetings were well organized. The union sponsored organizers and organizing generally among migratory and unskilled laborers in areas such as Long Beach and San Pedro. Jornaleros Unidos was affiliated with the AFL, which in this instance may have thought the local could be used as a counter-tool to the IWW's work among Chicanos and as a means of counteracting the alleged strikebreaking potential of Chicano workers. The longevity and success of Jornaleros Unidos is yet to be researched.

Another attempt at a general community-based union occurred in Texas. The Mexican Protection Association organized in 1911 was an early effort on behalf of agricultural laborers.[78] However, as has often occurred in Chicano organizing, this organization included diverse elements, perhaps too diverse for its purpose. The group was composed, in addition to agricultural workers, of property owners, shopkeepers, tenants, and others. It functioned as a mutual aid society and optimistically sought to mitigate the Anglo violence so endemic in Texas. An unstable membership, worsening economic conditions, and factionalism made its life tenuous. The unresolved contradictions flared into a final disruptive conflict between moderate and militant factions in 1914. A no-more-successful and even more short-lived effort in Texas was the Asherton strike of April 1912.[79] Onion clippers struck, apparently influenced by PLM-IWW politicalization, and secured half of their wage demand. But they refused it, insisting on their original proposal. The owners then hired other Chicanos and the strike failed.

Chicano workers also participated in the Wheatland, California, strike, a microcosm of the labor struggle in the West.[80] Aspects of it make it a classic, as well as a prototype of the strikes of the 1930s in California. The owners, operators of the Durst Ranch, were in a financial squeeze because of an economic recession that heightened capitalist competition and lowered prices. Through the use of extensive, misleading advertising a surplus of labor was achieved by the ruthlessly clever growers. Over two thousand and eight hundred men, women, and their children were recruited for half as many jobs. The owners sought to maximize their profit through drastically reduced wages, deductions from wages, rental of living quarters, providing minimum toilet facilities, sale of water, and so forth. A tightly controlled work force was insured by the owners' political influence, especially over local police agencies. In the surrounding area and the state, public opinion was manipulated against the workers. At the time of the strike there was an "enlightened" state governor, Hiram Johnson, who later, in the crunch, sided with the growers.

The Wheatland strike erupted on August 4, 1913. IWW organizers and sympathizers were present. They faced an almost wholly negative situation, partly due to the above external factors, other factors related to their ideological principles, and organizing tactics. The work force was divided into twenty-seven national groups and many of the workers spoke no English. Simply organizing them into some kind of a strike force was a feat. There was no immediate preparatory organizing much less a stable, disciplined union organization.

The conflict was short and violent. The courageous Richard "Blackie" Ford of the IWW assumed leadership and presented written demands that were pathetically minimal: water twice a day, separate toilets for women and men, and one dollar and twenty-five cents a hundred. At a public meeting Ford was slapped by Durst and a constable tried to arrest Ford. The workers objected. After surrounding the area the sheriff ordered the meeting disbanded. When a deputy sheriff fired, wounding a picker, the workers defended themselves, losing two of their own but killing the district attorney and a deputy sheriff. A posse of a hundred armed "lawful" citizens descended on the workers. Eventually, after Governor Hiram Johnson called in five units of militia, the strike was broken.

The depression of 1914 discouraged strike activity but desperate conditions brought on one widely known strike in Ludlow, Colorado, against the Colorado Fuel and Iron Company.[81] It was one more honorable chapter in United States labor history. Chicanos as well as Italians, Slavs, and others were part of the work force. The strike was called by the United Mine Workers for union recognition, wage increase, and better working and living conditions. Constitutionally guaranteed the freedom to exploit, the owners unleashed their armed guards and vigilante groups upon the workers and ejected them from company property. The workers set up makeshift dwellings on adjacent land. On April 20, 1914, the militia set fire to the camp, thus beginning the "Ludlow massacre." The Chicano tents and dugouts were among the first hit; of the eighteen victims nine were Chicanos, five of them children. Eventually the union rescinded the strike call.

In 1915 there were two tenuous efforts at founding community-based quasi-labor organizations. Heriberto Reyes, Agustín V. Galván, and the ubiquitous A. M. Villareal established the Unión Constitucionalista de Obreros Mexicanos in Los Angeles.[82] It was an early effort involving Mexican consular personnel with labor. La Unión Constitucionalista may have been primarily a politically motivated stratagem by partisans of Venustiano Carranza to use a populist tool to counteract PLM influence as well as conservative wealthy recent emigrants. An apparently similar effort took place in Phoenix, Arizona, in late 1915. Dionisio Men . . . [?], who was in correspondence with the Carranza government, sought to establish the Unión Nacional Mexicana (Central Fundadora).[83] It was opened only to *ciudadanos mexicanos* [Mexican citizens] and aimed at protecting them in their jobs, and securing employment for them, as well as providing support in personal and health problems. A lengthy set of statutes were written for the governance of the union and membership cards were printed. Its success is unclear, but certainly in Phoenix there was Chicano union organizing in the building trades.

> "Los mineros se reunieron y al verse negados con esa respuesta lograron un mítin y se engolillaron en recía protesta"
>
> corrido popular

MINEROS

Five thousand miners struck the Clifton, Morenci and Metcalf mines of Arizona on September 12, 1915.[84] Chicanos made up over 70 percent of the work force and generated the strike. The grievances were the double standard in wages, one rate for Anglos, a lower rate for Chicanos, and the brutality and corruption of foremen who sold jobs and lotteries to workers. Great hardship was suffered by Chicanos as a result of the nineteen-week shutdown. Historians have found the strike interesting because it is "remarkably" free of violence; actually it was only comparatively free of violence. It is far more interesting because of its politics. The strike was settled somewhat favorably to workers; the governor of Arizona, George P. Hunt, is awarded the credit.[85] His role was important in a negative sense, since he did not lend coercive state support to the owners and thus hindered the introduction of strikebreakers. On the other hand he convinced the workers to compromise. The *Los Angeles Labor Press* had a less personalistic analysis of who was responsible for the successful strike: "Everyone knows that it was the Mexican miners that won the strike at Clifton and Morenci by standing like a stone wall until the bosses came to terms."[86]

The historical development of the Chicano social labor relations of the Clifton-Morenci area would be an excellent case study. A summary of the antecedents of the 1914 strike and the aspects of the strike serve to indicate this. Prior to the coming of the Anglos, Mexican miners discovered and worked the copper deposits in Arizona. However, strife, the technology available, and difficult terrain determined the suspension of these efforts. The entrepreneurs Charles and Henry Lesinsky picked up claims in the Clifton-Morenci district around 1872.[87] Since they literally knew nothing of mining and since the dangerous conditions ruled out Anglo miners, who in any case would not have the specific skills necessary, they recruited Chicanos from El Paso and Chihuahua. Chicanos built, supplied, and developed the mines, often giving up their lives in the process. In especially hard times they even agreed to reduction in wages while the company was in financial difficulties. The company store earnings helped carry the entrepreneurs. James Colquhoun, former chairman of the board, confessed: "Indeed without that assistance Lesinsky would have been effectively stranded."[88] Colquhoun also acknowledged, "those Mexicans were brave, hardy and resourceful."[89] The Chicanos comprised nearly 99 percent of the population and did all the work. Further, they organized to sponsor cultural activities and maintain order. In 1882, Lesinsky handsomely sold out for one million and two hundred thousand dollars to Frank L. Underwood, who then sold to a Scottish concern, Arizona Copper Company, for two million dollars, six months later.[90] Their operations, as well as those of the Detroit Copper Company and Shannon Copper Company, expanded. Anglo workers displaced Chicanos at skilled levels during the 1890s. By 1914 operations were capitalized at over fifty million dollars.

At the turn of the century there was labor organizing and also strained relations between Chicano and Anglo workers. These general factors were the antecedents to the strike of 1915. The AFL tried to organize along craft lines in Globe-Miami, Bisbee, and Jerome, while the Western Federation of Miners (WFM) gave attention to unskilled labor. Labor disturbances occurred among the predominantly Chicano work force in 1903 when militia was called in to insure control; and there were disturbances in 1907. The unions were weak and torn by dissension. On the other hand the companies were doing well despite occasional recessions: Phelps Dodge in 1912 recorded 23 percent profit on its capital of forty-six million dollars, the Detroit Company paid a dividend of 146 percent, the Shannon Company paid one dollar and fifty cents per share listed at six and a half dollars.[91] The wages were the lowest for Arizona camps, two dollars and thirty-nine cents a shift for Chicanos, two dollars and ninety-eight cents for Anglos.[92] Management rationalized low wages by pleading that the ore quality was low and the labor inefficient.

The immediate root of the strike was the discontent present since January 1914. Responding to the depression, the copper companies cut wages by 10 percent.[93] Coincidentally, that year, the voters, with union support, passed a law restricting "alien" employment in any single company to 20 percent.[94] Be that as it may, as a result of the wage cuts, AFL affiliates and WFM and IWW locals called a walkout. The owners refused to deal with workers through union representatives but did accede to mediation by Governor George W. P. Hunt. An agreement was reached whereby the 10 percent wage cut was restored and a sliding pay scale pegged to copper price was instituted. Management thought itself magnanimous for initiating a sliding pay scale, a clever ruse on the workers. This round was hardly a victory for the workers.

Workers still harbored grievances, particularly the Chicanos. Throughout this period they had their own quasi organizations, and in fact, they were the best organized and the most politicized and aggrieved. Despite reasons to distrust unions, given union support for the Anti-Alien Law, the WFM, the more progressive union, was invited during the summer to the Chicano communities.[95] The organizers apparently were first tested. At rallies Chicano workers would put them on by shouting "We can't understand you, speak Spanish," then "Speak English, we can't understand." After a while the chant would start, "otro toro! otro toro!" [another bull!][96] Union leaders, as well as the owners, came to fear the Chicano anger. Nonetheless, preparatory organizing took place and on September 12 the workers struck for wages, just working conditions, and union affiliation; the Chicanos were nearly unanimous for the move, the Anglos hesitant. Almost immediately, the demand for union affiliation was set aside by the workers. The owners still rejected conciliation. In the process it became apparent that management was less concerned about wages and grievances than it was about eradicating WFM influence in the district.

Several aspects of the strike reveal its dynamics. Chicanos presided over the three locals, Juan Guerrera in Clifton, Carlos Carbajal in Metcalf, Abrán Rico in Morenci.[97] Rico had been involved in PLM activity.[98] Speeches by Anglos had to be translated. Gutiérrez de Lara, a PLM veteran, on one occasion translated for Governor Hunt. Pickets, meetings, and marches occurred throughout. A Mexican orchestra provided the music. The workers' chant was "abajo los Gerentes" (down with the bosses).[99] Chicano militants got rough. On one occasion several hundred ran through the town requiring union cards of everyone, no doubt to insure solidarity. Beatings on nonunion sympathizers occurred often and one union sympathizer was shot by an antagonist, both of them Chicanos. An *esquirol* [scab or strikebreaker] was paraded through the town with a sign hung around his neck. Militancy was also firm. Juan García and Ricardo Rodríguez, union officers, were forced to resign for showing signs of weakening. Chicano workers, nearly unanimously, consistently till the last, rejected compromises in the negotiations, usually booing and jeering when compromise was discussed. In contrast, the Anglo workers, equally unanimously, voted on every occasion to accept what management offered. There were lighter aspects. Many citizens, some businesses, and some unions provided food and clothing. On Christmas a big fiesta was held; local talent performed and a Chicano baseball team played against an all-Anglo one.

Through the skill of union leadership, Governor Hunt's efforts, and businessmen's pressure, the companies moved toward a compromise.[100] They were willing to grant higher wages and adjudication of grievances but no union recognition, and the workers had to abandon WFM. This was the position on January 1, 1916. The Chicanos were firm. However, Hunt's arguments and businessmen's pressure plus the willingness of some workers to compromise determined that on January 11, all the workers would abandon WFM. Management agreed to let the workers affiliate with AFL but did not recognize it. In effect management recognized the fact of unionism and had astutely maneuvered to determine the union. On that basis the workers settled the strike.

Labor conflict continued in Arizona mines and later in the fields. In Jerome and Bisbee Chicano miners were numerous and militant. *El Rebelde,* a militant Spanish language newspaper, was distributed. During May 1917 the Metal Mine Workers Industrial Union local #800 (IWW) and the International Union of Mine, Mill, and Smelter Workers local (formerly WFM) concurrently, but not jointly, struck the Jerome mines for higher wages.[101] The IUMMSW added the demand of the "checkoff." Quickly, the owners mobilized the Jerome Loyalty League, a "patriotic" citizen's association which functioned as an Anglo vigilante group. With the support of the local sheriff it began deporting "undesirables"; seventy Wobblies were soon shipped out. The strike was settled by a partial concession to the demands; the companies would not concede the checkoff demand but offered to accept a grievance committee of employees regardless of their union affiliation. Unresolved grievances resulted in a strike on July 7, 1917, at Jerome and on July 12 at the Bisbee mines.[102] The IWW went at it alone. Citizen groups and the sheriff's office deported sixty-seven strikers in Jerome and twelve hundred in Bisbee.

To the north, the Chicano railroad workers of the Rock Island Railroad organized the Benito Juárez Society; it was both beneficial and recreational.[103] Incorporated in 1918, by 1921 it disintegrated because of prolonged unemployment of the members.

"El burgués que nos humilla
Temblará ante nuestros ojos"

corrido popular

TOWN AND COUNTRY

During 1918, in Los Angeles, Chicano workers broke a strike. When the Moulders local #374 went out against the Baker Iron Works, management replaced the strikers with new workers, many of them Chicano.[104] The union could think of no better approach than to raise the issue of patriotic chauvinism. They appealed to the company that it was unpatriotic to hire non-English-speakers. Since management, when it is convenient, advances nativist appeals, the union perhaps believed that this argument would convince management not to hire non-English-speakers. It didn't. Chicano workers could hardly be induced to support the union position. The strike failed.

During April 1917, in Colton, California, the Portland Cement Company announced a 50 percent wage reduction for Chicano workers because they were "making too much money."[105] When workers complained, fifty were fired. The jobless Chicanos formed a union, Trabajadores Unidos, and called a strike. Those still on the job, about one hundred and fifty Chicanos, walked out in solidarity. The demands specified union recognition, rehiring of all workers, and a five-cent-an-hour raise. Because their work required experience and skill, the Chicanos were in a strong bargaining position. Scabs were hired but proved unsatisfactory. For two months the union held out. Portland Cement was forced to concede the three Chicano demands. The Colton strike was successful; however, in time, the union deteriorated to a fraternal lodge.

On August 16, 1919, Chicano and Anglo carmen and platform workers of the Los Angeles Railway struck.[106] They were joined, as in the past, by Chicano track workers from the Pacific Electric Railway. The workers demanded pay increase to two dollars and seventy-two cents a day, time and a half for Sunday, holiday, and night work, and collective bargaining. About fifteen hundred men were involved in this strike, which was backed by the Brotherhood of Railway Trainmen and division #835. Initially the union did not consider the Chicano workers though the Chicanos were interested.

They were allowed to participate when the Anglo unions realized they needed Chicano support to make the strike effective. The companies immediately launched a campaign to attract laborers to replace the strikers, paying them five dollars a day plus board and lodging. The strike failed.

As a result of the pressure for labor during World War I, increased acreage, and changes in technology and crops, larger numbers of Chicanos entered the agricultural fields. Concurrently, agricultural strikes occurred between 1917 and 1919. At Turlock, California, in 1917, labor conflict erupted causing a loss of a thousand carloads of cantaloupes for the growers.[107] The growers then enlisted the help of town citizens who drove out the militant workers and organizers, thereby ending the strike. The same year witnessed orange pickers out on strike at Riverside. Using the courts, the growers secured an injunction to prohibit strikers from interfering with strikebreakers.[108] In January 1919, citrus workers struck at San Dimas, Covina, San Gabriel, Azusa, Monrovia, and Duarte, California.[109] Supporting the growers, local newspapers red-baited the workers and announced an imminent Bolshevik conspiracy. Arrests broke the strike. Again in April, farm workers struck at Pomona, La Verne, and Ventura, and again arrests and intimidation broke the strikes. Strikes occurred in the Arizona cotton fields during 1920 involving four thousand Chicano workers.[110] Many of these workers had been specifically recruited in Mexico by another kind of entrepreneur that was to play a larger role in the future, the *coyote-enganchista* [type of rapacious labor contractor]. Violence, jailing of leaders, and deportations did not dishearten the spirit of the workers; and efforts, led by C. N. Idar, a Chicano from Texas, were made to adapt organizations to the changing labor-economic situation by establishing confederated locals of Chicano agricultural workers.

A MATTER OF CONVENIENCE

Changes in immigration laws parallel those in crops and labor recruitment. In 1917, the 1885 Alien Contract Labor Law was extended as it had been in 1891 and 1907.[111] It endeavored to curb the inducement of European aliens to the United States. However, the 1917 Act contained a proviso which permitted the Commissioner of Immigration and Naturalization to approve the temporary admission of aliens.[112] Significantly this clause provided discretionary authority to allow Mexicans to fill the increasing labor needs. By June 1918, growers were arranging the mass recruitment of labor in

Mexico through their representatives. During 1917, farm journals reported large groups of Mexican laborers, from San Felipe and Guaymas, arriving by truck to the Imperial Valley in units of fifteen hundred to twenty-five hundred.[113] Concurrently sugar beets, cotton, and winter vegetables were of increasing importance. The first bulk shipment of Mexican labor, two trainloads from El Paso, arrived in the western Colorado beet fields in 1918.[114] In February and April of 1920 the Department of Labor issued orders to permit Mexican labor to enter specifically for agricultural work, dispensing with the requirements of literacy and the head tax.[115] The farm journals of 1920 refer to the year as that of the "Mexican Harvest" and by 1921 the Chicano was the dominant labor force in California fields. In 1921, there was the first tentative effort to establish a confederation of Chicano unions.[116]

> "Siempre fuertes, siempre unidos otra sería nuestra vida"
>
> corrido popular

CONCLUSIONS

What the present essay indicates for research should be clear: much more information is needed. Surely what is known needs to be questioned and supplemented. The concern of researchers, however, should not be limited simply to expanding the pool of information. Research in labor history should involve the testing of available theories. It is perhaps in this area that findings and generalizations may prove most original.

There are five major theoretical approaches for the study of labor in the United States: the moral conditioning school; the economic interests analysis; the psychological-environment focus; the conventional Marxist approach; the the job monopoly theory.[117] None of these is universally viable for United States labor as a whole, much less for the Chicano. Their application to historical analysis is more valuable than their application to the present day which is of dubious value. It would be presumptuous to attempt to deal with them in this brief space. Nonetheless, it must be pointed out that each provides insight for particular aspects of the development of labor at a certain time. Certainly they must be tested in application to the problems of Chicano labor organizing and must be kept in mind in historical research. They are helpful in the negative by suggesting the following: many labor problems or features are not recent but historical. Chicano labor, as any other, must not be seen as an abstract struggling against abstract forces. Racial prejudice and authoritarian attitudes are not the property of some sectors and not others in the society. The study of the Chicano working class cannot be confined to the study of unions and exceptional labor conflicts. The Chicano labor force cannot be viewed as static or unchanging in its character. The Chicano has suffered as well as practiced job-consciousness but this alone explains only strictly economic concerns that are visible in Chicano labor organizing.

The broad labor movement and its relations to the Chicano worker is a study of contradiction. It sought power and solidarity. However, organized labor hid behind its self-serving argument: the Chicano worker was unorganizable, he took jobs from Anglo workers, and he depressed wages. With this as "Labor's" rhetorical argument, it would be too much to expect that "Labor" would unmask the issue of racism among workers or deal with the function of Chicano labor in a colonial underdeveloped area such as the Southwest. Rather than a strategy to bridge divisions among workers and to acknowledge their common problems in order to shape a common resistance to the employer, organized labor capitalized on the ethnic divisions among workers and gained partial concessions for a favored few of the workers and increased *their* purchasing power at the expense of the workers it excluded.

Comparatively, for the Chicano, the AFL was implicitly hostile and the IWW ineffectively sympathetic. The AFL explicitly opposed Mexican immigration. It blocked the enrollment of Chicanos as members with such patent obstacles as requiring naturalization papers for membership. Generally, it did not seek to organize migratory labor or urban semiskilled or unskilled labor except as a preventive measure or when presented with an accomplished fact. In contrast to the AFL elitist, liberal, collaborationist policy, the IWW believed its mission to be "subserve the immediate interest of the working class and effect their final emancipation." The IWW *did* organize general industrial and agricultural labor. Though members were not free of hostile attitudes toward Chicanos, IWW faced the issue of racism, appealed to worker solidarity, and facilitated Chicano participation. Nonetheless, the IWW, battered by repressive assaults, infatuated with its rhetoric, and faulty in its organizing did did not prove a viable alternative to the Chicano worker. At most, the AFL exploited Chicano discontent and the IWW sold left-wing pie in the sky.

Chicano labor history in the period from 1900 to 1920 reveals two major aspects and several secondary ones: Labor conflict is historical and its character is related to objective conditions and subjective attitudes. Chicanos struggled against the exploitation by management and the hostility of other workers. Conflict was pronounced in California, Arizona, Texas, Colorado, and New Mexico in that order. In this period, industrial labor conflict was more marked than agricultural. In terms of numbers and demands, those of the fields and the mines were the most impressive. The majority of the strikes failed and the reason for failure was repression, intimidation, deportation, and faulty organization. Violence was initiated by management or state agencies. Strikes were usually about work conditions, wages, rights to unionization, hours, and pay schedules. Chicanos organized in plural unions though there also were efforts at establishing Chicano unions. Thus, at the end of the twenty-year cycle, the Chicano was, as in the beginning, locked in mortal combat.

I am grateful to the following people for reading the manuscript: Miss Vivian Marone, Ginger Tonkin, and Professors Carlos Cortés, José Juárez, Alexander Saxon, Gary Nash, Carlos Vásquez, David J. Weber, Alberto Camarillo, Rodolfo Alvarez, and the editors of *Aztlán*.

Notes

1. General data on U.S. labor and society for this period is drawn from the following sources: Robert H. Bremner, *From the Depths: The Discovery of Poverty in the United States* (New York: New York University Press, 1956); Philip Foner, *History of the Labor Movement in the United States*, 4 vols. (New York: International Publishers, 1964); Samuel P. Hays, *The Response to Industrialism, 1885–1914* (Chicago: University of Chicago Press, 1957); Richard Hofstadter, *The Age of Reform* (New York: Knopf, 1955); Marc Karson, *American Labor Unions and Politics, 1900–1918* (Carbondale: Southern Illinois University Press, 1958); Ira Kipnis, *The American Socialist Movement, 1897–1912* (New York: Columbia University Press, 1968); E. C. Kirkland, *Industry Comes of Age: Business, Labor and Public Policy, 1860–1897* (New York: Holt, Rinehart and Winston, 1961); William E. Leuchtenburg, *The Perils of Prosperity, 1914–1932* (Chicago: University of Chicago Press, 1958); Arthur S. Link, *Woodrow Wilson and the Progressive Era, 1910–1917* (New York: Harper, 1954); Henry Pelling, *American Labor* (Chicago: University of Chicago Press, 1960); George Soule, *Prosperity Decade: From War to Depression, 1917–1929* (New York: Rinehart, 1947); Norman J. Ware, *The Labor Movement in the United States, 1860–1895* (New York and London: Appleton, 1929); and Robert H. Wiebe, *The Search for Order, 1877–1920* (New York: Hill and Wang, 1967).

2. Florence Peterson, *Strikes in the United States, 1881–1936* (Washington, D.C.: U.S. Bureau of Labor Statistics, Bureau of Labor Bulletin No. 651, 1937), pp. 21–26 and pp. 28–40.

3. Florence Peterson, *American Labor Unions* (New York: Harper & Bros., 1945).

4. Melvyn Dubofsky, *We Shall Be All, A History of the I.W.W.* (Chicago: Quadrangle Books, 1969), p. 12. This is the principal source for information on the I.W.W.

5. Statistical data are drawn from Luis Ortiz Franco, et al., "Chicano Statistical Abstract" (to be published).

6. Estimate. The accepted figure, which is probably an underestimate, for Mexican residents in the Southwest in 1848 is 75,000. Carey McWilliams, *North From Mexico* (New York: Greenwood Press, 1968). The U.S. census of 1890 recorded

Mexican-born *emigrant* population at 75,000. Neither of these figures takes into account the following: (1) numbers of offspring; (2) unrecorded residents and unrecorded crossings.

7. U.S. Bureau of the Census, *Statistical Abstract of the United States, 1970* (Washington, D.C.: Government Printing Office, 1971), p. 66.

8. Leo Grebler, et al., *The Mexican American People* (New York: Free Press, 1970), p. 64.

9. U.S. Bureau of the Census, *Statistical Abstract of the United States, 1970,* p. 65.

10. See the analysis of Mexican census data provided by Fernando Rosenzweig, "El Desarollo Económico de México de 1877 a 1910," *El Trimestre Económico,* vol. 32 (julio–septiembre, 1965), pp. 418–49.

11. Luke Dove, Deputy Collector of Customs, Del Rio, Texas to Captain W. S. Scott, August 10, 1907. National Archives, Department of Justice, File 90755, Record Group 60, Washington, D.C.

12. *Annual Report of the Commissioner General of Immigration, for the Fiscal Year 1911.* Comments on the loss of labor to the United States appear in the following: Bureau of Statistics, Department of State, *Special Consular Reports,* vol. 13, pt. 1, September 26, 1896, pp. 118–21; Juan R. Martínez, "Mexican Emigration to the United States, 1910–1930" (Ph.D. diss., Berkeley: University of California, 1957), p. 10; and Victor S. Clark, *Mexican Labor in the United States* (Washington, D.C.: Bureau of Labor Statistics, Bureau of Labor, Bulletin No. 78, 1908), p. 470. See also Archivo del Arzobispado de Guadalajara, Carpeta con correspondencia relativa al gobierno civil. Consulado de México, Nogales, Arizona, al Subsecretario de Gobernación, June 12, 1910.

13. See the following Mexico City newspapers: *Diario Oficial,* 23 diciembre 1904; *El Tiempo,* 4 enero 1906; *Diario Del Hogar,* 20 septiembre 1910; *El Tiempo,* 31 enero 1910 and 28 febrero 1910; and *El Imparcial,* 7 septiembre 1912.

14. Seminario de Historia Moderna de México, *Estadísticas económicas del porfiriato, Fuerza de trabajo y actividad económica por sectores* (México, D.F.: El Colegio de México, n.d.), pp. 25–26.

15. Raymond Vernon, *The Dilemma of Mexico's Economic Development* (Cambridge, Mass.: Harvard University Press, 1963), p. 44. See also Leopoldo Solís, *La realidad económica Mexicana: retrovisión y perspectivas* (México, D.F.: Siglo Veintiuno Editores, 1970); and Luís Nicolau d'Oliver, et al., *Historia Moderna de Mexico, El porfiriato, La vida económica,* Daniel Cosío Villegas, ed. (México, D.F.: Editorial Hermes, 1965).

16. Vernon, *The Dilemma,* p. 50.

17. Seminario de Historia Moderna de México, *Estadísticas económicas del porfiriato,* pp. 147–157.

18. *Ibid.,* pp. 40–46.

19. *Ibid.,* pp. 46–60.

20. Secretaría de Economía, *Estadísticas sociales del porfiriato, 1877–1910* (México, D.F.: Dirección General de Estadísticas, n.d.), p. 107.

21. *Ibid.,* p. 123.

22. *Ibid.,* pp. 123–127.

23. *Ibid.,* pp. 241–242.

24. *Ibid.,* pp. 42-63 and pp. 224–239.

25. Juan Gómez-Quiñones, "Nationalism in the Press, 1890–1911," unpublished manuscript.

26. For information on the congresses there are the following sources available: *Crónica del 1er Congreso Católica Celebrado en Puebla* (Puebla: Colegio y Salesianas de Artes y Oficios, 1903); *Segundo Congreso Católico de México y Primero Mariano Celebrado en Morelia* (Morelia: Talleres Tipográficos de Agustín Martínez Mier, 1905); *Congreso 3° Católico Nacional y 1° Eucarístico, celebrado en esta ciudad de Guadalajara,* 2 vols. (Guadalajara: Tipografía de "El Regional," 1908); for the fourth congress the source available is Eulogio Gillow y Zavalza, *Reminiscenias del Illmo y*

Rmo. Sr. Dr. Don Eulogio Gillow y Zavalza, Arzobispo de Antequera (Puebla: Linotipografía Salesiana, 1921), in the appendix of the volume, 41 pp., are the resolutions and 177 statements of purpose. For contemporary newspaper coverage consult: *El País* and *El Tiempo*, February and March 1903, October 1904, October 1906, January and February 1909. For secondary treatment, consult Ciro Hernández, "Some aspects of the Mexican Catholic Social Congresses, 1903–1909" (M.A. thesis, México, D.F.: University of the Americas, 1959).

27. Consult John M. Hart, "Anarchist Thought in Nineteenth-Century Mexico," (Ph.D. diss., University of California, Los Angeles, 1971), *passim*; see also Armanda List Arzubide, *Apuntes sobre la prehistoria de la revolución* (México, D.F., 1958), pp. 30–36.

28. Aníbal Sánchez-Reulet, "Panorama de las ideas filosóficas en Hispanoamérica," *Tierra Firme* (1936); see also Victor Alba, *Las ideas sociales contemporáneas de México* (México, D.F.: Fondo de Cultura Económica, 1960), pp. 101–110; and Manuel González Ramírez, *La revolución social de México*, 3 vols. (México, D.F.: Fondo de Cultura Económica, 1960). Actually the best evidence in addition to the secondary sources is provided by book catalogues and book advertisements that appeared in the press during this time period.

29. Moisés González Navarro, *Historia moderna de México, El porfiriato, La vida social* (México, D.F.: Editorial Hermes, 1957), pp. 350–356.

30. *Ibid.*, p. 298.

31. *Ibid.*

32. *Ibid.*, p. 299.

33. Consult Manuel González Ramírez, ed., *Fuentes para la historia de la Revolución Mexicana*, vol. 3. *La huelga de Cananea* (México, D.F.: Fondo de Cultura Económica, 1956), *passim*.

34. Moisés González Navarro, *El porfiriato, La vida social*, pp. 324–332.

35. Manuel Gamio, *Mexican Immigration to the United States* (New York: Arno Press, 1969), pp. 13–29, 204–207; see also Clark, *Mexican Labor in the United States, passim.*

36. Clark, *Mexican Labor in the United States, passim.*

37. *Ibid.*

38. *Ibid.*

39. McWilliams, *North From Mexico*, p. 168.

40. Clark, *Mexican Labor in the United States, passim.*

41. Paul S. Taylor, *Mexican Labor in the United States; Chicago and Calumet Region* (Berkeley: University of California Press, 1932), pp. 28–34, 133.

42. Clark, *Mexican Labor in the United States*; see also U.S. Bureau of Labor, *Bulletin*, No. 17, July-November, 1908.

43. Clark, *Mexican Labor in the United States, passim.*

44. *Ibid.*

45. *Ibid.*

46. *Cf.* Clark, 1908; Jamieson, 1945; Stowell, 1921; Paul Taylor, 1928, 1929, 1930.

47. *Ibid.*

48. Paul S. Taylor, *Mexican Labor in the United States; Dimmit County, Winter Garden District, South Texas* (Berkeley: University of California Press, 1932), p. 325.

49. Paul S. Taylor, *Mexican Labor in the United States; Valley of the South Platte, Colorado* (Berkeley: University of California Press, 1929), p. 101; and Clark, *Mexican Labor in the United States.*

50. Selig Perlman and Philip Taft, *History of Labor in the United States, 1896–1932*, 4 vols. (New York: Macmillan Co., 1935), vol. 4: 189–207; and Dubofsky, *We Shall Be All*, pp. 37–57.

51. In the National Archives, Washington, D.C., there is correspondence by Abraham Salcido in the Department of Justice Record Group 60; the Department of State Record Group 59 contains an extensive report by Captain W. S. Scott on organizing activities in the border area; also consult Luís Hernández, *Las tinajas de Ulúa* (México, D.F.: Editorial Hermida, 1943), pp. 39–40.

52. Stuart Jamieson, *Labor Unionism in American Agriculture* (Washington, D.C.: U.S. Bureau Department of Labor, Bulletin No. 836, 1945), pp. 56, 76, and Philip Foner, *History of the Labor Movement in the United States*, 4 vols. (New York: International Publishers, 1964), vol. 3: 276–277; see also McWilliams, *North From Mexico*, p. 190. As a result of the noticeable unrest the AFL convention at New Orleans, 1903, voted to assign an organizer to the California agricultural workers. A similar vote was made by the State Federation of Labor, January 1903. Nothing is known of the results in either case.

53. *Oakland Tribune*, April 21, 1903; *Oxnard Courier* and *Ventura Daily Democrat*, March 7 and March 28, 1903. Tomás Sánchez, a student at California State University, Northridge, has written an interesting research paper comparing the 1903 strike and the one in 1933.

54. *Oxnard Courier*, March 28, 1903.

55. *Ventura Daily Democrat*, March 1, 1903.

56. *Oxnard Courier*, March 7 and March 28, 1903.

57. *Ibid.*

58. *Oxnard Courier*, March 7, 1903.

59. *Ibid.*

60. *Ibid.*

61. *Oxnard Courier*, March 14, 1903.

62. *Ibid.*

63. *Ventura Daily Democrat*, March 24, 1903.

64. *Oxnard Courier*, March 28, 1903.

65. *Ventura Daily Democrat*, March 31, 1903.

66. *Ventura Daily Democrat*, April 4, 1903.

67. Louis B. Perry and Richard S. Perry, *A History of the Los Angeles Labor Movement, 1911–1941* (Berkeley and Los Angeles: University of California Press, 1963), p. 71.

68. Grace Stimson, *Rise of the Labor Movement in Los Angeles* (Berkeley and Los Angeles: University of California, 1955), p. 208.

69. *Ibid.*, p. 267.

70. Ruth Allen, *Early Chapters in the Organization of Labor in Texas* (Austin: University of Texas Press, 1941), pp. 96–100. For a description of conditions at Thurber see: *Journal of United Mine Workers*, September 24, 1903, and *Proceedings* of the Twelfth Annual Convention of the Texas State Federation of Labor, 1909, p. 89.

71. Juan Gómez-Quiñones, "Sembradores: Ricardo Flores Magón y el Partido Liberal Mexicano," *passim* (to be published). In Laredo, Texas, in contrast, there was continuing labor organizing.

72. Eugenio Martínez Núñez, *La vida heróica de Praxedis G. Guerrero* (México, D.F.: Biblioteca del Instituto Nacional de Estudios Históricos de la Revolución Mexicana, 1960), pp. 39–41, 80–85, 98–111.

73. Capt. W. S. Scott to Adjutant General, Acting Secretary of War, Fort Sam Houston, Texas, August 26, 1907, in the National Archives, Department of State, Record Group 59; Luís Hernández, *Las tinajas de Ulúa*, pp. 39–40; Florencio Barrera Fuentes, *Historia de la Revolución Mexicana* (México, D.F.: Instituto Nacional de Estudios de la Revolución Mexicana, 1955), p. 203; Ethel Duffy Turner, *Ricardo Flores Magón y el Partido Liberal Mexicano* (Morelia, México: "Erandi," 1960), pp. 124–125.

74. Clark, *Mexican Labor in the United States*, p. 180.

75. Dubofsky, *We Shall Be All*, pp. 184–189.

76. Stimson, *Rise of the Labor Movement*, p. 336; and Ira B. Cross, *A History of the Labor Movement in California* (Berkeley: University of California Press, 1935), p. 281.

77. Stimson, *Rise of the Labor Movement*, p. 336; *Regeneración*, 25 febrero 1911, and 11 marzo 1911 (Los Angeles, California).

78. Jamieson, *Labor Unionism*, pp. 260–261. This, in Chicano materials, is referred to as the Agrupación Protectiva Mexicana. It was associated with the efforts of the Primer Congreso Mexicanista (José Limón).

79. Taylor, *Mexican Labor in the United States; Dimmit County, Winter Garden District, South Texas*, p. 351.

80. Jamieson, *Labor Unionism*, pp. 60–63; Philip Foner, *History of the Labor Movement in the United States*, vol. 4: 260–272; Dubofsky, *We Shall Be All*, pp. 294–300.

81. Beshoar Barron, *Out of the Depths, The Story of John B. Lawson* (Denver: The Colorado Labor Historical Committee of the Denver Trades and Labor Assembly, World Press, 1942), *passim*; Perlman, *History of Labor in the United States, 1896–1932* 4: 37–40. See also Alvin R. Sunseri, "The Ludlow Massacre: A Study in the Misemployment of the National Guard," *American Chronicle: A Magazine of History*, vol. 1 (January 1972): 21–28. I am indebted to Sr. Jesús Leyva for information and insight on the Chicano role in the Colorado mines and the Ludlow strike.

82. Correspondence of A. M. Villareal to Venustiano Carranza. Archivo Carranza, Centro de Estudios de Historia de México, México, D.F.

83. Dionisio Men . . . [?] to Venustiano Carranza, Phoenix, Arizona, December 20, 1915. (Surname is unclear on document.) Archivo Carranza, Centro de Estudios de Historia de México, México, D.F. Particularly strong in Arizona at this time is the Liga Protectora Latina which claimed 5,000 members and was led by Pedro N. Salinas, Teodoro Olea, and others.

84. *Los Angeles Labor Press*, February 11, 1916 and April 14, 1916; James R. Kluger, *The Clifton-Morenci Strike, Labor Difficulty in Arizona, 1915–1916* (Tucson, Arizona: University of Arizona Press, 1970), *passim*.

85. Kluger, *Clifton-Morenci Strike*, pp. 57–68.

86. *Los Angeles Labor Press*, April 14, 1916.

87. James Colquhoun, *The Early History of the Clifton-Morenci District* (London: William Clowes and Sons, 1924), pp. 23–27.

88. *Ibid.*, p. 46.

89. *Ibid.*

90. Kluger, *Clifton-Morenci Strike*, p. 18.

91. *Ibid.*, p. 24.

92. *Ibid.*, p. 23.

93. *Ibid.*, p. 24.

94. *Ibid.*, p. 26.

95. *Ibid.*, p. 25.

96. *Ibid.*, p. 26.

97. *Ibid.*, p. 58.

98. Eugenio Martínez Núñez, *La vida heróica de Praxedis Guerrero*, pp. 39–41.

99. Kluger, *Clifton-Morenci Strike*, p. 38.

100. *Ibid.*, pp. 57–68.

101. Perlman and Taft, *History of Labor*, 4: 398–400; and Dubofsky, *We Shall Be All*, pp. 369–370, 385–391.

102. *Ibid.*

103. Taylor, *Mexican Labor in the United States, Chicago and the Calumet Region*, p. 34.

104. Perry and Perry, *History of the Los Angeles Labor Movement, 1911–1941*, p. 252.

105. Robert Pinger and Susan Pinger, "Colton," in *The Bent Cross: A History of the Mexican American in the San Bernardino Valley*, preliminary draft, forthcoming, courtesy of the editor, Professor Carlos Cortés.

106. Perry and Perry, *History of the Los Angeles Labor Movement*, p. 226.

107. Jamieson, *Labor Unionism*, p. 65.

108. *Ibid.*

109. *Ibid.*, p. 67; and Carey McWilliams, *Factories in the Field* (Santa Barbara and Salt Lake City: Peregrine Publishers, 1971 [first published 1935]), pp. 182–183.

110. *Arizona Labor Journal,* July 20, 1920.

111. Fred A. Schmidt, *Spanish Surnamed American Employment in the Southwest* (Los Angeles: Institute of Industrial Relations, University of California, Los Angeles, 1970), p. 62.

112. "Results of Admission of Mexican Laborers Under Departmental Orders for Employment in Agricultural Pursuits," *Monthly Labor Review* 11 (July–December 1920): 1095.

113. McWilliams, *Factories in the Fields,* p. 125.

114. Taylor, *Mexican Labor in the United States; Valley of the South Platte, Colorado,* p. 101.

115. "Results of Admission of Mexican Laborers Under Departmental Orders . . .," pp. 1095–1097.

116. For a published reference to this see: Jamieson, *Labor Unionism,* p. 195.

117. The major writings for the five schools are: (1) Richard T. Ely, *The Labor Movement in America* (New York: T. Y. Crowell, 1886); John A. Ryan, *Declining Liberty and Other Papers* (New York: Macmillan, 1927); (2) George E. Barnett, *The Printers* (Cambridge, Mass.: American Economical Association, 1909), etc.; (3) Carleton H. Parker, *The Casual Laborer and Other Essays* (New York: Harcourt, Brace, 1970); Robert F. Hoxie, *Trade Unionism in the United States* (New York: Appleton, 1919), Frank Tannenbaum, *The Labor Movement: Its Conservative Functions and Social Consequences* (New York: Putnam, 1921); (4) Anthony Bimba, *A History of the American Working Class* (New York: International Publishers, 1936), Nathan Fine, *Farmer and Labor Parties in the United States, 1828–1928* (New York: Rand School, 1928); Paul Bukle, "American Marxist Historiography, 1900–1940," *Radical America* 4 (November 1970); and (5) Selig Perlman, *A Theory of the Labor Movement* (New York: Macmillan, 1928). For discussion of labor theory see Mark Perlman, *Labor Union Theories in American Background and Development* (Evanston: Row, Peterson, 1958), and Paul J. McNulty, "Labor Problems and Labor Economics: The Roots of an Academic Discipline," *Labor History* 9 (Spring 1968).

Sources

I. Archival Material

Centro de Estudios de Historia de México, México, D.F. Archivo Ramón Corral.

Centro de Estudios de Historia de México, México, D.F. Archivo Venustiano Carranza.

National Archives, Washington, D.C. Department of Justice, Record Group 60.

National Archives, Washington, D.C. Department of State, Record Group 59.

II. Government Publications

Anonymous, "Results of Admission of Mexican Laborers Under Departmental Orders for Employment in Agricultural Pursuits," *Monthly Labor Review* 2 (July–December 1920): 1095–97.

Clark, Victor S., *Mexican Labor in the United States* (Bureau of Labor Bulletin No. 78), Washington, D.C.: United States Bureau of Labor Statistics, 1908.

Jamieson, Stuart, *Labor Unionism in American Agriculture* (Bureau of Labor, Bulletin No. 836, U.S. Department of Labor), Washington, D.C.: Government Printing Office, 1945.

Menefee, Selden C., *Mexican Migratory Workers of South Texas* (Federal Works Agency: Work Project Administration, Division of Research), Washington, D.C.: Government Printing Office, 1941.

Peterson, Florence, *Strikes in the United States, 1880–1936* (Bureau of Labor Bulletin, No. 651), Washington, D.C.: U.S. Bureau of Labor Statistics, 1938.

Secretaría de Economía. *Estadísticas sociales del porfiriato,* 1877–1910, México, D.F.: Dirección General de Estadísticas, n.d.

U.S. Bureau of the Census, *Statistical Abstract of the United States, 1970,* Washington, D.C.: Government Printing Office, 1971.

III. Newspapers

Diario Del Hogar (México, D.F.), 1900–12.
Diario Official (México, D.F.), 1900–12.
El Imparcial (México, D.F.), 1900–12.
El Tiempo (México, D.F.), 1900–12.
Labor Press (Los Angeles, California), 1916.
Oxnard Courier (Oxnard, California), 1903.
Oakland Tribune (Oakland, California), 1903.
Regeneración (Los Angeles, California), 1910–18.
Ventura Daily Democrat (Ventura, California), 1903.

IV. Dissertations and Other Unpublished Material

Anonymous, "Unionization of Migratory Labor, 1903–1930," Federal Writers Project, Bancroft Library.
Gómez-Quiñones, Juan, "Sembradores: Ricardo Flores Magón y el Partido Liberal Mexicano." To be published.
Hart, John M., "Anarchist Thought in Nineteenth-Century Mexico," Ph.D. diss., University of California, Los Angeles, 1971.
López, Espiridión B., "The History of the California State Federation of Labor," M.A. thesis, University of California, Berkeley, 1932.
Martínez, Juan R., "Mexican Emigration to the United States, 1910–1930," Ph.D. diss., University of California, Berkeley, 1957.
Ohno, Kakijiro, "History and Economic Significance of Mexican Labor in California," M.A. thesis, University of Southern California, 1931.
Ortiz Franco, Luis, "Chicano Statistical Abstract," to be published.
Wilson McEven, William, "A Survey of the Mexicans in Los Angeles," M.A. thesis, University of Southern California, 1914.

V. Articles

Anonymous, "Mexican Miners Going Back Home," *Survey* 39 (October 1917).
Coben, Stanley, "A study in Nativism: The American Red Scare of 1919–1920," *Political Science Quarterly* 79 (March 1964).
Lingquist, John H., and James Fraser, "A Sociological interpretation of the Bisbee Deportation," *Pacific Historical Review* (November 1968).
Oates, J., "Globe-Miami District," *International Socialist Review* 18 (August 1917).
Rosenzweig, Fernando, "El Desarollo Económico de México de 1877 a 1910," *El Trimestre Económico* 32 (julio–septiembre 1965).
Taylor, Paul, and Tom Vassey, "Historical Background of California Farm Labor," *Rural Sociology* 1 (December 1936).

VI. Books

Adamic, Louis, *Dynamite: The Story of Class Violence in America,* New York: Viking, 1931.
Alba, Victor, *Las ideas sociales contemporáneas de México,* México, D.F.: Fondo de Cultura Económica, 1960.
Allen, James B., *The Company Town in the American West,* Norman: University of Oklahoma Press, 1966.
Allen, Ruth, *Chapters in the History of Organized Labor in Texas,* Austin: University of Texas Publications, 1941.
Araiza, Luis, *Historia del movimiento obrero mexicano,* México, D.F.: Editorial Cuauhtemoc, 1965.
Barrera Fuentes, Florencio, *Historia de la revolución mexicana, Etapa precursora,* México, D.F.: Instituto Nacional de Estudios de la Revolución Mexicana, 1955.
Briggs, Asa, and John Saville, eds., *Labour History, 1886–1923,* London: Macmillan, 1971.
Brody, David, *Labor in Crisis, The Steel Strike of 1919,* Philadelphia: Lippincott, 1965.
Cerda Silva, Roberto de la, *El movimiento obrero en México,* México, D.F. Instituto de Investigaciones Sociales, U.N.A.M., 1961.

Clark, Marjorie R., *Organized Labor in Mexico*, Berkeley: University of California Press, 1934.

Colquhoun, James, *The Early History of the Clifton-Morenci District*, London: William Clowes, 1924.

Cosío Villegas, Daniel, ed., *Historia moderna de México*, 9 vols. México, D.F.: Hermes, 1955.

Cross, Ira, *History of Labor Movement in California*, Berkeley: University of California Press, 1935.

Dick, William, *Labor and Socialism in America: The Gompers Era*, Port Washington, New York: Kennikat Press, 1972.

Dos Passos, John, *U.S.A.*, New York: Houghton-Mifflin, 1937.

Dubofsky, Melvyn, *We Shall Be All: A History of the Industrial Workers of the World*, Chicago, Quadrangle, 1969.

Foner, Philip, *History of the Labor Movement in the United States*, 4 vols. New York: International Publishers, 1964.

Gamio, Manuel, *The Mexican Immigrant*, New York: Arno Press and the New York Times, 1969 (first published 1931).

———, *Mexican Immigration to the United States*, New York: Arno Press, 1969.

González Ramírez, Manuel, *La Revolución social de México*, 3 vols. México, D.F.: Fondo de Cultura Económica, 1960.

Grebler, Leo, et al., *The Mexican American People*, New York: Free Press, 1970.

Hernández, Luis, *Las tinajas de Ulúa*, México, D.F.: Editorial Hermida, 1942.

Jensen, Vernon, *Heritage of Conflict*, Ithaca: Cornell University Press, 1950.

Joll, James, *The Anarchists*, Boston: Little, Brown, 1965.

Kipnis, Ira, *The American Socialist Movement*, 1897-1912, New York: Columbia University Press, 1952.

Kluger, James P., *The Clifton-Morenci Strike: Labor Difficulty in Arizona, 1915–1916*, Tucson: University of Arizona Press, 1970.

Kornbluh, Joyce L., *Rebel Voices: An I.W.W. Anthology*, Ann Arbor: University of Michigan Press, 1969.

Lamar, Roberts Howard, *The Far-Southwest, 1846–1912: A Territorial History*, New York: Norton, 1966.

Laslett, John, *Labor and the Left: A Study of Socialist and Radical Influences in the American Labor Movement, 1881–1924*, New York: Basic Books, 1970.

Levenstein, Harvey A., *Labor Organizations in the United States and Mexico, a History of Their Relations*, Connecticut: Greenwood Publishing Company, 1971.

List Arzubide, A., *Apuntes sobre la prehistoria de la revolución*, México, D.F.· n.p., 1958.

López Aparicio, Alfonso, *El movimiento obrero en México*, México, D.F., 1952.

McWilliams, Carey, *Factories in the Field*, Boston: Little, Brown & Co., 1944.

———, *North From Mexico*, New York: Greenwood Press, 1968.

Martínez Núñez, Eugenio, *La vida heróica de Praxedis G. Guerrero*, México, D.F.: Biblioteca del Instituto Nacional de Estudios Históricos de la Revolución Mexicana, 1960.

Murray, Robert K., *The Red Scare: A Study in National Hysteria, 1919–1920*, Minneapolis: University of Minnesota Press, 1955.

O'Neill, William L., *Everyone Was Brave: The Rise and Fall of Feminism in America*, Chicago: Quadrangle, 1969.

Perlman, Selig, and Philip Taft, *History of Labor in the United States, 1896–1932*, 4 vols. New York: Macmillan, 1960.

Perry, Louis B., and Richard S. Perry, *History of the Los Angeles Labor Movement, 1911–1941*, Berkeley: University of California Press, 1963.

Renshaw, Patrick, *The Wobblies*, New York: Doubleday, 1967.

Rayback, Joseph G., *A History of American Labor*, New York: Free Press, 1966.

Rodea, Marcelo N., *Historia del movimiento obrero ferrocarrilero en México, 1890–1943*, México, D.F.: n.p., 1944.

Salazar, Rosendo, *Las pugnas de la gleba*, México, D.F.: Avante, 1922.

Saxton, Alexander, *The Indispensable Enemy, Labor and the Anti-Chinese Movement in California*, Berkeley: University of California Press, 1971.
Schmidt, Fred A., *Spanish Surnamed American Employment in the Southwest*, Los Angeles: Institute of Industrial Relations, University of California, Los Angeles, 1970.
Seminario de Historia Moderna de México, *Estadísticas económicas del porfiriato, Fuerza de trabajo y actividad económica por sectores*, México, D.F.: El Colegio de México, n.d.
Solís, Leopoldo, *La realidad económica mexicana: retrovisión y perspectivas*, México, D.F.: Siglo Veintiuno Editores, 1970.
Stimson, Grace, *Rise of the Labor Movement in Los Angeles*, Berkeley: University of California Press, 1955.
Stowell, Jay S., *The Near Side of the Mexican Question*, New York: George H. Doran Co., 1921.
Taylor, Paul S., *Mexican Labor in the United States; Chicago and the Calumet Region*, Berkeley: University of California Publications in Economics, vol. 7, no. 2, University of California Press, 1932.
———, *Mexican Labor in the United States; Dimmit County, Winter Garden District, South Texas*, Berkeley: University of California Publications in Economics, vol. 6, no. 5, University of California Press, 1930.
———, *Mexican Labor in the United States; Imperial Valley*, University of California Publications in Economics, vol. 6, no. 1, University of California Press, 1928.
———, *Mexican Labor in the United States; Valley of the South Platte, Colorado*, Berkeley: University of California Publications in Economics, vol. 6, no. 2, University of California Press, 1929.
Turner, Ethel Duffy, *Ricardo Flores Magón y el Partido Liberal Mexicano*, Morelia, México: Erandi, 1960.
Veblen, Thorstein, *Farm Labor and the I.W.W.* (n.p., n.d.).
Weinstein, James and David W. Eakins, *For a New America; Essays in History and Politics from Studies on the Left*, New York: Random House, 1970.
Wiebe, Robert, *The Search for Order, 1877–1920*. New York: Hill and Wang, 1967.

Twentieth-Century Search for Cíbola: Post–World War I Mexican Labor Exploitation in Arizona*

Herbert B. Peterson

Myths and tall stories stimulated the Spanish penetration of Arizona and the Southwest. After Cortés and his men bagged the treasure of the Aztecs, avaricious and optimistic Spaniards hoped to find a new bonanza just over the horizon. In 1536, when Cabeza de Vaca's party arrived, after several years of wandering across Texas and the Southwest, at the Sinaloa River in what is now northwest Mexico to meet Guzmán's slave hunters, the search for the Seven Golden

*This paper was presented at the annual Arizona Historical Convention in May 1971, at Tucson, Arizona.

Cities of Cíbola gained fresh impetus. Viceroy Antonio de Mendoza, titillated by Cabeza de Vaca's retelling of the Pimas' gift of five "emerald" arrowheads and of the towns of big houses and the many wealthy people who provided these arrowheads, lost no time in organizing a search for the now ever-closer Cíbola.

The Franciscan padre, Fray Marcos de Niza, and his guide, the Moor Estevanico (whom Niza borrowed from Dorantes of the Cabeza de Vaca entourage), broke trail first in 1539. Their return to Mexico with a "chamber of commerce report"—which later proved to be overly optimistic—spurred Mendoza to dispatch Don Francisco Vásquez de Coronado north in 1540. The subsequent disappointments of Coronado and disgrace of Marcos de Niza are well known. The Spaniards of the sixteenth century did not find their Cíbola gold. Had they been of an agricultural mind, the rich alluvial river valleys of Arizona might have excited them.[1] This discovery eluded their grasp as well as that of their modern-day followers, the Mexicans. It was left to greedy gringos to grasp the prize, only to discover in the twentieth century that it was impossible to fully extract the agricultural gold from the stubborn desert soil without the help of Mexicans.

The sprawling Salt River Valley (the site of metropolitan Phoenix) became part of the United States in the Mexican Cession of 1848. At that time the valley boasted no permanent inhabitants. The ancient Hohokams had departed for unknown reasons centuries before. Their descendants, the modern Pimas and Papago, lived farther south in the Gila River villages and the desert beyond. Raiding Apaches and Yavapais seldom visited this inferno. The only Mexicans were a few thousand clustered in what was to become the Gadsden Purchase along the Santa Cruz River in the hamlets of Tucson and Tubac. Even with the advent of mechanized farming spurred by the Deere plow and McCormick reaper it was not until 1867 that the first commercial crop of wild hay along the Salt River was sold by V. T. Smith to the cavalry at Ft. McDowell, some thirty miles upstream on the Verde River. It was then that the first Mexicans moved into the Salt River Valley to help with the menial farm labor.

Also in 1867 a canal company was organized to re-trench the canals the Hohokams had used to coax cotton, corn, and beans from the arid land a millennium or two before. More Mexicans drifted in to help build canals, level land, cut mesquite, build roads and railroads, and harvest the crops. Even with the completion of Roosevelt Dam—the nation's first large irrigation works—in 1911, ensuring permanent agricultural success for the valley, there was not yet a need for mass immigration of Mexican farm workers. However, concurrent with the taming of the Salt and Tonto rivers by Roosevelt Dam an important related project was nearing completion. It was this development that would soon demand Mexican workers by the thousands in the Salt River Valley.

It was perhaps ironic that Egyptian long-staple cotton would be bred into a new strain—Egyptian-American, later named Pima for the Indian tribe—in the very center of Hohokam cotton culture a thousand years before. It was no less a quirk of history that the early Spaniards bypassed this land as worthless in their search for the Seven Cities of Cíbola and that their descendants hearkened to a new siren call of riches represented by this new strain.

By 1912 Egyptian-American cotton had been planted on about three hundred acres by thirty-two farmers in the Salt River Valley. Arizona's cotton industry was well established by 1917; acreage of long-staple cotton had increased to thirty-three thousand and production to nearly sixteen thousand bales. "Thus, at two independent points in time separated by a thousand years, Arizona's climate and exploited river water had become the basis of a cotton ecology."[2] This new economy demanded huge amounts of cheap labor. World War I drained off most local farm workers to the armed forces or higher-paid jobs, just when the explosive growth of the cotton industry required thousands of workers. The cotton farmers turned their labor recruitment problems over to the Arizona Cotton Growers Association (referred to hereafter as the ACGA or the Association).

The ACGA in cooperation with other agricultural interests and the railroad lobby decided something must be done about legal obstacles to the importation of contract laborers from nearby Mexico, an easily accessible, potential source of nearly unlimited cheap labor. The Alien Contract Labor Act of 1885, which made it unlawful to import contract laborers, was continued in Section 3 of the Immigration Act of 1917. However, under pressure of the agricultural and railroad interests of the Southwest, the Ninth Proviso of that section stated an exception to the general prohibition in the event of a labor shortage.[3]

The United States had scarcely entered World War I when the ACGA, allied with the railroads and other interests, complained to the Bureau of Immigration that relief was needed in the imminent labor shortage. The labor commissioner acquiesced and in May 1917 issued orders permitting the entry of otherwise inadmissible aliens.

At the same time the secretary of labor issued orders outlining procedures to be followed in importing Mexicans under the Ninth Proviso.

Any employer who wanted Mexican nationals was to file an application with the Bureau of Immigration or the United States Employment Service, listing the number needed, kind of work, wages to be paid, and place of employment. He was also required to comply with the secretary's orders with respect to aliens admitted to his care. Housing and sanitation laws of the state where workers were employed were to be observed. In the event such laws did not exist housing was subject to approval by the secretary of labor. He was to report those laborers who broke their contracts by running off and to pay the return transportation to ports of entry of those laborers who after having skipped were apprehended by the Immigration Bureau. As a precaution against skipping the employer was authorized to deduct twenty-five cents per day from each worker's wages and deposit the money in a Postal Savings Bank. Identification cards issued to all aliens at border entry points under these procedures became their permits to enter Arizona to work in agriculture or on railroads. Periodic investigations were to be made by the Bureau of Immigration and the Employment Service to see that the labor secretary's orders were obeyed. The basic weakness of the program was lack of adequate enforcement machinery.[4]

These changes were made prior to the founding of the Border Patrol in 1924. The Immigration Bureau was already too undermanned to take care of both routine immigration and illicit entry. The bureau's sporadic investigations revealed that thousands of farm workers in Arizona were illegal "fence crawlers" (called wetbacks in Texas). The official count of temporary Mexican farm laborers who *legally* came to the state of Arizona in the fiscal year ending June 30, 1919, was 9,752. Illegal entries were perhaps double this figure. Because of lack of enforcement manpower, importation of temporary workers was subject to abuses as was candidly admitted by the inspector in charge at El Paso, Texas, in 1920.[5] Despite such abuses Mexicans were recruited by the thousands by the ACGA each year from 1917 to 1920. With the shortage of labor, the skyrocketing price of cotton, and the rapidly increased acreage of cotton plantings in the Salt River Valley, the need for cotton pickers was enormous. But, even so, why did the Mexicans come?

The bright picture of big money and the lush life in the United States, painted vividly for them by *enganchadores* (hiring agents or literally those who ensnare), eager for their commission of four dollars per head, found enthusiastic acceptance by the Mexicans. It held out promise of riches as compared with the nightmare of poverty at home. The editor of Mexico City's *Excelsior* wrote:

> It is necessary not to lose sight of the fact that the revolutionary disorder of our country played an important part in this northward movement [1914–20] . . . the chaotic state of our country because of internal strife, had paralyzed our economy, and therefore great numbers of workers became unemployed. In search of bread, fleeing from calamity . . . caused thousands of Mexicans to take refuge in the United States.[6]

So Mexicans came in droves, searching for their Cíbola gold but finding disillusionment in the muddy and dusty squalor of a farm labor camp in the rich Salt River Valley.

Disillusionment erupted into open protest by 1919, one year after the ACGA became a large user of Mexican labor under the Ninth Proviso. The Liga Protectora Latina (Latin Protective Association) on May 15, 1919, submitted a long list of complaints to Governor Thomas E. Campbell, first Republican governor of Arizona. The Liga charged that hundreds of Mexican contract workers were paid less than contractually agreed, paid with purchase orders in lieu of cash, and "housed" in dirty, unsanitary tents pitched on the burning sands of the Salt River's edge in Tempe contrary to contract agreement; and the Liga charged the ACGA with full responsibility.

The Liga directed their ire particularly at the overseer of the ACGA, Rafael Estrada (former Tempe town marshal), who issued food orders to his son's grocery in Tempe. Of course this "company store" operation had all the usual pricing abuses the Liga charged. Estrada received the Mexican workers' pay and in turn reimbursed the store. This receipt and disbursement of their wages was without the Mexican's consent. Estrada forced the Mexicans to remain camped in the sun (where temperatures were over one hundred degrees in mid-May) although only three hundred yards from their camp stood a grove of shady cottonwoods. Estrada prohibited movement to this shady glen under penalty of jail or deportation.[7]

Governor Campbell referred the charges to the ACGA in Tempe. W. H. Knox, secretary-manager of the ACGA, defended Estrada as being a trusted interpreter, not an overseer. Knox denied all charges except that some deductions from wages had been made by the Association for food advances. He denounced the attack on Estrada as a political vendetta of P. G. Lama, secretary of the Liga, "one of the principal agitators of this complaint." Knox claimed that all the Mexicans received fair treatment and had sanitary living conditions; also that the immigration officials, a United States Army officer, and the Mexican consul after a joint inspection concurred with this claim.[8] This inspection tour had all the appearances of a whitewash.

Inspector-in-Charge Sterling G. Robertson, of the Phoenix office of the Immigration Service, reported to the governor that he and the Mexican consul in Phoenix, Francisco Paredo, had inspected the camp on a tour guided by Knox of the ACGA. They found everything in order, Robertson stated, despite the fact that he ended his report with the statement, "I made satisfactory adjustments both to the alien and the grower."[9]

This writer interviewed Rafael Estrada's son Pedro Estrada, proprietor of the store, and his cousin Juana Estrada Peralta about the incident. Pedro Estrada stated that his father was well liked by the Anglos, Mexican-Americans, and aliens. His father had few enemies and was affectionately called Güero (because of his light, sandy hair and ruddy complexion). Pedro claimed that the vast majority of the aliens were contented, except for a few "malcontents" whom he labeled *broncos.* He inferred that these agitators were sent back to Mexico by the ACGA (perhaps before the inspection tour).[10] Juana, who lived across the road from the Mexicans' camp, declared that the workers were allowed to move from the sun-baked edge of the Salt River into a grove of trees and also into a shed-like building near La Casa Vieja (The Old House), boyhood home of Senator Carl Hayden (perhaps also just before the inspection tour).[11] These two accounts, although meant to be favorable to Rafael Estrada and the ACGA, more than hinted at a housecleaning just prior to the inspection tour. There seems some doubt, however, whether the matter was resolved to the Mexicans' satisfaction. Perhaps the ACGA swept the dirt under the rug only to see it exposed later in more serious confrontations between the growers and the alien workers.

Meanwhile, growing dissent was heard about the whole program of Ninth Proviso recruitment of farm laborers. The national secretary of the American Federation of Labor (AFL), Frank Morrison, requested southwestern union officials to wire information in regard to local labor conditions. The consensus of union officials in Houston, Albuquerque, and Phoenix was that no labor shortage existed. The Phoenix local of the AFL added that the imported Mexican labor had lowered wages of all common labor to a point where Americans could not compete and still maintain an American standard of living.[12] Carey McWilliams in *North from Mexico* reported that a Department of Labor investigation in 1920 (with two AFL officials on the committee) disclosed that the Mexicans who had been imported during the war years had not come into competition with or displaced whites (Anglos). This was undoubtedly true, as Anglo workers were no longer interested in this type of labor. However, it seems that the report failed to mention how many

Mexican-American laborers were displaced or were forced to work for lower wages than they otherwise could have demanded.[13]

Editor Mills in the *Phoenix Messenger* also raised questions not answered by the Department of Labor committee:

> Our immigration laws forbid letting down the bars. . . . No official has a right to waive the law unless there is an actual and imperative need staring us in the face. . . . Our courts are congested with the trials of criminal cases, arising from depredations committed by these underpaid, half civilized people who creep all along the International line. This extra cost comes off the entire community and not from those who enjoy special privileges.[14]

González Córdoba, the Mexican consul in Phoenix, complained in a letter to General Alvaro Obregón, president of Mexico, on February 8, 1921, that "because of the low culture of these Mexican masses [Ninth Proviso workers] the companies and associations that hire them, exploit them and many times the same authorities put them in jail, accusing them of crimes that receive long sentences." Eduardo Ruiz, Mexican consul in Los Angeles (on special duty in Phoenix), revealed in a letter to President Obregón dated February 18, 1921, that "these Mexicans are of such naiveté and ignorance that if they are not protected like children they expose themselves at anytime to go through the most terrible trials and tribulations."[15]

Ramón P. Denegri, consul general of Mexico in New York City, on a visit home on February 9, 1921, put it to a reporter of *Excelsior* in even more shocking terms: "It is very sad to say: the penitentiaries of the United States are full of Mexicans who have committed crimes of all kinds, especially of passion instituted by hunger. . . . Because of the inclement weather our compatriots become ill and lacking resources become obliged on numerous occasions to commit robbery or murder." Denegri went on to say that despite efforts of Mexican consuls in the United States it is impossible to get the offenders out of jail. Much more, the workers are judged and condemned before the consuls even know of the accusation. In many of the farm labor camps, far from a consulate, the Mexican workers are meted unjust punishment. Through ignorance of the language and laws, they often are railroaded into prison without even benefit of legal counsel.[16]

It became obvious to both the AFL and the Mexican workers in the Phoenix area in 1920 that because of these problems self-protection was needed. An organizing drive under the aegis of Lester B. Doane, Arizona State AFL president, began in the cotton fields of the Salt River Valley. The new recruits to AFL ranks were largely Ninth Proviso workers. Trouble erupted almost immediately because the business leaders of Arizona simultaneously mounted an open-shop drive—designed to have less union workers in the state, not more.

The ACGA fought back by illegally deporting the organized Mexican workers. The Arizona AFL claimed this was a common ploy and cited a case involving six Mexican workers who were picked up on a farm near Glendale, Arizona, on June 21, 1920, and hauled to the city jail in Tempe, twenty miles away. Arrested without any warrant or legal authority, they were summarily deported by the ACGA the following day. AFL President Doane talked to these men (Apolonio Cruz, José Berdugo, Bruno Rodríguez, Pablo Mora, Antonio Lial, and Juventino Martínez) at the Tempe jail. They advised Doane that they were brought to Arizona under contract by the ACGA to work for two dollars and fifty cents per day until their indebtedness was repaid. Finding it impossible to live on this, they asked for more money, were declared strikers by the ACGA agents, and were incarcerated. Cruz's eight-year-old son was left on a ditch bank after the family was deported. Friends later brought the boy to Tempe and the Association shipped him off to Mexico, alone.

Inspector Robertson of the Immigration Service assured AFL counsel that he had deputized no one to deport persons, he had not been consulted on these deportations, and his office had no knowledge of the matter until it was brought to his attention after the deportation. This of course violated the rules under the Ninth Proviso. AFL officials found this procedure to be so common that it excited no comment. Tempe police looked upon deportation as an ordinary, legal procedure. The ACGA claimed that the deportees went back to Mexico willingly. The area's leading newspaper, the *Arizona Republican*, failed to even report these incidents.[17]

These deportations did not slow the rail traffic north from Mexico. Mexico City's *Excelsior* reported that six cars were added to the regular train that left the Nogales, Sonora, depot for the Arizona fields on June 28, 1920:

> These wretched families presented a truly sorry picture with their scattered pots and pans around the station, shattered trunks, pieces of well-worn luggage, large knots of tattered clothes, that proclaims the miserable state of poverty in which they lived in the interior of our country. . . . From Phoenix, they write saying there are over two thousand Mexicans who were contracted to work but are unemployed and without means of support.[18]

One cannot help wondering how many of these two thousand were released from work because they joined the AFL.

R. M. Sánchez and E. M. Flores, AFL farm worker organizers, decided to move the action to the international scene. They advised provisional President Adolfo de la Huerta (meeting him in Mexico City) that the contracts offered to Mexican citizens lacked provision for decent living, housing, and fair pay by American cost-of-living standards. They advised that Mexican workers must stop being deceived by the ACGA *enganchadores*. President de la Huerta ordered the governor of Sonora to halt emigration to Arizona temporarily, until the government could set up the Office of Protection of Mexican Workers at Nogales, Sonora. Five *enganchadores* of the ACGA were jailed in Mexico for "coming in conflict with the labor laws of Mexico and orders of President de la Huerta." The editor of the *Arizona Republican* no longer remained silent. On July 27, 1920, he editorialized that labor leaders were making it hard for cotton growers. He accused them of doing all they could in both Mexico City and Washington to prevent the importation of Mexican labor.[19]

Meanwhile, the enraged cotton foremen "threatened rough stuff." They attempted to prevent a farm workers' union meeting in Avondale, Arizona. At this meeting, on July 7, 1920, AFL President Doane also was threatened by the ACGA foremen. Whether this action resulted from the union's part in closing the border to further unregulated influx of Mexican workers or from the organizing efforts among the alien workers by the AFL is not clear. It is clear that Governor Campbell and Alvaro Obregón (then de facto president of Mexico) met in Nogales, Arizona, and Nogales, Sonora, to discuss the recent events.[20]

Doubtless spurred by the meeting with Obregón and news that two hundred Mexican laborers had just been cut adrift without pay, Governor Campbell began an investigation of charges that Mexican workers in Arizona had been abused. Campbell appointed John D. Petty, Arizona representative of the United States Employment Service, to investigate. Abelardo B. Sobarzo, special commissioner of the government of the state of Sonora, Mexico, sent by Sonora Governor F. A. Bórquez, and the Mexican consul in Phoenix, E. C. González, initiated an independent inquiry. The three submitted a joint report on the living conditions of the alien farm workers to Governor Campbell. However, a separate report was sent to the ACGA by the Mexican officials only.

The report to Governor Campbell revealed that between twelve and fifteen thousand aliens were housed mostly in tents in the Salt River Valley. (Maricopa County's total population in the 1920 census was less than ninety thousand including approximately twenty thousand Mexican-Americans.) Recommendations included: more shade over the tents to reduce the intense heat (July temperatures in the shade often top one hundred and fifteen degrees), enforcement of proper sanitary conditions, and payment of no less than thirty five cents per hour for a ten-hour day with time and one half for overtime. The report further asserted that even under such poor living conditions the workers were generally contented and satisfied. (This probably speaks more for the terrible postwar conditions in Mexico than for the "good" conditions in Arizona.)

Somewhat more critical observations marked the report to the ACGA. The Mexican officials complained of: poor and inadequate housing that caused suffering and hardships, wholly inadequate and expensive medical care, deceptive hiring methods, crowded and degrading transportation facilities, abusive treatment by the ACGA foremen, and illegal deportation methods. González and Sobarzo requested an early reply from the Association.[21]

The ACGA's decision was stated in a letter to González dated August 14, 1920, and signed by A. J. Milliken, secretary-treasurer. The thrust of the reply advised an increase in the cotton-picking rate to four cents per pound. Milliken ignored the grievances enumerated by the Mexican officials. The Association official maintained that the pay increase was the result of the consul's advice, not agitation and union activity. In a report to President Obregón six months later, Eduardo Ruiz, Mexican consul in Los Angeles, accused Milliken of "being ruthless and treating the Mexican workers with extreme harshness, having the belief that all are thieves and try to cheat the company."[22]

Governor Campbell advised Governor Bórquez of the findings of the investigation conducted by Sobarzo, González, and Petty. The Arizona governor seemed happy to inform Bórquez that "many of the rumors regarding the treatment of the cotton workers were totally false, and not stated on fact."[23] Campbell concluded that their only complaint seemed to be wages, which had been favorably acted upon. Apparently a considerable communication gap plagued the Arizonan and Mexican officials. Nevertheless, again a crisis was averted through the mediation of Governor Campbell. But dark foreboding clouds gathered in the superheated summer air of Arizona which heralded the approach of a new storm. Because of the precipitous decline in long-staple cotton prices (which began in May 1920) and the collapse of the cotton market, Arizona growers faced ruin.[24]

Against this background the ACGA moved to cancel the agreed increase in cotton pickers' wages. R. M. Sánchez girded the Mexicans for this new struggle with the growers. On November 6, 1920, agents of the United States Department of Justice swooped down on the AFL hall in Phoenix, arrested Sánchez, and jailed him without a warrant, without charges, and without bond. Not until November 19 was Sánchez finally charged with being a "deserter" from the United States Army and turned over to the military authorities at Nogales, Arizona, for trial before a military court. AFL officials declared that Sánchez's sole offense was being active in organizing Mexican cotton workers in the valley. They felt that it was more than coincidental that Sánchez was held without charges for nearly two weeks, the United States district attorney finally charging him with desertion on the day before a mass meeting of growers on November 20 called by the ACGA to propose cutting the pickers' pay scale.

For unexplained reasons it took the daily *Arizona Republican* a week to report the incident on November 14, labeling Sánchez as an undesirable alien and a radical. The phoniness of the charge became apparent when the military acquitted and released Sánchez on February 3, 1921. As coincidence would have it, his incarceration covered the remainder of the cotton harvesting season. Despite this desperate move the ACGA was unsuccessful in cutting the pickers' wages. At a second meeting on November 24, the growers decided against the cut, on the advice of bankers and because some growers were fearful of a strike.[25]

Cotton prices fell so low that the question of a pay cut became academic. The United States Department of Agriculture reported that Arizona farmers' sales in 1920 fell twenty million dollars below those of 1919. The steady, although artificially high, price of long-staple in the early spring of 1920 had caused cotton acreage to double. The cost of recruiting Mexican pickers rose from one hundred and twenty-five thousand dollars in 1919 to two hundred and ninety-six thousand dollars in 1920 because the need for pickers also doubled. An Association official estimated that this imported labor saved the growers two million eight hundred thousand dollars.[26] With the collapse of the cotton boom the savings were ephemeral. Many growers, unable to sell their crops except at a great loss, merely cut their pickers adrift, often without final pay. Chaos ensued.

The *Tucson Daily Citizen* on January 22, 1921, banner-headlined a story, "Penniless Mexican Laborers By Thousands Are Stranded Over Salt River Cotton Valleys." The story quoted the Mexican consul who protested that from fifteen to twenty thousand Mexican laborers were stranded in Arizona because cotton growers had not paid them. Two days later the *Citizen* reported that ten thousand cotton laborers were returning to Mexico, all of them hungry. R. C.

Davidson, official of the Southern Pacific Railroad, claimed the railroad agreed to transport these ten thousand back to Nogales, Arizona, on the international line.[27]

Dave Loeb, president of the Nogales (Arizona) Chamber of Commerce, wired Governor Campbell on January 25, 1921, that the movement of thousands of Mexican cotton pickers to the border from the Salt River Valley was causing a serious situation in ambos Nogaleses (both Nogaleses, the twin cities of Nogales, Arizona, and Nogales, Sonora). He felt it was the moral responsibility of the ACGA to return these people to their homes free of expense. Loeb described their condition as deplorable and sickening. The *Nogales Daily Herald* described the condition of the workers as follows:

> Hundreds of Mexican cotton pickers are stranded in Nogales, Sonora. They are eating and sleeping in the open (the temperatures go well below freezing in Nogales in January). Dr. Gutsetter reports much suffering in the camp near the line. He stated little children are without sufficient clothing and food. The laborers are sleeping in ditches and under bridges. The fence built by the U.S. government along the border is being used to hang pieces of canvas upon, under which many rude huts have been built in the arroyo near the border and alongside the residence formerly occupied by President Obregón.[28]

Loeb's wire, together with complaints from González Córdoba (Mexican consul in Phoenix), stirred Governor Campbell to action. He informed Knox of the ACGA of the grievances and requested immediate rectification.

At the same time Consul Córdoba alerted Mexico City. President Alvaro Obregón fired a telegram off to Eduardo Ruiz, Mexican consul in Los Angeles:

> In view of the critical situation Mexicans in Arizona cotton camps are going through due to sudden lack of work and broken promises by ensnaring companies, by executive order you are ordered to proceed to Phoenix at once, conferring with Governor Campbell and other authorities of that state concerned with the problem so that the crisis may be resolved in an expedient manner for our compatriots. You must leave immediately upon receipt of this message.[29]

Governor Campbell also received a wire from Obregón informing him of Ruiz's impending visit to Phoenix as his personal envoy.

Ruiz lost no time entraining for Phoenix. February 1, 1921, found him in conference with Consul Córdoba and Governor Campbell. Ruiz informed Campbell that he had no bias against anyone but meant to learn the truth about the plight of Mexicans in Arizona. Campbell offered full cooperation, suggesting a meeting with the ACGA officials, Mexican officials, and himself after Ruiz had the opportunity to investigate fully. Ruiz also requested that some members of the chamber of commerce and Adolfo Pecina, president of the Liga Protectora Latina, be present, to which Campbell agreed. After a field investigation of the cotton camps Ruiz reported to President Obregón.

The ACGA, he revealed, took charge of contracting for Mexican laborers on various parts of the border. It mediated for companies and the men, called *enganchadores* or *negreros* (slave traders), who received and distributed the laborers to the ranchers "with the greatest of indifference as if they were herds of cattle." In good years the Mexicans received enough pay to establish themselves in the United States. In the present instance, the harvest was bad and the price of cotton low, which caused the Association to demonstrate the "same harshness and indifference that almost all American corporations demonstrate towards their workers." He further accused the ACGA of being to blame for poor housing, contrary to promises. Often the Mexican men, women, and children simply sprawled in the fields.

Consul Ruiz further criticized the Association for default in payment to workers. He censured the ACGA for not repatriating the Mexicans who did not find work. The organization was morally, if not contractually, obligated to find employment for the imported field hands. Many of the complaints by the Mexican workers about the Association were caused by its ruthless overseers, Ruiz further charged. He singled out the manager, A. J. Milliken, as noted above, and Rafael Estrada, "a blond Christ who is the epitome of a *cacique*" [boss]. Ruiz described Estrada as "a renegade Mexican who is in charge of choosing who shall be repatriated, preferring those who have paid him or those from whom he has collected valuables or jewels of some kind to allow them to board the train."[30] One Felipe Alanis swore under oath that he was personally acquainted with one Estrada, who was known among the Mexicans as Güero Cristo, and that Estrada was employed by the ACGA. Alanis testified that Estrada took whatever amount of money the repatriated Mexicans had as they boarded the Nogales-bound train. He said that on one occasion, on or about January 25, he "saw Estrada take from an old lady from Sinaloa a pair of earrings, when she stated she had no money, and put them in his pocket."[31] Ruiz reported that the ACGA's general manager, J. S. Knox, was a kindly man but that he seemed influenced by Milliken.

Obregón's special envoy next took to task the Mexican Labor Association. It was a labor subcontractor, working for the ACGA under the management of a Mr. Manning, an American, and A. L. González, a Mexican, and authorized by D. Flavio Bórquez, former governor of Sonora. Ruiz charged this company with deceit and torpidity in the contracts for engaging Mexican workers for the ACGA. The contract read, ". . . give employment in the states of Arizona and California to ————, Mexican agricultural worker during the term of no more than six months." Ruiz scored the ACGA for using this clause to hire for as few as ten or fifteen days, and claimed that the Association should have promised to give work to each Mexican for *no less than* six months. Ruiz felt that despite this defect in the contract the ACGA should have felt morally if not legally bound to find work for the aliens for more than a few weeks after bringing them as many as a thousand miles from home.

Ruiz further castigated the Mexican Labor Association for: not having an inspector at the labor camps, charging immorally four to seven dollars per head, sending in late November 1920 large numbers of Mexicans to the Salt River Valley knowing there was no work, illegal collection of moneys from the Mexicans, and deceitful and untruthful statements in recruiting laborers.

Consuls Córdoba and Ruiz found on their field investigations of the labor camps that the condition of the Mexicans hired in late November was the most disastrous. Those who either did not work more than a few weeks or did not receive pay at all numbered around three thousand. Some were owed as much as five hundred dollars. Many lived in the open and were near the point of starvation. The consuls took depositions from hundreds of laborers. Two typical cases:

> Alejandra Ramírez was brought by the ACGA three months ago. She is a widow with two children. Last employed by the Chandler Improvement Company, she was ordered on February 2, 1921 to leave her tent and seek shelter elsewhere. She immediately proceeded to move out her belongings, as well as many others nearby. Before she could get her things out the tent was pulled down on orders of a Mr. Cook, exposing her to the elements. What little she had to eat was ruined. . . . Jesús Norzagary, was working for a rancher near Glendale who owed him $7.00. His wife had no more clothes on than the law allows, his children poorly dressed, one of his babies, about four, was entirely naked. There was no food. The rancher had quite a few chickens. Jesús offered to take his pay in chickens but was refused.

Ruiz felt that if it had not been for the intervention of President Obregón many would have perished from starvation.[32]

The Mexican press lashed the ACGA. *El Universal* wrote on March 5, 1921, that the Mexicans "were dying of hunger in Phoenix and were treated as if they were animals by the contractors," and that some of the contracting companies would better be named "slave traders" and were treating Mexicans brutally, forcing them from their miserable camps by denying them food or water. *El Demócrata* even more vociferously charged that the ACGA treated the Mexican workers "worse than Negroes" and that the cotton camps were "infernal concentration camps." It described one of these camps:

> When they arrived at Phoenix a party of Mexican workers were taken to Tempe and introduced to a concentration camp that looks like a dung-heap. . . . Once in this camp the worker is dispatched to a rancher and is now at the mercy of the master they get . . . not free in any way. He can not change bosses without permission of the ACGA which is seldom granted . . . concentration camp costs, between jobs, are charged to the workers, eating up his meager savings. Those who do not wish to contract these debts and abandon the camp are considered deserters and then the Association acts as immigration officials, look[s] for them with blood-hounds, return[s] them to camp, threaten[s] them with deportation. . . . many are jailed as if they were criminals. . . . handcuffed and tied, with the Company the sole judge of what shall become of those who refuse to be a slave.[33]

Excelsior reported that thousands were deprived of a means of livelihood and numerous reports of death by starvation had been received from Arizona.

The reactions of the Arizona press varied from that of the liberal *Arizona Labor Journal* to that of the conservative *Arizona Republican*. The *Arizona Journal*'s reporter described conditions as he saw them:

> The city jail congested with vagrants [unemployed Mexican aliens] and tents strung alongside roads. . . . many families in actual want without subsistence or money to return home. . . .
>
> Now the cotton season is over. . . . farmers lost money, country deluged with undesirable citizens. . . . No good record of families imported and while the cotton association was supposed to return entrants to Nogales, have not done so with regularity. . . .
>
> [The] experiment has been a costly one. . . . shouldn't be repeated. . . .[34]

The *Arizona Republican* seemed more concerned with diplomatic pressures. It reported that President Obregón had expressed to Governor Campbell his concern about the crisis. The *Arizona Republican* hoped for an adjustment of this most embarrassing matter.

Several meetings were held between the Mexican officials and the ACGA officials with Governor Campbell as mediator in an attempt to make adjustments satisfactory to all concerned. Consul Ruiz stated that the ACGA greatly resisted reaching an agreement. The Association based its intractability on the premise that the vagueness of the contracts protected it. Ruiz agreed that this was true of many of the articles in the contracts. Finally, in a meeting on

February 5, 1921, at the capitol in Phoenix, the principals signed an agreement.

All present agreed that the Arizona Cotton Growers Association would transport back to the Mexican border all those Mexican cotton pickers who were without funds, without cost to said pickers. The ACGA agreed to sign new contracts to this effect and further agreed to pay the Mexicans sums owed them by the ranchers, who for the most were broke. The Mexicans in turn would transfer such debts in favor of the ACGA so it could collect in the future from the ranchers. The Mexican consulate in Phoenix stipulated it would send an unbiased representative to the ACGA office in Tempe to help investigate and decide which pickers should be sent back at ACGA expense. The Association further agreed to compel its member ranchers to transport the unemployed Mexicans to the Tempe office for entrainment to the border. Eduardo Ruiz affixed his signature as the emissary of President Obregón of Mexico and W. H. Knox signed as general manager for the ACGA.[35]

Ruiz wrote to Obregón that the ACGA relented only after pointed reminders of the friendship of Obregón and Campbell and of the consequences if their promises were broken: members of the ACGA would not be able to depend in the future on Mexican workers to harvest their crops. Although he gave credit to Campbell for his good services, Ruiz pointed out to Obregón that the governor, who greatly owed his election to the ACGA, had to be prodded to see that the moment had arrived to prove his friendship to Mexico and its president. In a letter to Campbell from the Phoenix consulate Ruiz unqualifiedly commended him for his good services in the settlement and gave high praise to the ACGA.[36]

After Ruiz returned to his consulate in Los Angeles, he must have had uneasy second thoughts. A letter dated February 14, 1921, to Governor Campbell indicated that although arrangements were then in progress for the transportation of Mexican cotton pickers to Mexico, Ruiz hoped the matter would be satisfactorily and definitely settled. Apparently Ruiz's intuition served him well.

Nearly three weeks after the agreement was concluded, the *Tucson Daily Citizen* carried the story that organized labor (AFL) established a soup-and-bread line in Phoenix and fed one thousand Mexican men, women, and children each day. *The Tucson Daily Citizen* also reported that the Arizona Fifth Legislature had considered the problem of hungry and unemployed cotton pickers and had suggested that the federal government should take over, since the Immigration Service admitted the workers to Arizona. The Immigration Service curtly retorted that it permitted the Mexican laborers to enter the United States and work in the Salt River Valley because the cotton men demanded that it do so; therefore it suggested that the cotton growers "do their duty."[37]

The *Arizona Labor Journal* put it more bluntly, claiming that outside of Phoenix thousands of Mexicans were sitting on ditch banks, most with no shelter, "starving, literally starving." The *Arizona Labor Journal* further proclaimed that Phoenix union men dug into their own pockets to feed Mexican victims of the "American Plan" (the open-shop, cheap-labor theory) fostered by the ACGA, which had now also repudiated its pledge to return them to Nogales. Nearly five thousand claims for back wages had been filed with the Mexican consul in Phoenix. Furthermore, arrangements by the ACGA to settle these wage claims had not been honored.

The Maricopa County Board of Supervisors on March 3, 1921, investigated the AFL soup kitchens and immediately pledged one hundred dollars for food purchases. Supervisor Guy Vernon also called Knox at the ACGA and informed him to get on with his program, agreed to on February 5. Vernon also sent a telegram to Secretary of Labor Wilson, who in turn instructed Phoenix Immigration Agent Robertson by wire to see that the agreement was enforced.[38]

J. H. Hamill, editor of the conservative *Globe Record*, wrote this about the treatment accorded Mexican cotton pickers:

> [An] example of man's inhumanity to man, . . . shameful treatment of the Mexican cotton picker in the Salt River Valley surpasses in heartlessness anything that has occurred in Arizona since its organization as a territory 57 years ago. . . . hard to believe that any group of persons claiming to be human could be so lost to all sense of honor as to abuse the confidence of President Obregon and his representatives after they had so graciously expressed thanks to Governor Campbell for his efforts in behalf of the unfortunate Mexicans and their confidence in the promises of that particular group that had previously broken faith with Mexico and brought discredit on Arizona.
>
> Yet it now appears the Arizona Cotton Growers Association had no intention of righting the wrong done to the Mexican workers in the valley.

The editor of the liberal *Arizona Silver Belt*, H. S. McClusky, pointed out that it was so seldom that a paper friendly to the big corporations, such as Hamill's *Globe Record*, took the part of the underdog that it should be copied by every paper in the Southwest and read before the Arizona legislature.[39]

President Obregón apparently got the picture. He authorized the secretary of foreign relations to pay out two hundred and fifty thousand pesos for the repatriation of unemployed Mexican workers in Arizona. The Confederación Regional Obrera Mexicana warned Mexican workers not to accept a contract of employment in the

United States unless the conditions of employment were spelled out in detail and iron-clad. *El Universal* advised that many Mexicans had to travel on foot to the border at Nogales, ragged and dying of hunger.[40]

The crisis did not end for months, and the basic, underlying problem of Mexican farm workers in Arizona and elsewhere in the Southwest remains in 1973. The Arizona State Legislature in 1972 passed a vicious anti-Mexican, antiunion farm workers law. Conservative Republican Governor Jack Williams signed the bill in great haste. The organizing efforts of César Chávez have scared the agricultural corporate giants of today, just as those of Doane and Sánchez did in their day.

Seeking a union to improve their lot was and is the Mexicans' greatest error. Carey McWilliams charged that the growers "in the area of labor relations are spoiled, stupid, and arrogant. Until fairly recent years, they or their predecessors have had such undisputed airtight control of local and state authorities that what they want they get, as by divine right."[41]

As long as Mexico cannot provide work with decent pay to so many of her people, the siren call of modern-day Cíbolas to the north will continue to entice hapless Mexican immigrants to the United States, thereby compounding the problem of a decent living for so many of their cousins—the Mexican-Americans.

Notes

1. John Francis Bannon, *The Spanish Borderlands Frontier, 1513–1821* (New York, 1970), pp. 12–27.
2. Harland Padfield and William E. Martin, *Farmers, Workers, and Machines* (Tucson, 1965), pp. 84–87.
3. Otey M. Scruggs, "The First Mexican Farm Labor Program," *Arizona and the West* 2 (Winter 1960): 320; Leo Grebler, "Mexican Immigration to the United States. The Record and Its Implications," in *Mexican-American Study Project Advance Report 2, UCLA, 1966*, chap. 4, pp. 10–13; and J. B. Given, "Back and Forth to Mexico," *Survey*, October 6, 1917, p. 10. The Ninth Proviso provided that the commissioner general of immigration, with the approval of the secretary of labor, could issue rules and prescribe conditions, including exaction of such bonds as were necessary to control and regulate the admission and return of otherwise inadmissible aliens applying for temporary admission. The commissioner was further authorized to temporarily set aside literacy, head tax, and contract labor provisions of the law, if convinced of a labor shortage.
4. Scruggs, "First Mexican Farm Labor Program": 321–25.
5. U.S. Department of Labor, *Annual Report of the Commissioner General of Immigration, Reports of the Department of Labor, 1920* (Washington, D.C.: Government Printing Office, 1921), pp. 168, 428.
6. *Excelsior* (Mexico City), May 9, 1921, p. 3.
7. Liga Protectora Latina to Campbell, May 15, 1919, Campbell File, Arizona State Archives.
8. Knox to Campbell, May 30, 1919, Campbell File, Arizona State Archives.

9. Robertson to Campbell, May 16, 1919, Campbell File, Arizona State Archives.

10. Pedro Estrada, in interview, April 11, 1970.

11. Manual Peralta and Juana Peralta, in interview, May 5, 1970.

12. *Arizona Labor Journal,* April 30, 1920, p. 3.

13. Carey McWilliams, *North From Mexico* (New York: Greenwood Press, 1968), p. 186.

14. *Phoenix Messenger,* May 7, 1920, p. 1.

15. Córdoba to Obregón, February 8, 1921, and Ruiz to Obregón, February 18, 1921. *Secretaria Particular de la Presidencia de la República,* Sección de Archivo, Palacio Nacional, México, D.F., Período Obregón-Calles (años de 1921–1928), Paquete 40–1, Legato 9, Clase 407–14–2.

16. *Excelsior* (Mexico City), February 9, 1921, p. 1.

17. *Arizona Labor Journal,* June 25, 1920, p. 1, and Carey McWilliams, *Ill Fares the Land* (Boston, 1942), p. 78. McWilliams gives as the sources of the incident *Arizona Labor Journal* and *Arizona Republican,* June 28, 1920. This writer found no story of the incident in the *Republican* of that date or in any issue between June 21 and July 1, 1920.

18. *Excelsior* (Mexico City), July 3, 1920, p. 5.

19. *Excelsior* (Mexico City), July 1, 1920, p. 5, and July 22, 1920, p. 5; *Arizona Labor Journal,* July 2, 1920, p. 1; and *Arizona Republican,* July 27, 1920, p. 4.

20. *Tucson Daily Citizen,* July 9, 1920, p. 1, and *Arizona Labor Journal,* July 9, 1920, p. 1.

21. Patty, Sobarzo, and González to Campbell, July 20, 1920, and Sobarzo and González to the ACGA, July 31, 1920, Campbell File, Arizona State Archives.

22. Milliken to González, August 14, 1920, Campbell File, Arizona State Archives, and Ruiz to Obregón, February 18, 1921, Archivo Palacio Nacional, México, D. F.

23. Campbell to Borquez, August 2, 1920, Campbell File, Arizona State Archives.

24. *Southwestern Stockman-Farmer,* April 30, 1921, p. 6, and *Arizona Republican,* October 14, 1920, p. 9. In this six-month period long-staple cotton prices slipped from as high as one dollar and twenty-five cents per pound to as low as twelve cents per pound.

25. *Arizona Labor Journal,* November 11, 1920, p. 4, November 18, 1920, p. 4, November 25, 1920, p. 4, December 2, 1920, p. 4, and February 3, 1921, p. 4; and *Arizona Republican,* November 14, 1920, p. 7.

26. Malcolm Brown and Owen Cassmore, *Migratory Cotton Pickers in Arizona* (Washington, D.C.: Government Printing Office, 1939), pp. 55–65. Brown and Cassmore quote an ACGA official as stating that the ACGA maintained a steady, low level of wages throughout its territory and that the Mexicans were their best source of cheap labor. Brown and Cassmore state that the ACGA habitually overestimated its real labor needs—"When they say they need one hundred pickers, you would be about right if you sent them fifty."

27. *Tucson Daily Citizen,* January 22, 1921, p. 8, and January 24, 1921, p. 2.

28. Loeb to Campbell, January 25, 1921, Campbell File, Arizona State Archives; and *Nógales Daily Herald,* January 24, 1921, p. 1, and January 29, p. 1.

29. Obregón to Ruiz, January 29, 1921, Sección de Archivo, Período Obregón-Calles, Paquete 40-1, Legato 9, Clase 407-14-2.

30. Ruiz to Obregón, February 18, 1921, Sección de Archivo, Período Obregón-Calles, Paquete 40-1, Legato 9, Clase 407-14-2.

31. *Partial Report on Mr. Ed Ruiz, et al.,* February 5, 1921, p. 42, Arizona State Archives, Document No. 58468.

32. *Ibid.,* pp. 6 and 33; Ruiz to Obregón, February 18, 1921, Sección de Archivo, Período Obregón-Calles; and *La Prensa* (Los Angeles), February 19, 1921, p. 1.

33. *El Universal* (Mexico City), March 5, 1921, p. 1; *El Demócrata* (Mexico City), January 28, 1921, p. 1, and March 21, 1921, p. 1; and *Excelsior* (Mexico City), February 5, 1921, Hemeroteca Nacional, México, D.F.

34. *Arizona Labor Journal,* January 27, 1921, p. 4, and *Arizona Republican,* February 6, 1921, p. 12.

35. Ruiz to Obregón, February 18, 1921, Sección de Archivo, Período Obregón-Calles; Knox-Ruiz agreement, February 5, 1921, Campbell File, Arizona State Archives; and *Excelsior* (Mexico City), February 8, 1921, p. 1.

36. Ruiz to Obregón, February 18, 1921, and Ruiz to Campbell, February 9, 1921, Campbell File, Arizona State Archives.

37. *Tucson Daily Citizen*, February 24, 1921, p. 1, and February 25, 1921, p. 2.

38. *Arizona Labor Journal*, February 17, 1921, p. 1, February 24, 1921, pp. 1, 4, and March 3, 1921, p. 4.

39. *Arizona Record*, March 1, 1921, p. 4, and *Arizona Silver Belt*, March 1, 1921, p. 1.

40. *Excelsior* (Mexico City), February 17, 1921, p. 1, and February 18, 1921, p. 1; *El Universal* (Mexico City), April 5, 1921, p. 1.

41. Carey McWilliams, "A Man, a Place, and a Time," *American West*, May 1970.

Chapter Four

World War II and the Mexican-Americans

World War II, despite the death, mutilation, and suffering it brought, has been acknowledged as an event that wrought some beneficial consequences for minorities, especially the Mexican-Americans. According to some writers, as a result of the war formerly closed jobs were opened, segregated living was weakened, and the Mexican-American first recognized that he too was an American. However, the war also had some extremely disillusioning effects upon the Mexican-American community.

In this chapter Robin Fitzgerald Scott and Patricia Rae Adler have written penetrating essays on wartime life and events that caused some patriotic and thinking Mexican-Americans to become disillusioned with the treatment given to some members of their people. Scott's selection treats "Wartime Labor Problems and Mexican-Americans in the War." Adler's essay presents a historical picture and analysis of the pachuco riots of 1943.

Wartime Labor Problems and Mexican-Americans in the War*

Robin Fitzgerald Scott

WARTIME LABOR PROBLEMS

The labor problems of the Mexican-American existed before World War II but they were intensified as the war progressed. Although not openly advocating evacuation of the Japanese from the West Coast after Pearl Harbor, the Mexican-Americans were hopeful that their economic prospects would be brighter as a result. During the 1940s the Japanese had developed truck gardens, and these proved financially successful. Japanese were also hired as gardeners—some even owned their own nurseries.[1] The Mexican-Americans had hoped to assume these positions. They were disappointed for a time. "There was an increase in frustration as well, when the war-time evacuation of the Japanese did not bring about the economic miracle expected and the strain of war increased the level of tension in the community."[2]

In the United States the Mexican-American people and their supporters charged that discriminatory practices were built into the Selective Service Act of 1940.[3] Workers in the defense industry—few of whom were Mexican-Americans—were granted occupational deferments, whereas workers in the essential agricultural industry—with a heavy concentration of Mexican-Americans—were granted no deferments. Nearly all of the able-bodied Mexican-Americans were eligible for the draft.[4] Mexican-Americans in the United States were drafted while the United States government imported workers from Mexico to replace them. The President's Commission on Migratory Labor stated that the wartime Mexican labor program of 1943–47 placed farm workers in twenty-four states.[5] Some of these Mexican workers did replace Mexican-Americans who shifted from agricultural work to the industrial plants.[6] Concessions were given to the Mexican government regarding these workers, concessions that the Mexican-Americans had never been able to obtain. The President's Commission on Migratory Labor described the statutory differences that American and Mexican negotiators encountered:

---

*From Robin Fitzgerald Scott, "The Mexican-American in the Los Angeles Area, 1920–1950: from Acquiescence to Activity" (Ph.D. dissertation, University of Southern California, History Department, 1971).

> The Mexican and United States representatives do not approach negotiations with equal freedom for bargaining. Mexico, by law, prescribes minimum standards in several respects for her nationals leaving for employment abroad whereas we, by law, prescribe no minimum standards for domestic agricultural workers. If we had legislative standards for farm workers equal to those we have for industrial labor, most of the obstacles confronted in [our] Mexican labor agreement negotiations and administration would vanish.[7]

Study of the possible importation of Mexican workers to meet the labor shortage in the United States is complicated by the fact that two distinct programs must be considered, one for agricultural workers and the other for railroad or nonagricultural laborers. Although the programs were fundamentally similar, they were to be administered separately. The peculiarities of the two industries as well as the different points of view of the personnel involved had to be considered.

The fact that the governments of the two countries were interested made these programs significant. During the 1920s, Mexicans came to the United States with the urging of private enterprise, and many were to stay permanently. In the 1940s, both the Mexican and United States governments made sure that this mass immigration was controlled and that most of the workers imported during this decade had to return to Mexico.

In the latter part of 1942 the Southern Pacific Railway Company, which had so quickly reduced rates for Mexican repatriates during the Great Depression, requested permission from the Immigration and Naturalization Service to import Mexican workers for temporary maintenance-of-way work. Considerable opposition to this proposal was offered by organized labor, and the application was withdrawn. In May 1942 the Southern Pacific stated it had 949 positions vacant, and it filed another application. Again organized labor delayed a decision.[8]

On April 29, 1943, an agreement was reached between the United States and Mexican governments for a recruitment of nonagricultural workers to be started. The program was placed under the War Manpower Commission. Many guarantees were included in the agreement: Imported Mexican workers were to be paid the same salary that domestic workers received for the same job. The minimum wage was established at forty-six cents per hour (later raised to fifty-seven cents per hour). The imported Mexican worker was to be returned to his place of recruitment when the contract had been fulfilled, at the expense of the employer or the War Manpower Commission.[9]

By the end of 1944, a total of 80,273 Mexican nationals had been recruited, and most of these were delivered to employers for railroad work. Later these braceros began to play an important role in the agricultural industry. Many communities, particularly on the Pacific Coast, felt that the Mexican workers saved particular crops. At one time they made up 8.9 percent of the farm workers on the Pacific Coast.[10] Most of the Japanese-Americans had been relocated and were no longer available in the fields.

The numerous importations of Mexican workers spelled difficulties for the Mexican-Americans. Kaye Briegel found that the coming of the braceros into agricultural work forced many Mexican-Americans into the urban areas. They then "found the war had created new stable jobs for them in California cities. Urban Mexican-Americans also found the demand for wartime workers helped them find better jobs at higher wages."[11]

Robert C. Jones, author of *Mexican War Workers in the United States,* believed that the bringing of contract Mexican nationals into the United States was an important factor in determining the relations between Mexico and the United States. He felt that although Mexico had recognized this fact, the United States did not. Jones further pointed out that furnishing war workers was not Mexico's only contribution to the United States. Mexico had been helping to supply manpower for the United States for two decades: "According to estimates based on the 1940 census, there were 383,360 persons resident in the country who had been born in Mexico. . . . Of these 208,080 were between 12 and 45 years of age and of the additional 699,220 native born persons whose parents had been born in Mexico 295,820 fell into the same age classification."[12]

California alone received 63 percent of the Mexican laborers in 1945.[13] It received more than just contract labor, however, since large numbers of immigrants from south of the border settled in many cities of California without any labor-contract protection.[14] Neither the legal, contract laborers nor the "wetbacks" should be confused with the Mexican-Americans. Most of the wartime labor group had only a temporary stay in the United States. Unfortunately, many Anglo-Americans equated the Mexican-American with the bracero and the wetback, and unfairly applied the stigma of foreigner to all Mexican-Americans.[15]

Discrimination was felt keenly during the war years. Mexican-Americans were not hired in citrus-packing plants or defense industries because "Americans simply will not work with Mexicans."[16] A 1944 report of the Los Angeles City and County Civil Service Commission showed that only 2.5 percent of the Mexican-

Americans held local government jobs, despite the fact that 10 percent of the total population of the area was Mexican-American.[17] Mexican-American youths were denied work in the war industries but were encouraged to enter the armed services.[18]

In order to bypass discriminatory practices used by local governmental agencies to deny aid to Mexican-American families, in 1944 the Committee on Economic Organizations and Agencies advised the Spanish-speaking people to start asking for economic help from the federal agencies. The Social Action Department of the National Catholic Welfare Conference in its second report issued in October 1944 listed the federal agencies that would help Mexican-Americans solve the problem of job discrimination, as follows:[19]

Committee on Fair Employment Practices
United States Employment Services
Farm Security Administration
Fair Labor Standards Act, Wages and Hours Division
National War Labor Board
National Labor Relations Board

Federal agencies also helped in obtaining employment for Mexican-Americans. It was stated that "because of the FEPC [Fair Employment Practices Commission] many local Mexican-Americans were employed in war plants in towns nearby San Dimas."[20] Problems of Mexican-Americans in the wartime labor market intensified their feelings of rejection by the majority group.

MEXICAN-AMERICANS IN THE WAR

The war had a profound effect on Mexican-Americans and the greater Los Angeles community. "That so large percentage of American troops captured or killed at Bataan were Mexican-Americans merely served to stress the intensity with which the Spanish-speaking identified themselves with the Allied cause."[21] Between three hundred seventy-five thousand and five hundred thousand Mexican-Americans served in the armed forces during the war. Mexican-Americans constituted less than 3 percent of the population of the United States.[22]

The sons of Mexican immigrants who served in the armed forces were changed. They learned how it felt not to be treated like Mexicans. "In the service most of them were treated like gringos."[23] Unlike the Negro youths, the uniformed Mexican-Americans were not denied the freedom of choice for which they were asked to fight, nor were they segregated.

Many of the Mexican-American boys who immigrated to the United States as babies were, however, turned down when they attempted to enlist in the armed services. "For men who considered America their country, the refusal of the service centers to allow them to enlist was a bitter experience."[24] They were not exempted from the military draft, however, and most of them were eventually taken. Once they were in the military service the Spanish-speaking youths strove to become paratroopers. In this they were highly successful. "These Mexican-American and Spanish-speaking paratroopers took part in all the major airborne attacks of World War II."[25] Raúl Morín in his study of Mexican-Americans in World War II and the Korean conflict answered the puzzling question, Why were so many Mexican-Americans paratroopers, and why did so many more want to be?[26]

1. This was a new and different branch of the service.
2. They liked the uniform.
3. They liked flying into space.
4. The physical requirements for the airborne fitted them to a "T"—young, alert, tough, daring, and of short stature. The latter alone had eliminated many young Mexican-Americans from other branches of their choosing.
5. They liked the extra pay.

William D. Altus made a study of the Mexican-Americans rejected by the service centers. He found that the army had made an effort to salvage some of the soldiers who were classified as illiterate after they took the army's intelligence tests. Beginning in 1943 a center was set up for such inductees, where they spent twelve weeks in special training. At the end of that period they were either discharged for ineptness or assigned regular army duty. In the Ninth Service Command, the Special Training Center served the eight western states. Approximately 48 percent of those taking the special training for illiteracy were of Mexican ancestry. "There [were] more maladjusted among the American-born and American-reared non-English-speaking Mexicans than among the corresponding group lately arrived in the United States."[27] Altus discovered that the Spanish-speaking (non-English-speaking) Mexican-American born in the United States did not score as highly in tests as did the foreign-born, Spanish-speaking Mexican who had recently arrived from Mexico. Perhaps the schools these Mexican-Americans had attended could be blamed for part of the problem. As to those who had recently arrived from Mexico: "None of this group had any literacy in English, though the average grade achieved in American schools, mainly those of California and Arizona, was between the second and third grade, the highest grade achieved by any of this group being the seventh."[28]

Perhaps this is evidence of what some experts in Mexican-American affairs have long maintained: public schools in Mexico are better than those in the United States.[29]

The Altus study of the center for illiterates also uncovered other information about Mexican-Americans in California. It revealed many factors that were keeping their culture alive in California. Newspapers printed in Spanish were widely read by Mexican-Americans. *La Opinión* of Los Angeles had a circulation of twelve thousand. Mexican motion pictures were extremely popular with the Spanish-speaking groups. Bookstores that featured Spanish-language periodicals and literature contributed to the retention and enlargement of the Mexican culture. Spanish names of places and streets throughout California kept alive in the memory of Mexican-Americans their Spanish and Mexican ancestors and heritage.[30]

There was no discrimination in the national draft lottery—the Mexican-American had an equal chance not to be drawn. Raúl Morín described the results of the first draft lottery: "On October 29, 1941, Pedro Aguilar Despart of Los Angeles was the holder of number 158 in the national draft lottery, the same number pulled out by President Roosevelt; and thus, became the first Angeleno to be drafted for selective service in World War II."[31]

After Pearl Harbor even the alien noncitizens in the United States were classified 1A and were drafted. Many Mexican-Americans were later given the opportunity to become citizens while they were in the services.

Raúl Morín, author of *Among the Valiant: Mexican-Americans in World War II and Korea,* was drafted in 1944. He wrote: "On the first night at the reception center, all the *palomilla* [gang], approximately 30, as if by a prearranged plan automatically gathered outside the barracks to get better acquainted."[32] The music of the guitar provided a pleasant accompaniment to the talking, singing, laughing, and drinking. Morín discovered in camp that the zoot-suit riots in Los Angeles had left a poor impression of Mexican-Americans throughout the United States. One serviceman from Los Angeles, who at that time was stationed in Fort Greely on Kodiak Island, Alaska, remembered that the pachuco riots of June 1943 were in all the headlines, even in Alaska. He recalled how uncomfortable he was when his buddies stationed at the same camp gave dirty looks and asked, "What kind of citizens are those Mexican zoot-suiters that would beat up our own Navy men?"[33] Morín believed that had it not been for the many young Mexican-Americans in Camp Roberts,

California, he never would have remembered that camp: "Every evening after getting back to camp from the long hikes and hard field problems, you could always see them jostling around. Young "pachuquitos" [little zoot-suiters]—who often bragged of being veterans of the Pachuco–Zoot-Suit War—would be wrestling, fighting, cursing, and yelling. No one could figure out how they could generate so much energy."[34]

A change was noted in the Mexican-Americans as they left the United States for overseas duty. Although they were still full of energy, now they were treated as seasoned and experienced American soldiers. Morín explained the difference: "No longer were we chided and shunted by other GIs and Army officers. Where we had been held in contempt by others who disliked us because of our constant Spanish chatter or our laxity in military discipline, we were now admired, respected, and approved by all those around us including most of our commanding officers."[35]

It may have been that the exploits of Mexican-American fighting men in action changed the Anglo-American image of the Mexican-American soldier. A tremendous number of men with Spanish names were found on the rolls of the military at Bataan. Mexican-Americans fought in the North African Campaign in 1942. "All of us Spanish-speaking GIs got a kick out of listening to the Spanish news that came over the ship's radio as we crossed the Gibraltar Strait. . . ."[36] The late Ernie Pyle in his wartime book *Brave Men* mentioned the many Spanish-speaking soldiers who were with the Forty-fifth Infantry Division in Sicily.[37]

Lists of American soldiers killed and wounded in action were saturated with the names of Mexican-Americans. Beatrice Griffith reported that in Los Angeles alone, where Mexican-Americans comprised about one tenth the population, in ten random lists printed in the papers "about one fifth of the names on the casualty lists and about the same proportion on the lists of awards were the names of men of Mexican ancestry."[38] Incidentally, during World War II, thirty-nine Congressional Medals of Honor were awarded to Mexican-Americans. Most of these were given posthumously.[39] The Japanese occupation of Attu in the Aleutian Islands shocked the American public, but it also brought recognition to Mexican-American soldiers for their valor and fighting abilities. All America marveled at the exploits of one Mexican-American fighting man: "The career of José P. Martínez in Attu assumed great importance, not only as United States History but to all Americans of Mexican descent because he was the first draftee enlisted man in the Pacific Theatre to distinguish himself in battle by winning the Congressional Medal of Honor in World War II."[40]

When Mexican-American veterans returned from overseas they no longer considered themselves foreigners. They had been respected in the armed services, whether in the mess hall or in the foxhole—just like any other United States citizen.[41] The rigors, the dangers, and the boredom involved on the fighting fronts made the GI see, at least temporarily, the artificiality and senselessness of his racial and other prejudices. The American of Mexican ancestry, however, returned to the United States to find the same old prejudices on the home front: certain restaurants still would not serve him, swimming facilities were barred to him, and his children or brothers and sisters were still being segregated in the schools.

Ralph Guzmán summed up the disillusionment of the Mexican-American soldier returning home. He wrote that the Mexican-American now "knows that valor in war brings no vantage in peace."[42] It was up to the Mexican-American veteran to change his status after he returned home. Another kind of war was necessary—a war to end discrimination. The Mexican-American was now ready to wage that war and he prepared himself for it, in education and in political activism. The postwar period would prove eventful in the changing status of the Mexican-American.

Notes

1. Christopher Rand, *Los Angeles: The Ultimate City* (New York: Oxford University Press, 1967), p. 121.
2. Robert A. Valdez, "Incident at Sleepy Lagoon," mimeographed (Fullerton: California State College, 1966), p. 1.
3. Carey McWilliams, *North from Mexico: The Spanish-Speaking People of the United States* (Philadelphia: J. B. Lippincott Co., 1949), p. 269.
4. Elis M. Tipton, "What We Want is Action," *Common Ground* 7 (1946): 76.
5. President's Commission on Migratory Labor, *Migratory Labor in American Agriculture* (Washington, D.C.: Government Printing Office, 1951), p. 39.
6. Edward C. McDonagh, "Status Levels of Mexicans," *Sociology and Social Research* 33 (1949): 458.
7. President's Commission, *Migratory Labor*, p. 50.
8. Robert C. Jones, *Mexican War Workers in the United States: The Mexico-United States Manpower Recruiting Program and Operation, 1942 to 1944 Inclusive* (Washington, D.C.: Pan American Union, 1945), p. 26.
9. *Ibid.*, p. 27.
10. *Ibid.*, pp. 39–40.
11. Kaye Briegel, "The History of Political Organizations Among Mexican-Americans in Los Angeles since the Second World War" (M.A. thesis, University of Southern California, 1967), p. 7.
12. Jones, *Mexican War Workers*, pp. 41, 44.
13. President's Commission, *Migratory Labor*, p. 28.
14. John A. Ford, *Thirty Explosive Years in Los Angeles County* (San Marino: Huntington Library, 1961), p. 134.
15. Celia S. Heller, *Mexican American Youth: Forgotten Youth at Crossroads* (New York: Random House, 1968), p. 11.
16. Tipton, "What We Want is Action," p. 76.
17. Beatrice Griffith, *American Me* (Boston: Houghton Mifflin Co., 1948), p. 267.

18. Ruth D. Tuck, *Not With the Fist: Mexican-Americans in a Southwest City* (Durham: Duke University Press, 1954), p. 140.
19. National Catholic Welfare Conference, Social Action Department, *The Spanish Speaking of the Southwest and West, Second Report* (n.p.: National Catholic Welfare Department, 1944), p. 17.
20. Tipton, "What We Want is Action," p. 80.
21. McWilliams, *North from Mexico,* p. 239.
22. *Ibid.* Also see Griffith, *American Me,* p. 256.
23. Briegel, "The History of Political Organizations," p. 7.
24. Griffith, *American Me,* p. 258.
25. *Ibid.,* p. 259.
26. Raúl Morín, *Among the Valiant: Mexican-Americans in World War II and Korea* (Los Angeles: Borden Publishing Co., 1963), p. 212.
27. William D. Altus, "The American Mexican: The Survival of a Culture," *Journal of Social Psychology* 29 (1949): 217.
28. *Ibid.,* pp. 213–214.
29. *Ibid.,* p. 217.
30. *Ibid.,* p. 218.
31. Morín, *Among the Valiant,* p. 25.
32. *Ibid.,* p. 83.
33. *Ibid.,* p. 56.
34. *Ibid.,* p. 89.
35. *Ibid.,* p. 256.
36. *Ibid.,* p. 44.
37. *Ibid.,* p. 57.
38. Griffith, *American Me,* p. 264.
39. Consuelo Salcedo, "Mexican American Socio-Cultural Patterns: Implications for Social Casework" (M.A. thesis, University of Southern California, 1955), p. 42.
40. Morín, *Among the Valiant,* p. 49.
41. Griffith, *American Me,* p. 264.
42. As quoted by Inter-Agency Committee on Mexican-American Affairs, *The Mexican American: A New Focus on Opportunity* (n.p.: Inter-Agency Committee on Mexican-American Affairs, 1967), p. 246.

The 1943 Zoot-Suit Riots: Brief Episode in a Long Conflict*

Patricia Rae Adler

Los Angeles during World War II was a tense, fevered place. The overcrowded city was strained and resolute, and at the same time like an unplanned carnival. Defense workers with new security badges packed into the streetcars. On the waterfront, the night shifts worked in a blaze of light along the keels of Liberty ships. Downtown, near the bus station, servicemen on leave watched families from Arkansas and Oklahoma and the deep South unload-

---

*From a study by Patricia Adler, prepared for a course in the History of the Mexican-American in the Southwest, at the University of Southern California.

ing children from their used-up cars, trying to get their bearings, asking where to find a job. Sailors stood in line for the movie theaters, eyeing their reflections in the plate glass department store windows, restless, with more money than there was time to spend. Everyone was restless. The city's disquiet intensified and burst out, in early June 1943, in a sudden pageant of violence—the zoot-suit riots.

After Pearl Harbor, Los Angeles had braced itself for a sea attack, for a strike by Japanese invaders coming onto the beach from submarines or perhaps flying in on bombing raids out of the undefended Pacific skies. The Japanese fishermen on Terminal Island and the families growing vegetables on the bluffs along the coast were immediately suspect. Military and civilian authorities came to swift agreement that not only these, but all Japanese, must be moved inland, away from the vulnerable shoreline.

The Japanese were the most conspicuous but not the only source of anxiety in Los Angeles. The Southern California penchant for supporting outlandish political schemes gave a basis for the suspicion that Hitler's agents might be able to raise a fifth column here. Communists, too, had seemed to multiply during the depression, despite a campaign to suppress them and what nonunion Los Angeles considered their labor agitation programs.

A series of books on the question of American loyalties which appeared in 1940 were read and discussed in Los Angeles as relevant to the local problem—Martin Dies's *Trojan Horse in America,* Harold Lavine's *Fifth Column,* and Lawrence Dennis's *Dynamics of War and Revolution.* The America First movement gained adherents. In January 1941 the California State Legislature created a joint senate-assembly committee to investigate Communist, Fascist, Nazi, and other foreign-dominated groups. It was to "ascertain, collate and appraise all facts causing or constituting interference with the National Defense Program in California or rendering the people of the State, as a part of the Nation, less fit physically, mentally, morally, economically, or socially."[1]

This Joint Fact-Finding Committee on Un-American Activities in California, the "Little Dies Committee" headed by State Senator Jack B. Tenney, held its first hearing in Los Angeles in July and October, 1941. It came primarily to investigate the CIO strike at North American Aircraft Company which it considered the outgrowth of local Communist activity.[2] It returned soon after Pearl Harbor to study the subversive organizations found to be active in the Southern California Japanese community. While the bulk of the committee's first report deals with Communism, local Nazi

Bundists, and Fascist front groups, it also includes testimony on the Shinto religion and Japanese state philosophy which the committee found to be a fanatic nationalism gripping American citizens of Japanese parentage as well as immigrants from Japan. The committee recommended strict and continuing surveillance of all Japanese, regardless of their claims of United States citizenship.

Late in 1942, alerted by newspaper accounts of violence in the Mexican community, the committee launched an investigation of the *Sinarquistas,* an anti-Communist society seeking to influence politics in Mexico and charged with subversion in the barrios of Los Angeles. The committee was quickly convinced that sinister forces were at work. Its hearings, continued through the war years, contributed a semiofficial respectability to the city's xenophobic suspicions of the Mexican minority.

Another factor which predisposed the city to suspicions of its Mexican-Americans was a mounting obsession with juvenile delinquency which was, at the time, associated in the public imagination with the Mexican gangs of downtown and East Los Angeles. After the relocation of the Japanese was completed, in March 1942, the old hotels and rooming houses they vacated in Little Tokyo filled with incoming war workers and their families. Rental housing had always been in short supply in Los Angeles. During the war families moved into store fronts and garages, doubled up with relatives, and poured into wartime housing projects as soon as they were built. In downtown Los Angeles, children responded to the crowded quarters and the tensions of their parents with mischief, truancy, and a wildness which appeared to the authorities to be a wave of delinquency. Delinquency was measurably worse in the most urbanized areas—juvenile arrests by the Sheriff's Department declined while arrests increased in the metropolitan precincts of Los Angeles. Although arrests of white boys increased at about the same rate as did arrests of nonwhites, the police and the public were particularly impressed with Mexican delinquency due to the belief that violence was peculiar to Mexican gangs.

In a survey of wartime juvenile delinquency the Los Angeles district attorney protested that, "The declaration of war in December, 1941, did not cause any abrupt change in the delinquency trend (except in regard to auto cases). There was a considerable increase in delinquency in 1941 so that the further increase which occurred in 1942 was particularly serious. However, the 1942 increase in delinquency was unduly exaggerated in the public mind due to the fact that *many incidents of violence and gang activity which ac-*

tually involved adults was attributed to juveniles." [Emphasis appears in the report.] He also pointed out that Mexican boys appearing in juvenile court made up only 26.3 percent of the total, contrary to the public's belief.[3]

A comparison of local news reports in the Los Angeles press during 1942 and 1943 with the statistics compiled by the district attorney, and later confirmed by other officials, indicates that the newspapers, especially those published by William Randolph Hearst, were presenting a highly distorted picture of delinquency. Beginning a few weeks after the Japanese relocation story had left the front pages, the war news was frequently interspersed with news about roving gangs of Los Angeles teen-agers and the crimes of violence they supposedly committed. It was not, however, an entirely new theme. The morning papers of August 17, 1941, had carried the first sensationalized story—the report of the death of two boys after a party-crashing fight in the Rose Hill section. An invading gang had rammed and overturned a car full of departing guests—allegedly members of a rival gang. Both gangs were composed of Mexicans—as the papers called them without distinction as to their individual citizenships—and some of the boys were dressed in the bizarre style favored for "jive" dancing, the "zoot-suit."

The existence of gang fighting and zoot-suit styles in the Mexican district did not come as a revelation, but rather as a confirmation, of the Los Angeles stereotype of Mexican conduct. According to the stereotype, there was always violence in the barrios, hidden behind the picturesque "Old California" facade which fascinated the tourists. At the same time, Mexicans were thought of as ignorant and lazy. The nature of this stereotype invited the hostility of the majority community. It also blocked all sincere efforts at understanding when the outbreak of violence made understanding of crucial importance. The majority community could see the "Mexican problem," but never the actual Mexicans.

The stereotype had developed long before. A feature writer for the *Los Angeles Times* had written as early as 1925,

> We always picture Mexico as a cactus-covered desert populated exclusively by bloodthirsty natives whose chief interest in life is cutting one another's throats. . . . Yet, we have in Los Angeles one hundred thousand Mexicans living in different sections of the city, apart from our social life, in a miniature world all their own. All along South Main Street and North Spring Street, you see them in the Mexican theaters and restaurants. . . . As you watch them at play in a large group you realize the numerous bloods blended in their veins . . . and in their humble and quiet manner you read the history of a great and romantic people.[4]

This ambivalence in the Anglo stereotype of the Mexicans persisted into the war years, was clearly evident during the zoot-suit riots of 1943, and dominated public debate in the aftermath of the riots. Social workers shared this attitude, and perpetuated it. Since the first great migrations from Mexico in 1910, they had explained the obviously substandard Mexican sections of the city in terms of the uncivilized habits transplanted from south of the border. The barrios were "the result of years of oppression . . . the heritage of generations who have been forced to adapt themselves to bitter poverty and insupportable tyranny," rather than a reflection of American conditions.[5] This notion continued to prevail despite the fact that Mexicans born and raised in Los Angeles had outnumbered those of Mexican upbringing since the 1930s.

Although the Mexican immigrants in Los Angeles had an inordinately high rate of crime, social workers did not consider this as evidence of inherited criminal tendencies not present in other ethnic groups. It was the Police Department which accepted the theory that criminal tendencies were hereditary and based on ethnic factors. The Los Angeles Police Department tabulated crimes according to race until 1950, using the categories "White," "Black," "Red" (Indian, i.e., Mexican), "Yellow," and "Brown" (Filipino). The department published in its annual reports tables of statistics on the nationality of offenders, and offenders' parents.

As a prominent University of Southern California sociologist analyzed Mexican criminality, it was a cultural disability: "His crimes are usually elemental, simple, overt. Lack of self-control and of social control in a complex and perplexing environment are major explanations. Mexicans rank abnormally high in crimes of personal violence against each other. They have brought their customs with them relative to settling their disputes. These methods, which are sometimes honorable in an elementary culture level, are 'crimes' in our sophisticated civilization."[6] English and American common law had long ago rejected this aspect of chivalry and interposed the mediating arm of the state. The Police Department could not, in the twentieth century, be governed by ancient social customs in their task of applying the statutes.

The primitive Mexican custom of socializing outside the home, in bars and on the sidewalks, appeared to social workers as another unfortunate anachronism which ought to be abandoned. Boys especially, in America, were expected to be kept off the street. Police shared this idea, and both police and social workers were backed by the firmly held conviction of the dominant class in America that idleness, under any circumstances, was morally wrong.

Yet another conviction written into law and at odds with Mexican folkways was that drunkenness, at least in public, was an offense against the community. As a sympathetic commentator on the barrios of Los Angeles wrote, "for the adult Mexicans the trouble is 'drunkenness,' as a rule uncomplicated by any other charge. The offenders are, largely, the laborers of middle age and over. . . . The *colonia* [Mexican community] is not proud of these befuddled oldsters, but it has a certain sympathy for them. 'Those police cars are like *zopilotes* (buzzards). They circle these streets. It doesn't make any difference how quiet a man is. If he is alone on the streets at night, he is stopped. If he has had a drink or two, he is drunk.' "[7]

The police, who stood for the white, Anglo-Saxon Protestant norms of conduct, at the same time represented to the Mexican community the weakness of the proclaimed American democratic principles, when it came to the application of these principles to people who did not share the conduct norms. The community remembered the deportations to Mexico during the depression, when families had been herded into railroad cars without a chance to prove their United States citizenship. The police were constant reminders of the arbitrariness of American policies, and of the background Anglo hostility toward the Mexican way of life. Conflict with the police was a fixed condition of existence in the barrios, outlasting the riots, and the investigations, and the recommended changes, and the exhortations of innumerable citizens' committees.

For their part, the police regarded the Mexican family as a prime source of antisocial behavior in the city. A sociologist noted that, "in many instances the parents are ignorant of child training methods. . . . The officers spend some time in giving parents instruction. 'Mexican peon parents have no ideas about raising children.' "[8] The notion of the Mexican family as a defective Anglo family proved to be unshakable in the thinking of both social workers and the police.

There had long been a recognition of the fact that the second generation was rebellious. The riots seemed to be a demonstration of this, and the postriot handling of the "Mexican problem" was predicated on the same assumptions about the causes of the rebelliousness which had become established years before. Social workers considered it typical for the families of immigrants from all countries. Mexican parents should be no more baffled by the behavior of their children than the parents of second-generation Polish- or Italian- or Irish-Americans had been.

Parents tended to accept the restlessness of youth as part of the North American environment. They, as well as the police and social workers, were aware of the conflict long before World War II. "The pachucos [hoodlums] existed long before the zoot-suits came into style," one social worker wrote. During the unrest and dislocations of the depression years, teen-agers had been sharply aware of their inability to compete for jobs with the schooled, protected, "American" youths, and had reacted with displaced and disguised hostility. They had revolted "against not one but two cultures. They neither understood nor wanted any part of either. . . . Being lost, they looked for a means of expressing their group solidarity. They found it in hostility to the established order and in the pleasures of shocking public opinion."[9] The Mexican community was fully as shocked by *pachuquismo* as the Anglo community.

Between midsummer 1942 and midsummer 1943, the institutionalized Calvinist conscience of Los Angeles—the Police Department, the time-honored apologetics of the social workers, the scapegoating operations of the Tenney Committee, the war mood of the press, the restlessness of the crowded city, and the rebelliousness of the pachucos all came together to produce mob violence—the zoot-suit riots.

As hot weather began in 1942, the press played up a series of "midnight battles" between the Belvedere gang and the Palo Verde gang in East Los Angeles. A party-crashing fight between two other gangs on August 1, according to police accounts, preceded the slaying of a young Mexican-American, José Díaz. His death beside an East Los Angeles swimming hole, the "Sleepy Lagoon," appeared to be one more episode in an inexcusable succession of Mexican outrages. The police rounded up twenty-four youngsters, all alleged to be gang members. The grand jury returned indictments against nineteen, with two of these youths asking and receiving approval for a separate trial. The remaining seventeen were convicted January 13, 1943, on various charges of manslaughter and assault after a poorly conducted trial with neither the fact of murder, the murder weapon, or the presence of the accused at the scene being established. There was unrestrained prejudicial comment by the press throughout the period of the trial.

The broader "Mexican problem" was put on trial in the press at the same time. The Tenney Committee returned to Los Angeles to begin hearings on Communist party agitation in the Mexican community, and the Los Angeles County Grand Jury called members of the Police and Sheriff's departments to give explanations of the underlying causes of Mexican delinquency.

In efforts to "get to the bottom of this thing," the 1942 grand jury provided a forum for the expounding of the police theory that crime was fundamentally a matter of race. The Mexican propensity for violence was an inherited trait, according to the well-publicized police statements. One concerned member of the grand jury managed to have scientific refutations of this ancient fallacy presented in open session, and the final report of the 1942 grand jury includes no recommendations which would implement the racist theories, but the damage to the public concept of Mexican-Americans was not undone. It was reflected the following year, in the recommendations of the 1943 grand jury for removing all delinquent and "pre-delinquent" Mexican youths to special facilities. It was also reflected in the proposal that juvenile court jurisdiction be denied for participants in zoot-suit gang offenses, which was advanced by the grand jury's Special Committee On Older Youth Gang Activity in Los Angeles and Vicinity.[10]

While the Mexican population was being tried by various committees and the press, the Police Department redoubled its efforts to get the gangs under control. Chief Horrall's assistant was soon able to report,

> The Los Angeles Police Department in conjunction with the Sheriff, California Highway Patrol, the Monterey, Montebello, and Alhambra Police Departments, conducted a drive on Mexican gangs throughout Los Angeles County on the nights of August 10 and 11. All persons suspected of gang activities were stopped. Approximately six hundred persons were brought in. There were approximately one hundred and seventy-five arrests for having knives, guns, chains, dirks, daggers, and any other implement that might have been used in assault cases. . . . Present plans call for drastic action. . . .[11]

On October 30, 1942, seventy-two Mexican youths were arrested by the newly activated "LAPD Riot Squad," following a party-crashing fight in the Crenshaw district.

Following the conviction of the Sleepy Lagoon murder defendants, a group of Los Angeles liberals organized a committee to bring to public notice what seemed to them a miscarriage of justice, and to raise funds for an appeal. It was headed by an able magazine editor and writer, Carey McWilliams. The committee worked to good effect. It succeeded in mounting an appeal which led, in 1944, to the reversal of the convictions, the dismissal of charges, and a reprimand of the trial judge for his conduct of the court proceedings.

Meanwhile, the "riots" which had been reported by the police and the press for months actually assumed riot proportions. The violence, when it erupted, was not between gangs but was an outburst of Anglo hostility against Mexicans identified as hoodlums by their wearing of the flamboyant zoot-suits. It began June 3, 1943, with off-duty policemen staging a hunt for zoot-suiters who had allegedly attacked eleven sailors entering the Mexican district. The police "Vengeance Squad," the papers reported, had failed to find the culprits. The following night two hundred sailors hired a fleet of taxicabs and cruised through the Mexican district, stopping to beat lone zoot-suiters and rip their clothing. The police followed along and arrested the victims. With variations, the violence was repeated on June 5, 6, 7, and 8. On June 8, Mayor Bowron told reporters, "sooner or later it will blow over," and County Supervisor Roger Jessup said, "All that is needed to end lawlessness is more of the same action as is being exercised by the servicemen." The Los Angles City Council passed an ordinance making the wearing of zoot-suits a misdemeanor.[12] On June 9, military authorities placed downtown Los Angeles "Off Limits," and the violence came to a halt.

Immediately after the riots the Tenney Committee returned to pursue the question of Communist agitation in the barrios. The original charges that the Los Angeles Mexican-American community harbored a Nazi-supported fifth column called the *Sinarquistas* had been made by Mrs. LaRue McCormick, an acknowledged member of the Communist party. The committee proved to be more concerned with investigating Mrs. McCormick and her Communist ties than the *Sinarquistas*. *Sinarquista* affiliations with Nazi agents in Mexico were established by committee investigators, but the matter was dropped because of difficulties presented by Spanish-language testimony, the rudimentary nature of the local organization, and the paltry sums of money actually received from abroad.

It is difficult to understand the priorities or the logic of the Tenney Committee. It operated on a guilt-by-association principle and often lost itself in a web of its own tracing by following membership lists into other membership lists, and implicating suspected Communists who served in turn to reimplicate each other. However, its 1943 and 1945 reports suggest that the highest priority in the *Sinarquista* investigation was to tie the label of Communist on the entire Sleepy Lagoon Defense Committee by showing that it was contaminated not only by the presence of Mrs. McCormick, but by CIO organizers identified by the committee as Communists during its investigation of the North American Aircraft Company strike.

The committee became solicitous of the *Sinarquistas* in the process. It reported that, "The Communist press, Communist spokesmen, loud-mouthed Communist sympathizers and fellow travelers charged the *Sinarquistas* with the responsibility for the riots," but that, in fact, it had been the other way around.[13] The committee offered its proof that it had been the foes of the *Sinarquistas*, the

Communists, who had started the riots, having realized that, "The pachuco, or so-called zoot-suit fad among Negro and Mexican youth in Los Angeles's east side was a golden opportunity for Communist racial agitation. . . ."[14]

Carey McWilliams, as chairman of the Sleepy Lagoon Defense Committee, was called to testify on his activities among Mexican-American youths prior to the riots.

"While the [Sleepy Lagoon murder] case was pending on appeal," he writes, "several members of the committee, including myself, were subpoenaed by the Committee on Un-American Activities in California . . . and grilled at great length. Naturally these various grillings were reported in the press in a manner calculated to make it most difficult for us to raise money for the appeal."[15]

McWilliams deplores, but does not analyze, the innuendoes of the committee's line of attack. It wished to publicize the Communist threat to the moral as well as the military and political safety of the state. Communists, according to the committee, wanted to promote miscegenation, which was a foreign notion inimical to American moral well-being. The defenders of the zoot-suiters in Los Angeles were to be exposed as believers in miscegenation. The committee wanted the press and the public to have the benefit of its information while the causes of the riots were being discussed and analyzed.

Senator Tenney himself questioned Carey McWilliams. The committee report summarizes the testimony which Tenney considered routine, while the exchanges he considered significant are given in full, headed: "McWilliams's views on racial intermarriage are identical with COMMUNIST PARTY ideology." The report reads in part:

Q. (Chairman Tenney) I would like to ask you what you think of miscegenation.
A. (McWilliams) I think miscegenation statutes are a reflection of prejudice in the community.
Q. Do you think they should be abolished?
A. I do.
Q. You think there should be free intermarriage?
A. I don't think there should be a legal prohibition against intermarriage. . . .
(Long interchange on same lines)
Q. I don't think you have answered my question. . . . Do you favor intermarriage?
A. I say it is presumptuous upon me to say that 'A' should marry 'B.'
Q. I understand. I am not talking about 'A' and 'B,' I am talking about negroes and whites.
A. I am not advocating. I think the prohibition should be removed.[16]

McWilliams may have been unaware of the relationship between miscegenation and Communism in the thinking of the Tenney Committee, and of at least some law enforcement officials. An example of police thinking on the subject had been read into the minutes earlier. It came from a paper on Communist tactics presented at a state conference of the California Peace Officers Association. The Communist party was seen as "trying to discard its more barbarous and loose libertinism for the attempted appearance of respectability. But within the party's ranks there existed a situation where white women openly consorted with Negro men; white, Japanese, Mexican and Filipino members had set up their own little alliances. . . . 'Communist marriages,' not blessed by benefit of clergy, founded upon this color-and-race combination basis, abounded. . . ."[17]

A sexual aspect of the zoot-suit rioting was present not only in the ties with Communist ideology as publicized by the Tenney Committee but directly, in the persons of the Mexican girl friends, the *pachuquitas,* over whom the initial clash of zoot-suiters and sailors took place. The Mexican *pachuquitas* were very appealing to American servicemen, and jealously guarded by the Mexican-American boys. They scandalized the adults of the Anglo and Mexican communities alike, with their short, tight skirts, sheer blouses, and built-up hairdos. The pursuit and beating of zoot-suiters and the destruction of the "drapes," or costumes, by mobs of servicemen were so many defeats of Mexican manhood and symbolic conquests of at least the access to the then-undefended *pachuquitas.*

Chief of Police C. B. Horrall seemed to recognize the sexual aspects of the riots. In his opinion, they made the violence less serious. He testified before the Tenney Committee:

> These disturbances, of course, started with the Latin-American gang situation, which was among themselves up until approximately a year ago. . . . However, about a year ago we had a little difficulty down at San Pedro, wherein they got mixed up with the sailors down there. . . . The latest disturbance started in the north end up here around the 1700 block on North Main Street, as apparently the result of some sailors making advances to some Mexican girls or talking to them. I don't know whether it went any farther than that . . . reached a point where it got some publicity in the papers, and that was what caused the gangs to congregate downtown that night and brought all the crowd out. However, some people have chosen to call it riots; I don't think it should be classified as that. Quite a few of the boys had their clothes torn off, but the crowds weren't particularly hard to handle. And the feeling in general among them was one of fun and sport rather than malice.[18]

Carey McWilliams recalled the mood of the crowd quite differently in his book, *North From Mexico.* He wrote:

> Marching through the streets of downtown Los Angeles, a mob of several thousand soldiers, sailors, and civilians proceeded to beat up every zoot-suiter they could find. . . . Streetcars were halted while Mexicans, and some Filipinos and Negroes, were jerked out of their seats, pushed into the streets, and beaten with sadistic frenzy. If the victims wore zoot-suits, they were stripped of their clothing and left naked or half-naked on the streets, bleeding and bruised. . . . From affidavits which I helped prepare at the time, I should say that not more than half of the victims were actually wearing zoot-suits. A Negro defense worker, wearing a defense-plant identification badge on his workclothes, was taken from a street car and one of his eyes was gouged out with a knife. Huge half-page photographs showing Mexican boys stripped of their clothes, cowering on the pavements, often bleeding profusely, surrounded by jeering mobs of men and women, appeared in all the Los Angeles newspapers.[19]

According to McWilliams, overt racism was finally checked in Los Angeles by the overturning of the convictions in the Sleepy Lagoon murder case. He acknowledges, however, that the police resumed their raids and the press resumed its stories after a few months' time. If racism is considered in broader terms than the Mexican issue, it is difficult to demonstrate that the court action produced any improvement. A survey of the Negro newspapers, the *California Eagle* and the *Los Angeles Sentinel,* shows that police harassment of minority groups increased, "shoving incidents" on the crowded streetcars were common, and, by 1946, the Ku Klux Klan was again burning crosses in Los Angeles.

The Negro press bears out Carey McWilliams's contention that racial prejudice was a basic cause of the riots—an important point to establish in view of the many statements by Los Angeles officials and social workers to the contrary. On the other hand, the Negro press does not equate the Los Angeles riots with those occurring elsewhere during 1943, as McWilliams does. In his estimation, "The week-long zoot-suit riots which began in Los Angeles . . . touched off a chain reaction of riots across the country. Similar disturbances were reported in San Diego on June 9; in Philadelphia on June 19; in Chicago on June 15; and in Evansville on June 27."[20]

These outbursts were triggered in some but not all cases by zoot-suit wearers, but lacked the Mexican gang element. They were directed against Negroes. The major riots which McWilliams saw as related to the Los Angeles events—the Detroit riot of June 20–21 and the Harlem riot of August 1–2—were very little concerned with zoot-suiters. They stemmed from fear of the Negro minority on the part of the dominant white community. No comparable fear of the attacked minority entered into the zoot-suit riots of Los Angeles.

The aftermath of the zoot-suit riots was contained in the inception of the riots. The whole thing was a continuum. The week of violent debauchery by white mobs changed nothing in the attitude of the police. It failed to shake the stereotype of the Mexican in which the social workers believed, nor did it alter the Anglo assumption that the problem to be handled was the minority race. The hearings and exposés of the Tenney Committee continued, and the formation of citizens' committees to study the Mexican problem went on at a rapid rate.

Ignacio L. López of Pomona College wrote a few years after the riots:

> In Los Angeles, out of the guilt of the dominant group, arose a faddism for the Mexican-American. Committees gave birth to litters of other committees. Coordinator battled coordinator. There was a new set of resolutions every morning. Still, when the emotional fever and the defensiveness subsided, few real gains had been made for or by the Mexican-American group. They were basically where they had been for twenty-five years, and the flare of faddish interest was dying.[21]

In a series of articles entitled, "Los Angeles's Answer to Bigotry," the *Los Angeles Examiner* was more optimistic. It reported:

> The wartime "zoot-suit" riots in Los Angeles sent such a huge counter-army of community organizations into the field to prevent further disorders that by 1946 they were stumbling all over each other. They overlapped in services, duplicated one another's work, and sapped their effectiveness by adding to the general confusion. The Welfare Planning Council, stepping in to find out how to bring order out of these well-meaning but chaotic efforts, found in a survey there were no less than fifty agencies working in the field of community relations. In 1947 the Welfare Planning Council invited these organizations . . . to coordinate activities.[22]

The affiliation of these organizations produced the Community Relations Conference of Southern California, which has continued to serve the Los Angeles area. Accomplishments of the conference in the years following the zoot-suit riots included the negotiated end of racial segregation in public housing projects, a part in ending racial segregation policies of the Los Angeles City Fire Department, and assisting the Police Department to establish a human relations course.

Among the conference's early member organizations was a Mexican political action group, the Community Service Organization, which had its beginnings in the riots in 1943. José Antonio Villarreal wrote that he joined the group when a "touch of conscience began to work on the educated Mexican who had made the transition and joined the main-stream of his society. Lawyers and teachers and businessmen of Mexican descent began to make demands upon the authorities, to formulate plans for the emancipation of a people."[23]

Of deeper significance than the committees which came out of the riots was the beginning self-understanding of individual young people of Mexican descent. Although it has been a slow and private conceptualization which may not properly be regarded as the aftermath of any one event, it is related to the trauma of the zoot-suit years. The trauma has gone deeper than the beatings and harassments of the mobs in 1942 and 1943. It included the animosity and rejection by the Mexican community of the pachucos who had presented it with an irreducible dilemma. To defend the youths was to affirm the racial over the superficial causes of the violence. It meant opposing both the explanations and the remedies offered by the Anglos and, in fact, to contend with the whole community including the police. To sympathize with the pachucos required a reconciliation the older generation of Mexicans was not prepared to make. Yet, to deny them was to deny that prejudice and discrimination existed which might justify their revolt. The Mexican press attempted a middle way by rejecting *pachuquismo* and treating the mob violence as abstractly as possible.

The leading Spanish-language newspaper in Los Angeles, *La Opinión,* warned the Mexican-American community that wrongdoers would incite the mobs of servicemen to continue invasions of the barrios. By wrong-doers the paper meant pachucos. It warned that few would escape the wrath of the sailors. Idlers would be beaten, "y pagaron justos por pecadores," the just would pay for the misdeeds of the guilty.[24]

A member of the district attorney's staff said of *La Opinión:*

> I don't think you will find any criticism in that newspaper of the prosecution or of the police or the sheriff in regard to that case [the Sleepy Lagoon trial], or any similar case. You'll find the better elements in the community, both Mexican, colored and white, all believe in law enforcement with respect to those matters. But this group of radicals. . . .[25]

The "radicals," the members of the Sleepy Lagoon Defense Committee, presented in their attempts to gain public support a picture of the pachucos which contrasted strikingly with the picture in the Mexican press. Guy Endore, the committee's chief propagandist, wrote:

> These were nothing more than neighborhood gangs of frolicsome kids. Their escapades were always on Saturday night, pay-day night, for they

were hard workers the rest of the week. There was no leader, no membership, nothing of the sort. These boys and girls simply lived near each other, knew each other, liked each other, and hung around together.[26]

The pachucos themselves, in retrospect, describe still another picture. Gabe Villaseñor recalled in 1954 that:

> We were kids, anxious to be wanted but we just couldn't make the grade. We were openly discriminated against in public swimming pools. There were no recreational facilities to speak of. We could only raise hell in the streets. Gangs gave us a feeling of being tough, of not caring what the adults thought of us. I don't want to defend what we did. It was bad. But the police didn't help any. They were unnecessarily cruel with us. I think the newspaper headlines helped incite public opinion against us, too. We felt rejected and wanted revenge.[27]

The largest of the gangs on the outskirts of the east side was the Clanton–14th Street, composed of about eighty boys. Tony Chávez, a leader of the Clantons during the riots, recalled, "I was scared all the time, but I had to keep up a front. I could not let down. When I faced myself alone at night, I felt horrible. But I liked the power I had. I couldn't let go."[28]

Mike Durán, a deputy probation officer and once a zoot-suiter, said of the riots, "I wish I could close my mind on it, the senseless fighting, the constant insecurity and guilty feelings unless I was with the gang. I had great resentment, but it was a resentment I couldn't define."[29]

The Mexican-American youths who did not become zoot-suiters also suffered deep frustrations. Raúl Morín, who spent the war years in the army, wrote in his chronicle, *Among the Valiant,* of "the constant struggle to make our Anglo neighbors see and realize that we were no longer the stereotype Mexican they had always pictured us to be. . . . We were placed in the categories of cheap laborers, thriftless, lazy, unorganized, lacking in leadership, unkempt, and uneducated."[30]

To Carey McWilliams, looking back over the nationwide changes in attitudes which occurred in the 1940s, it seemed that, "within the last decade, the whole mythology of race as a determinant of culture has been demolished with interacting and far-reaching consequences. . . . Even those who advocate white supremacy are today aware of the fact that they speak as poets of hatred and not as scientists."[31]

The fact that they spoke as "poets of hatred" did not, however, prevent the racists from continuing to speak in Los Angeles. They were heard from after the "Bloody Christmas" of 1951, when seven Mexican-American youths were beaten by police officers in Lincoln

Heights jail. They were heard from in the *Los Angeles Times* in 1953, exactly ten years after the zoot-suit riots, in a series of articles following the killing of a businessman during a gang fight in downtown Los Angeles. The headline reads, "5000 L.A. Hoodlums Belong to Violence-Dealing Gangs." The writer relied on his readers to know that these gang members were all Mexicans. He doesn't state it until the sixth paragraph. The article goes on, "Anyone who has driven around Los Angeles streets at night has seen the gangs. They're the groups of laughing, joking boys who hang around the hot dog stands and street corners, just standing around. . . . They don't look vicious, particularly, and they don't act vicious, particularly. But anyone who doesn't think they can become killers without batting an eye is just kidding himself. It happens all the time. . . ."[32]

Notes

1. *Report of the Joint Fact-Finding Committee on Un-American Activities in California* (Sacramento: State of California, 1943), p. 5.
2. *Ibid.*, pp. 52–53.
3. Fred N. Howser, district attorney, "Report on Juvenile Delinquency in Wartime Los Angeles," mimeographed (Los Angeles: County of Los Angeles, 1943), p. 3.
4. Agnes Pallen, "Mexicans in Los Angeles," *Los Angeles Times*, May 3, 1925, in *Los Angeles Clippings*, Vol. 3 (compiled by staff, USC Library), items 43–44.
5. Elizabeth Fuller, *The Mexican Housing Problem in Los Angeles*, Studies in Sociology Monograph No. 17 (Los Angeles: University of Southern California Press, 1920), p. 1.
6. Emory S. Bogardus, *The Mexicans in the United States*, School of Research Studies No. 5 (Los Angeles: University of Southern California Press, 1934), p. 53.
7. Ruth D. Tuck, *Not with the Fist: Mexican-Americans in a Southwest City* (New York: Harcourt Brace and Co., 1946), p. 213.
8. Bogardus, *Mexicans in the United States*, p. 56.
9. Beatrice Griffith, "Who Are the *Pachucos*?" *Pacific Spectator* (Summer 1947), p. 355.
10. "Summary of Recommendation and Progress to Date of the Special Committee on Older Gang Youth Activity in Los Angeles and Vicinity," in *Final Report of the Los Angeles County Grand Jury, 1942*, p. 48.
11. Joseph F. Reed, administrative assistant, to C. B. Horrall, chief of police, Los Angeles, August 12, 1942, quoted in Carey McWilliams, *North from Mexico: The Spanish-Speaking People of the United States* (New York: Monthly Review Press, 1961), pp. 235-36.
12. McWilliams, *North from Mexico*, p. 250.
13. *Report of the Joint Fact-Finding Committee on Un-American Activities in California* (Sacramento: State of California, 1945), p. 172.
14. *Ibid.*, p. 160.
15. McWilliams, *North from Mexico*, p. 232.
16. Carey McWilliams, "Testimony Before the Committee," in *Report . . . Un-American Activities . . .* , 1945, p. 194.
17. California Peace Officers Association, "Report of the State Conference, Fresno, October, 1940," in *Report . . . Un-American Activities . . .*, 1945, pp. 92–93.
18. C. B. Horrall, "Testimony Before the Committee," in *Report . . . Un-American Activities . . .* , 1945, p. 161.

19. McWilliams, *North from Mexico*, pp. 249–250.
20. *Ibid.*, p. 256.
21. Ignacio L. López, introducing Ruth D. Tuck, *Not with the Fist*, p. vii.
22. *Los Angeles Examiner*, "Let-Live Policy Wins," Feb. 22, 1960, reprinted in *Los Angeles' Answer to Bigotry* (Los Angeles: *Los Angeles Examiner*, 1960), p. 5.
23. José Antonio Villarreal, "Mexican-Americans in Upheaval," *West Magazine, Los Angeles Times*, September 18, 1966, p. 22.
24. "Alarma en el Barrio Mexicano," *La Opinión*, June 6, 1943, p. 1.
25. Clyde Shoemaker, "Testimony Before the Committee," in *Report . . . Un-American Activities . . . , 1945*, p. 181.
26. Guy Endore, *The Sleepy Lagoon Mystery* (Los Angeles, Sleepy Lagoon Defense Committee, 1944), p. 14.
27. Marina Mireles, "The Zoot-Suit Era: From Gangs to Respectability," *Herald-Examiner*, April 20, 1954.
28. *Ibid.*
29. Mireles, "The Zoot-Suit Era."
30. Raul Morín, *Among the Valiant* (Alhambra, Calif.: Borden Publishing Co., 1966), p. 23.
31. Carey McWilliams, *Brothers under the Skin* (Boston: Little, Brown & Co., 1964), p. 13.
32. Bob Will, "5000 L.A. Hoodlums Belong to Violence-Dealing Gangs," *Los Angeles Times*, December 17, 1953.

Chapter Five

The Postwar Years: Two Quiet Decades?

Despite the disillusionment that some Mexican-Americans felt during and after World War II, they received undreamed benefits from it. They had become Americanized by being in the services or by working alongside Anglos. They had received the G.I. Bill of Rights and could receive either an education or on-the-job training. Unfortunately, the Mexican-Americans, despite their excellent war records, were unable to take full advantage of the new opportunities offered them. Whether because it was too great a step for them to make, because of their previous positions in life or because there still existed a virulent anti-Mexican prejudice among the older Anglo "establishment" that did not see service, the Mexican-Americans of the postwar decade did not make any great strides in achieving positions of leadership in the Anglo world.

Manuel Servín, who feels that the postwar period offered previously undreamed benefits, is somewhat critical of his own generation—a nonachieving generation. In his article, "The Post–World War II Mexican-Americans, 1925–65: A Nonachieving Minority," he compares the achievements of the pre–World War II generations with those of the postwar period. Servín's findings and conclusions, which may be overly critical, are not sympathetic to his own generation.

Kaye Briegel, an authority on the history of Mexican-American political organizations, presents a viewpoint somewhat opposed to Servín's thesis. Briegel in her study, "Alianza Hispano-Americana and Some Mexican-American Civil Rights Cases in the 1950s," cogently demonstrates that the postwar generation did achieve some notable success in the area of civil rights.

The Post–World War II Mexican-Americans, 1925–65: A Nonachieving Minority*

Manuel P. Servín

The Mexican-American resident in the United States constitutes this nation's most unique, if not mystifying, minority group. Descendant of the aboriginal American inhabitants and of the first European settlers in the New World, the Mexican-American, despite the fact that he preponderantly lives in areas that were wrested from him, has until the recent war years been considered not an American but a foreigner. This fact has been so evident that even European immigrants, whose accents patently reveal their very recent arrival in the United States, did not hesitate to regard the Mexican-American not as an American but as a Mexican, whom they considered less American than themselves.

That such an attitude should prevail is clearly understandable to those possessing a historical insight to early Anglo-Mexican relations. Incredible as it may seem, the Mexicans became a minority group not when they immigrated to the North American republic, but rather when the North Americans migrated to Mexican Texas and California, finding a very poor class of settler. Consequently, despite his residence on his own national soil, it was the Mexican who became the backward, somewhat unassimilable foreigner.

This attitude toward Mexicans, particularly in Texas, was further intensified by the Texas and the Mexican wars. With the few exceptions of the *ricos* who passed themselves off as Spaniards, Mexicans truly became a minority group in the worst sense of the word. Generally despised in Texas, dispossessed of his lands in California, and denied his racial heritage in New Mexico, he lacked an acknowledged Mexican aristocracy—social, economic, and clerical—which would visibly prove to him that he was capable of achieving success and status.

The plight of Mexicans in the United States, however, did not reach its lowest depth with the Texas and Mexican wars. Notwithstanding Mexican treachery at Goliad, cruelty at San Antonio, and lack of bravery at San Jacinto, Santa Fe, and Monterey, the image

*This essay was originally delivered at the Annual Conference of the Western History Association on October 15, 1965, at Helena, Montana. A slightly revised first section, "The Pre–World War II Mexican-American: An Interpretation," appeared in *California Historical Society Quarterly* 45 (December, 1966).

of Mexicans was to be even further denigrated. The discovery of gold in California attracted an even less cultured Mexican—the *Norteño* [Northern Mexican] or Sonoran—than even the early settlers of New Mexico, Texas, and California. Little Mexicos, called "Sonora towns," sprouted throughout the gold routes of the Southwest and California. These towns and their residents represented the least civilized and least urbane element of Mexico.[1] The towns were far from rivalling Querétaro, León, or San Miguel de Allende—that is, far from being centers of culture, virtue, art. Sonora towns were, as Los Angeles was, a home for thieves, murderers, and unappetizing *putas* (prostitutes).[2] Consequently, while some of the less puritanical gringos enjoyed the life of this somewhat depraved but enjoyable minority, such was not the case with the majority of the Americans. This was especially true after the opening, in the 1880s, of the southern transcontinental railroad lines which transported the hordes of solid, but perhaps sanctimonious and prosaic, midwesterners to California, Arizona, and Texas.

The decades that followed the North-Americanization of the Southwest and that preceded the early-twentieth-century wave of Mexican immigration are in a historical sense extremely quiet concerning North American and Mexican-American relations. Perhaps it would not be too rash to surmise that the Mexican-American of this period generally resigned himself to a fate that previous historical events had cast upon him. He was, at least in the eyes of the North American, an inferior being, a half-breed, if not a *coyote* [no-good]; he was unassimilable, especially if he was dark-skinned; he was treacherous; he was cowardly; he was lazy; and thus he was not an American but a Mexican whose lot was to exist in poverty, subservience, and isolation.

That such was the fate of Mexicans after the 1880s is attested to by the treatment of the Mexican immigrant who arrived in the United States after the fall of Don Porfirio Díaz (May 1911). Unfortunately for this new immigrant, he was neither prepared for the treatment that he would receive nor would he be able to understand the reasons for it. Because of the great changes, relative progress, and social and political stability imposed upon Mexico by the benevolent dictator Don Porfirio Díaz, the twentieth-century Mexican immigrant was a different person than his early predecessor in the borderlands. He was far from lawless—Díaz's *rurales* [rural police] had created respect for law and order. He was not the idle, lazy greaser so eloquently characterized by early American writers—he had been oppressed in peonage for much too lengthy a period. Generally speaking, he was a moral and religious man—

almost without exception he had emigrated from the highly religious areas of Mexico. Finally, he was meek and submissive—Díaz's policy of *pan ó palo* [bread or the club] had been effective.

It was this humble and meek person who arrived in great numbers beginning in 1901. His increasing immigration reflected the chaotic condition of revolutionary Mexico and the North American need of cheap labor. Thus in 1901–10 over ninety-three thousand Mexicans legally entered the United States; in 1911–14, approximately seventy-seven thousand; in the war years of 1915–19, about one hundred and thirty-seven thousand; in 1920–24, over one hundred and thirty-five thousand; and in 1925–30, just under one hundred and nine thousand.[3] By 1930 about six hundred and seventeen thousand Mexicans had entered the United States legally, constituting almost one half of the Mexican population in the nation.[4] Actually, however, it is quite safe to state that if the illegal entrants—the predecessors of the wetbacks and fence-climbers—were taken into account, the majority of the Mexicans then residing in the United States were foreign-born.[5] And, perhaps even more significant than the number of foreign-born Mexicans, is the sound evidence that they were not predominantly a rural group (as is often asserted) but were in the majority emigrants from urban and semiurban areas.

This wave of legal and illegal Mexican immigration, plus the birth rate of Mexicans in the early Spanish borderland, swelled the total 1930 Mexican population in the United States to just under one and a half million.[6] Although Mexicans migrated in some numbers to such states as Michigan, Illinois, Kansas, and Indiana, it was in the Southwest, the former Mexican territory, that the overwhelming majority—some one and a quarter million—settled.[7] By 1930, Texas, long reputed among Mexicans as the most racially bigoted state, had the largest Mexican population, some six hundred and eighty-three thousand; California had approximately three hundred and sixty thousand; New Mexico, at least two hundred thousand (although only fifty-nine thousand of these throwbacks to colonial times confessed to being Mexican to the census takers); Arizona hosted just over one hundred and ten thousand; and Colorado, about fifty-seven thousand.[8]

Contemporary materials on the life of the early-twentieth-century Mexican, particularly of the poor, ignorant, docile immigrant, are sparse. Had it not been for foresight and imagination of Professors Paul S. Taylor and Emory S. Bogardus, of the Universities of California and Southern California, respectively, little would have been written of his ignominious suffering. It is basically from their works (particularly those of Taylor), from the interviewing of immigrants of the period, and from my boyhood recollections that the following brief picture of the plight of the pre–World War II Mexican has been reconstructed.

The panoramic view of early-twentieth-century Mexicans is an interesting, and compared with that of the post–World War II Mexican-American, a more respectable one. Arriving in poverty, unable to speak English, and inheriting the anti-Mexican prejudice engendered decades before, he was definitely at a disadvantage and greatly in need of help. Unfortunately, such help was not given, particularly by the groups from which Mexicans expected aid. The Spanish-speaking aristocracy—old Mexicans who disguised their heritage under such euphemisms as Californios, Spanish-Americans, and Hispanos—not only ignored but apparently despised the immigrant.[9] The Roman Catholic church, aside from building churches and stationing refugee Mexican priests in Spanish-speaking parishes, did little to aid materially or socially.[10] Paradoxically, it was certain Protestant churches, especially the Methodist, that appeared to be most cognizant of the plight of the immigrant.[11] It is therefore not strange that bitterness toward the Spanish-speaking aristocracy and some antipathy toward the church should have developed—a bitterness that characterized the "aristocracy" as *una junta de cabrones* [a bunch of bastards] and resulted in the conversion of many Mexicans to Protestantism.

Unaided by their own groups and unable to obtain work in their previous occupations, Mexicans were forced to take the lowest-paying jobs as well as the hardest work. In the agricultural areas of Texas, Colorado, and California they became neglected, underpaid, exploited migratory farm workers. In the north-central areas of the nation they performed various forms of low-paid, unskilled labor. In the Chicago and Calumet area, for example, they worked in the railroad sections and in the meat-packing plants. In Minnesota they worked in the sugar beet industry. And, in the area of Bethlehem, Pennsylvania, they became unskilled steel workers. Thus were the Mexicans consciously relegated to the lowest working positions.[12] Perhaps the classical example of this policy was best expressed by an executive in the Chicago and Calumet area who bluntly stated the hiring policy found in the area. "We use Mexicans. We have more refined work and have not had to resort to greasers. They use them for rough work and around blast furnaces."[13]

But regardless of the demeaning nature of the work which they were assigned, the Mexicans, according to conflicting testimony, appear to have been good but not excellent workers. Preferred in

California and Texas as farm laborers, the Mexicans—despite the remarks of California's brilliant Irish-surnamed Senator [Murphy]—did not merit this preference because they were built closer to the ground and possessed a physical advantage. The preference was simply economic: they were unorganized, apparently docile, and did not demand decent wages and living conditions.[14] In the industrial areas their record, as in the farming areas, was respectable. The reports compared them favorably with the Slovaks, Wends, Negroes, and Irish, both on the farms and in the plants.[15] Perhaps the most favorable report on the Mexicans' work occurred in Bethlehem, Pennsylvania, when Taylor interviewed a number of executives, one of whom stated that he

> rated the Mexicans as equals or possibly the superior of the two important groups of Europeans available for the same work: "The Mexicans are a good class of men as a whole; the majority are good steady workers. As a class their intelligence is above the Slavish (Slovaks) and Wendish. They are a bright, keen race, and good workers." And in response to my [Taylor's] observation that in other localities some persons regard Mexicans as possessing low intelligence, he added, "If some people think the Mexicans are dumb, they should see some of our Irish. . . ."[16]

Notwithstanding the Mexicans' at least average work record, they, along with the Negroes, were the lowest paid of the workers, both on the farms and in the plants. Unlike the Japanese, who were disliked by their fellow workers because of their industriousness and efficiency, Mexicans were unacceptable to their co-workers for a number of reasons. The most generally cited were that they lowered wages and weakened union organization.[17] But the racial differences, the dark skin, unhygienic appearance, and quaint dress habits appear to be, at least to me, the more basic reasons. Following a pattern that was almost identical to the well-known segregation that existed in Arizona, California, and Texas, Mexicans had difficulty renting in the Chicago area's better neighborhoods. The litany of such forced segregation makes interesting but sad reading:

> The principal colony of Mexicans near the stockyards is located on the west side. The fact that its development was checked on the east side, where the Mexicans appeared first, and subsequently stimulated on the west side was attributed by local residents chiefly to the resistance of the Irish (including the second generation) living on the east side. . . .[18]
>
> The movement of Mexicans west of the yards was also opposed. There they encountered violent attacks of the Poles. . . . The Poles and Lithuanians . . . declined to rent to Mexicans in their well-established neighborhood. . . .[19]
>
> In South Chicago a good deal of hostility was manifested toward Mexican neighbors, especially when they sought to move out from the

> more restricted and poorer locality which they occupied, largely among Negroes. An old resident, a German, found the Mexicans satisfactory neighbors. . . . But others, particularly young Poles, probably American-born, expressed vigorous complaints. . . .[20]

The low wages received by Mexicans, regardless of area, plus cultural and racial discrimination, of course had a very essential influence upon their living conditions. While Texas has always possessed among both Mexicans and dogmatic liberals the worst reputation for oppressing Mexicans and for retaining them in the lowest substandard living conditions, it is my judgment—as a person who was born and has traveled in Texas, attended school in New Mexico, journeyed extensively through Arizona, and was reared in California—that the living conditions, with some very few exceptions in New Mexico, were equally as poor in utopian California as in Texas, Arizona, and other areas.[21]

Southern California, whose record for indiscriminate, hypocritical discrimination is difficult to excel, possessed perhaps the Southwest's most blatant contrast in living conditions between the white North American and the Indian-Spanish Mexican. Few Mexican barrios could compete in poverty with that of Maravilla Park in Los Angeles where two and sometimes three shacks built of scrap lumber, old boxes, and other salvage were erected on one small lot; where there were forty houses to a city block; where the average family income in 1928 was seven hundred and ninety-five dollars; where almost all workers were unskilled laborers; and where out of 317 houses only 10 had cesspools connected with flush toilets.[22]

But in reality Maravilla Park was not an exception in California. Similar living conditions could be found in El Centro, San Fernando, and the outskirts of Montebello, Whittier, and El Monte—and, incidentally, in various cities of the San Joaquin Valley, even today.[23]

Actually, such poverty was not unknown to the Mexican in his home country, and would not be a great source of unhappiness. What did strike the Mexican was the irrational prejudice and disdain that he encountered. In many areas he could not eat in the same restaurants with the American, nor could he swim in the same pools. In other areas he could not attend the same theatres or, if allowed to do so, he would have to sit in a segregated area. Naturally, the Mexican generally had to attend segregated schools and churches; but this segregation, similar to his living among his own people, did not seem to bother him—perhaps he inwardly considered himself equal or even superior to the Americans in some areas.[24]

Yet despite all the disheartening and degrading conditions that he encountered, the pre–World War II Mexican not only maintained a good record but made certain remarkable achievements.

Although he inherited the poor reputation for crime from the early Mexican settlers, his crime record, basing it on random examples, was not outstandingly bad.[25] In the Chicago and Calumet area, a two-year survey, 1928–29, revealed that 1.4 percent of all persons arrested were of Mexican nativity, while the Mexican population constituted only .57 percent of the total population.[26] In Los Angeles City the 1927–28 percentage of Mexican arrests—revealing narcotics (probably marihuana), drunkenness, and vagrancy as the raising element—amounted to 17.5, while the Mexican population of the city was slightly over 10 percent.[27] In California's Imperial Valley, an important farming area, where Mexicans in 1925 were supposed to be responsible for 75 percent of all crimes, it was authoritatively found that they were responsible for only one fourth, while they constituted approximately one third of the population.[28] Thus, seeing that the rural crime rate was less in proportion to that of the urban, one might conjecture (perhaps somewhat dangerously) that since the Mexican population in the United States was almost equally divided between rural and urban, its crime rate was in proportion to, or even lower than, its total population.

A similar picture is found in California regarding juvenile delinquency—a reflection of family life. In Los Angeles County in 1928, 19 percent of the Mexican boys and 28 percent of the Mexican girls were on probation—figures which were far above the Mexicans' estimated 11 percent of the total population.[29] Yet in the Imperial Valley the picture was reversed. The percentage of Mexican children involved in juvenile court was proportionately much less than the total Mexican population, and incidentally also less than that of old North American stock.[30]

Besides possessing rather good work records and not bad adult and juvenile crime rates, Mexicans also possessed fairly good records in marital relations and relief. Insofar as married life was concerned, there is no doubt that their divorce rate was less than that of either Negroes or whites.[31] Mexicans' public relief record, based upon statistics of California—the nation's most magnanimous, or perhaps most foolish, state—was not quite as good, but it was below their proportional maximum. Despite unfavorable relief records in Los Angeles, Orange, and Riverside counties, and despite the low and seasonal wages they were paid, it is evident from Governor C. C. Young's 1930 report that Mexicans in California were not only not a burden on the state but that they did not receive a just proportion of relief funds.[32] That such seems to have been the case throughout the nation appears most plausible from the report of the Governor's Interracial Commission in Minnesota and from the Mexicans' practice of organizing societies for helping each other financially and otherwise.[33]

Undoubtedly the Mexican's area of least success and greatest failure was in obtaining an education. Coming from a culture that did not prize mass education, finding it necessary to put even his elementary-school-age children to work, and perhaps feeling frustratedly that an education would not help him overcome the prejudices and disdainful treatment he received throughout the Southwest, the Mexican failed drastically to take advantage of the educational opportunities opened to him. Of all the groups listed in the United States census of 1930, he had the lowest percentage of school attendance—a factor of course that in the long run militated and still militates against him and his future advancement.[34]

Yet despite the prewar Mexican's lack of educational interest, language barrier, and racial and cultural prejudice, he made some formidable breakthroughs in addition to changing gradually his portrait in the areas of work, crime, family life, and relief. Unlike some other persecuted minorities, he established a good, culturally conscious press, as exemplified by *La Opinión*. He broke into the motion pictures and produced respectable and respected stars such as Ramón Novarro, Dolores del Río, and Gilbert Roland. In the East he yielded such distinguished professional men as Harold Medina, the jurist, and Alonso E. Escalante, American Maryknoll missionary bishop for Mexico. In crime, he at least showed some ability to "think big" as exemplified in the case of the fugitive Los Angeles police lieutenant, Peter Del Gado.[35] In music he developed popular crooners such as Andy Russell and more serious singers as José Mojica and Tito Guízar. And in higher education he came forth with such academic limelights as historian Carlos Eduardo Castañeda and educationist George Isidore Sánchez, both from the University of Texas.

Breakthroughs into North American life were not, however, the only achievement of the prewar Mexican. He also made some contributions to United States culture—and I do not mean just the adding of tacos, tamales, and margaritas to the North American diet. He contributed, as Henry López's interview with Katherine Anne Porter in *Harper's Magazine* indicates, an incentive for enriching American letters.[36]

The era of the pre–World War II Mexican in the United States came to an end with opening of hostilities late in 1941 and early in 1942. The young Mexican of the postwar period was in secondary or elementary school—that is, the young Mexican-descended person who was born after 1925 or 1926—encountered entirely different social and economic conditions than his predecessors had. He now became an American, though a hyphenated one. Jobs previously denied to his ethnic group were open to him. Positions of authority, previously unattainable, were much more within his grasp. He could also swim in the same pools and eat in the same restaurants with North Americans. Furthermore, the war made it possible, at least for the older Mexican-Americans, to obtain a college education as the result of the GI Bill of Rights.[37]

Unfortunately, a minority of the postwar Mexican-Americans, the pachucos or zoot-suiters, reacted in a most un-Mexican-like manner. Dressed outlandishly, as they followed the styles of less acceptable minorities, they quickly undid the hard-earned reputation of prewar Mexicans. Despite the pious lamentations of social workers, the pachucos in a rat-pack manner attacked United States servicemen and, regardless of justification or guilt, gave the Mexican community—which incidentally condemned them as much as did the North American—an undeserved reputation for lawlessness, cowardice, and disloyalty.[38] As a result, the heroic service of the Mexican-Americans in the Philippines as well as the outstanding bravery of the proportionately numerous Medal of Honor winners were ignored by the North American whites and blacks.[39]

It has been over a score of years since the zoot-suit riots, a quarter of a century since opportunities somewhat opened up with World War II, and forty years since the first of the postwar Mexican-Americans were born. In this period—admittedly a period too brief to make any definitive judgments, but definitely long enough to give evidence of progress or regression—the post–World War II Mexican-Americans have been a nonachieving minority.

In education, where his legacy and language barrier have placed him at a great disadvantage, the Mexican-American has the poorest record of all minority groups recorded in the 1960 United States census. For instance, in the Southwest the median number of years in school for Mexican-American males is 8.1, but 8.3 for Negroes and Filipinos; and, to make the situation even worse, the achievement rate of the Mexican youth appears, at least to some educators, to be declining.[40] Whatever may be the reasons for this lack of achievement, it is this writer's belief that the Mexican-American cannot entirely blame the North American community for his lack of achievement in this area. Certainly, the Mexican-American, despite whatever discrimination there may exist, does not suffer from the same extreme racial and caste disadvantages that the Negroes and the Filipinos endure.

But a more disturbing educational and professional situation is the one that concerns the Mexican educator and professional man. Admittedly, there are more persons of Mexican descent in professional positions now than prior to the war, but this increase is found mostly in the fields of less prestige, such as elementary and secondary teaching, social work, and real estate work. In the prestige areas, however—the fields of relatively difficult entrance such as medicine, dentistry, engineering, science, and college instruction—the numbers are indeed few, and far out of proportion to the total population. A case in point: there are only a few more Mexican-descended college history instructors today than there were in the 1930s. And, if I may be honest, they are not in the same class as the older group. Much as I have searched books, records, and minds, I fail to find any post–World War II Mexican-American professor of the caliber of a Carlos Castañeda or George I. Sánchez.[41]

This lack of excellence pervades not only higher education, where many instructors waste more time in political activity than in scholarly endeavor, but also other fields. There are for instance few Mexican-American lawyers like Raúl Magaña who merit the respect and admiration of their fellow lawyers.[42] While the medical men appear to have a sound, solid training, outstanding men with Spanish-sounding names are indeed difficult to identify. In regard to science the situation is of course greatly aggravated—a situation attributable to our nonscientific culture.

More depressing than the lack of outstanding men in the lucrative professions is the absence of outstanding personalities in fields where Mexicans in New Spain and in Mexico have had, and have, a heritage of distinguished achievement. In religion, for example, renowned Mexican-American priests are a rarity. There is, as far as I have been able to determine, not one Mexican-American Roman Catholic bishop, not even an auxiliary bishop, in the United States.[43] While it is true that the Irish-Americans have unhumbly latched onto ecclesiastical offices, this is in my opinion an insufficient reason for lack of achievement in this area where Mexico is now producing scholarly and saintly priests, who, in my observation, are in many cases superior to the North American clergy.

A similar situation exists in the arts, both plastic and musical. With the exception of Joan Baez, the ballad musician, and Trini López, the teen-age idol and singer—a far cry from a Carlos Chávez or Agustín Lara—Mexican-American musicians have not risen above mediocrity. Accentuating the problems in this area is the fact that no Mexican-American music has developed or even appears to be developing. Perhaps a reason for this lack of development is the proximity of Mexico and authentic Mexican musicians, but it should be noted that this propinquity has not inhibited the development of a Mexican-American patois.

While it is easier to accept and to explain the lack of Mexican-American achievement in the professions and the arts, where excellence plays an important role, it is difficult to understand the political failure of the Mexicans. With a population of some three and a half million in the Southwest, the Mexican-Americans outnumber the Negroes but have not capitalized on the opportunities offered in this area where mediocrity is far from a disadvantage. Presently possessing one United States senator and two United States congressmen, the Mexicans, outside of New Mexico, are grossly underrepresented and flagrantly ignored in political appointments. In California in 1964 they had one congressman, one state legislator, three superior court (county) judges, two persons in the attorney general's staff, and at least three city mayors. Curiously the most significant appointments are in the Department of Education whose director, Max Rafferty, has proved to be more understanding than is the liberal Democratic administration.[44] In Texas the Mexicans are better represented. In 1961 they had four members of the United States House of Representatives, two superior court judges, and at least five mayors of cities—one of whom governs the important city of El Paso with a population of two hundred and seventy-six thousand.[45] In Colorado, where the Mexican population is decreasing, the Mexican-Americans have virtually no representation at all.[46]

But if Mexican-American political organization and leadership has proved disillusioning, the behavior of the whole post–world war generation has been less than encouraging. It has become increasingly difficult to obtain noncomplimentary data on minority groups, but it can be logically conjectured that the crime rate of the postwar Mexican-American has increased. In California, a relatively unbiased state, his felon population in state prisons is 17.1 percent and in state camps 20.7 percent, far out of proportion to his total state population percentage of approximately 9.1.[47] A similarly disheartening but revealing datum is that about one half the "local Aid to Needy Children" caseload in the Los Angeles area is among Mexican-Americans in East Los Angeles.[48] It is quite evident from these limited data in the largest Mexican-American population center that the Mexican-American has not only failed to achieve but that in comparison with his predecessors of the 1910s, 1920s, and 1930s he has lost ground in the spiritual and dignified aspects of life.

Perhaps this loss of personal dignity could be somewhat overlooked had the Mexican-American made contrasting material gains.

Unfortunately, this has not been the case. Despite the large crime record among postwar Mexicans, there are no famous criminals, no Anastasias, O'Banions, or Siegels—there is no achievement. In a more serious vein, the Mexican-American, whose unemployment record in California for males is not too bad (7.7 percent compared to 5.5 percent for North Americans), certainly has not made a relative achievement in income; while in 1959 he received a median income of $3,849, the white obtained one of $5,109.[49] And according to my interpretation of the Los Angeles County 1960 Census Map of Family Income,[50] the predominantly Mexican neighborhood had a family income on the average of $1,000 less than that of the predominantly Negro sections, including the Watts area.

The picture that documentation has portrayed of the Mexican-American in the Southwest, particularly in California, is not a happy one. Whatever the causes of the lack of achievement may be, the basic fact of nonachievement cannot be denied. Perhaps it has been partially due to racial prejudice, perhaps to a general lessening of acquisitiveness among all North Americans, or to the decline in drive that is generally found among the children of immigrants. There is no doubt in my mind, however, that there was some truth in Hans Zinsser's autobiography (which I read as a twenty-year-old) when he stated, "give the Mexican a good home diet, cheaper beer, and tons of soap and flea powder, and we shall have a great, tranquil, and friendly neighbor." Perhaps this is what happened to the Mexican-American. He was happy. He was isolated and insulated. But he is changing. He has seen the Negro advance and surpass him. And he is seeing his blood-brothers in Mexico recognized and respected. Thus he sees that his Mexican-American culture has failed to give him the drive for such recognition and success. He is becoming aware of his status; he is developing leaders, particularly in the labor field;[51] and he is receiving help from his former tormentors—the North Americans. Perhaps the next score of years will reveal a picture of achievement similar to that of Mexico whose record for nonachievement was once much dimmer than that of the present-day Mexican-American.

Notes

1. Concerning the Sonorans see J. M. Guinn, "The Sonoran Migration," *Annual Publications of the Historical Society of Southern California* 8 (1909–1910): 30–36; Carey McWilliams, *Southern California Country* (New York, 1946), pp. 55–68.

2. An interesting description of Los Angeles is found in Robert Glass Cleland, *History of California: The American Period* (New York, 1922), pp. 312–322.

3. U.S. Bureau of Census, *Fifteenth Census of the United States, 1930: Population* 2 (Washington, D.C., 1933): 498.

4. *Ibid.*, pp. 25, 27, 405.

5. *Ibid.*

6. *Ibid.*, p. 27; Enrique Santibañez, *Ensayo acerca de la inmigración Mexicana en Los Estados Unidos* (San Antonio, 1930), pp. 47–48.

7. *1930 U.S. Census: Population* 2: ix, 35.

8. *Ibid.*

9. Of the various older Mexican immigrants I have interviewed, not one has had a kind word for the early Hispanic settler in California and the Southwest.

10. The Rev. Francis J. Weber, "His Excellency of Los Angeles: The Life and Times of the Most Reverend John J. Cantwell," manuscript in Archives of the Archdiocese of Los Angeles (Los Angeles, n.d.), pp. 96–103; "Notes: Outline of Protestant Proselytism in the United States," in Archives of the Archdiocese of Los Angeles (Los Angeles, 1945), pp. 1–8, 54–55, 66–82; Kathryn Cramp *et al.*, "A Study of the Mexican Population of Imperial Valley, California," manuscript in Bancroft Library, Berkeley, California (Berkeley, 1926), p. 23.

11. To obtain a true insight of the zeal and efforts of the Methodists in working with Mexicans of the period it is only necessary to read the *Minutes of the Southern California Conference of the Methodist Episcopal Church, 1879–1939*. For a very limited view into Methodist church activities see Edward Drewry Jervey, *The History of Methodism in Southern California and Arizona* (Los Angeles, 1960), pp. 90–100.

12. For the work the Mexican performed see Paul S. Taylor, *Mexican Labor in the United States*, published in the University of California Publications in Economics. Taylor's different studies utilized in this essay and cited individually are: *Mexican Labor in the United States; Imperial Valley* (Berkeley, 1928); *Mexican Labor in the United States; Valley of the South Platte, Colorado* (Berkeley, 1929); *Mexican Labor in the United States; Dimmit County, Winter Garden, South Texas* (Berkeley, 1930); *Mexican Labor in the United States; Bethlehem, Pennsylvania* (Berkeley, 1931); *Mexican Labor in the United States; Chicago and the Calumet Region* (Berkeley, 1932). Also see Kathryn Cramp *et al.*, "A Study of the Mexican Population in Imperial Valley"; Santibañez, *Ensayo acerca de la inmigración Mexicana en los Estados Unidos*, especially p. 53; The Governor's Interracial Commission, *The Mexican in Minnesota* (Minneapolis, 1953); and Carey McWilliams, *North from Mexico* (Philadelphia, 1949).

13. Taylor, *Mexican Labor; Chicago*, p. 80.

14. For a summary of Mexican attempts to unionize agriculturally in early 1900s see Federal Writers Project, "Organization Efforts of Mexican Agricultural Workers," manuscript, Bancroft Library (Oakland, 1939). For other areas see Cramp *et al.*, "A Study of Mexican Population in Imperial Valley," pp. 6–11; George L. Cady, *Report of Commission on International and Interracial Factors in the Problem of the Mexicans in the United States* (1926), pp. 11, 21; State of California, *Mexicans in California: Report of Governor C. C. Young's Mexican Fact-Finding Committee* (San Francisco, 1930), pp. 159–171, especially 171, and also pp. 123–150, 176–179; Sister De Prague Reilly, "The Role of the Churches in the Bracero Program in California (M.A. thesis, University of Southern California, 1969), p. 125.

15. Taylor, *Mexican Labor; Chicago*, pp. 77–80; Taylor, *Mexican Labor; Bethlehem*, pp. 13–14.

16. Taylor, *Mexican Labor; Bethlehem*, p. 13.

17. For examples see Taylor, *Mexican Labor; Chicago*, pp. 77–80.

18. *Ibid.*, p. 222.

19. *Ibid.*, pp. 222–223.

20. *Ibid.*, p. 224.

21. The information compiled by Cady, *Report of Commission on International and Interracial Factors in the Problem of the Mexicans in the United States*,.as well as Taylor's studies on Mexican labor in California, Texas, Colorado, Chicago, and Calumet, very definitely appear to bear out this writer's evaluation.

22. *Mexicans in California: Report of Governor C. C. Young's Mexican Fact-Finding Committee*, pp. 177–178. For an inclusive view of the poverty of Mexican communities in Chicago, Colorado, Texas, New Mexico, Arizona, and California

see W. Rex Crawford, "The Latin American in Wartime United States," *Annals of the American Academy of Political and Social Science* 223 (September 1942): 127.

23. *Mexicans in California*, pp. 178–179.

24. A fine example of almost complete segregation is contained in Cramp *et al.*, "A Study of the Mexican Population in Imperial Valley." A partial list of segregated living and school districts in California is found in *Mexicans in California*, pp. 176–177. Also see Bogardus, *The Mexican in the United States*, pp. 28–29, for an area in which the Mexican did not consider himself inferior to the North American.

25. Cady in his *Report of Commission on International and Interracial Factors* gives a fine example of pre–World War II exaggeration, p. 10.

26. Taylor, *Mexican Labor; Chicago*, p. 144.

27. *Mexicans in California*, pp. 203, 175.

28. Cramp, *et al.*, "A Study of the Mexican Population in Imperial Valley," p. 11.

29. *Mexicans in California*, p. 204.

30. Cramp, *et al.*, "A Study of the Mexican Population in Imperial Valley," pp. 10, 25.

31. *1930 U.S. Census: Population* 2: 842.

32. *Mexicans in California*, pp. 190, 195.

33. *The Mexicans in Minnesota*, pp. 44–45; Taylor, *Mexican Labor; Bethlehem*, p. 17; Taylor, *Mexican Labor; Chicago*, pp. 124, 128–129, 132–133; Cramp *et al.*, "A Study of the Mexican Population in Imperial Valley," pp. 13–14; interview with José M. Bravo, Los Angeles, September 11, 1965.

34. *1930 U.S. Census: Population* 2: 1094–1095; Pauline R. Kibbe, *Latin American in Texas* (Albuquerque, 1946), p. 92, a fine example of the frustration encountered by enthusiastic Mexican students.

35. Interview with Richard Rodríguez, Los Angeles, September 29, 1965.

36. Katherine Anne Porter, "A Country and Some People I Love: An Interview by Hank López," *Harper's Magazine* 231 (September 1965): 58–68.

37. For examples of the World War II's resulting emancipation see Ruth D. Tuck, *Not with the Fist: Mexican-Americans in a Southwest City* (New York, 1946), p. 198; Kibbe, *Latin Americans in Texas*, pp. 100, 105.

38. This writer has yet to find an older, pre–world War II Mexican or Mexican-American defending or offering an apology for the pachucos. The pachuco's viewpoint is cogently presented by Beatrice Griffith in *American Me* (Boston, 1948).

39. Raúl Morín, *Among the Valiant: Mexican-Americans in World War II and Korea* (Los Angeles, 1963), *passim*.

40. U.S. Bureau of Census, *United States Census, 1960: Persons of Spanish Surname*, p. 12; *United States Census, 1960: Nonwhite Population by Race*, p. 9; interview with Rudolph Acuña, Los Angeles, September, 1965.

41. Dorothy Hancock, ed., *Directory of American Scholars: A Biographical Directory. Volume 1, History* (New York: 1963), and *Volume 4, Philosophy, Religion, and Law* (New York, 1964).

42. Confidential interview with a United States district court judge, Los Angeles, September 8, 1965; interview with Rudolph Acuña, Los Angeles, September, 1965; *Martindale-Hubbell Law Directory*, 1: 489.

43. *The Official Catholic Directory, Anno Domini 1963* (New York, 1963), *The American Catholic Who's Who, 1966 and 1967* (Grosse Pointe, 1966), p. 123, names Bishop Alonso Escalante, but he is stationed in Mexico.

44. Frank M. Jordan, comp., *Roster of Federal, State, County, and City Officials, 1964 (Sacramento, 1964)*, pp. 1–26.

45. *Texas Almanac, 1961–1962* (Dallas, 1961), pp. 450–459, 399–403.

46. *The Book of the States: Supplement I, February 1965: State Elective Officials and the Legislatures* (Chicago, 1965), pp. 3, 24, 25.

47. State of California, Department of Corrections, "Characteristics of Felon Population in California State Prisons by Institution" (Sacramento, June 30, 1963). Also see the *Los Angeles Police Department 1963 Annual Report* (Los Angeles, 1964), pp. 18–19, for a comparison in the Negro, Mexican, and white precincts.

48. "Summary of Proceedings of the Southwest Conference: Social and Educational Problems of Rural and Urban Mexican American Youth," Occidental College, April 6, 1963, p. 59.

49. State of California, Department of Industrial Relations, *Californians of Spanish Surname* (San Francisco, 1964), p. 17.

50. These maps are produced by the Brewster Mapping Service, 5110 Huntington Dr. South, Los Angeles, California 90032.

51. "Mexican-American Labor Leaders—Los Angeles Area 1965," enclosed in Louis M. Bravo to Manuel P. Servín, La Puente, September 20, 1965.

Alianza Hispano-Americana and Some Mexican-American Civil Rights Cases in the 1950s*

Kaye Briegel

One of the most important events in United States history occurred in 1954 when the Supreme Court declared racial segregation in public schools to be illegal. This 1954 decision reversed an 1896 ruling of the Court that established the principle of Separate But Equal. Under the earlier decision, racial groups could be segregated in public facilities, including schools, if equal facilities were provided for all. In 1954, however, the Supreme Court ruled that Separate could never be Equal and that to restrict people to specified facilities because of their race deprived them of equal protection of the law. This equal protection is guaranteed by the Fourteenth Amendment to the United States Constitution.

It was also in 1954, in another case, that the Supreme Court found Mexican-Americans to be an identifiable ethnic group who have been systematically discriminated against in certain situations. This was the first case involving Mexican-Americans, as a group, to be decided by the Supreme Court.[1] Neither Mexican-Americans, in this case, nor blacks, who were involved in the other 1954 case, won their decisions without previously establishing a long record of protest against legal segregation.

Both of these 1954 decisions also required long years of preparation. The preparation included legal and social research as well as fighting related cases in lower courts. This preliminary struggle was supported by organized activities to raise money for legal expenses and to create a climate of favorable public opinion. In the 1954 decision against racial segregation in public schools, the support was provided by the National Association for the Advancement of

*This essay by Kaye Briegel, who is writing her doctoral dissertation on the Alianza Hispano-Americana at the University of Southern California, was written for publication in this anthology.

Colored People (NAACP). The 1954 decision concerning Mexican-Americans was supported by the American Council of Spanish-Speaking People. Another Mexican-American group who have been active in supporting these struggles for legal equality is the League of United Latin-American Citizens. The LULAC established a record of protest against legal segregation of Mexican-Americans beginning in the 1930s. None of the cases that they took to court, however, was decided in their favor.[2]

Probably the first case that was decided in favor of equal access to public facilities for Mexican-Americans concerned a swimming pool. The decision was announced in 1944, in a case initiated by Ignacio López. López was the editor of *El Espector,* a local San Bernardino, California, area newspaper. He was also a graduate of Chaffey Junior College, Pomona College, and the University of Southern California. Recently he had served as head of the Spanish Department in the Office of Foreign Languages, Division of War Information, in Washington, D.C., and as Spanish-speaking director of the Office of Coordinator of Inter-American Affairs in Los Angeles.[3]

Both of the agencies that employed López were active in promoting support for the United States in World War II. One of these employers, the Office of the Coordinator of Inter-American Affairs, was directed by Nelson Rockefeller and charged with organizing support for the war among Latin-Americans in this country and south of the border. Toward this goal, Rockefeller's office operated programs to integrate Mexican-Americans into United States society and to provide them with opportunities for advancement. Educational opportunities, for example, were made available including college scholarships.[4]

As director of the Los Angeles office, López ran these kinds of programs to encourage Mexican-Americans to support the war effort for Rockefeller's office. While he worked in the Division of War Information, he also participated in programs to organize ethnic minorities in the east into Liberty Leagues to support the war. Later, when López returned to San Bernardino, he began to organize similar groups, called Unity Leagues, among local Mexican-Americans. The purpose of these Unity Leagues, however, was to support the Mexican-Americans' struggle against discrimination. Even before the war, in the 1930s, as a local newspaper editor, López had been active in fighting discrimination against Mexican-Americans. He saw the Unity Leagues as a more effective way of continuing the struggle.[5]

After he began organizing these Unity Leagues, López received assistance from the American Council on Race Relations. The council sent an organizer, Fred Ross, to help expand the Unity Leagues' activities. The goal of these organizations was to increase political awareness among Mexican-Americans by encouraging them to become citizens, register to vote, and support Mexican-American candidates for local public offices. Using these organizations for support, López sought to fight discrimination in public accommodations in San Bernardino.[6]

Even before López began organizing the Unity Leagues, he had established a record of fighting discrimination against Mexican-Americans in public accommodations. In 1939 he brought about the integration of the swimming pool at Chaffey Junior College. Previously, the pool was integrated only while school was in session; Mexican-Americans and other students swam together as participants in the same classes. When the pool was open to the public, however, it was segregated; Mexican-Americans were allowed to use it only on Mondays. López's public protests in his newspaper resulted in a change in official policy and the opening of the Chaffey College swimming pool to everyone in the public whenever it was open to the public.[7]

In 1944, however, the tactics that López had previously found successful failed to secure the admission of Mexican-Americans to Perris Hill Plunge, San Bernardino's public swimming pool. López therefore took the case to court. He and others claimed that by being excluded from the pool they had been denied their constitutional right to equal protection of the law.[8] López was joined in his suit by the Rev. R. N. Núñez, a parish priest of Mexican descent at Guadalupe Church in San Bernardino, and by Eugenio Noguera, who was a San Bernardino editor and publisher, a veteran of service in the United States Army, and a Puerto Rican. These three were also joined in the suit by two students, Virginia Prado and Rafael Muñoz. Each of the petitioners said that he had been denied entrance to the swimming pool because he was of Latin-American descent.[9] The petitioners asked that the federal court enjoin the city of San Bernardino from continuing this practice of exclusion. The court complied on February 5, 1944. It ruled that the petitioners had been denied equal protection of the law as specified in the Fourteenth Amendment when they were excluded from the public swimming pool.[10]

The San Bernardino swimming pool case became a precedent for others involving Mexican-Americans and their attempts to end discrimination and segregation. Following this precedent, another case was taken to court two years later. This next case, however, involved school segregation. In February 1946 Gonzalo Méndez and some others sought an injunction in a federal court to restrain several Orange County, California, school districts from continuing to practice the segregation of Mexican-American children in their schools. Méndez, William Guzmán, Frank Palomino, Thomas Estrada, and Lorenzo Ramírez sued the school districts of Westminster, Garden Grove, El Modena, and Santa Ana.[11]

In reply to the suit, the school administrators of the districts involved explained their policies to the court. They claimed that Mexican-American children had to be segregated because of language difficulties. The Mexican-American children, they claimed, did not have sufficient command of the English language to be taught in the same classes with those who came from English-speaking homes. Segregation, for this reason, was necessary for an efficient school system serving all the children in the districts. The school officials failed, however, to show that any test other than nationality was applied to determine which children would be assigned to the Mexican school. None of the districts used standardized tests to measure language competence; they simply assigned children with Spanish surnames to the Mexican school.[12]

The evidence in this case clearly showed that Mexican-American children were segregated on the basis of nationality and that no other test was used. The federal court therefore ruled that the segregation must be ended.[13] This decision, which required the desegregation of four Orange County school districts, was appealed, but the ninth circuit court upheld it in April 1947. *Amici curiae* briefs (statements of information relative to the case) were filed, on the appeal, by an impressive list of organizations and people. They included

Thurgood Marshall, Robert Carter, and Loren Miller for the National Association for the Advancement of Colored People
Will Maslow, Pauli Murray, and Anne H. Pollock for the American Jewish Congress
Julien Cornell, Arthur Garfield Hays, Osmond K. Frankell, A. L. Wirin, and Fred Okrand for the American Civil Liberties Union
Charles Christopher for the National Lawyers Guild
A. L. Wirin and Saburo Kido for the Japanese-American Citizens League
Robert Kenney, attorney general of California, and T. A. Westphal, his deputy[14]

Despite the urging of some of these briefs, the court refused to regard the case as a test of the Separate But Equal principle. Some of the *amici curiae* briefs argued that this would be a good case with which to test that decision because it was admitted by the Mexican-Americans and their attorneys that the segregated schools their children attended were equal to those which served other children in these districts. The court, however, ruled that segregation was illegal in this case, not because Separate could never be Equal but because segregation of Mexican children was specifically prohibited in the California Education Code. Whatever the legal details, however, four Orange County school districts, as a result of the *Méndez* decision, were desegregated and Mexican-Americans won another battle against discrimination.[15]

After the precedents of *López* and *Méndez,* the Alianza Hispano-Americana took up the fight for desegregation of public facilities in 1951, following the example of the National Association for the Advancement of Colored People and the League of United Latin-American Citizens in supporting these legal struggles for equality.

Alianza Hispano-Americana may seem an unlikely organization to take up this struggle. It is a fraternal insurance society that was first organized in 1894 in Tucson, Arizona. The Alianza offers low-cost life insurance and social activities to its members, much as do other fraternal societies such as the Woodmen of the World, Ancient Order of United Workmen, and Sons of Norway. Although the Alianza's headquarters remained in Tucson, it soon organized local lodges in California, New Mexico, Texas, Colorado, Nevada, Wyoming, and Mexico. The Mexican and United States branches of the society separated, however, in 1938 when the United States lodges failed to conform to Mexican insurance laws. By 1950 the Alianza's membership, like that of many of its gringo counterparts, was slowly but steadily declining. This decline was a result of competition from other social activities and commercial insurance companies. In 1950, however, the society maintained almost twelve thousand members,[16] and even as late as 1968 the Alianza remained the best-known Mexican-American organization in Los Angeles.[17]

The Alianza was directed by conservative leaders in the 1930s and 1940s. However, in the 1920s the society's policies were less conservative toward existing American values. During this earlier period, articles appeared in the *Alianza* magazine protesting the portrayal of Mexicans in United States movies. In the movies, it was claimed, Mexicans always seemed to be less than honest and honorable people.[18] Also, in 1921, the supreme lodge took the apparently unprecedented action of asking the governor of California to commute the death sentence that had been given Aurelio Pompa.[19] This clearly was also a protest against the quality of justice available to people with Spanish surnames in the United States.

In the 1930s and 1940s, the Alianza's leaders were more concerned about internal conflicts and maintaining the society's solvency than reforming the larger society. In the 1950s, however, the Alianza's leaders again became concerned about the quality of justice available to Mexican-Americans. In 1951 the supreme executive council petitioned the governor of Arizona to grant a stay of execution to a convicted murderer, Angel Serna, until new evidence in his case could be presented in court.[20] This petition was only the first example of the Alianza's renewed interest in reform and in asserting the civil rights of Mexican-Americans.

The first civil rights action that Alianza attorneys officially entered in the 1950s was a school desegregation case in Tolleson, Arizona. Gregorio García, Alianza supreme president, and Ralph Estrada, the society's supreme attorney, went into federal court in Phoenix to represent Porfirio González, Fuastino Curiel, and their children in a suit against the Tolleson school district. The court ruled again, as it had in the *Méndez* case, against segregation. In this case, however, the decision was based on a different principle. In *Tolleson,* the court found that the schools assigned to Mexican-American children were demonstrably inferior to those provided for other children. The deficiency was not only in buildings but also in equipment and personnel. Again the segregation of Mexican-American children was ended, but this time in only one district.[21]

Also in 1950 an alliance was made among Estrada, López, and Gustavo García, an attorney from Texas. Included, in addition, were Bernardo Valdez of Colorado and Tibo Chávez, lieutenant governor of New Mexico. The organization was headed by George Sánchez, professor of education at the University of Texas and a leader in the Mexican-Americans' struggle for equality. Arturo Fuentes, the Alianza's new supreme president, was on the executive council. The aims of the new organization were

1. To eliminate segregation of Mexican-American students in those schools where such a practice still exists
2. To eliminate racial segregation in government housing
3. To increase participation of Mexican-Americans on juries and in public offices
4. To secure equal service in public facilities.
5. To end discrimination in the employment of Mexican-Americans in government agencies[22]

The alliance, called the American Council of Spanish-Speaking People, assisted the Alianza in its next school desegregation case. The council and the Marshall Trust Fund also provided financial support to the Alianza for the legal battle.[23] With the support of these new allies, Alianza attorneys attempted a new strategy. They realized that one desegregation victory, such as that in the *Tolleson* case, would not end all school segregration in Arizona. In 1952 the *Alianza* magazine reported, for example, that segregation continued in the schools in Glendale, Douglas, Miami, and Winslow. An attempt was then launched to challenge segregation of Mexican-American students in all Arizona schools. In this case, Estrada represented Ricardo Ortiz, Jessis B. Leyva, and their children in a suit against not only the school district of Glendale but also against the Arizona Board of Education. In suing the state Board of Education as well as the local one, Estrada sought to challenge the segregation of Mexican-American children wherever it existed in the state.[24]

Unfortunately for this plan, however, the officials of Glendale decided that they would not fight the case in court. Instead, they closed the Mexican school and committed themselves to building a new school that all the children in their district would attend together.[25] Other matters then occupied the attention of Estrada and other Alianza civil rights activists, so the fight to end segregation in the rest of Arizona's schools was put aside.

In 1954 the Alianza became involved in another desegregation case. It was not, however, another school desegregation case but concerned, instead, the issue that led to the first successful Mexican-American desegregation decision in the 1940s. Ten years after a federal court first decided that Mexican-Americans could not legally be excluded from public swimming pools, another case of this kind had to be taken into court. The swimming pool that remained segregated in 1954 was in Winslow, Arizona. Unlike the swimming pool in San Bernardino, California, however, the one in Winslow did not completely exclude Mexican-Americans. Their use of the pool was limited to only one day a week. That day was Wednesday; it was also the day before the pool was emptied and cleaned.[26]

In this case Alianza attorneys brought suit for Mollie Baca, Caroline Leyva, Margarita Vallejos, and Margarito Reyes. They were all members of the Alianza lodge in Winslow and all had been denied use of the pool except on Wednesdays. This case, like the Glendale school case, was settled out of court because city officials realized that they had no legal grounds on which to fight. Winslow city officials then, to avoid a trial, agreed voluntarily that they would no longer limit Mexican-Americans' use of the public swimming pool to one day a week. In the future, Mexican-Americans would be admitted to the pool whenever it was open to the public.[27]

Also in 1954 another member of the American Council of Spanish-Speaking People argued a case before the United States Supreme Court, and the result was the first civil rights decision for Mexican-Americans handed down by the court, as discussed above.[28] The attorney in the case was Gustavo García, who represented Pete Hernández, a convicted murderer. The Court in a unanimous decision agreed with García's arguments and reversed Hernández's conviction. The decision was based on the argument that Hernández had been denied a fair trial in Texas. In that state, García argued, Mexican-Americans are systematically excluded from juries although many are capable and willing to serve. The Court agreed with this argument and found that Mexican-Americans are a distinct and identifiable ethnic group who were being discriminated against in Texas. This discrimination had denied Hernández a fair trial by his peers; he had been denied the equal protection guaranteed under the Fourteenth Amendment to the United States Constitution.[29]

Following this 1954 victory before the Supreme Court, the Alianza formalized its activities in this field when the supreme president, Ralph Estrada, announced the establishment of an Alianza Civil Rights Department in 1955.[30] The Department was to be directed by Ralph Guzmán, a community organizer who was educated in East Los Angeles. He was graduated from Garfield High School and East Los Angeles College.[31] Under his direction the new department opened an office in Los Angeles to help Mexican-Americans fight against violations of their civil rights. In many cases Guzmán and the Alianza referred the complaints they received to other organizations or agencies including the American Civil Liberties Union.[32] In some cases, however, the Alianza Civil Rights Department took action itself.

Probably the most noted of the cases handled by the Alianza Civil Rights Department was involved in a struggle to desegregate the schools of El Centro, California. In this case the Alianza, represented by Guzmán and Estrada, cooperated with attorneys for the National Association for the Advancement of Colored People to investigate the situation and file suit against the El Centro Board of Education.[33]

In El Centro there were two elementary schools, Douglass and Washington, which served black and Mexican-American students. Although other families lived near the two schools, their children attended elementary schools farther away. All the black teachers and administrators in El Centro were assigned to these two schools whose faculties were entirely black except for one white principal. Beyond elementary school, students in El Centro attended integrated classes, although none of these secondary classes was taught by a black teacher. Of the students at Douglass and Washington elementary schools, 60 percent were black and 40 percent Mexican-American.[34]

In response to this situation of clearly segregated student and faculty assignments in El Centro, the NAACP in 1954 brought pressure on the Board of Education. The board then ruled that those children who lived in the neighborhoods served by Douglass and Washington schools must attend them and could not transfer to other elementary schools farther away from their homes. This ruling was announced at the end of the spring semester, and parents of the affected students were informed that they might avoid the necessity of sending their children to school with Negroes and Mexicans by withdrawing from the El Centro school district and joining the adjacent but already overcrowded Meadows Union school district. The Imperial County Board of Supervisors approved the transfer from El Centro to Meadows and, when school resumed in the fall, Douglass and Washington remained segregated.[35]

In January 1955 the Alianza became interested in the case and began to work with the NAACP. Representatives of both organizations advised the parents of the students at Douglass and Washington that no solution seemed to promise success except legal action. When the parents agreed to this, the attorneys for both the NAACP and the Alianza chose to begin their action in a federal court.[36]

There was a reason for beginning the legal action in a federal court. The *Westminster* and *Tolleson* cases had been decided in a federal court, but there was yet another reason. In an interview with *La Opinión,* Alianza Supreme President Ralph Estrada explained: it is important for this and similar civil rights cases to have direct access to the federal courts. If this were established, he said, "No Mexican or Negro would have to fear, in the future, the prejudice of local judges. If their civil rights were violated they could obtain justice in the federal courts directly."[37]

In the first court test, however, a problem arose. A judge, Pierson Hall, of the federal district court in San Diego, ruled that the case must first be tried in the state courts before it could be brought before the federal courts.[38] The attorneys, however, challenged this decision before the ninth circuit court of appeals. That court reversed Judge Hall's ruling and affirmed the right of the federal courts to hear such cases in the first instance. It was also affirmed that El Centro practiced illegal, segregative student and faculty assignment procedures, and the court ordered them changed. The El Centro School Board asked for and received a delay in putting the ruling into effect. Subsequently, however, the district decided against further appeals and came to a settlement out of court. In an article in *Frontier* magazine, published in 1956, Guzmán listed the basic points of the settlement.[39] They were

1. To hire and assign teachers on merit and without reference to race, creed or color
2. To draw school zones upon a basis of pupil population, regardless of race, color, religious creed, or national origin
3. To enroll pupils from kindergarten through the sixth grade on the basis of proximity of their residence to the respective school and to assign all older pupils to three central, integrated schools

4. To require a written application for inter-zonal transfers, the same being granted only for good and sufficient cause, and the question of race, color, religious creed or national origin not being deemed a good and sufficient cause[40]

The *El Centro* case was an important victory for both Mexican-Americans and blacks against school segregation. It was also significant that the Alianza and the NAACP cooperated to achieve this victory. Although the two groups seem to have similar interests in ending segregation and discrimination, the Alianza has not always acknowledged this fact. Earlier in its history, in fact, the society specifically excluded members of the "black and yellow races" from membership.[41] By 1957, however, the Alianza had awarded an honorary membership to Louis Armstrong, "While he was in Tucson . . . on a personal appearance tour."[42] In 1956 the society's Civil Rights Department also acknowledged the civil rights of blacks by cooperating with the NAACP in a struggle against school desegregation.

Another case handled by the Alianza's Civil Rights Department concerned a criminal matter. Three young men of Mexican descent, Manuel Mata, Robert Márquez, and Ricardo Venegas, were tried and convicted of murder and conspiracy. The person they were convicted of killing was William D. Cluff. He died during an altercation at Seventh and Broadway in Los Angeles on December 6, 1953. The altercation involved the three young men and a young member of the United States Marine Corps, John W. Moore. Cluff interfered in the altercation and died. Expert medical testimony indicated that Cluff died not as a result of injuries received in the altercation but as a result of an enlarged heart, advanced arteriosclerosis of cerebral blood vessels, and arterial heart disease. The three young men were, however, convicted of his murder.[43]

The Alianza's attorneys believed that the conviction of the three young men was a result of sensational newspaper publicity concerning the incident, and the Civil Rights Department therefore helped them in their appeals of the case. On one appeal the Alianza filed an *amicus curiae* brief in their behalf documenting the sensational coverage given Cluff's death in Los Angeles newspapers.[44] Although this first appeal failed, a subsequent one succeeded in obtaining a new trial.[45] Once more, the Alianza had questioned the quality of justice available to Mexican-Americans, and this time found it less than adequate without involved appeals.

Another Mexican-American group also was involved in questioning the quality of justice available to people of Mexican descent in the United States in 1950. This group was the Community Service

Organization. The CSO had first been organized to help elect Edward Roybal to the Los Angeles City Council. It was assisted in this activity by Fred Ross, a veteran of work with López and the Unity Leagues. After Roybal was elected in 1949 the group turned to other problems that affect Mexican-Americans. One of these is the relationship between law enforcement agencies and Mexican-Americans.[46]

The CSO became involved in police-community relations problems as a result of the Ríos-Ulloa case. Anthony Ríos was the president of the Los Angeles CSO, a leader in a CIO union local, and a delegate to the Los Angeles Central Committee of the Democratic party. Ríos and a companion, Alfred Ulloa, claimed that on January 27, 1952, they attempted to stop a fight behind an East Los Angeles restaurant. Unfortunately for Ríos and Ulloa, however, two of the men involved in the fight were plainclothes policemen. They arrested Ríos and Ulloa and charged them with interfering with officers.[47]

The help of Councilman Roybal secured their prompt release on bail, and, with the support of the CSO, Ríos and Ulloa pleaded not guilty to the charges. They were acquitted. Their statements at their trial, that they had been taken to the Hollenbeck police station, stripped, and beaten, brought demands by Councilman Roybal and others for an investigation of police brutality in Los Angeles.[48]

Other cases and investigations followed. Perhaps the best known was that of January and February, 1952, when the Los Angeles grand jury indicted eight Los Angeles policemen in the Bloody Christmas case. Policemen were accused of participation in an orgy of beating seven young Mexican-American prisoners in the Lincoln Heights police station during a Christmas Eve drinking party in 1951. The youths had been picked up after a brawl with police near a bar and charged with battery and interfering with officers. As a result of this case, police officers were disciplined by the Police Department and some of those indicted were convicted and sent to jail.[49]

Another case in which the CSO was interested also involved the Alianza's Civil Rights Department. The case was that of David Hidalgo. Hidalgo was a Los Angeles high school student who, through his guardian, Manuel Domínguez, brought a civil suit against the Los Angeles County Sheriff's Department. He charged that on May 8, 1953, he received an unprovoked beating from a deputy while other deputies watched and did not come to his aid. On March 2, 1956, the suit was decided in Hidalgo's favor and he received both actual and compensatory damages of more than a thousand dollars. Hidalgo's was an important moral victory for Mexican-Americans against police brutality.[50]

Together with police brutality, criminal, and desegregation cases, the Alianza Civil Rights Department was concerned with the problems of Mexicans and Mexican-Americans who have become naturalized United States citizens; these people had problems with United States immigration and naturalization laws. In particular, in the 1950s there were problems with the McCarren-Walters Immigration and Naturalization Act of 1952. This act not only perpetuated most of the features of prior immigration and naturalization legislation but also provided for denaturalization of persons not fit to be United States citizens. This provision was used against Mexican-Americans, and the government seemed to apply it in an especially rigorous manner in the 1950s. That was a period of economic downturn in the United States. Perhaps in response to high unemployment figures, the government also instituted Operation Wetback, a program to deport Mexicans who had entered the United States illegally. In one year during the operation of this program, 1953, more than a million aliens were deported to Mexico. In this climate of economic recession and of strict enforcement of immigration laws, Mexican-Americans also needed organizations to help them secure equal justice in this area.[51]

The Alianza helped several people prove their right to be in the United States. One, for example, was Daniel Casteñeda González. González was threatened with losing of his citizenship because he lived in Mexico during World War II. The Department of Immigration and Naturalization contended that since he did not return to the United States to fulfill his responsibility to serve in the armed forces during the war he should lose his citizenship. The Alianza's lawyers had to take González's appeal all the way to the Supreme Court to maintain his United States citizenship against this charge. They argued that the fact that González did not serve in the armed forces during the war did not prove that he went to Mexico to avoid serving. González said that he went to Mexico to stay with his relatives and did not know that he was obliged to return to the United States to serve in the army. The Supreme Court, in 1955, agreed with the Alianza's attorneys that the government had failed to show that González intentionally avoided serving in the army, and the Court prevented the Department of Immigration and Naturalization from revoking González's citizenship.[52]

In the late 1950s, as Alianza membership continued to decline, interest in civil rights cases also declined. Alianza leaders at this time exhibited a new interest in partisan politics. The son-in-law of Supreme President Estrada, Carlos McCormick, was national chairman of the Viva Kennedy! Clubs, John Kennedy's organization among Mexican-Americans to support his 1960 presidential campaign.[53]

Following Kennedy's victory, Estrada received an appointment with the Agency for International Development in Latin America.[54] The head of the Civil Rights Department, Guzmán, also received an appointment, with the Peace Corps in Venezuela.[55] McCormick succeeded to the supreme presidency when Estrada took his new position,[56] and with the departure of Estrada and Guzmán, the civil rights program of the Alianza was forgotten.

Notes

1. Guadalupe Salinas, "Mexican-Americans and Desegregation," *El Grito* (Summer 1971), p. 39.
2. *Ibid.*
3. Ruth Tuck, "Sprinkling the Grass Roots," *Common Ground* (Spring 1947), pp. 80–83; Carey McWilliams, *North from Mexico: The Spanish-Speaking People of the United States* (New York: Greenwood Press, 1968), p. 280; and 71 *F. Supp.* 769. (This legal form indicates that the decision was reported in volume 71 of the *Federal Supplement* beginning on page 769.)
4. Pauline R. Kibbe, *Latin Americans in Texas* (Albuquerque: University of New Mexico Press, 1946), p. 23.
5. "Ignacio López, Foreign Language Division, Office of War Information," *Alianza* (March 1943), p. 9, and interview with Ignacio López, March 21, 1965.
6. *Ibid.* and McWilliams, *North from Mexico*, p. 280.
7. Ruth Lucretia Martínez, "The Unusual Mexican: A Study in Acculturation" (Master's thesis, Claremont Colleges, 1942), pp. 35–38.
8. 71 *F. Supp.* 669.
9. *Ibid.*
10. *Ibid.*
11. McWilliams, *North from Mexico*, pp. 280–84; Beatrice Griffith, *American Me* (Boston: Houghton Mifflin Co., 1948), p. 155; 64 *F. Supp.* 544; 161 *F. Supp.* 774.
12. *Ibid.*
13. 64 *F. Supp.* 544.
14. 161 *F. 2d.* 774.
15. *Ibid.*
16. Kaye Briegel, "La Alianza Hispano-Americana, A Fraternal Insurance Society, 1894–1965" (Ph.D. diss., University of Southern California, 1973), *passim.*
17. Leo Grebler, Joan W. Moore, Ralph C. Guzmán, *et al.*, *The Mexican American People: The Nation's Second Largest Minority* (New York: Free Press, 1970), p. 547.
18. There are a few of these movies in the New York Public Library.
19. Tomás Serrano Cabo, *Las Crónicas* (Tucson: Alianza Hispano-Americana, 1929), p. 184.
20. Alianza Hispano-Americana, "Acta Oficial de la Sesión Extraordinaria del Consejo Ejecutivo Supremo" (Tucson, July 27–28, 1950); Serna's appeal is reported in 211 *p. 2d.* 455.
21. "Golpe al Discrimen," *Alianza* (January 1951), pp. 5, 13; and 96 *F. Supp. 1004.*
22. "Organización Contra el Discriminen Racial," *Alianza* (July 1951), pp. 7, 14.
23. "Un Triunfo Más de la Alianza," *Alianza* (April 1951), p. 5.
24. *Ibid.*; "Lucha Contra la Discriminación," *Alianza* (October 1951), p. 7, and "Labor Aliancista: Lucha Contra la Segragación," *Alianza* (March 1952), p. 3.
25. *Ibid.*
26. "Alianza Group Files Suit on Racial Matter," *Arizona Daily Star*, December 3, 1953, p. 68; "Pool in Winslow Ends Segregation," *Arizona Daily Star*, June 29,

1954, p. 9A; and "Cuando Terminará Esto? Discrimen Racial en Winslow, Arizona," *Alianza* (January 1954), p. 3.

27. *Ibid.*

28. Salinas, "Mexican-Americans and Desegregation," p. 39.

29. *Ibid.*; David Sierra, "Gus García Jr. High Honors Chicano," *Forumeer* (December 1972), pp. 1, 3–4; and 347 *U.S.* 475.

30. Ralph Estrada, "New Horizons and New Techniques: Introducing Our New Civil Rights Department," *Alianza* (March 1955), pp. 7–8.

31. *Ibid.* and "Ralph Guzmán Appointed Assistant Project Director," *Progress Report* No. 1 (Mexican-American Study Project, Graduate School of Business Administration, University of California, Los Angeles, January 1965), pp. 1–2.

32. "First Annual Progress Report of the Civil Rights Department," *Alianza* (August-September 1965), p. 12.

33. Ralph Guzmán, "How El Centro Did It: The End of Segregation in One School System," *Frontier* (February 1956), pp. 13–16, and also in *Alianza* (February-March 1956), pp. 19–20.

34. *Ibid.* and 131 *F. Supp.* 818.

35. *Ibid.*

36. *Ibid.*

37. "Triunfo de la AHA en los Tribunales; Obtuvo que se oigan sus quejas; la Corte Federal oirá el caso de la segregación," *La Opinión* (Los Angeles), October 16, 1955, pt. 2, p. 1.

38. Guzmán, "How El Centro Did It," and 131 *F. Supp.* 818.

39. *Ibid.*

40. Guzmán, "How El Centro Did It."

41. Serrano Cabo, *Las Crónicas,* p. 23.

42. "Musician Louis Armstrong is awarded an honorary membership . . . ," *Alianza* (October-November 1957), p. 15.

43. 280 *P. 2d. 175*; and 283 *P. 2d.* 372.

44. 280 *P. 2d.* 175; "Enérgica Defensa de 3 Jovenes que fueron convictos en el Caso Cluff; intervino en su favor la Alianza H. Americana," *La Opinión,* March 6, 1955, pt. 2, p. 1; and *Alianza* (June-July 1956), p. 15.

45. 283 *P. 2d.* 372.

46. Kaye Briegel, "The History of Political Organizations Among Mexican-Americans in Los Angeles Since the Second World War" (Master's thesis; University of Southern California 1967), pp. 24–26.

47. Mike Glazer, "The LA CSO Story: American Democracy is Not a Fake" (Los Angeles: Community Service Organization, 1965), p. 4, and interview with Anthony Riós, March 9, 1966.

48. *Ibid.*

49. *Ibid.*; "8 Policemen Indicted for Bloody Xmas Beatings," *Los Angeles Mirror,* May 13, 1952, p. 3; and *Los Angeles Daily News,* January 24, 1952, p. 4.

50. Glazer, "The LA CSO Story," p. 5; and "David Hidalgo Wins Damages Against L.A. Sheriff's Dept.," *Alianza* (February-March 1965), p. 29.

51. Marion T. Bennett, *American Immigration Policies: A History* (Washington, D.C.: Public Affairs Press, 1963), pp. 133–93; and Grebler, Moore, Guzmán, *et al., Mexican American People,* p. 521.

52. "Interviene la Alianza; lucha contra la Ley que priva de la Nacionalidad," *La Opinión,* November 30, 1955, pt. 1, p. 7; *Alianza* (June-July 1956), p. 17; 215 *F. 2d.* 955; and 349 U.S. 943.

53. "J. Carlos McCormick, Supreme President," *Alianza* (May 1962), p. 2.

54. "Nobramiento del Hno. Ralph Estrada," *Alianza* (May 1962), p. 8.

55. J. Carlos McCormick, "Spanish-Speaking Americans, A People's Progressing," *Alianza* (December 1962), p. 13.

56. "J. Carlos McCormick, Supreme President," *Alianza* (May 1962), p. 2.

Chapter Six

An Awakened Minority

After two postwar decades of slow, quiet progress, Mexican-Americans awakened and demanded equality and justice from the Anglo world. They became militant in seeking social justice and their rights. New leaders, most notably the incomparable César Chávez of California and Arizona, emerged throughout the Southwest. Chicano students, who previously had been so criticized for their lack of interest in education, organized and sought better educational facilities, relevant curriculum programs, and well-prepared teachers and administrators.

In this final chapter, six selections, from previously published materials as well as from original articles, concerning the new leaders are presented to the reader. Curtis J. Sitomer, of the *Christian Science Monitor,* presents an unbiased picture of Chávez's farm union work and of César Chávez himself in a brief article. Clark S. Knowlton captures the reader with his account of Reies López Tijerina and of the New Mexican Alianza Federal de los Pueblos Libres as they seek to recover their lands. Armando Rendón, in an excerpt from his book, *Chicano Manifesto: The History and Aspirations of the Second Largest Minority in America,* discusses Rodolfo "Corky" Gonzales and his Crusade for Justice in Colorado. José Angel Gutiérrez, founder of La Raza Unida party in Texas, talks about the new party in his speech, "Mexicanos Need to Control Their Own Destinies." Dolores Huerta, vice-president of the United Farm Workers Organizing Committee and the outstanding female leader in the Chicano awakening, talks about Republicans, César, children, and my home town. In the sixth selection, Geoffrey P. Mawn, a doctoral student in history, presents a biographical picture of "Raúl Castro of Arizona," the state's foremost Democratic leader.

In addition to the selections on leaders, this chapter contains succinct articles on important Chicano activities and protests. Kaye Briegel, who is completing her doctoral dissertation on the *Alianza Hispano-Americana,* analyzes the Los Angeles blowouts in her article, "Chicano Student Militancy: The Los Angeles High School Strike of 1968." Christine Marín, the coordinator of the Chicano Studies Project at Arizona State University, presents a study of the militant Brown Berets' activities in "Go Home, Chicanos: A Study of the Brown Berets in California and Arizona." Patricia A. Adank, a teacher of Mexican-American history, discusses the Mexican-American students' and parents' boycott of Phoenix Union High School in "Chicano Activism in Maricopa County —Two Incidents in Retrospect." Finally, José Angel de la Vara, an active member of MECHA at Arizona State University and a law school student, reviews and interprets the events that led to the death of the distinguished Chicano journalist, Rubén Salazar, in "The 1970 Chicano Moratorium and The Death of Rubén Salazar."

Harvest of Discontent*

Curtis J. Sitomer

UNION DRIVE RIPENS IN VINEYARDS

The broiling summer sun bakes this central California valley with one-hundred-ten-degree temperatures.

It's preharvest time. And out in the hot, muggy fields a lush grape crop and a labor movement are ripening together.

At stake is a half-million dollars in grapes and the fortunes of eighty thousand migrants who pick them.

What happens may force a redirection of California's $3.8-billion-a-year agricultural economy, which peaks right here in this fiery furnace in late August and September.

César Chávez's farm labor union has been picking up momentum for two years—since its dramatic grape strike here in the fall of 1965. At the same time, [the] migrant workers' civil rights movement also crystallized.

---

*Reprinted by permission from *The Christian Science Monitor* of August 9 and 10, 1967.

Contract Push Planned

Now with tens of thousands of acres of fruit ready for harvesting, the union plans its greatest push ever for collective-bargaining contracts.

Some three hundred growers in this San Joaquin Valley will be under pressure. Many may be forced to sign with the union or lose their crop for lack of labor.

Other factors make this perhaps the most meaningful harvest ever for the growers. In recent years, their profits have steadily dwindled as overhead soared. Higher labor costs, forced by unionization, could drive some growers out of business.

A successful union thrust in the next few weeks could mean [for the migrants] higher wages, . . . a better standard of living, improved housing, and a boost from society's cellar.

But if the union drive fails, the entire farm labor movement and its attendant civil rights cause may be set back for a decade.

Immigrants Transform Soil

But no matter which way [the union drive] goes, California's agriculture—the state's biggest business—will not be left unchanged.

Delano is a farm community. It has been since the turn of the century, when a group of ambitious Yugoslav immigrants settled on its barren soil and turned worthless land into a garden.

Since then these growers and their progeny have ruled the valley. Their sons and grandsons, who inherited the now-fertile acres, are the backbone of the community. They not only own the farms, they invest heavily in the supporting services—banks, retail stores, and machinery and equipment outlets.

The growers sit in the city council and the board of supervisors and the local school board. Nor is their influence bounded by the borders of Delano. It reaches far into the northern farm country in Tulare County and all the way to the state capitol in Sacramento.

Up to two years ago, this was the story of Delano—rich farmland and its landed gentry.

La Causa Hits

Then came La Causa.

Suddenly, dramatically, at the peak of the 1965 grape harvest, a strike hit Delano's vineyards and with it a full-scale social and economic rebellion. The Mexican farm worker, virtually silent and anonymous for more than half a century, sprang from beneath the arbors and demanded a share of "the good life." He called his uprising La Causa.

He was prodded by the simple but pungent dialogue of one of his own kind, soft-spoken César Chávez, a man whom an admirer has called "a quiet explosion."

Chávez and his newly formed farm workers' union masterminded the grape strike. With it, in their untutored ways, they struck a brash chord for a migrant workers' civil rights movement that has since echoed across the land.

The *huelga* (strike) pounded home the poverty of the migrant pickers: an annual income of less than two thousand dollars for a family of six or eight or more; often pre–Industrial Revolution working conditions; no unemployment insurance or welfare coverage; and labor camp housing—a remarkable remnant of that tin-shack era described by John Steinbeck in *The Grapes of Wrath*.

Inroads Made

Through his new union, the migrant asked for reform. From the grower, he demanded guaranteed wages, better working conditions, and collective-bargaining agreements with a union contract and closed shop. From the government, he demanded coverage under the National Labor Relations Act, unemployment and disability insurance, and Social Security.

Now almost two years old, the *huelga* has jumped from place to place—from the lush fields of central California to, most recently, the fertile Rio Grande Valley on the southern Texas border.

The union so far has won only three major contracts. But these are with growers who sell in national markets.

CHÁVEZ: A MILD MANNER WORKS AN EXPLOSION ON THE FARM

A gentle-looking Mexican-American [walks briskly out of] an old, dilapidated house on the west side of the tracks in Delano.

He pauses, turns to another man—also a Mexican-American—painting a picket fence. The two exchange words in Spanish. Then the first continues toward his car.

"Viva la huelga, César," the man painting the fence calls after him.

"Viva La Causa, Umberto," the first man waves as he leaves.

The painter continues his work with quicker strokes. He has just personally talked with a symbol—a social force—the embodiment of a new revolution in American labor.

To Umberto and thousands of other migratory workers, mild-mannered, quiet, affable César Chávez is all of these things. He is a sort of "quiet explosion."

They call him César. He leads seventeen thousand seasonal farm workers who comprise the nation's most heralded—and controversial—agricultural union.

Goal Described

For the migrant, César embodies the *huelga*—the union's two-year-long strike for recognition by three hundred growers in California's lush San Joaquin Valley.

And he embodies La Causa—the dramatic civil rights–type movement aimed at pulling the poverty-stricken, uneducated, and up to now almost ignored, Spanish-speaking migrant into labor's mainstream.

César is short and sturdy. He has wavy, black hair and a dark, youthful complexion.

His eyes are searching and penetrating. And they seem to add to the credibility of the simple but sometimes explosively eloquent phrases which verbalize La Causa.

"We are more than a union," he says. "But we are also less than a union."

In the first instance, he is talking about an extra dimension which most other unions don't possess. Some of the Chávez associates here call this "social conscience." He himself refers to it as "personalized service."

Activities Listed

For example, his United Farm Workers of California (UFWOC) operates a social-service center right at union headquarters. Nearby, it manages a discount gasoline station. And it now is building a medical and dental clinic for farm workers and their families.

At the service center, the migrant can get help filling out his immigration forms. He can find out if he is eligible for welfare or other government aid. And he can get information—in both Spanish and English—about interest rates on the ice box or used car he wants to buy on time.

The union will help him pay a traffic fine or refer him to free legal aid if a civil suit is leveled against him. It will even advise him on domestic problems.

"We must do these things," says Mr. Chávez. "Our members are unique. We are a union of have-nots. So we must satisfy basic needs before other things."

In some ways, César Chávez, as a union leader, is reminiscent of the past. He is the union—much in the tradition of Samuel Gompers and, later, John L. Lewis.

Battle Already Won

The Walter Reuthers and George L. Meanys of today's multistructured AFL-CIO don't personally embody a cause. They don't need to. Their battle—[for] living wages, adequate working conditions, Social Security, unemployment insurance, and the right to bargain collectively—was basically won many years ago.

But the American migratory worker has no such framework—yet. For this reason, he, too, recalls the past. And his union in that respect, as Chávez says, "is less than a union."

The migratory worker is not covered under the National Labor Relations Act. He is usually ineligible for unemployment insurance. He is without specific health and welfare protection. And he has no guaranteed minimum wage.

Recognition Sought

Against this backdrop, La Causa fights the migrant's battle on three fronts. It presses the grower for union recognition and collective-bargaining contracts. It lobbies the state and federal governments for legislation to protect the agricultural worker. And it makes a broad appeal to the public to end social discrimination against the migrant.

"Our aims are still very elementary," explains Mr. Chávez. "The big goal is union recognition by the growers. And even when we get this, we have to teach the growers the very meaning of negotiations. Hopefully, they will then get together themselves and set up management-labor relations departments. Now they have no such thing."

Legislation giving benefits to migrants as a group [is] almost nonexistent.

"What we need in a state like California," says Mr. Chávez, "is a Little Wagner Act which would spell out our right to organize and engage in collective bargaining."

"On the national level—for the past thirty years—federal policy has said that workers in general have a right to join a union. We want this extended specifically to farm workers."

The soft-spoken migrant leader is optimistic that such coverage will come. "We have history on our side," he says.

Coverages Explored

And he may not have to wait long. Even now a congressional subcommittee on migratory labor is discussing the extension of certain coverages to farm workers under the National Labor Relations Act.

La Causa's thrust to gain widespread public sympathy for the ongoing *huelga* is central to the Chávez approach.

Driven by this, the union's cause is dramatically spilling beyond Delano's vineyard.

College students—caught up with La Causa—now march in picket lines across the land in front of food markets selling certain farm products without the union [label].

Members of the migrant ministry talk up the *huelga* to church and club groups.

Leadership Recognized

And national labor chieftains [pour] into Delano each month thousands of dollars from union coffers to keep the strike going and sustain unemployed migrants.

But again—in the eyes of an untutored farm laborer like Umberto—his greatest power and the fulfillment of his dreams lie in one man, César Chávez.

And the Chávez precepts are nonviolent.

"We don't slash tires or cuss at crossers of our picket lines," he says. "Instead we may say a prayer—or turn the other cheek if we are attacked physically."

"It takes more power to win in this manner. It's slower and takes more money and more people. But once you get it this way, you keep it."

Some of the union's ardent critics insist that UFWOC is easy prey for left-wing and other subversive groups. A few—including growers who have adamantly resisted the union's infiltration among their workers—charge outright that La Causa is Communist-inspired and that Mr. Chávez was trained by the "Reds."

Charge Answered

Mr. Chávez responds to this branding: "People who Red-bait us are saying, ironically, that only Communists care for people and are concerned with social problems. They seem to disregard the religious philosophy which says that man is concerned for his brother."

César Chávez is a patient man. He realizes that it may take ten years or longer for his union to make real headway. In its first two years of operation, UFWOC has signed with only three of the three hundred growers in central California.

And although he doesn't particularly like to think of La Causa as a civil rights movement, Mr. Chávez knows that constant public exposure of the abject poverty and deprivation of the farm worker is essential to the momentum of his movement.

"Our situation," he says, "is really no different from that which exists in the Negro ghettos in other parts of the country."

Sensitivity Noted

"We have a tremendous capacity," he explains—speaking of people in general—"to hurt our fellow human beings—and then to deny that anything is happening."

Mr. Chávez is extremely sensitive to human feelings. Perhaps this is one of the reasons he personally carries La Causa with him and with it often touches his legion of individual Umbertos.

And the migrant—caught up with hope and emotion—often responds to this softly administered, electric charge of César Chávez.

"Viva la huelga," he shouts at the union meeting. And then "Viva La Causa." And finally he is moved to complete the cycle: "Viva César Chávez."

Tijerina, Hero of the Militants*

Clark S. Knowlton

Reies López Tijerina, leader and founder of the largest Spanish-American militant organization in New Mexico, the *Alianza Federal de Los Pueblos Libres,* was found innocent in an Albuquerque courtroom December 14 [1968] of the capital charge of kidnapping and of the lesser charges of false imprisonment and assault on a jail. These charges originated in the Alianza raid on the Tierra Amarilla courthouse, June 5, 1967. The unexpected verdict was harshly condemned by the New Mexican press. It also shocked the dominant Anglo-American political and economic establishment of northern New Mexico. The verdict was wildly cheered, on the other hand, by large numbers of impoverished Spanish-Americans living on dreams of the past and on welfare in the slums of Albuquerque and Santa Fe, and by numerous Spanish-American small ranchers and farmers hurt severely by recent National Forest regulations. The Alianza, badly battered by two years of constant court battles, has now sud-

*From *The Journal of Mexican American Studies,* I, No. 2 (Winter 1971), 91–96 and the *Texas Observer,* December 9, 1966. Reprinted by permission of the author, and the *Texas Observer.*

denly become again a threat to the political and economic groupings that control northern New Mexico. Convoys of cars from rural Spanish-American villages again visit the shot-up Alianza headquarters in Albuquerque.

Tijerina, the most important Spanish-American leader in New Mexico, was born into a poor migrant family near Falls City, Texas, September 21, 1923. He lost his mother at an early age. His father, [who lost] three wives, supported his family of ten children by sharecropping in South Texas. Tijerina states that he saw his family driven away three times from Anglo-American farms at gunpoint when the harvests were in by farmers who refused to pay the family their share of the crop. The meek but Anglo-hating father finally settled his family in San Antonio. During the spring, summer, and fall, they moved [with] the migrant stream in the Midwest and West Texas, wintering as best they could in San Antonio. Although his father is still living, Tijerina says very little about him. He prefers to dwell with admiration upon his paternal grandfather and great-grandfather. He explains that his great-grandfather owned a small ranch on a land grant near Laredo. Anglo-American ranchers wanting his land, according to Tijerina, drove branded cattle onto the ranch and accused his great-grandfather of cattle rustling. Six Texas Rangers hung the accused man in front of his family. The man's son, Tijerina's grandfather, became a border raider attacking Anglo-American settlements and ranches along the border.

Tijerina is thus a product of the bitter border fighting between aggressive Mexican-hating Anglo-American ranchers and Rangers and the resident Mexican-American population in the lower Rio Grande Valley.

Tijerina's early history is somewhat shadowy. He relates that he grew up as a migrant worker, attending school very infrequently. Somewhere along the line he managed to acquire a decent knowledge of the English language. A Baptist missionary, distributing the New Testament to midwestern migrant labor camps, visited the Tijerina family. Reies, a boy in his middle teens, read the book through. That night he dreamed that God had called him to lead his people out of bondage and poverty. Interpreting this as a religious call, he enrolled in the Assembly of God Bible School at Ysleta, Texas, now part of El Paso. Finishing his training, he was licensed as a minister and sent to assist revivals in and around Santa Fe. He soon acquired a reputation as a fiery, unconventional preacher and missionary. Within a few years he lost his license to preach. He asserts it was because he argued that the church should provide financial and spiritual assistance to the poor rather than the poor donating money to the church.

Somewhat disoriented, he drifted around northern New Mexico, finally settling around the age of twenty-three in Tierra Amarilla. A half-abandoned Spanish-American frontier settlement, Tierra Amarilla has always been a center of anti-Anglo-American agitation. The people of the area were robbed of their land grant by Anglo-American lawyers and politicians toward the end of the nineteenth century. The inhabitants, refusing to abandon their ancestral lands, have periodically cut the fences, burned the ranch buildings, and slaughtered the livestock of intruding Anglo-American ranchers.

Married and with a growing family to support, Tijerina finally left Tierra Amarilla (date uncertain). For thirteen years [while he was] an itinerant Pentecostal preacher he and his family moved from California to East Texas and from the Mexican border to the Midwest as migrant workers. Developing a devoted following, he finally formed a small communal settlement of around seventeen families on purchased land near Casa Grande, Arizona, in the early 1950s. The settlers built their homes [and] a small church and worked for the neighboring farmers and ranchers. Friction over land questions soon developed with Anglo-Americans in the vicinity. The small settlement was burnt out. Tijerina, charged with trying to help an imprisoned brother escape, fled to Mexico.

He remained there for six years. During this period, he claims that he studied the history of land grants in Mexico and in the Southwest. Some evidence exists that he became involved in the activities of militant Mexican peasant groups and was deported by the Mexican government. His Mexican contacts have helped him raise funds and secure a sympathetic audience in Mexico. No evidence exists that he was ever a Castro sympathizer or Communist. Entering Mexico as an itinerant religious leader, he left it deeply motivated by the philosophy of the Mexican revolution.

Returning to Tierra Amarilla sometime in the early 1960s, he was accused of joining clandestine groups of Spanish-American night-riders [who were] trying to burn out encroaching Anglo-American ranchers from Texas and Colorado. The ranchers blamed Tijerina for the recurrence of night-riding activities and threatened him. Several attempts on his life may have taken place. At any rate, he moved to Albuquerque. Securing employment around 1962 as a janitor in a local Presbyterian church, he began to organize the Alianza Federal de Mercedes, the Federal Alliance of Land Grantees. His first wife finally left him, as he was seldom able to support his family.

The Alianza at first attracted primarily the landless, impoverished, aging, rural Spanish-American immigrants living in the slums of

Albuquerque and Santa Fe. Forced to migrate to the city because of land lost to Anglo-American ranchers and merchants and because of the decline of the village economic systems, they exist upon welfare and upon their dreams of recovering their lands. More profoundly isolated from Anglo-American urban society than ever, [like] the inhabitants of Negro urban ghettos, large numbers of them are found in almost every city in New Mexico.

Around 1965 the composition of Alianza membership changed rapidly. Thousands of bitter Spanish-American small ranchers and village farmers became members. Angered by what appeared to them to be harsh, unfair, and capricious decisions by the National Forest Service that were forcing many of them to migrate, or to seek employment outside of agriculture, they appealed for redress to state and federal agencies. Unable to secure a hearing, they turned to Tijerina and the Alianza. As members, they caused the Alianza to become more militant. Forest Service personnel living in the rural villages of northern New Mexico began to move to the larger cities, as resentment against them spread. [Forest] Rangers were shot at on mountain trails. Many fires were deliberately set in the National Forests of New Mexico.

The Forest Service may have had good reasons for its policy decisions, but these reasons were never communicated to the Spanish-Americans. Grazing permits for small herds of cattle and sheep upon which so many Spanish-Americans depend were sharply cut. The grazing season was reduced from nine to six months. Those holding grazing permits were required to fence their allotments and to move their herds and flocks from one allotment area to another. The fencing was usually beyond the ability of poor Spanish-Americans to purchase or to install. Although Anglo-American ranchers with their cowboys could move their animals without difficulty, it was very difficult for a Spanish-American farmer or small rancher, often with other employment, to do so. Permits for Spanish-Americans to graze milk cows and work horses were cancelled even though Anglo-American ranchers were permitted to graze their work horses. This decision intensified malnutrition and threatened to force hundreds of Spanish-American farmers out of agriculture. They cannot afford to buy tractors for their small acreage and have no range for their work stock. The Forest Service claims that erosion in the forests has forced it to make these decisions. However, [the service spends] far more on recreational developments for the Anglo-American hunter, fisher, tourist, or camper than . . . on the improvement of grazing or the control of erosion. Spanish-Americans, dependent upon the National Forests that once were part of their land grants, are today convinced that the National Forest Service would like to eliminate the Spanish-Americans and replace them with Anglo-American ranchers and tourists.

The Alianza message to the rural Spanish-American village people was very simple and convincing. Tijerina and Alianza organizers repeated it in dozens of villages throughout 1965 and 1966. By now very few Spanish-Americans have not heard it:

> You have been robbed of your lands by Anglo-Americans with some Spanish-American accomplices. No one is willing to help you recover your lands, protect your water rights, or secure your grazing permits. The federal and state governments are not interested in you. Join the Alianza. Together we will get your lands back or adequate compensation for them, and protect your grazing and water rights. This will be done preferably through court action. If the courts do not respond, then we will have to resort to other methods.

These words endlessly repeated have deeply affected the thinking of Spanish-American people in northern New Mexico.

Alianza tactics were also simple and rather naive. The Forest Service, owner of so much of Northern New Mexico, was selected as the primary target. National Forest lands in northern New Mexico were carved out from Spanish-American land grants. Spanish-American land titles were not completely extinguished. Forest boundaries were carelessly surveyed and often included entire villages. As the Forest Service has now become the major focus of rural Spanish-American hostility, it was not difficult to mobilize Spanish-Americans for activities against the National Forest Service.

Selecting a former community land grant, the San Joaquin del Rio Chama (now part of the Kit Carson National Forest), Tijerina announced in 1966 that the original village community, now uninhabited, had been reconstituted as the Pueblo Republica de San Joaquín del Río Chama and would assert its rights to the land grant. Community members were drawn from the inhabitants of the surrounding Spanish-American villages, some of whom were descendants of the original villagers. In an open meeting, . . . a complete set of village officials [was selected]. To emphasize their claim, a series of camp-ins were held at the Echo Amphitheater, a public campsite on the grant within the Kit Carson National Forest. Finally, on October 22, 1966, a brief altercation broke out between two nervous Forest Rangers, trying to sell camping permits to the hostile Spanish-Americans, and Alianza members.

The following Wednesday, Tijerina, his brother Cristóbal, and two members were arrested on a federal warrant, charged with assault upon two Forest Rangers and appropriating government property to personal use. On a change of venue, the case was transferred from friendly Rio Arriba County, where conviction would have been impossible, to hostile Las Cruces. After several postponements the trial was finally held in November 1967. A jury, all Anglo-American except for two Mexican-Americans, found the defendants guilty. The federal judge sentenced Tijerina to two years in jail, his brother to two years with eighteen months suspended, and two other defendants to sixty days. All were allowed bail. The verdict was appealed.

The tempo of events accelerated during the spring of 1967. In one meeting after another, Tijerina and other Alianza leaders in ever stronger language demanded the return of the land grants and harshly criticized state and federal governments. Fires were set on the National Forests. Anglo-American ranchers hired more gunmen as their fences were cut and property destroyed. Finally a mass meeting for June 3, 1968, was called at Coyote, New Mexico, during which plans would be made to take over the land. The Anglo-American press began to demand that law enforcement agencies repress the Alianza and curb its activities.

In 1966, David F. Cargo, a liberal, maverick Republican, had, unsupported by the regular Republican leaders, won the governor's office with considerable Spanish-American support. While in office, he married a Spanish-American girl who had been a member of the Alianza. He began to visit many Spanish-American villages [and listened] to the bitterly expressed problems, resentments, and needs of the village people. He published a number of statements expressing his sympathy for the Spanish-Americans, calling them an exploited, neglected minority. The Albuquerque papers reacted coldly to his description of northern New Mexico. He also met several times with Alianza leaders and succeeded in moderating somewhat their ferocious attacks upon state and federal governments. The day before the Coyote meeting, Governor Cargo flew to Michigan to participate with Governor Romney in a fund-raising banquet.

Cargo's plane had scarcely left the ground when District Attorney Alfonso Sánchez, the Democratic district attorney for Rio Arriba County, former Alianza attorney, and personal enemy of Tijerina, and Captain Joseph Black, commander of the [State Police], announced that the Coyote meeting was illegal and therefore banned. Any person attempting to attend the meeting would be arrested. They also stated that Tijerina was a "con man," the Alianza members were dupes, and the organization was Communist-inspired.

Roadblocks went up on all highways leading into the area. Warrants of arrest were issued for Alianza leaders.

Angry, not understanding the division of power in the state government, and feeling that they had been betrayed by the governor, the refugee Alianza leaders, headed by Tijerina, slipped through the roadblocks and met near Canjilon to decide future policy. Learning that a hearing was to be held at Tierra Amarilla on June 5, 1967, for Alianza members arrested while trying to attend the Coyote meeting, they decided to send a raiding party of around twenty men to release their people and to make a citizens' arrest of District Attorney Sánchez. Tijerina gave orders to the group to avoid violence.

The raiding party entered the courthouse in the early afternoon of June 5, 1967. Two deputies and a janitor were wounded by tense raiders. Unable to find the arrested Alianza members, who had been bound over for trial and released on bail at an early morning hearing, or Sánchez, who had not come for the hearing, the raiders held the courthouse for several hours. Then, seizing two hostages—a newspaper reporter and a deputy sheriff—they fled to the mountains near Canjilon, releasing their hostages before disappearing into the hills.

Panic and confusion swept the governorless state administration when news of the raid arrived in Santa Fe. Rumors that Alianza guerrilla bands led by Cuban guerrilla experts were moving toward Santa Fe, massacring Anglo-Americans on the way, were widely believed. Other rumors had it that Alianza arson and assassination squads were infiltrating Albuquerque and Santa Fe. National guardsmen equipped with tanks and artillery moved along mountain roads but did not penetrate into the mountains. Apache tribal police from Dulce, New Mexico, Anglo-American sheriffs' posses from central and eastern New Mexico, and State Police units manned roadblocks and searched for Alianza members. Guardsmen and their allies swept through Spanish-American villages around Canjilon, breaking into homes without warrants, confiscating property, holding suspected men, women, and children for many hours without food or water in temporary concentration camps. A large part of Rio Arriba County was treated as though it were enemy territory in the process of occupation. No state emergency or martial law was declared and no warrants were issued. One of the most massive violations of the American civil rights in recent years took place without protests or open investigation by any state or federal agency.

Governor Cargo returned to New Mexico early on the morning the next day, June 6. Within forty-eight hours the guardsmen were sent home along with the Apaches and the Anglo-American posses. Contact was established with the refugee raiders. Given the assurance that their lives would be spared, the majority surrendered or were conveniently arrested by state and local police. Preliminary hearings were held. The defendants were bound over for trial on charges, among others, of kidnapping, assault on a jail, and destruction of government property. Within forty-five days all were out on bail. The immediate crisis was over. However, the serious, unpunished violation of civil rights and the mistreatment of so many rural Spanish-Americans will have long-lasting effects upon relationships between Anglo-Americans and Spanish-Americans and upon the attitudes of the local people toward both state and federal governments.

Before the state had recovered from the impact of the raid, Eulogio Salazar, one of the deputies wounded in the raid and a star state's witness, was found beaten to death by unknown assailants on a road near Tierra Amarilla on January 3, 1968. Once again a pall of fear and insecurity covered northern New Mexico. Local people refused to discuss the murder, the Alianza, or local problems with strangers.

The state press and law enforcement agencies all automatically assumed that Tijerina and the Alianza were responsible for the murder. The governor revoked the bonds of the Alianza defendants and they were immediately jailed. Their lawyers appealed the jailing to the state supreme court. Under questioning from the court bench, District Attorney Sánchez admitted that no evidence connecting the defendants with the murder existed. The court ordered all the defendants released on bond except Tijerina who was charged with a capital crime of kidnapping. In time he also was released when the charges against him were reduced by Judge Joe Angel.

The murder has not yet been solved. Rumors emanating from Tierra Amarilla implicate militant Anglo-American groups anxious to besmirch the Alianza's reputation. Other rumors hint that the deputy may have been murdered [because] he was about to change his testimony. Local observers are rather curious [about] why he was never given police protection as an important state's witness against the raiders. And still others believe that a local feud may have been responsible for the death of the state's witness. The state trial for the courthouse raid was assigned to State District Judge Joe Angel of Las Vegas, New Mexico. On February 8, 1968, the judge held extensive hearings, and, as a result, reduced the charges against Tijerina and ten other raiders from first-degree kidnapping to false imprisonment. They were bound over for trial and then released on bail. Charges against nine other defendants including Tijerina's charming nineteen-year-old daughter were dismissed.

Sánchez, disgruntled at the reduction in charges, hastily impaneled a grand jury of his own choosing in Rio Arriba County and reinstated the original capital charges that had been reduced by Judge Angel. Amidst legal controversy, the state supreme court shifted jurisdiction of the case from Judge Angel to District Judge Paul Larrazolo. This judge was a bit miffed when he found out that Sánchez had sworn in thirteen men for the grand jury rather than the twelve men specified by law and that seemingly very scanty records had been kept of grand jury proceedings. Nevertheless, he allowed the charges to stand. At the request of the prosecution, the case was shifted from Rio Arriba County to Albuquerque. Tijerina was allowed to conduct his own defense with the assistance of two court-appointed attorneys.

The constant legal battles have been costly to the state and federal governments. They have effectively slowed down Alianza activities. Many members dropped out because of fear and pressure from law enforcement agencies. Others suspended their membership, as the Alianza was acquiring a reputation for violence. Alianza funds were drained away to pay heavy bail charges and to secure expensive legal assistance. Tijerina and many other Alianza leaders were spending most of their time in jail or in the courtroom. Militant Anglo-American groups have made several attempts upon Tijerina's life. Alianza headquarters in Albuquerque have been bombed and shot at. In one attempt, an Anglo-American deputy sheriff from Bernalillo County lost most of one arm when a dynamite charge misfired as he set it against the door of the Alianza headquarters. Although the police were faithfully notified, no charges have been pressed and no one is in custody.

Tijerina has become the hero of every militant Spanish-American and Mexican-American group in the Southwest. He and the Alianza have decisively broken through the apathy and hopelessness of the Spanish-Americans. They have [created] a gulf of fear and antagonism between Anglo-Americans and Spanish-Americans in the state of New Mexico. The old political structure of northern New Mexico has been destroyed. Younger men are now organizing groups far more militant and inclined to violence than the Alianza has ever been. Unrest is growing rapidly. Unless programs come into existence to resolve the land question, secure water and grazing rights, ameliorate poverty, build roads, and recognize the existence of the Spanish language and the Spanish-American culture, violence in rural New Mexico is almost inevitable.

A New Faith—Hope for Change*

Armando B. Rendón

In northern New Mexico, in the whole Southwest, justice could be based solely on land, its products, its permanence, and its beauty. Yet there is another justice, one that depends not on legalities but on what we refer to as La Raza, a cultural entity rather than a purely racial sentiment. Rodolfo "Corky" Gonzales—a short, stocky Chicano who has in recent years become a poet and a playwright after years of earning his living and a reputation with his fists—began to preach a new faith to Mexican-Americans in Denver, Colorado, as far back as 1963. He founded Los Voluntarios, a Chicano group that a year later effectively protested police tactics against La Raza. As owner of a bail-bond business, he had financed in 1959 a barrio newspaper called *Viva,* the first of its kind in the city. The Crusade for Justice, which began in April 1966, soon published *El Gallo,* one of the first Chicano newspapers. The organization and its newspapers became central dissemination points for La Raza thought and action.

It can be said, in truth, that the Crusade, and Gonzales specifically, have instilled the Chicano revolt with much of its spirit and ideology. Back in 1967, Gonzales was probably the first Chicano leader to oppose publicly the Vietnam war. His opposition [was based] not on pacifist convictions but on the nature of the war which [was] taking a toll of Chicano lives in order to subdue a people as oppressed and impoverished as Chicanos themselves. The concept of Aztlán [see the last page of this article] originated at the Youth Liberation Conference held March 27–31, 1969, at the Crusade headquarters with a group of Chicanos who prepared a position paper regarding the Chicano movement which was to issue from the conference. From the Crusade also, through the genius of Manuel Martínez—perhaps the best true Chicano muralist in the nation—came the mestizo head: a three-profile head depicting the Indian mother, the Spanish father, and the fusion of the two—the mestizo, el Chicano.

To Gonzales, Chicano nationalism is "the key or common denominator for mass mobilization and organization." Commitment to the concept of La Raza and the Plan of Aztlán, Gonzales has said,

---

*Reprinted with permission of Macmillan Publishing Co., Inc. from "A New Faith—Hope for Change," pp. 167–170 and 327–337, in *Chicano Manifesto: The History and Aspirations of the Second Largest Minority in America,* by Armando B. Rendón.

implies a commitment to social, economic, cultural, and political independence. "Our struggle then must be the control of our barrios, campos, pueblos, lands, our economy, our culture, and our political life. El Plan de Aztlán commits all levels of Chicano society: the barrio, the campo, the ranchero, the writer, the teacher, the worker, the professional—to la causa." Nationalism is not merely an instrument of organization, Gonzales is saying, but a necessary readjustment of our own values that the Chicano must make away from Anglicization, if La Raza is to survive whole and sane in a fragmented and insane environment.

Very conscientiously, Gonzales and Crusade members make every effort to instill a sense of La Raza, of brotherhood, of *Chicanismo,* into the youngest and the oldest Chicano and in every way possible. At a conference, Gonzales will stress the use of the Chicano handclap rather than the more common Anglo applause; the Chicano style is simply to begin at a slow, even pace, then accelerate until there is a final burst of applause. Usually this form of clapping conveys the audience's approval more readily than straight applause. It seems more deliberate, communal, intense, and dramatic. Crusade meetings, such as the Fishermen's meetings each Wednesday evening at the Downing Street center near downtown Denver, forego parliamentary procedure for consensus. Young or old can participate in what amounts to a family gathering—a strictly non-Anglo form of discussion.

In December 1969, during a teachers' strike in the Denver City schools, the Crusade conducted a Freedom School for some one hundred and fifty to two hundred *Chicanitos* from all over the city. Basic curriculum subjects—math, English, and history—were provided by volunteer teachers [who were] on strike and Crusade members. But courses in Chicano history, in Chicano culture, and in Spanish also were taught, or rather communicated, principally by Gonzales and Crusade instructors. A similar program had been offered the past summer with great success and no dropouts! The program had a dual purpose, to continue the regular instruction of the students but also to Chicanoize them. This little poem was left on a classroom desk by Ruth Núñez, age twelve, following a lesson that ranged from basic Spanish to *pachuquismo* [the study of zootsuiters]:

"Poesia Aztlán"

Viva la raza
Don't let them down
Be proud of your color
Brown, brown, brown.

Down the halls of the Crusade building, the young students six to sixteen years old would come, yelling, "Chicano Power!" Even some of the teachers, Chicanos who had earned their certificates and had taught for years in the Denver school system, were themselves radicalized by the classes.

Those young people, and a few of the older ones who had forgotten, expressed a hunger and a thirst for the life-giving sustenance of that which made them what they are, Chicanos: not just tacos, mariachis, and La Virgen de Guadalupe, but their color, which they might be led to deny was bronze, their language, which had nearly been ripped from their tongues, certain inclinations of spirit in the family and among *carnales* (fellow Chicanos), and complex psychology governing relationships within and without the family.

THE SPIRITUAL PLAN OF AZTLÁN

(Crusade for Justice Youth Conference, Denver, Colorado, March 31, 1969)

In the spirit of a new people that is conscious not only of its proud heritage, but also of the brutal "gringo" invasion of our territories, *we*, the Chicano, inhabitants and civilizers of the northern land of Aztlán, from whence came our forefathers, reclaiming the land of their birth and consecrating the determination of our people of the sun, *declare* that the call of our blood is our power, our responsibility, and our inevitable destiny.

We are free and sovereign to determine those tasks which are justly called for by our house, our land, the sweat of our brows, and by our hearts. Aztlán belongs to those that plant the seeds, water the fields, and gather the crops, and not to the foreign Europeans. We do not recognize capricious frontiers on the Bronze Continent.

Brotherhood unites us, love for our brothers makes us a people whose time has come and who struggles against the foreigner "gabacho" [Anglo] who exploits our riches and destroys our culture. With our heart in our hand and our hands in the soil, we declare the independence of our mestizo Nation. We are a bronze people with a bronze culture. Before the world, before all of North America, before all our brothers in the Bronze Continent, we are a Nation. We are a union of free pueblos. We are *Aztlán*.

To hell with the nothing race.

All power for our people.

Mexicanos Need to Control Their Own Destinies*

José Angel Gutiérrez

As you know, there is a new political party in southwest Texas. It's called La Raza Unida party. The history of this party is rather interesting.

For years the Chicano farmworker has made up the majority of the population in the South Texas counties. But he goes trucking across this country on his "summer vacation" . . . ., and so he's never there to vote. Yet this is precisely the time the primaries are held—in May. And he is already vacationing in his resort area by the time the runoffs are held in June. So, you see, we are in fact not even able to vote.

We have had other problems which we have known about for a long time. For instance, the fact that the Mexicano can't cope with the culture of the monolingual creatures that abound in South Texas. You see, we're literate in Spanish, so we can't recognize the name of John Waltberger on the ballot, but we sure as hell recognize Juan García. . . .

Supposedly in this kind of a democratic society the citizenry is encouraged to participate in the political process—but not so in South Texas.

Someone asked me recently whether I thought any type of system other than the American political system could work in South Texas. I thought about it for a minute and suggested that the question be reworded because we ought to try the American system first. . . .

They accuse me and Mexicanos in Cristal [Crystal City], in Cotulla and Carrizo Springs, of being unfair. One gringo lady put it very well. She was being interviewed around April 6, right after the school board elections and before the city council elections. The guy from *Newsweek* asked her to explain the strange phenomena that were occurring in these counties: a tremendous voter turnout and a tremendous amount of bloc voting. She said, "Well, this is just terrible! Horrible! A few days ago we elected a bunch of bum Mexicans to the city council." And the reporter said, "Well, they are 85 percent of this county." And she replied, "That's what I mean! They think they ought to run this place!"

---

*From "Mexicanos Need to Control Their Own Destinies," in *La Raza Unida Party in Texas* (New York: Pathfinder Press, Inc., 1970). Reprinted by permission of Pathfinder Press, Inc.

By all these little things you can begin to understand how to define the word "gringo," which seems to be such a problem all the time. It's funny, because the Mexicano knows what a gringo is. It's the gringos themselves that are worried about what the hell it is. . . . Let me elaborate on it.

I'm not going to give you a one-sentence thing on them; I feel they deserve at least two sentences. . . . The basic idea in using the word "gringo" is that it means "foreigner." The gringos themselves say, "It's Greek to me." So the Mexicano says, "It's griego [Greek] to me." That is one explanation of its origins, according to Professor Américo Paredes of the University of Texas. Another is, of course, the traditional one about the United States troops coming into Mexico with "green coats." The Mexicanos would say, with our own pronunciation, "Here come the 'green coats.' " And there are other explanations.

The word itself describes an attitude of supremacy, of xenophobia—that means you're afraid of strangers. I pick up a fancy word here and there. This attitude is also found in institutions, such as the Democratic party. It's in policies like the one that says you can't speak Spanish in school because it's un-American. It's in the values of people who feel that unless Mexican music is played by the Tijuana Brass or the Baja Marimba Band it's no good. You can't eat tacos de chorizo [sausage tacos] around the corner for twenty cents. You've got to go up there to La Fonda [fancy Anglo-owned Mexican restaurant] and eat a three-dollar-and-fifty-cent plate that gives you indigestion. . . .

The formation of [La Raza Unida] party came about because of the critical need for the people to experience justice. It's just like being hungry. You've got to get food in there immediately, otherwise you get nauseous, and get headaches, and pains in your stomach.

We were Chicanos who were starved for any kind of meaningful participation in decision-making, policy-making and leadership positions. For a long time we have not been satisfied with the type of leadership that has been picked for us. And this is what a political party does, particularly the ones we have here. I shouldn't use the plural because we only have one, and that's the gringo party. It doesn't matter what name it goes by. It can be Kelloggs, All-Bran, or Shredded Wheat, but it's still the same crap.

These parties, or party, have traditionally picked our leadership. They have transformed this leadership into a kind of broker, a real estate guy who deals in the number of votes or precincts he can deliver or the geographical areas he can control. And he is a tape recorder—he [plays back] what the party says.

A beautiful example of this is Ralph Yarborough [Democratic senator from Texas]. The only thing he does for Chicanos is hire one every six years. He's perfectly content with the bigoted sheriff and Captain Allee [Texas Rangers] and the guys that break the strikes in El Rio Grande City and with [Wayne] Connally [brother of former Texas governor John Connally] and all these other people. Well, he gets beaten, and he knows why. The Republicans, the Birchers, the Wallaceites and all these people went over to support Bentsen in the primaries. Yet I just read in the paper this afternoon that he said, "As always, I will vote a straight Democratic ticket in November." . . .

There is only one other kind of individual who does that kind of work and that's a prostitute. . . .

Four years ago, when the guy who is now running for commissioner in La Salle County in La Raza Unida party ran in the Democratic primaries, it cost him one third of his annual income! That's how much it costs a Chicano with a median income of $1,574 per family per year. With the third party [La Raza Unida] it didn't cost him a cent.

On top of the excessive filing fees, they have set fixed dates for political activity, knowing that we have to migrate to make a living. We are simply not here for the May primaries. Did you know that in Cotulla, Erasmo Andrade [running in the Democratic primary for state senator in opposition to Wayne Connally] lost by over three hundred votes because the migrants weren't there? In the Democratic primaries you're not going to cut it. In May there are only sixteen more Chicano votes than gringo votes in La Salle County. But in November the margin is two and one-half to one in favor of Chicanos.

So you see that what's happening is not any big miracle. It's just common sense. The trouble is that everybody was always bothered and said, "We can't get out of the Democratic party. Why bite the hand that feeds you?" Well, you bite it because it feeds you slop. . . . Others say, "Well, why don't you switch over and join the Republican party?" Well, let's not even touch on that one.

Why can't you begin to think very selfishly as a Chicano? I still haven't found a good argument from anyone as to why we should not have a Chicano party. Particularly when you are the majority. If you want to implement and see democracy in action—the will of the majority—you are not going to do it in the Democratic party. You can only do it through a Chicano party. . . .

But you see there is another, more important, reason, and that is that Mexicanos need to be in control of their destiny. They need to make their own decisions. We need to make the decisions that are going to affect our brothers and maybe our children. We have been complacent for too long.

Did you know that not one of our candidates in La Salle County had a job the whole time they were running [for office], and that they still can't get jobs? The same thing happened in Dimmit County. In Uvalde this is one of the reasons there's a walkout. They refused to renew the teaching contract of Josue García, who ran for county judge. That's a hell of a price to pay. But that's the kind of treatment that you've gotten.

You've got a median educational level among Mexicanos in Zavala County of 2.3 grades. In La Salle it's just a little worse, about 1.5 grades.

The median family income in La Salle is $1,574 a year. In Zavala it's about $1,754. The ratio of doctors, the number of newspapers, the health, housing, hunger, malnutrition, illiteracy, poverty, lack of political representation—all these things put together spell one word: colonialism. You've got a handful of gringos controlling the lives of muchos Mexicanos. And it's been that way for a long time.

Do you think things are going to get better by putting faith in the Democratic party and Bentsen? Or that things are going to get better because you've got a few more Chicanos elected to office now within the traditional parties? Do you think that things are going to get better now that the United States Commission on Civil Rights has officially claimed that there is discrimination against Mexicanos? They've finally found out it's for real—we're discriminated against! . . . Do you think that things are going to get better simply because kids are walking out of schools—kids who can't vote, who in many cases can't convince the community to stand behind them?

No, it's not going to get better. We are going to have to devise some ingenious ways of eliminating these gringos. Yet they don't really have to be too ingenious. All you have to do is go out there and look around and have a little common sense.

It stands to reason that if there are two grocery stores in town and we are the ones who buy from them, then if we stop buying from them they are going to go down. If you talk about transferring the wealth, that's how you do it. . . .

In 1960 there were twenty-six Texas counties in which Chicanos were a majority, yet not one of those counties was in the control of Chicanos. If you want to stand there and take that you can. You can be perfectly content just like your father and your grandfather were, "con el sombrero en la mano" [with hat in hand].

That's why most of our traditional organizations will sit there and pass resolutions and mouth off at conventions, but they'll never take on the gringo. They'll never stand up to him and say, "Hey, man, things have got to change from now on. 'Que pase lo que pase' [let whatever happens happen]. We've had it long enough!"

That is what we've got to start doing. If you don't go third party, then you've got to go the independent route, because there is no other way you are going to get on the November ballot. And don't try to put in a write-in candidate. That never works. . . .

The recent elections here in April for school board and city council demonstrated something that many people knew was a fact. It was almost like predicting that the sun is going to come up in the morning; if you can count, you know what the results are going to be. But an interesting factor is going to enter in now. We won in an off year in the nonpartisan races, which means that we were able to elect a minority to these positions. So now the establishment has all summer long to figure out how to stop the Mexicano. This is where we get back to the old tricks and lies of the gringo.

They tried the "outside agitator" bit on me but it didn't work because I was born in Crystal City. So they changed gears. Then they tried the "Communist" one for a while, until they found out I was in the United States Army Reserves. . . . Then somewhere they dug up my "kill a gringo" thing of about a year ago, when I said that I would kill a gringo in self-defense if I were attacked. . . .

Another lie is the white liberal approach. "I like Mexican food. Oh, I just love it!" And this is the kind of guy who's got the *molcajete* [Aztec mortar and pestle for cooking] sitting as an ash tray in his living room. . . .

This kind of character is the one that cautions you: "Be careful. Don't be racist in reverse. It's bad enough that gringos don't like 'Meskins' and 'Meskins' don't like gringos. You have to talk things over. You have to turn the other cheek. You've got to be nice. You've got to be polite. You can't use foul language in public. You have to have a constructive program."

They ask us, "What are you going to do for the schools in Crystal City?" And when we answer, "Bring education," they don't know what the hell we're talking about.

You see, that's another thing about the liberals. They always love to make you feel bad. And oh, my God, we hate to hurt the feelings of a good Anglo liberal, don't we? Well, hell, tell them the truth!

We've been hurting for a long time. They think we've got education, but we know different. How come we have 71 percent dropouts in Crystal City? It's miseducation. We ain't got teachers down there, we've got Neanderthals.

These are the kinds of problems we are going to be faced with by the time November comes along. But a lot of people ain't going to buy it. The kids in the schools aren't going to stand for it. They see what this whole gringo thing has done to their parents, what it's done to our community, what it's done to our organizations. And nothing is going to prevent them from getting what is due them.

There's no generation gap in Crystal City. To the old people who are experienced this is nothing new. The older people in Crystal City, who have experienced years and years of humiliation and blows to their dignity, know what's going on. There was a problem for a while with the twenty-five- to forty-five-year-olds who were trying to be gringos. But that's no longer true. You see, those are the parents of these kids, and these kids got their parents straight very early in the game. . . .

You know, civil rights are not just for those under twenty-one. They're for everybody—for grandma, for daddy and mama, and *los chamaquitos* [youngsters] and *primos* [cousins] and sisters, and so on. We've all got to work together. That means that all of us have to pitch in. And this is why in Crystal City you no longer hear "Viva La Raza" and "Chicano Power" and "La Raza Unida" all over the place. We don't talk about it anymore because it's a reality. You see, there "la familia mexicana está organizada" [the Mexican family is organized]. Aztlán has begun in the southwest part of Texas. . . .

Our actions have made "La Raza Unida" more than just a slogan. Beginning with the walkout, we began organizing and moving in to counterattack every time the gringo tried to put pressure on the Mexicano. Boycott his store. Point the finger at him. Expose him for the animal that he is. Bring in the newspapers and photographers and the tape recorders. Let the world see it. . . .

So don't let anybody kid you. We are the consumers, we are the majority. We can stop anything and we can make anything in South Texas if we stick together and begin using common sense.

This third party is a very viable alternative. It's a solution. For once you can sit in your own courthouse and you don't have to talk about community control because you are the community. And we are not talking about trying to run for Congress because you are sitting on the school board and then four years from now you're going to run for county judge. That's not the name of the game either.

We are talking about bringing some very basic elements into the lives of Mexicanos—like education and like making urban renewal work for Mexicanos instead of being the new way of stealing land. We got screwed once with the Treaty of Guadalupe Hidalgo and now we're getting it under "Model Cities" and urban renewal. . . .

You can be as imaginative as you want and do almost anything you want once you run units of government. I'll give you an example. Everyone publicizes the fact that the Panthers are feeding kids all over the country. And everybody pours out money at cocktail parties and gets very concerned about little kids eating in the morning.

Well, the gringos in Cristal pulled out another one of their gimmicks and just a few days before the elections they decided to experiment with a pilot program of feeding kids in the morning. It was going to last for six weeks and feed thirty kids. They were going to watch them. They were going to experiment, study, conduct a survey to see if they grew an inch. . . .

Well, right now in Crystal City any kid who wants to eat can eat. Free breakfast in all the schools. You can do that, you see. You can also be very, very friendly to your opposition. You can rule them out of order when they get out of hand. You can slap them on the hand: "That's a no-no!"

They can't hold an illegal meeting—like they tried yesterday with the school board while I was out of town. They tried to take advantage of the fact that I was out of town to hold a special meeting. But the law says you must give three days' notice. So the gringos failed in their attempt to hire a principal to their liking. We don't need to be experts in parliamentary procedure. All we have to do is follow the book and tell them, "No, no! You can't do that!" . . .

Let me be serious for a few minutes because I think we have laughed enough. Mario [Campean] was talking about having a third party in Bexar County by 1972. Good luck, Mario. . . .

It doesn't matter if you don't agree with MAYO because this thing is no longer just MAYO [the Mexican-American Youth Organization]. The response that we've had to this third party in all sections of our communities has been overwhelming. You saw the results. You can count votes just as I did.

The third party is not going to get smaller. It's going to get bigger.

You have three choices. First, you can be very active in this thing. For once we are not talking about being anti-Democratic or pro-Republican or pro-Democrat and anti-Republican. We are talking about being for La Raza, the majority of the people in South Texas. So there are a lot of things you can do and be very actively involved in.

If you don't choose that route, you can stay home and watch baseball and just come out and vote. But otherwise stay home. Don't get in the way.

The third thing you can do is lend your support, your general agreement. Often we are too critical of ourselves, and the gringo misunderstands that. He says, "You're disorganized, there's no unity among you." Hell, he can't understand an honest discussion when he hears one.

So, you've got these three roles that you can play. Or you can get very, very defensive and say, "This is wrong, this is un-American because you're bloc voting." But don't forget that the Democrats do it too. You can say that this is racism in reverse, but don't forget that we are the majority. And you can say that this is going to upset the whole situation in the state of Texas because we will never be able to elect a senator, because we're segregating ourselves and cutting ourselves apart and that this is not what we should be trying to do, that we should be trying to integrate, etc., etc. Well, before you go on your warpath or campaign, come down and tell that to my sheriff. Tell him how much you like him. Or, better yet, move on down the road a bit and tell it to Ranger Allee himself.

Build your constituency, build your community—that's how we will be electing three and possibly four congressmen in the very near future. There's going to be another congressman in Bexar County, and there's not room for all of them on the north side [Anglo section of San Antonio]. . . . So we have some very interesting developments coming up. . . .

To the gringos in the audience, I have one final message to convey: Up yours, baby. You've had it, from now on. . . .

Chicano Student Militancy: The Los Angeles High School Strike of 1968*

Kaye Briegel

By Friday, March 8, 1968, students demonstrating for educational reform had caused disruptions of classes in at least seven Los Angeles high schools.[1] The leaders of the demonstrations, which had begun earlier in the week in East Los Angeles, were Chicanos. They cited impressive statistics to support their claim that Los Angeles schools were failing to give Mexican-Americans an adequate education.

Failure of the East Los Angeles high schools, the Chicanos suggested, is defined in part by dropout statistics. For example, nearly

*This essay was delivered originally at the Annual Meeting of the Western History Association in October, 1970, at Reno, Nevada.

50 percent of the students who entered east side high schools in the 1960s did not graduate. Many other young Chicanos never even entered high school.[2] Of those Chicanos who did finish high school, very few went on to college. In 1966, for example, only 76 out of 26,083 students enrolled in the University of California at Berkeley were Chicanos although one Californian in ten is of Mexican descent.[3] The failure of the educational system in the case of the Chicanos may also be seen in 1960 United States Census figures. For Los Angeles, these figures indicate that the total population had completed, on the average, twelve years of school and nonwhites had completed eleven years. Chicanos, however, had completed only nine years.[4] The special census of south and east Los Angeles, conducted in 1965, showed substantially the same result—that Chicanos are even less educated than blacks.[5] The students used such statistics to support their claim that change was necessary.

The set of changes called for by the students to improve these statistics began with bilingual and bicultural programs and textbooks and curricula dealing with the achievements of Mexicans and Chicanos. They also sought to have their classes taught by people who are at least apparently unprejudiced against Mexican-Americans. Specifically related to problems on the east side, the students proposed to have their schools brought up to the same standard as that of other Los Angeles high schools, including new buildings to replace old and dilapidated ones and construction of swimming pools, lighted athletic fields, covered lunch areas, and better libraries. Also in this category were changes relating to the employment of community aides and the requirement that teachers live in the community where they work. The remainder of the set of proposed changes called for expanded student rights including the end of corporal punishment, removal of fences, freedom of speech, and the free dissemination of information on campus. In addition there were proposals for general educational improvements, such as smaller classes, improved counseling and industrial arts programs, and the accountability of teachers to the community.[6]

These proposals, put forth by the demonstrating students, were not original. Mexican-Americans had been discussing many of them for some time. A group of Los Angeles Mexican-Americans had begun a struggle to have similar reforms adopted early in the 1950s. At first their struggle centered around the Education Committee of the Council of Mexican-American Affairs. The committee was comprised of educated, professional Mexican-Americans who sought educational reforms through accepted channels. They took their cause to hearings, press conferences, symposia, and meetings of all kinds to acquaint legislators, school officials, and the general public with the failure of the public schools to educate Mexican-American children. The details of the reform programs they advocated were strikingly similar to parts of the set of changes proposed during the student strike.[7]

Many of those Mexican-Americans who were involved in the Education Committee also participated in the 1965 campaign to elect a Mexican-American, Ralph Poblano, to the Los Angeles Board of Education. Although the campaign did not succeed, it led to the formation of another educational pressure group, the Association of Mexican-American Educators. This group was formed from the Council of Mexican-American Affairs Education Committee and those who were active in the school board campaign. With an expanding membership this new organization of educators pursued a program of trying to improve opportunities for Mexican-American students and educators. Although it declared itself nonpolitical, the new organization's members were also active in the successful campaign to elect Julían Nava to the Los Angeles Board of Education in 1967. These educators were the most visible Mexican-Americans in Los Angeles in the 1960s.[8]

Despite the victory of Nava, a Chicano and an advocate of improved education for Chicanos, nothing seemed to change in East Los Angeles high schools. Dropout rates continued to be high and college admissions low. There was frustration among the students. They had watched the older activists seek reform through the established channels and they had worked to elect Nava. Yet there did not even seem to be a recognition of the need for change.

The Los Angeles Chicano high school students had no trouble finding models, other than the older Mexican-American activists, of people who sought reform. There were examples of more direct action by Mexican-Americans in the 1960s which seemed to lead to more successful results. The most publicized and successful action of this kind was the grape strike and boycott by the National Farm Workers Association (which later became the United Farm Workers of California). The farm workers struck central California factory farmers beginning in September 1965. They refused to pick grapes without recognition of their union and the guarantee of a safe job and a decent wage. Support came first from liberal churches and from civil rights groups. Later the strike was supported also by organized labor. Through the nationwide, and then worldwide, boycott of California table grapes, the farm workers captured national attention, sympathy, and support. The nonviolent manner in which the strike was conducted, after it was begun without support from any other group except the primarily Filipino Agricultural Workers Organizing Committee, won respect for the strikers and their leader, César Chávez.[9]

Another widely publicized Chicano leader in the 1960s was Reies López Tijerina. He used direct and violent action to focus national publicity on the cause for which he was fighting. Tijerina organized Chicanos in rural New Mexico around the idea of regaining land granted to them by the Spanish crown and guaranteed to them by the Treaty of Guadalupe Hidalgo. Their land, according to Tijerina, had been stolen. The New Mexico farmers, whose attempts to seek redress through existing channels had been unsuccessful, believed in Tijerina's program. They staged marches and other demonstrations to gain public support. Their most publicized act, however, was a raid on the Tierra Amarilla courthouse. In the confusion of the raid, several wounded courthouse officials were left behind when the raiders fled. National publicity was focused on this event when the New Mexico National Guard, with tanks and other similarly useless heavy equipment, was called out to track down a few escaped raiders in the rugged New Mexico mountains.[10]

The tactics of Tijerina and Chávez, which were aimed at publicizing rural problems and trying to bring about their solution, were not the only models of direct action available to Los Angeles Chicano high school students. Other Chicano leaders also have taken direct action against the government. The high school demonstrators could also find precedents in the actions of Mexican-Americans apparently accepted by the "establishment" as well.

In 1966 a group of Mexican-American leaders from throughout the Southwest was invited to bring their problems before a meeting of the Federal Equal Employment Opportunities Commission in Albuquerque. The delegates represented such organizations as the League of United Latin-American Citizens, the American GI Forum, and the Political Association of Spanish-Speaking Organizations. When these delegates arrived at the meeting, however, they found that only one commissioner was present and that none of their previous complaints had even been investigated. The Mexican-American delegates believed that nothing could be accomplished under these circumstances, so they walked out. As they left, the delegates sent a series of resolutions to President Johnson explaining their actions and seeking a solution to their charges against the federal agency. They also stated that they would not again meet with the commission until a Mexican-American commissioner had been appointed. This walkout would not have been of such significance if the delegates had not organized themselves into the Ad Hoc Committee Against the Federal Equal Employment Opportunities Commission, and publicized their action by issuing press releases and holding a banquet in their own honor.[11]

Another example of Mexican-American protest against government policies occurred in October 1967. The occasion was an extraordinary hearing held by several members of President Johnson's cabinet in El Paso, Texas. The meeting, incidentally, coincided with a meeting between President Johnson and the President of Mexico, Gustavo Díaz Ordaz, to sign a treaty ending the Chamizal border controversy (the Chamizal is a strip of land in El Paso which formerly belonged to Mexico). While some Mexican-Americans were presenting testimony before the cabinet committee, others held their own meeting in an El Paso barrio. This second meeting was a protest against the exclusion of leaders such as Tijerina from the official one. The unofficial meeting was presided over by labor organizer and scholar Ernesto Galarza. It also drew support from farm workers and student groups in California, Texas, and other parts of the Southwest and eventually led to the formation of La Raza Unida party, which has since became an important political force among Chicanos.[12]

Chicano high school students, especially in Los Angeles, also had the example of another minority group that took action to show its frustration and desire for change. The Watts riot of 1965, together with examples of growing Chicano militancy, offered both a lesson and a challenge for Chicanos.[13]

Before the 1965 riot, none of the programs (Head Start, Teen Posts, Neighborhood Youth Corps, etc.) available under the Equal Opportunities Act of 1964 had begun to operate in Los Angeles. After the riot, jurisdictional conflicts, which had blocked operation of the programs, were put aside and the programs were begun. The amount of aid and attention, under these programs and others, that seemed to pour into South Los Angeles suggested to many Chicanos that action was necessary to bring about change or even recognition. Chicanos realized that they were the largest minority group in Los Angeles and that Los Angeles has the largest concentration of people of Mexican descent outside of Mexico. Yet it remained for blacks, using violence, to force Los Angeles community leaders to begin antipoverty programs in the area.[14]

This lesson, along with the 1960 United States Census figures that showed Chicanos even less educated than blacks, began to lead Chicanos to a comparison between their own situation and that of blacks. Black militant action seemed to have brought some results. A notable result was the appearance of black faces in advertisements not aimed primarily at a Negro market. Chicanos, however, still seemed to be represented by the "Frito Bandito." It also seemed to many Chicanos that blacks were receiving more help from programs such as those operated under the Equal Opportunities Act than were Chicanos. A Chicano community newspaper claimed, for example, that in 1968 only 88 Chicanos were entered in Educational Opportunity Programs from five Los Angeles high schools with large Chicano enrollments. At the same time, 202 students from other backgrounds received help under the program from the same five schools.[15]

Chicano frustration and discussion of the lessons of other groups came to focus in the late 1960s in two small Chicano community newspapers. One, *La Raza,* was aimed at the Chicano community as a whole and the other, *Inside Eastside,* was written and edited by high school students—the same students who participated in the blowouts discussed below. Both papers were effective in stirring interest in educational deficiencies and the need for change.[16]

Thus Los Angeles Chicano high school students had examples of black and Chicano action. They also knew the statistics cited by the older activists in their struggle to improve educational opportunities. The students could, in fact, validate these statistics in their everyday experience. They knew that Chicanos were not receiving an adequate education despite the efforts of the older activists. And now they also had *La Raza* and *Inside Eastside* to publicize their frustration. The schools needed to be improved, the students believed, and so there were blowouts.

Although such a blowout may not be in any dictionary, it is now a part of the vocabulary of many Chicanos. It refers to the Los Angeles high school strike of March 1968. The strike was largely peaceful, although there were a few arrests and incidents of things being thrown at police. The main concern of the striking students, however, was to bring about an improvement in the quality of the education they received in East Los Angeles schools.

The plan was just to threaten a blowout. "The original plan was to go before the Board of Education and propose a set of changes without walking out—to hold that back to get what they wanted," according to Sal Castro, a teacher at largely Chicano Lincoln High School and advisor to the students. An incident at an east side high school, however, triggered the blowout before the scheduled appearance before the Board of Education. At Wilson High School, which is about 20 percent Chicano, the principal decided that a play, "Barefoot in the Park," which was being rehearsed was not suitable and could not be performed. He made this decision in what seemed to be an arbitrary manner without seeing the rehearsals and on the recommendation of only one other administrator. The students and their advisor, who were preparing the play, protested the principal's action. In the climate of frustration that already existed, this incident was enough to initiate a school strike. Although the original schedule seemed to have been forgotten, the goals of the blowouts remained the same. Improvement of educational opportunities in East Los Angeles was to be the criterion for returning to classes.[17]

On Tuesday, March 6, 1968, the *Los Angeles Times* reported "Classes Boycotted by Student Groups at 2 High Schools." The *Times* reporter estimated that "About 2,700 of the 3,750 predominantly Mexican-American students at Garfield [High School] congregated across the street from the school during the noon lunch recess [and] . . . did not return to the campus until about 2:30 p.m." The principal at Garfield, Reginald Murphy, told the *Times* that leaflets calling for a wide range of educational reforms, including smaller class sizes, more emphasis on Mexican-American figures in textbooks, and expanded student rights and also urging the walkout, had been circulated on campus for more than a week.[18]

By the next day, the blowout had spread to Roosevelt and Lincoln high schools, which also have overwhelmingly Chicano enrollments. Disruptions continued at Garfield as "250 students marched two blocks from the campus to Atlantic Park in a boycott of morning classes." During this demonstration Francisco Martínez was arrested for picketing and shouting slogans in front of the school. He was a student at nearby California State College at Los Angeles and a member of the United Mexican-American Student chapter there. Martínez is an example of the "outside agitators" who were blamed by many observers for causing the blowouts.[19]

On the same day, "at Lincoln . . . about 500 youngsters left classes at 10 a.m. and paraded 10 blocks to the school district's area offices." At Roosevelt, "about 400 students assembled in front of [the school]. Police were called . . . when students began hurling objects at passing motorists. One patrol car was pelted with eggs. . . . One policeman was knocked down by a bottle when officers sought to disperse [the students]." By this time, the *Times*' awareness of student demands had also come to include "firing insensitive teachers, an updated industrial arts program, the replacement of old buildings, . . . a more liberal dress code, and Mexican-American oriented cafeteria menus."[20]

On Thursday, March 8, Belmont High School, which is only about one third Chicano, also joined the blowouts. Jefferson High School, which is in a black neighborhood, was experiencing a simultaneous strike. There were also disruptions at Wilson High School, where the original incident had occurred, and at Venice School, where only about one third of the students belong to minority groups. By Friday, since classes had not resumed at the struck schools, a special meeting of the Board of Education was scheduled for Monday, March 11, to hear the Chicano student proposals for change.[21]

At the March 11 board meeting, the students and their adult supporters, largely centered around the Educational Issues Coordinating Committee, were allowed to voice their opinions. At this meeting they demanded amnesty for those involved in the blowouts and a meeting of the Board of Education in East Los Angeles to discuss a proposed set of changes in the education offered Chicanos in Los Angeles. The board agreed to both demands and scheduled the meeting for March 26 at Lincoln High School. As a result of the agreement, classes began to resume. The situation, however, did not return to normal.[22]

The March 26 meeting at Lincoln drew twelve hundred people and lasted four hours. As a result of this meeting, the Board of Education agreed to "Go on record opposing the discipline of students and teachers participating in the week long boycott [and]. . . . Plan meetings of the Board's urban affairs committee with the Educational Issues [Coordinating] Committee to discuss further the students' demands." The most significant thing about the meeting, according to the *Los Angeles Times,* however, was that the Chicano students walked out when they became convinced that no part of the set of changes that they proposed would be implemented.[23]

It seemed, at the end of the March 26 meeting of the school board, that the blowouts had accomplished nothing. The proposals presented at the meeting were turned down as being too expensive or impractical. Otherwise, the blowouts had resulted in the arrest of some Chicano students (who might or might not be granted amnesty) and the loss of some school time for thousands of others. The blowouts had, in fact, accomplished a good deal. They were an example of action by Los Angeles Chicanos. It was appropriate that this action should be against the school system, since its inadequacy in dealing with Chicano students and teachers had been given so much attention in the 1950s and 1960s.

The aspects of the blowouts most noted by the mass media, however, seemed to be violence (such as throwing eggs), arrest of "outside agitators" (who seemed to be mostly Chicano college students who knew from their own experience what kind of education Chicanos get in the public schools) and the refusal of high school students to obey the law and return to classes. At the March 26 Board of Education meeting, and in a feature article in the Sunday, March 17, *Los Angeles Times,* however, the students presented their proposed set of changes. On the whole, the set was neither unreasonable nor illegal. Many of the proposals were, in fact, changes previously proposed by teachers' groups, professional educators, and concerned parents. The idea behind the blowouts was to bring these proposals before the Board of Education and the public and to secure their implementation.

Although the blowouts had the positive result of focusing attention on educational inadequacies, the outcome for some of those directly involved did not seem positive the following June. On June 2, 1968, the *Los Angeles Times* reported "13 Indicted in Disorders at 4 L.A. Schools; Arrests Under Way." The indictment charged the thirteen with a felony: conspiracy to disrupt the educational process. Most of the thirteen charged were Chicano college students; many were members of United Mexican-American Students and several were employed by government antipoverty programs. Also among those arrested were the editor of *La Raza* and a teacher at Lincoln High School, Sal Castro.[24]

After his release on bail, June 4, Castro was not allowed to return to teaching his classes. The Board of Education explained that since Castro faced felony charges, he had been reassigned to other work outside the classroom until his case had been disposed of in the courts.[25] The school board's pledge of amnesty did not seem to extend to Castro.

Castro continued his work outside the classroom for the few days remaining in the semester. By September, when the schools were scheduled to open again, the case of the thirteen accused conspirators had not yet been disposed of in the courts. School district policy still kept Castro out of the classroom. A group of Chicanos representing those involved in the blowout, the Educational Issues Coordinating Committee, United Mexican-American Students, and other organizations, appeared before the Board of Education Friday, September 28, to demand Castro's return to the classroom. When no action was taken on their demand, the group vowed to remain until Castro was allowed to return to Lincoln as a teacher. Thirty-five persons remained when the Board of Education offices were closed at 6 P.M.[26]

Those thirty-five remained, in fact, until the following Wednesday. Chicanos declared the Board of Education "liberated." On Wednesday, the liberators were removed by security guards. The next day, however, the board voted to allow Castro to return to his classes at Lincoln.[27]

The sit-in at the Board of Education had accomplished its purpose of returning Castro to his classes. More importantly, perhaps, it had shown Chicanos that they could change the policy of the school board. They had not, however, secured the dismissal of the indictments against the thirteen accused conspirators or amnesty for all those arrested during the blowouts.

Later in October, in fact, Francisco Martínez, who had been arrested at Garfield on March 6, was convicted of picketing and the shouting of slogans on the sidewalk outside the school, discussed above.[28] The conviction of Martínez, the only person ever brought to trial for his part in the blowouts, was later reversed.[29] After much legal activity, the charges against the thirteen were finally dropped.[30]

The positive results of the blowouts cannot, unfortunately, be reckoned in terms of educational improvements in East Los Angeles high schools. A few classes in subjects more directly relating to Mexico and Chicanos have been added, and there are more teachers with Spanish surnames. There are also, however, more security officers to protect the same old buildings and equipment. The Educational Issues Coordinating Committee, which became the spokesman for the blowouts, was subsequently co-opted by the Board of Education and transformed into an official Mexican-American Educational Commission.[31] It was funded to survey and make recommendations about improvements in Chicano education. Of course there was no money to implement those recommendations.[32]

Many of the people involved in the blowouts have gone on to colleges and universities which offer programs to recruit Chicano students and encourage them to compensate for the deficiencies in their secondary education while they are working toward college degrees. The agitation that began with the blowouts has, in addition, resulted in the initiation of Chicano studies programs in several colleges and universities. The aim of these programs is not only to encourage more Chicanos to go to college but also to encourage the study of their history and culture. Money to operate even these programs is now becoming scarce.

Notes

1. For other accounts of this see Charles Erickson, "Uprising in the Barrios," *American Education* (November 1968), pp. 25–27; Phil Kerby, "Minorities Oppose Los Angeles School System," *Christian Century* (September 1968), pp. 1119–22; and Dial Torgerson, " 'Brown Power' Unity Seen Behind School Disorders," *Los Angeles Times*, March 17, 1968, pt. C, pp. 1–5. Erickson and Torgerson are also collected in John Burma, ed., *Mexican-Americans in the United States: A Reader* (Cambridge, Mass.: Schenkman Publishing Co., 1970). My own interpretation of the blowouts is influenced by an interview with Sal Castro, Frank Cruz, and Fred Sánchez, September 9, 1970.

2. Kerby, "Minorities Oppose," p. 1121.

3. *Progress Report* (Mexican-American Study Project, University of California at Los Angeles, June 1966), p. 9.

4. State of California, Division of Fair Employment Practices, *Californians of Spanish Surname* (San Francisco: State of California, May 1964).

5. State of California, Division of Fair Employment Practices, *Negroes and Mexican-Americans in South and East Los Angeles* (San Francisco: State of California, July 1966).

6. Kaye Briegel, "The History of Political Organizations Among Mexican-Americans in Los Angeles Since the Second World War" (Master's thesis, University of Southern California, June 1967), pp. 32–33.

7. Jack McCurdy, "Demands Made by East Side High School Students Listed," *Los Angeles Times*, March 17, 1968, pt. C, pp. 1–5.

8. Briegel, "History," pp. 69–72.

9. For more information about Chávez, his movement, and his influence, see Eugene Nelson, *Huelga: The First Hundred Days of the Great Delano Grape Strike* (Delano: Farm Worker Press, 1966); John Gregory Dunne, *Delano: The Story of the California Grape Strike* (New York: Farrar, Straus and Giroux, 1967); and Peter Matthiessen, *Sal Si Puedes: César Chávez and the New American Revolution* (New York: Random House, 1970).

10. For more information about Tijerina, his movement, and his influence, see Michael Jenkinson, *Tijerina: Land Grant Conflict in New Mexico* (Albuquerque: Paisano Press, 1968); Peter Nabakov, *Tijerina and the Courthouse Raid* (Albuquerque: University of New Mexico Press, 1969); and Richard Gardner, *Grito! Reies Tijerina and the New Mexico Land Grant War of 1967* (New York: Bobbs Merrill Co., 1970).

11. Briegel, "History," pp. 66–68.

12. Armando Rendón, "La Raza—Today Nor Mañana," *Civil Rights Digest* (Spring 1968), pp. 7–17; also collected in Burma, *Mexican-Americans in the United States.*

13. Erickson, "Uprising in the Barrios," p. 26.

14. Governor's Commission on the Los Angeles Riots, *Violence in the City—An End or a Beginning?* (State of California, December 2, 1965), *passim.*

15. "Conspiracy Against Chicano Education," *La Raza* (April 30, 1969), p. 11

16. Erickson, "Uprising in the Barrios," p. 26.

17. Torgerson, "Brown Power," p. 1.

18. "Classes Boycotted by Student Groups at 2 High Schools," *Los Angeles Times*, March 6, 1968, p. 3.

19. Jack McCurdy, "Student Disorders Erupt at 2 High Schools," *Los Angeles Times*, March 7, 1968, pp. 3, 26.

20. *Ibid.*

21. Jack McCurdy, "School Board Yields on Some Points," *Los Angeles Times*, March 27, 1968, pp. 3, 26.

22. *Ibid.*

23. Jack McCurdy, "Angry Students Stalk Out of Board Meeting," *Los Angeles Times*, March 27, 1968, pp. 3, 21.

24. Ron Einstoss, "13 Indicted in Disorders at 4 L.A. Schools; Arrests Under Way," *Los Angeles Times*, June 2, 1968, p. 2.

25. "Chicanos Liberate Board of Education," *La Raza—Special* (October 15, 1968), p. 12.

26. *Ibid.*

27. *Ibid.*

28. "Francisco Martínez Found Guilty," *La Raza* (October 15, 1968), p. 12.

29. "Judgement Reversed," *La Raza* (July 1969), p. 16.

30. Oscar Zeta Acosta, "The East L.A. 13 vs. L.A. Superior Court," *El Grito* (Winter 1970), pp. 12–18.

31. "Is the deal phoney?" *Inside Eastside* (March 10–23, 1969), p. 5.

32. "The Mexican-American Educational Commission," *La Raza* (July 1969).

Nyle C. Frank, "An Analysis of the March 1968 East Los Angeles High School Walkouts" (Master's thesis, University of North Carolina, 1968), came to my attention too late to be considered in this paper.

Go Home, Chicanos: A Study of the Brown Berets in California and Arizona*

Christine Marín

The plea for a unified Raza has been resounding throughout the Southwest as a direct result of the climactic Chicano movement of the 1960s. The movement was one in which the Mexican-American became the catalyst for educational, political, and social change. It was the highly vocal and active participant within the movement, however, who sought valid recognition for the Mexican culture, language, and tradition. It was also this participant who, in some instances, was perhaps ignorant of the history and experience of his own people. Such was the case with the controversial Brown Berets during their stay in Arizona during the two-month period of October and November 1971 in those mining towns with large populations of Mexican-Americans.

The Brown Berets were originally organized in Los Angeles in late 1967 by David Sánchez, Carlos Móntez, and Ralph Ramírez. At that time the youths were active leaders of the Young Citizens for Community Action, later changed to Young Chicanos for Community Action.[1]

Acting as advisors supposedly in behalf of the Mexican-American community in the area, the group originally hoped to ease the strained relationships existing between the community and the Police Department. When their efforts grew fruitless, the young men disbanded the group to form a more forceful and vocal unit and called themselves the "Brown Berets." They wore brown berets and "mixed cast-off army fatigues and boots"[2] and quickly "adopted the brown color signifying La Raza."[3] Thus the group became a symbol of militancy and of violence, a "forceful element of the Chicano's search for liberation."[4] Proclaiming himself the "Prime Minister" of the group, David Sánchez proceeded to expose the "insensitivity and corruption of establishment bureaucracy."[5]

THE BROWN BERETS IN CALIFORNIA

The year 1968 in Los Angeles signaled an emotional and violent encounter between Mexican-Americans and the "establishment." Such beginnings were to become the stepping-stones for active par-

---

*This essay by Christine Marín, the Mexican-American Bibliographer at the Arizona State University Library, was prepared for a course in the History of the American Southwest.

ticipation in the struggle for Chicano self-determination. The Brown Berets were to play an important role in focusing direct attention to the problems facing the Chicanos in the Southwest.

High school blowouts (strikes), demonstrations, protests, walkouts, and public meetings staged in the city of Los Angeles by Chicano students began during the week of March 5, 1968. The manner in which the Brown Berets rallied to these demonstrations struck a forceful blow against the Anglo "establishment" banner of prejudice and discrimination. Such school disorders were to initiate police investigations at four Los Angeles high schools, as Kaye Briegel discusses in this volume. "The schools involved [were] Roosevelt High School in Boyle Heights, Garfield High School in East Los Angeles, Lincoln High School in Lincoln Heights, and Jefferson High School on the southern edge of downtown Los Angeles."[6] School officials at Lincoln reported that approximately four hundred students refused to attend classes. They were urged "to attend a rally at a nearby park by a bearded youth who wore the uniform of the 'Brown Berets,' a militant Mexican-American group."[7] Police officials continued to clash with the youthful demonstrators. At Roosevelt, police called a tactical alert, whereby "five police divisions surrounding the area were placed on standby readiness."[8] The boys' vice-principal, Ted Siegel, estimated that "about 200 of the school's 3,200 students left the campus during the lunch hour at the urging of outsiders, including members of the Brown Berets, a militant Mexican-American group."[9] At Garfield, the Garfield High School Strike Committee issued a list of student demands to Principal Reginald Murphy. At the predominantly Negro Jefferson High School, students complained of insensitive teachers, incompetent counselors, and the lack of minority administrators.

These demonstrations were only the beginning of the violence that was to come later in the early 1970s in Los Angeles, when Chicanos would be met with shattering bullets. But why were these youthful Chicanos staging such protests, issuing demands, and refusing to stay in the classrooms? The schools were guilty of being ignorant of the role of the Chicanos in the American democracy. The schools were guilty of destroying the cultural and linguistic heritage of the Chicanos. The students, on the other hand, were saying that they wanted courses implemented in the curriculum to teach them new ways of reviving, enriching, and maintaining their own heritage and culture. One student declared: "Chicanos owe it to themselves . . . to eradicate that system which cannot teach but simply reflects decadence and prejudice. The student strike, walkout, boycott are all the same. They are about the only weapons the students have against racist and incompetent administrators. . . . The walkouts confronted the system and declared, 'de aquí, no pasa. Ya basta!' (from here, it goes no further. It's already more than enough!)."[10]

Soon, other students would participate in school demonstrations. Students from Belmont High School complained of inadequate cafeteria facilities and the poor quality of food. Venice High School students in West Los Angeles angrily complained that police "attacked youngsters who school officials indicated were non-students of Venice or organizers of the walkouts."[11] Demonstrations were staged also at Alexander Hamilton High School, Hollywood High School, and Wilson High School. Thus began the first acts "of mass militancy by Mexican-Americans in Southern California."[12]

Associated with this type of militancy were the Brown Berets. They were "accused of inciting high school students to riot, using narcotics, being Communists."[13] David Sánchez, "at a press conference in the offices of the [Los Angeles] *Free Press*, denied charges that the Brown Berets incited the East Los Angeles High School walkouts."[14] He complained of police harassment and stated that "sixty-five Brown Berets have been arrested in the past month. There are warrants out now for five of us because of the school walkouts. . . . We were at the walkouts to protect our younger people. When [the police] started hitting with sticks, we went in, did our business, and got out." The "business" consisted of "putting ourselves between the police and the kids, and [taking] the beating."[15]

That the Brown Berets initially played a major role in awakening the Mexican-American community to the poor quality of the education their children were receiving cannot be overlooked. The March blowouts in Los Angeles were, however, only indications of the growing power and influence of the group. The police continued to look upon the group as militants and instigators of the growing unrest among the Chicano community. Brown Beret members were arrested on May 31, 1968, following a secret grand jury probe of school unrest and demonstrations the previous month of March. Charges of conspiracy to commit a riot were filed against David John Sánchez, chairman; Ralph L. Ramírez, minister of discipline; Frederic Bernard López, minister of communications; and Carlos M. Móntez, minister of public relations and Holy Grace. Others indicted, all alleged members of the organization and, like the others, nonstudents, were: Gilberto Cruz Olmeda, Richard Vigil, Joe Angel Razo, Henry N. Gómez, Carlos Muñoz, Jr., Moctezuma Esparza, and Juan Patricio Sánchez.[16] The investigation connected Brown Beret members with all the walkouts at Garfield, Lincoln,

Roosevelt, and Wilson high schools. The walkouts, investigations showed, were planned off campus by nonstudents. The court proceedings were to continue until early October of the same year. The "Brown Beret Conspiracy Trial" further served to indicate that the Brown Berets became "the official representatives of Brown Power."[17] Thus, the Brown Berets became associated with the most forceful element of the Chicano movement—militancy.

The militant approach of the organization was to create further dissension between the Los Angeles Police Department and David Sánchez, now the prime minister of the group. Police had suspected the Brown Berets of setting fires at an East Los Angeles Safeway store on April 10, 1969. Again, on April 24, 1969, a series of fires raged through the fourteen-story Biltmore Hotel in downtown Los Angeles. It was there that Governor Ronald Reagan was to address an educators' conference in which the participants would discuss the educational problems of Mexican-Americans in the Southwest. Ralph Ramírez, minister of discipline for the Berets, was arrested and charged with arson and conspiracy. Sánchez disavowed any knowledge of the incident and later claimed that if any Brown Berets were involved in arson, "they did it as individuals and not as Brown Berets."[18]

Late in May 1969 the Los Angeles Police Department's Special Operations Conspiracy Squad raided the main headquarters of the Brown Berets in Los Angeles. Leading the raid was a detective from the Hollenbeck division, a Sergeant Armas, who claimed that the raid was made because "we had cause to arrest two people on a charge of conspiracy to commit burglary."[19] Sánchez, on the other hand, felt the raid occurred because "the police were irritated by recent intelligence activities by the Berets which have reportedly uncovered two undercover agents from the police department in their membership."[20] Two Beret members, Chris Cebada and Jess Ceivallos [*sic*], were arrested and incarcerated.

The Brown Berets continued to operate their East Los Angeles Free Clinic. "With financial help from the Ford Foundation"[21] and the volunteer help of professionals, the clinic offered free medical, social, and psychological services to Mexican-Americans. Through the clinic, similar services were also provided by the Mexican-American Legal Defense Fund, also "financed by the Ford Foundation."[22] But such efforts were to be overshadowed by the arrests and convictions of those Brown Berets who allegedly created fires and disturbances in the Biltmore Hotel on April 24, 1969. Soon, the medical and legal services of the East Los Angeles Free Clinic would cease. But the violence in the streets in the form of demonstrations and social protests would continue. And a contingent of the Brown Berets would continue to participate in a show of "Brown Power" and militancy.

The Brown Berets claimed to have Beret chapters in twenty-seven cities other than Los Angeles in 1969. Some of those were San Francisco, Fresno, Berkeley, Sacramento, and Oxnard. Other chapters were begun in Denver and San Antonio.[23] David Sánchez called his organization "the shock troops of the Chicano Movement," and stated that the "Brown Berets [recruited] from the rebels without a cause and [made] them rebels with a cause."[24]

While in jail for disturbing the peace, Sánchez wrote the philosophy of the Brown Beret organization in a Brown Beret manual. The manual stressed personal cleanliness, strict discipline, prohibition of drugs and excessive drinking, and strict attendance at all meetings, demonstrations, and drills. The manual further indicated that the Berets were neither a violent nor nonviolent organization. Instead, Sánchez pointed out, the Brown Berets were "an emergency organization." Thus the Berets were always ready for any direct confrontation with any foe and always prepared for action with the police.[25]

The Brown Berets also wrote, printed, and distributed their official newspaper, *La Causa,* which bore the crossed-rifles insignia of the organization. Daniel Rodríguez, captain of national communications and circulations for the organization, was in charge of distributing the newspaper to all Beret chapters. On October 21, 1970, he was killed by the Los Angeles police during a demonstration and rally in MacArthur Park.[26] The newspaper repeatedly pointed out the "Brown Beret 13 Point Political Program," a program outlined "to unite all our people under the banner of independence. By independence we mean the right to self-determination, self-government, and freedom!"[27] The "political program" consisted of the following demands:

1. We want all land that was stolen from our people returned.
2. We demand the immediate end to the occupation of our community by the facist police.
3. We want an end to the robbery of our communities by capitalistic businessmen.
4. We want all Chicanos exempt from military service.
5. We want all Chicanos being held in all jails released.
6. We demand a judicial system relevant to Chicanos and therefore administered by Chicanos.
7. We demand Chicano control of Chicano education.
8. We want full employment for all Chicanos.
9. We demand housing fit for human beings.
10. We demand an end to the destruction of our land and air by the corrupt Capitalist ruling class.

11. We demand that all border lands be open to La Raza whether born north or south of 'the fence.'
12. We as Chicanos stand in solidarity with all revolutionary peoples who are engaged in the struggle for self-determination and freedom.
13. We denounce the U.S. System—Capitalism and Imperialism.[28]

La Causa newspaper was circulated to all those movement newspapers which belonged to the Chicano Press Association, "an informal confederation of community papers dedicated to promoting the movement of La Raza for self-determination and unity among our people."[29]

While the Berets in the Los Angeles chapter were circulating their *La Causa,* those in the San Diego chapter were printing and circulating their own "official" newspaper of the organization, *El Barrio,* published by "the San Diego *Free Press.*" In the June 26, 1970, issue, in a section titled "Brown Berets in Action," a member states: "We, the Brown Berets, consider ourselves to be the revolutionary youth of La Raza. It is our task to unite and educate our people, to serve the community, and to prepare La Raza for the struggle for liberation. We will achieve these ends by any means necessary. Even if it means the death of every Brown Beret, La Raza must be free."[30]

Meanwhile, confrontations between Chicano youths and the police were continuing in Los Angeles. On December 20, 1969, "chanting 'Chicano Power!' and led by sharp-marching Brown Berets, nearly a thousand Chicanos marched down a hill and spilled into Obregón Park in East Los Angeles . . . in a Chicano Moratorium protest against the war in Vietnam. Another five hundred, predominantly young Chicanos, joined the marchers for a rally in the park. Although the general feeling among Chicanos has been in opposition to the war in Vietnam, this was the first Chicano anti-war demonstration of any proportions."[31] Again the Brown Berets would be credited with organizing the demonstration. And again, the police were present to observe the day's proceedings and to keep a watchful eye on the Brown Berets. According to the spokesman for the organization at the rally, one of its originators, Carlos Móntez: "We're here to protest the high death rate of Chicanos and to protest U.S. aggression against the Vietnamese people."[32]

David Sánchez and other Brown Beret members participated in another antiwar rally in Los Angeles on February 28, 1970. "In addition to denouncing the war in Vietnam and stressing the fact that Spanish-surnamed GI's [were] dying at about twice the rate of other service personnel, several speakers insisted on the need for Chicanos to break with the capitalist Republican and Democratic parties and develop independent political action."[33] The rally signaled the entrance of the Chicano movement in its visible protest against the war in Vietnam. This rally also ushered in a new wave of violence and destruction which would be known as the Year of Decision for the Chicano movement.

"Students, barrio activists, professors and parents" from various sections of the Southwest traveled to Houston to participate in the "third annual Texas statewide Chicano student conference" on March 7 and 8, 1970. The theme of the conference was: "1970: Year of the Chicano."[34] The Brown Berets were there too. The conference sought to form a national Chicano political party and called for the end of the Vietnam War. Brown Beret members sympathized with both issues.

Later in the month, March 25 through March 29, members of the Brown Berets "served as security guards [and] frisked each [participant] and searched every handbag, briefcase, or package"[35] at the National Chicano Youth Liberation Conference in Denver. This four-day conference called for the unification of all Chicanos throughout the Southwest to form an independent political party. It also sought to form a "Chicano National Congress to advise and coordinate boycotts and school walkouts during the year."[36] Whether the Brown Berets actually played major roles in the formation of these two Chicano conferences is debatable. It is a fact, however, that their presence at such gatherings caused deep concern among members of the press, who were "required to sign a statement waiving ownership rights to anything they [recorded] or [photographed]."[37] Thus, the Brown Berets continued to be of interest to the newspaper media.

Several Brown Beret members were held responsible for causing and initiating "a major riot" in Coachella, California, on April 5, 1970. Police Chief Lester O'Neil felt that the rioting began after a farm workers' rally in which two opposing Chicano groups, the Brown Berets and the Progresitas, "a Mexican-American fraternal organization," began quarreling among themselves. At issue was the use of the city park for a rally. Each group had obtained a permit to use the park. "The Brown Beret rally was staged peacefully from noon to 6 P.M., when its permit expired, according to police. Members of the other organization, whose permit ran from 6 P.M. to 10 P.M., began arriving shortly after the Berets' rally. . . . Two men seized a public-address system and presumably ordered members of Progresita to leave the park." Police estimated that four hundred persons, many of them Brown Berets, took part in the "citywide disturbance." A police patrol car was overturned and burned; several policemen suffered "minor injuries" when "hit by rocks or bottles or shattered window glass." Police Chief O'Neil was aided by the

Highway Patrol, the Border Patrol, sheriff's deputies, and policemen from Indio, Banning, and Palm Springs in quelling the riot. Rioters broke windows at "all three schools in the city and at the post office." The home of Coachella Mayor Nick Abdelnour was set afire but was not heavily damaged.[38]

Those Brown Beret members arrested and "booked on suspicion of disturbance, inciting to riot and felonious resisting of arrest"[39] were Carlos Basabe and Ernesto Calles, students at Riverside City College. Later, Chief O'Neil would clear César Chávez and his United Farm Workers of any blame for the incident. In an interview with a reporter from the *Los Angeles Times,* Ricardo Chávez, brother of César Chávez, would deplore the violence and state: "We just don't condone these things. It was very unfortunate it happened the same day we had this rally. . . . We just don't conduct ourselves this way."[40] This statement would indicate the differences between the philosophy of César Chávez's United Farm Workers and that of David Sánchez's Brown Berets. While Chávez continued to expose the working conditions of the field workers through peaceful and nonviolent protest, Sánchez would continue to exploit the angry mood of the Chicano movement through visible forcefulness and aggressive demonstrations. That opposite factions existed within the movement only served to indicate the diversity of the goals of Chicano self-determination.

The confrontations between Chicano youths and the police continued. And again, whenever those confrontations occurred, the Brown Berets would be the most active participants. One such clash took place in Pomona, California, on May 30, 1970. "Two Pomona police officers [attempted] to make a drunkenness arrest within a predominantly Mexican-American crowd of 150 persons in Sharkey Park. . . . The crowd, mostly Mexican-American youths angered by a massive show of force by police during the melee at the park, retreated as officers moved upon them with batons. . . . The park . . . was crowded with families on outings, and with groups of young people . . . believed by police to be members of the militant Brown Berets."[41] That the police may have overreacted to the presence and possible threat of the Brown Berets was made obvious by subsequent action on the part of the Pomona Police Department and Lieutenant Richard Zbinden. An urgent police alert requested that all available units unite at the park. The radioed alert brought the following response: "Every Pomona officer on duty. Thirty patrol units from the Los Angeles County Sheriff's Department [many of the cars carrying more than two men]. Six units from the California Highway Patrol. Six units from smaller police departments around Pomona. . . . The tense situation caused the Pomona police to request a 100-man contingent of the Sheriff's Department special enforcement bureau."[42] It is no wonder, then, that the youths were prepared to physically confront police officers in a public park. Rocks and bottles were thrown at the police. One officer, Sheriff's Sergeant James R. Ware, was struck in the chest with a railroad spike. Altogether, thirteen people were hurt: eight civilians and five police officers. Windshields were smashed as the "protesters" threw objects at patrol units. The officers continued to retaliate with "batons and chemical irritants."[43] Thus, the incident would further serve to increase the bitterness and the hatred existing between the "militants," the Brown Berets, and the "system"—the police forces. Meanwhile, "in the traditionally quiet town of Pomona . . . a crowd of Mexican-American parents, not known for their civic participation, recently applauded Brown Beret speakers. The importance of this [was] that a year ago it would [have been] impossible to find Mexican-American parents hobnobbing with Brown Berets."[44]

Protests and public demonstrations against the tyranny of police brutality would continue in Los Angeles. Soon the August 29 National Chicano Moratorium would test the validity of such a charge. What began as a peaceful protest against the Vietnam War would soon end in violence, death, destruction, and bitterness. Such brutal confrontations between Chicanos and the police would become of major interest to the rest of the Chicanos throughout the Southwest. The need for thorough and complete investigations into the causes for such civil strife was quite obvious to the Chicano community. That their pleas were ignored and rejected by the legal system only served to widen the chasm between the Chicanos and the police. The Brown Berets continued to expose the indifference and the bias of the Anglo-Americans, who repeatedly ignored the anger and frustration of those Mexican-Americans who sought only equal representation in terms of education and employment.

The antiwar statements made by the Brown Berets and by approximately twenty thousand others who participated in the Chicano Moratorium on August 20, 1970, only served to point out a drastic need for communication between the Chicanos and the Anglos. The fact that these statements were made in a peaceful, orderly, and nonviolent manner was to go unnoticed by those who condemned the Chicanos for their protest. Members of the Brown Berets who participated in the moratorium rally helped to dramatize the disproportionate number of Spanish-surnamed men serving in Vietnam. That "outside agitators" were to be blamed for causing the violent confrontation that occurred later among the participants cannot be the justification for the ugly display of clubbings, gassings, kickings, and beatings on the part of the Los Angeles police. It is no wonder, then, that the Brown Berets became even more alienated from the "Anglo establishment."

One member of the Brown Berets, Lieutenant Lynn Ward, was killed by a "pig's exploding tear gas canister"[45] during the riot. Ward, a fifteen-year-old youth, belonged to the El Monte, California, chapter. He "was an instructor in the El Monte unit for tactical maneuvers and also worked in the unit's intelligence division."[46] His death was viewed as a Brown Beret symbol of resistance by the members of the organization.

The Berets participated in another antiwar rally at Belvedere Park in Los Angeles on January 31, 1971. The rally, organized by the Chicano Moratorium Committee, was also to serve as a protest against police brutality against Chicanos. What began as an orderly and nonviolent parade and rally would again end in violence. "The only violence seen at the park took place when Chicanos forcibly ejected salesmen of Progressive Labor Party literature from the park. A member of the militant Latin group, the Brown Berets, punched a PLP paper vendor in the mouth. . . . A spokesman for the Brown Berets said the news vendors, some of whom wore the clenched-fist badge of the Students for a Democratic Society, were 'attempting to stir up trouble.' "[47] Further violence, however, would occur at the East Los Angeles sheriff's substation, located in Belvedere Park. After the rally, a crowd of fifty young men attacked the substation. "A concussion grenade or a large cherry bomb exploded with a roar in the parking lot of the substation, and rocks, bottles and dirt clods fell [among] sheriff's deputies guarding the doors."[48] Violence continued, meanwhile, six blocks away, on Whittier Boulevard. Places of business were looted, and fires raged through the area. Again, confrontations between the sheriff's deputies and Chicano youths were unavoidable. One person was shot to death, more than twenty-five were injured, and seventy places of business were burned or damaged as a result of the encounters.

David Sánchez, Brown Beret prime minister, had previously spoken at the rally. Other members acted as monitors and organizers. Sánchez was reported to be "Cochairman of the Chicano Moratorium."[49]

THE BROWN BERETS IN ARIZONA

Sánchez was to organize, direct, and lead the Berets into another phase of confrontations with law enforcement officials outside of his home state of California. The vehicle created to carry the Brown

Beret ideology was La Caravana de la Reconquista (The Caravan of the Reconquest). The group was mobile, having initially "marched" from Calexico to Sacramento, California. They toured and "set foot on almost all of California," with a purpose "to unify an understanding that 'ALL CHICANO [*sic*] throughout the Southwest are being discriminated against' and because of this we are travelling to spread the word 'CHICANOS UNITE.' "[50] Thus, the caravan was formed "to reconquer [Chicanos'] rights to be treated like people, and not like second-class citizens."[51]

"La Caravana De La Reconquista began its first tour and deployment [on] October 6, 1971, from Palm Springs, California, and [was] travelling in a convoy movement to Arizona, New Mexico, Colorado, Texas, and California. [The Brown Berets were] also recruiting Raza from [various barrios] for leadership training."[52]

Sánchez was with this contingent of Brown Berets during a demonstration and rally in Phoenix on October 9, 1971. Seeking to recruit Chicano youths into the organization, various members distributed leaflets and handbills explaining the purposes of their visit.[53] The rally was a small one, and local newspapers did not report the rally; nor was any coverage given to the second rally held at Harmon Park in Phoenix on October 23, 1971.

Among the handbills distributed at the Harmon Park rally was a ten-page "manual" outlining the philosophy of the Brown Berets, written by David Sánchez. In a section titled "3 Steps To Chicano Power," Sánchez wrote:

> In order to have power to control our communities, we must create power to take control. . . . Organization is a form of people power. Power is to exert strength, and to persuade. In order to motivate someone of something towards change, pressure must sometimes be applied. . . . Attack without negotiating, because the negotiating table has evaded question number one, that what is rightfully ours. Attack until the [Anglo] invader gives us power to control our community, which he will refuse, so we will have to take it by continuous attacks.[54]

This type of confrontation strategy did not work for the Brown Berets in any of the copper-mining towns in which they traveled, i.e., Globe, Miami, Superior, and Douglas, or in the urban areas of Phoenix and Tucson.

The Berets were to begin their "tour" in Arizona between October 21 and November 20, 1971. Arizona newspapers originally placed the group in the Globe-Miami-Superior area on Monday, October 25. Their presence in Superior created distrust and suspicion among the residents and also among Pinal County and city officials, who reported that "15 to 20 [members] were in [the] community . . . while others were in Miami."[55]

On the morning of Wednesday, October 27, David Sánchez and members of the group met with the principal of Superior High School, Milton Dubsky. The Berets "had asked permission to show a movie at the school."[56] "And according to . . . Dubsky, the group was [also] given permission to speak at an assembly at the high school."[57] A controversy arose, however, over the wearing of the Beret uniforms, which included the display of "military-type bayonets strapped to [the] left leg."[58] The Berets "were told they couldn't come in [to the school] without removing their scabbards, so they left."[59]

A spokesman for the Berets in Superior, "Aljandro [*sic*] Noriega, who identified himself as the 'minister of information' of the Brown Beret national headquarters in Los Angeles . . . described the group as 'soldiers for the Chicano people' . . . [and when] asked why his people [wore] knives, he answered, 'This year we had a march in Los Angeles until the 'pigs' [police] came out and shot at 50 of us.' "[60]

"In protest to [the] expulsion of the Brown Berets from the school because they would not remove their bayonets,"[61] a walkout "of about 50 students"[62] from Superior High School occurred. Pinal County Sheriff Coy DeArman felt that the Berets were "trying to agitate the school kids. We had rumbles . . . that they were going to fake trouble, involve the local deputies and then take over Superior."[63] Whether the students who participated in the walkout were in full sympathy with the Brown Berets' departure is difficult to ascertain. One unidentified high school student was reported to have been involved in a scuffle, however, and was beaten. "Pinal County Sheriff's Sgt. Marshall Snyder said the boy had refused to join a group of student agitators. 'They beat him up,' Snyder said, 'but he was escorted back to school by a deputy.' He did not specify if the beating was administered by Berets or local sympathizers."[64]

Meanwhile "a state of emergency was declared by the City Council" in Globe, just twenty-four miles east of Superior. "More than 40 state and Pinal County law enforcement officers were called to [the] . . . area, which also [included] the towns of Miami and Superior."[65] Berets were in the Globe-Miami area "recruiting people to their cause."[66] The Globe City Council stipulated that the declaration of emergency would last ten days. Various Beret members, nevertheless, would journey back and forth from Superior to Miami, eighteen miles to the east, and continue to Globe. Superior, however, was to serve temporarily as the group's home base.

In Globe various members of the group were seen browsing through various shops and casually mingling in front of the Gila County Courthouse.[67] None of the members became involved in major confrontations with the police officials; nor did they meet with the high school principal. One local Mexican-American society reporter questioned the presence of the group, however, in her column:

> It is difficult to determine why these brown-garbed individuals entered [Globe and Miami]. . . . Is it possible that the small group of about 20 men who wore the armband reading 'Chicano power' was but a pilot move designed for the purpose of studying attitudes of area residents? Were they sent here to lay the groundwork for a larger movement by using the power of suggestion in making their presence known? Then again, were they sent to Arizona solely to recruit followers as they claimed? Whatever their reason for coming to this area was, it was obvious from the attitudes and opinions voiced by many of our residents of Mexican descent that these 'Brown Berets' weren't welcome.[68]

Clearly, their presence was felt, and this created suspicion in the Mexican-American community in Globe.

In Miami, meanwhile, the Berets were creating distrust and anger among the Mexican-American students at Miami High School. According to the student president, the reaction of the majority of Chicano students to the Brown Berets was totally negative. The Anglo students, on the other hand, remained uninterested and unaware of the Berets on the Miami High School campus.

The incident that occurred at Miami High was completely unlike that which was taking place in Superior. Three members of the organization went to the high school, confronted Principal Silver Barreras, and demanded that an assembly be called so that the Berets could discuss the problems of prejudice and discrimination encountered by Mexican-Americans in mining towns. The Beret spokesmen further demanded that the public-address system be made available. If the demands were not met, the Beret spokesmen promised "to force a walkout in [the] school and . . . [tell the] Chicano students to walk out with [them]."[69]

Principal Barreras dismissed such demands as unrealistic and asked the Beret members to leave the campus. As they were leaving they attempted to talk to several Chicano students walking on the campus. The students discouraged any discussion with the Berets and "told [them] to leave, that they didn't want them there."[70] Before leaving, however, the Berets "started asking the kids on the mall for handouts and for money."[71] This act further alienated the Chicano students at Miami High School and discouraged direct contact and communication with the Brown Berets. The walkout failed.

In the meantime the Berets were planning another "Chicano Power Rally" in nearby Superior. The rally took place on Saturday, October 30, in the parking lot at Kennedy Elementary School. David Sánchez addressed the sparse audience, most of whom were young school children and high school students. They were there mainly as curiosity-seekers rather than as the followers of "Brown Power" and the militant supporters Sánchez expected.[72]

In his speech Sánchez "extolled the virtues of La Raza and denounced categorically the schools, church and sheriff's deputies in Superior. . . . He [also] took time to deliver a verbal blast at Governor Reagan of California, President Nixon and Vice-President Agnew for their intolerance of the Mexican-American ethnic group and what it stands for."[73]

There were no incidents between Beret members and local police at the rally or at the parade that followed. In fact, "during the entire week some 30 sheriff's deputies, sheriff's posse and highway patrolmen—called in from various parts of the county—kept a close tab on the caravan but there never was any kind of confrontation between the two groups."[74] Many Mexican-American residents in Superior viewed the presence of the Berets as disruptive and undesirable.

Various citizens wrote their opinions and views in letters to the editor of the *Superior Sun*. Art Iberri, a Mexican-American merchant who conducted the convenience market, "Art and Lola's," stated: "Rumors have been circulating that I was sympathetic to the cause of the Chicano Brown Berets. . . . This is not the truth. . . . Some of [them] came to our store and asked if I would give them money. I refused and gave them, instead, a half gallon of milk and two boxes of cinnamon rolls in order to get rid of them. . . . I told them that . . . I . . . did not sympathize with their cause."[75] Another Mexican-American citizen, Dennis Gómez, Sr., wrote: "We do not need people like the militant Brown Berets in Superior. It is them [*sic*] who should stay out of Superior and Arizona and out of the nation, for that matter."[76] Miguel Rojo's letter expressed similar sentiments: "The one thing we don't need . . . is . . . outsiders telling us how to think. . . . Through a virtuous education, our own endeavors and the blessings of God we stamped out discrimination [here]. . . . GO HOME CHICANOS! The only thing you can do here is destroy the heritage which we have so proudly built for our children, and the mutual respect that exists [here] between Anglo-Saxons and Mexican-Americans . . ."[77] At a public forum held at the library's community center, other residents were interviewed by Phoenix television producer Polo Rivera. Rivera's weekly program, *"Este Eres Tu"* ("This Is You"), deals with issues directly relating to Arizona's Mexican-American population. Those interviewed were: "Ethel Wilson, office manager of *The Superior Sun;* Yolanda Chávez, eighth-grade teacher at Roosevelt [School]; Tony Tamerón, President of the USWA [United Steel Workers of America], local #938;

Manuel Machado, member of the Superior Sanitary District Board; Sam Rúa, high-school biology teacher; and Jennie Macías, high school student."[78] The discussion centered around the activities of the Brown Berets in the community. Ethel Wilson, a three-year resident of Superior, commented that she had not been aware of any problems existing between Anglos and Mexican-Americans in the community. She expressed a dislike for the Berets' wearing of any kind of weapons, however, and felt that their not being allowed to speak at the school assembly was a result of the Berets' refusal to remove them. Tony Tamerón agreed with Wilson: the "knives" were not appropriate. He criticized Sheriff's Sergeant Marshall Snyder, nevertheless, for overreacting to the situation. Snyder's calling in " 'an excessive amount' of law enforcement officers to patrol the town"[79] was unrealistic. Manuel Machado felt "the community was doing good and had no need for outsiders like the Brown Berets to stir up trouble."[80] Sam Rúa stated that the Berets' allegations that they were denied entrance to the school assembly were completely untrue; their refusal to "relinquish their bayonets" led to their dismissal. High school student Jennie Macías was among the small group of students who left the school "to talk with the Berets to see what they had to offer. She said she didn't feel that the Berets came to Superior to start any trouble but they were wrong in saying that Mexican-American students in Superior were being treated as second-class citizens. Asked pointedly by Rivera if any of the Anglo teachers had shown any signs of prejudice, she answered that she didn't feel that any of her teachers were in any way prejudiced against her."[81] Clearly, the panelists agreed that the Brown Berets definitely created a negative reaction in the community, and that the wearing of any kind of bayonets, knives, or similar weapons in the school was totally unnecessary.

David Sánchez stated his reactions to this negative climate in Superior in a letter to the editor of the *Superior Sun:*

> It is very strange that everytime we leave an area, the press along with others, take part in oppressing [*sic*] the truth. One store reported that there were things missing and . . . accused some berets [*sic*]. If this was so, then why wasn't this case taken to the court of law with proof of evidence. The matter is that there was no evidence or truth to this accusation. We ask the people to realize that self-interest[ed] business people, more than anyone else, do not have the social conscience for civil rights. And rather than understanding the social evils of this society, they would rather react with hostility and irrational accusations.[82]

Sánchez and his caravan were to encounter the same negative reactions in other areas of Arizona to which they journeyed. Their departure from Superior and trip to Tucson, approximately ninety miles to the south, was noted by Police Chief William J. Gilkinson and Truman Lovlis, chief investigator for the Tucson Sheriff's Department.[83] The arrival of the caravan the evening of November 2, 1971, was without fanfare, however. They carried "two large army-green trunks filled with materials, including literature handouts. [Their] van [was] a mobile closet and also [contained] attaché cases, tape recorders, cameras and a portable television set."[84] No one greeted the small group of fifteen, and no one prevented their entering the city.

The Berets' method of operation in Tucson was similar to that in Superior, Globe, and Miami. Leaflets and handouts were distributed in areas inhabited by Mexican-Americans. The people remained unconcerned. Pete García, a Brown Beret member, said "that his group was not 'going around arousing the people.' . . . In fact, Chicano movement movies that the Berets [showed], the speeches they made and the marches they conducted during their stay [appeared] to [go] unnoticed by the majority of the Mexican-American barrio people to which they directed their campaign."[85] A thirteen-mile march from the historic San Xavier Mission to Northwest Park and a rally were scheduled for November 10, 1971. The rally was a failure. "Berets marched by themselves to chants of 'Viva la causa' and 'Chicano power.' When they arrived at the park, only a few children were there to greet them."[86] Their ten-day stay in Tucson remained uneventful.

The Berets continued their journey southward to Douglas, the copper-mining community located one hundred and twenty miles away. They arrived on Sunday, November 14. Mexican-American community members allowed the Berets to stay at La Raza Unida Hall, used by Mexican-Americans in the community.[87] That the Berets were supposedly well received by the Mexican-American community was, perhaps, indicative of the willingness of the community to cooperate with the objectives of the group. Whereas they encountered suspicion and distrust in Globe, Miami, and Superior, and met with indifference and apathy in Phoenix and Tucson, it seems that they were welcomed in Douglas.

On Wednesday, November 17, the Berets participated in a parade that marked the grand opening of the Armed Forces Recruiting Station in Douglas. "The parade was a highlight of the Berets' stay in Douglas. . . . Joining in the parade were Joe Borane, Chief of Police, and Mayor Pro-Tem Esther Gutiérrez, who gave the welcoming speech."[88] Other participants in the parade included the 37th Army Field Band from Fort Huachuca and military recruiters representing the army, marines, and navy. That the Berets and the local military and law enforcement officials jointly appeared in a public function marked a sharp contrast to the previous encounters between activist Brown Berets and "establishment" law officials. What the local newspaper, the *Dispatch,* failed to make clear, however, was that the Berets staged and participated in their *own* parade as a protest against the war in Vietnam.[89] Thus there were two parades that day. Nevertheless, no incidents occurred either during or after the parades.

By permission, on November 19 the Berets conducted a public meeting at the Little Theatre, located on the campus of nearby Cochise College. David Sánchez addressed the crowd, comprised mainly of Mexican-Americans, and, according to one observer, aroused "anti-gringo feelings."[90] In letters to the editor of the local paper, Mexican-American citizens indicated their disagreement with the statements made by Sánchez. They also indicated a strong objection to the presence of the Berets in their community. Victor Grajeda felt that "the people involved in the little theatrics at the Little Theatre left a lot to be desired as representatives of what they possessively call the 'raza'. I consider myself a member, a proud member of that race and I deplore the fact that such a group should choose to represent me. . . . I truly believe that if . . . they went to a school and worked for a degree . . . they would do a hell of a lot more for the Mexican-American and the Mexican-American image."[91] Frank Guerrero remained objective in his views: "I am not a Brown Beret and do not agree with every [*sic*] they say and do, however; they are a fraction of the Chicano Movement and any one with an open mind will take time to find out more about any controversial group and why they were organized. . . . To try to understand and look at both sides of an issue is to be fair."[92] Such remarks were to become familiar and were typical of the feelings and views held by those Mexican-Americans in Arizona who were exposed to the Brown Berets. That negative attitudes continued to plague and follow the Berets wherever they journeyed cannot be overlooked. The Berets left the Douglas area on November 22, 1971. That they caused suspicion and unrest in the areas where large populations of Mexican-Americans resided cannot be ignored. The irony of their two-month stay in Arizona lies in the fact that it was the Mexican-American citizen himself who did not accept the Beret ideology of Chicano unity. That the Berets knew little of the attitudes of their fellow Mexican-Americans in Globe, Miami, Superior, Phoenix, Tucson, and Douglas was indicative of their naiveté in assuming that they could become the true representatives and spokesmen for Mexican-Americans in Arizona.

The Brown Berets were viewed by some Mexican-Americans in the barrios as crusaders in the early stages of the student blowouts. To some they carried the banner of the Chicano movement. They appeared to dedicate themselves to the elimination of the enemies of the movement, i.e., racial prejudice and injustice. Perhaps, to the oppressed the Berets became symbols of protest. To the oppressors, however, they became viewed as symbols of violence and destruction. Thus the Brown Berets became pseudo folk heroes simply because they were rebels. One cannot deny the validity of issues such as the discrimination and prejudice displayed toward a hard-working, productive, and achieving group, the Mexican-Americans. One can, however, challenge the manner in which these issues were presented. It is important to note, nevertheless, that Mexican-Americans are dedicated to the eradication and elimination of such issues, and that they will continue to contribute greatly to the further development of the United States. Whether the Brown Berets actually sought full equality and participation in educational, political, social, and economic opportunities or were the misguided, alienated, and militant products of the Chicano movement is debatable. The Brown Berets' impact upon the Mexican-Americans in Arizona was a negative one. The negativism displayed by Mexican-Americans further served to signal the demise of Brown Berets activities in Arizona.

Perhaps this demise can be exemplified by a former Brown Beret member who was with the group in Arizona. He ironically observed that

> There are a lot of people who felt the Brown Berets were a militant faction of the *Movimiento.* What they don't understand is that there are different levels of involvement and dedication within the *Movimiento.* The Brown Berets were simply at a different level too. This difference . . . only serves to show how diverse the Chicano himself can be. I see a lot of people doing a lot of different things in their own ways and making changes the best way they can. The Berets didn't know what to do when they were turned off in the mining towns. The Chicanos in the mining towns know that injustice exists, but how can they go out and change things when they're barely making it themselves? We were supposed to tell the people about the problems of prejudice in the barrios or wherever Chicanos lived, but we didn't even know enough about them and their own culture to see how everyone related to the *Movimiento.* What the Berets should have done was go on a walking campaign throughout Arizona, just talking to Chicanos wherever we went, to learn about them and from them. Then we could have used all that knowledge to be able to judge where and how changes could be made for the Chicano, wherever he happened to be.[93]

Notes

1. Armando B. Rendón, *Chicano Manifesto: The History and Aspirations of the Second Largest Minority in America* (New York: Macmillan Co., 1971), p. 205.
2. Dial Torgerson, " 'Brown Power' Unity Seen Behind School Disorders," *Los Angeles Times*, March 17, 1968.
3. Rendón, *Chicano Manifesto*, p. 204.
4. *Ibid.*
5. Ruth S. Lamb, *Mexican Americans: Sons of the Southwest* (Claremont, Calif.: Ocelot Press, 1970), p. 124.
6. "School Disorders Stir Police Probe," *Los Angeles Herald Examiner*, March 7, 1968.
7. *Ibid.*
8. Jack McCurdy, "Student Disorders Erupt at 4 High Schools; Policeman Hurt," *Los Angeles Times*, March 7, 1968.
9. *Ibid.*
10. Raúl Ruiz, "One Year Ago, 1968," *Chicano Student Movement* (March, 1969): 1, 3.
11. Jim Osborn, "High School Walkouts, Demonstrations Sweep L.A. Area, Students Protest Sub-Standard Facilities, Faulty Curriculum," *Los Angeles Free Press*, March 15, 1968.
12. Torgerson, " 'Brown Power' Unity."
13. *Ibid.*
14. Osborn, "High School Walkouts, Demonstrations."
15. Torgerson, " 'Brown Power' Unity."
16. "Swift Reaction to Brown Beret Arrests. Orderly Protests At LAPD Building," *Los Angeles Herald Examiner*, June 2, 1968.
17. Ralph Guzmán, "The Gentle Revolutionaries: Brown Power," *Los Angeles Times, West Magazine*, January 26, 1969.
18. Rubén Salazar, "Brown Berets Hail 'La Raza' and Scorn the Establishment," *Los Angeles Times*, June 16, 1969.
19. Lin Farley, "Brown Berets Hit With Police Raid," *Los Angeles Free Press*, May 30, 1969.
20. *Ibid.*
21. Salazar, "Brown Berets Hail 'La Raza.' "
22. *Ibid.*
23. Rubén Salazar, "Brown Berets' Goal Is To Fight Establishment," *Los Angeles Times*, June 16, 1969.
24. *Ibid.*
25. *Ibid.*
26. *La Causa* (Los Angeles) 1 (December, 1970): 10.
27. *Ibid.*, p. 17.
28. *Ibid.*, pp. 16–17.
29. *El Chicano: The Only Bi-lingual Publication in the Inland Empire* (San Bernardino, Calif.), August 7, 1970, p. 3.
30. *El Barrio: El Organo Oficial de los Brown Berets de San Diego* (San Diego, Calif.), June 26, 1970, p. 4.
31. Della Rossa, "West Coast Chicanos Hit Viet War," *Militant*, January 16, 1970.
32. *Ibid.*
33. Della Rossa and John Gray, "Chicanos Hold Mass March in L.A. Despite Downpour," *Militant*, March 20, 1970.
34. Cándida McCollam, "Texas Chicano Students Hold Conference," *Militant*, March 27, 1970.
35. Richard Vásquez, "Chicanos Pour Into Denver for National Parley; 3,000 to 4,000 Attend As Brown Berets Police Big Crusade for Justice," *Los Angeles Times*, March 28, 1970.
36. "Youths Go To Denver Rally," *Los Angeles Times*, March 26, 1970.

37. Vásquez, "Chicanos Pour Into Denver."

38. "Riot Breaks Out After Farm Workers Rally; Coachella Mayor's House Fired," *Los Angeles Times*, April 6, 1970.

39. *Ibid.*

40. "Riot After Chávez Rally Termed 'Spontaneous'; Police Chief Says Actions of Brown Beret Appears To Have Touched Off Disturbance," *Los Angeles Times*, April 7, 1970.

41. Robert Kistler and Tom Paegel, "47 Arrested As Melee Breaks Out in Pomona," *Los Angeles Times*, June 1, 1970.

42. *Ibid.*

43. *Ibid.*

44. Rubén Salazar, "Don't Make The 'Bato Loco' [crazy simpleton] Go The Way Of The Zoot Suiter," *Los Angeles Times*, June 19, 1970.

45. *La Causa* (Los Angeles) (December, 1970): 10.

46. *Ibid.*, p. 10.

47. Frank Del Olmo and Dial Torgerson, "Sheriff Station Attacked After Rally of Chicanos," *Los Angeles Times*, February 1, 1971.

48. *Ibid.*

49. Baxter Smith, "L.A. Cops In Brutal Assault on Chicano Protest," *Militant*, February 11, 1971.

50. "La Caravana De La Reconquista Is Coming." [Publicity handout distributed by the Brown Berets, n.p., n.d.]

51. *Ibid.*

52. Handbill distributed at a "Chicano Power Rally," October 21, 1971, Phoenix, Arizona.

53. Anonymous interviewee, Tempe, Arizona, February 12, 1973.

54. David Sánchez, prime minister, Brown Berets, *Chicano Power Explained*. [N.d., pp. 6, 7.]

55. Ted Lake, "Knife-wearing Group Accused Of Inciting Student Walkout," *Arizona Republic*, October 28, 1971.

56. Vince Taylor, " 'Berets' Continue To Recruit in Pinal," *Arizona Republic*, October 29, 1971.

57. " 'Chicano Power' Rally Fails To Entice Community," *Superior Sun*, November 4, 1971.

58. Taylor, " 'Berets' Continue To Recruit In Pinal."

59. *Ibid.*

60. Lake, "Knife-wearing Group Accused."

61. " 'Brown Berets' In Globe Bring State of Emergency," *Phoenix Gazette*, October 29, 1971.

62. Lake, "Knife-wearing Group Accused."

63. Taylor, " 'Berets' Continue To Recruit in Pinal."

64. *Ibid.*

65. " 'Brown Berets' In Globe Bring State of Emergency," *Phoenix Gazette*.

66. Lake, "Knife-wearing Group Accused."

67. Anonymous interviewee, Globe, Arizona, Feb. 23, 1973.

68. Alice Carrizosa, "Reflections," *Arizona Record*, November 4, 1971.

69. Interview with Ernest Dórame, Tempe, Arizona, February 6, 1973. (Dórame was student president at Miami High School.)

70. Anonymous interviewee, Tempe, Arizona, February 12, 1973.

71. Interview with Ernest Dórame, Tempe, Arizona, February 6, 1973.

72. Interview with José Carlos Santa Cruz, Tempe, Arizona, January 12, 1973. (Santa Cruz was present at the rally and at the parade that followed. His cousin, Ramond Rivera, a fifteen-year-old student, was one of the students who later left with the Berets "for excitement.")

73. " 'Chicano Power' Rally Fails To Entice Community," *Superior Sun*, November, 4, 1971.

74. *Ibid.*

75. "Has No Sympathy for Brown Berets," *Superior Sun*, November 4, 1971.
76. "Rojo Expressed Writer's Sentiment," *Superior Sun*, November 18, 1971.
77. "Chicanos, Twenty Five Years Too Late," *Superior Sun*, November 4, 1971.
78. "Panelists' Reaction To Brown Berets Televised," *Superior Sun*, November 11, 1971.
79. *Ibid.*
80. *Ibid.*
81. *Ibid.*
82. "The Press Holds Down The Truth," *Superior Sun*, November 11, 1971.
83. John A. Winters, "Brown Berets Have Come To Arizona," *Tucson Daily Citizen*, October 29, 1971.
84. "Brown Berets Arrive Here Preaching Chicáno Power," *Tucson Daily Citizen*, November 4, 1971.

In an interview with a former member of the Brown Berets, it was learned that the Berets received money and electronic equipment from the National Chicano Research Foundation, a program funded by the Ford Foundation. This former member, who wishes to remain unidentified, stated: "They ripped off a lot of money from the Ford Foundation. They had a lot of photographic equipment, but who knows whatever happened to the rest of the money? They didn't need that money."

85. Adolfo Quezada, "Brown Berets Go Largely Unnoticed in Tucson Barrios," *Tucson Daily Citizen*, November 11, 1971.
86. *Ibid.*
87. "Brown Berets 'Invade' Douglas Quietly; Seek Néw Membership," *Douglas Dispatch*, November 16, 1971.
88. "Joint Recruiting Station Opens; U.S. Military, Berets March," *Douglas Dispatch*, November 17, 1971.
89. Anonymous interviewee, Tempe, Arizona, March 6, 1973.
90. Victor Grajeda, in "Letters To The Editor," *Douglas Dispatch*, November 22, 1971.
91. *Ibid.*
92. Frank Guerrero, in "Letters To The Editor," *Douglas Dispatch*, December 2, 1971.
93. Anonymous interviewee, Tempe, Arizona, February 7, 1973.

Chicano Activism in Maricopa County—Two Incidents in Retrospect*

Patricia A. Adank

Chicanos have asserted themselves in the urban heart of Arizona. Maricopa County, in the southern and central portion of the state, counted nearly a million residents in 1970. In this region where cacti and rocks alternate in the landscape with sprawling, irrigated greenery, a population density of about one hundred and five persons per square mile belies the fact that almost 95 percent of Mari-

*This essay was prepared for a graduate course in the History of the American Southwest.

copa County residents are city-dwellers. In the black, white, and Indian population of this desert county are close to one hundred and fifty thousand Spanish-speaking Americans. Simmering discontent with social and economic conditions in this racial kaleidoscope boiled over into articulated protest by the Chicano urban community.[1] Active protest came, however, in the form of concerted action by pressure groups directed toward influencing policy and structure in established institutions rather than in an explosion of mindless, destructive mob violence. There were no burnings, no lootings, no bombings. Whether overt terrorism will ever occur is by no means clear. That it did not occur, in at least two specific examples of emerging Chicano activism, is significant.

Chicano students spearheaded a confrontation with the administration of a major state university, and Chicano students and parents boycotted the largest high school in the inner city of Arizona's capital, Phoenix. Nearly half a decade has lapsed since the first incident, three years since the second. Reexamination of these two occurrences indicates certain fundamental correlations. This account suggests a rationale for the absence of violence in the two situations and discerns a pattern of attitudes that may affect future activity.

In the autumn of 1968 sunbathed Maricopa County seemed untouched by the summer race riots, the screaming ghetto and student protests, which had ripped the fabric of social tranquility in cities and schools across the nation. The tattoo of contractor's hammers marked an advance from the urban centers of the county outward to new suburbs where increasing numbers of buyers sought homesites that offered quiet streets, model schools, and the indispensable swimming pools. Bigger and better buildings moved from drawing board to reality on the campuses of the county's burgeoning junior college system. New commercial and industrial structures rose throughout the Phoenix area. There was talk of a gleaming civic center for downtown Phoenix. A few miles from downtown a building expansion program offered more comfortable facilities for students who, in the near future, should number thirty thousand at Arizona State University (ASU). While the campus newspaper carried feature articles on the phenomenon of long hair sported by male students and debated retaining the traditional freshman beanie, a handful of Mexican-American students coalesced into a new organization that challenged self-contentment in the Valley of the Sun.[2]

Contacts with students from other Mexican-American campus organizations in Arizona and California provided an impetus to form a new local group at ASU. In mid-October an organizational meeting sought to hammer out a statement of goals and structure. Some saw the new group as being designed solely for Mexican-American students; others wanted to include "active Mexicans and any gringos who are concerned."[3] One point was agreed upon from the start. The service and social orientations of older, similar student groups would not do. MASO, the Mexican-American Student Organization, emerged as a new vehicle to allow and encourage Mexican-American participation in discussions of and solutions to community as well as student problems. Despite early talk regarding an emphasis on literary activism, MASO rapidly found itself in the center of political action.[4]

MASO gave public support to the efforts of striking California grape workers, and in response the university food service halted further grape purchases for university menus. A MASO representative indicated that support of the national campaign to boycott grapes was but one goal of the new student organization: "We plan to organize Mexican-American students on campus in an effort to hold them together to serve as an example to the rest of the community."[5] Deep involvement in a community-based situation was not long in coming.

CONFRONTATION AT ARIZONA STATE UNIVERSITY

The campus of Arizona State University is just a fifteen-minute drive from the inner city of Phoenix, where a sizeable Spanish-speaking community lives and works and where many MASO members made their homes. The university held a laundry service contract with a company in the inner city. When charges of promotion and salary discrimination on the part of the laundry were brought to MASO by a union representative involved in a labor contract dispute with the laundry, MASO organized a protest demonstration on the university campus. The action had widespread support both on and off campus.[6]

A morning rally brought over one hundred campus organizations to officially support the MASO-led petition that the school sever its service contract with the laundry. Two Protestant ministers and a Catholic priest from inner-city congregations shared the speaker's platform with MASO representatives and other student leaders. Clearly, the issue was not confined to Chicano students or even to Chicano community residents. Black, white *and* brown faces were in the crowd that milled, listened, then marched in the hot early afternoon sun to the administration building. MASO representatives, after a confrontation in which they presented petitions bearing thousand of signatures and demanded cancellation of the controversial contract, returned the following morning to the administration building and received the university president's decision. An investigation of the charges was promised and, should the allegations be proved true but no steps be taken by the laundry to remedy them, the university would take its business elsewhere.[7]

The incident, in retrospect, seems a tempest in a teapot. Quite possibly other issues involving the university might have been more worthy of the organization's efforts. Possibly the administration overreacted and moved precipitously—and, some critics said, from unwarranted fear—to conciliate the demonstrators.[8]

In an assessment of the choice of the laundry issue as a "cause," the MASO confrontation with the university has been described as "the first real attempt to do something we weren't sure of."[9] The laundry contract was apparently the first issue that presented an opportunity for the newly formed organization to generate interest for a specific grievance outside academic boundaries but still "close to home." It focused on alleged economic and racial discrimination within the inner city, and so drew wide nonstudent support. Any other incident that might have arisen at the same time, had it offered similar emotional and readily identifiable conditions, would probably have prompted the same broad-based fervor and agitation for change. It was not so much that the contract issue was the only significant cause. It was that Mexican-American students and residents grasped it as an opportunity to focus the opinions and activities of themselves and others upon a single issue.

As for the university's almost immediate and favorable response to that focus, and the later criticism that the institution had knuckled under out of fear: in 1968 half a dozen students with picket signs were sufficient to conjure images of impending violence as citizens and administrators alike recalled the hundreds of sometimes bloody disruptions that had occurred in student-led protests elsewhere. MASO members were well aware of the psychological value of the temper of the times and the pattern of action they had chosen. They recognized that the vocal presence among the demonstrators of members of the Young Socialist Alliance (YSA, formerly Students for a Democratic Society) heightened a feeling of urgency.[10]

That certain limitations had been self-imposed by MASO organizers, however, was made clear by their insistence on nonviolence and nondestructiveness. Urgings of YSA members that the afternoon demonstration illegally occupy the administration building were rejected. The day following the confrontation at the administration building, MASO scrupulously handed over to university officials a ninety-nine-cent check in payment for an ashtray inadvertently smashed the previous afternoon. The meaning was clear: those who sought to emulate newsreel martyrs in dramatic violence had the wrong parade! To further clarify its stance, MASO ultimately made a public statement of disassociation from the radical YSA group.[11]

By that time several other points were clear. The new organization had been established and had developed some interior structure capable of directing a concerted action, and MASO now saw itself as a separate and distinct voice by which Mexican-American students could challenge or support conditions affecting them in school or community.

The hyphenated designations, Spanish-speaking and Mexican-American, as well as Latin-American and Spanish-surname, fell more and more into disuse as the term Chicano was employed in speech and print by MASO.[12] General awareness of the designation Chicano spread far more rapidly than did agreement on what the term denoted. At times, Chicano appeared to be a synonym for militancy, with a Spanish sound. At other times its application to all Spanish-speaking, Mexican-American, Spanish-surnamed persons was advocated as a means to promote and symbolize unity among all Americans with Hispanic ethnic and cultural ties. Chicano, apparently, was a word one fully understood only if one was on the "inside." The outsider was slightly confused and often tongue-tied by indecisive terminology, in much the same uncomfortable way he was in the days before black seemed quite acceptable yet when Negro felt somehow outdated and colored was definitely out![13] Attempts to define and apply the term Chicano were symptomatic of a generalized process of emerging awareness by and about the Chicano, which MASO activities played a role in stimulating.

Recognition of the presence of such awareness, and belief in a need to foster and encourage it, was evidenced by an increasing insistence that Chicano studies programs be instituted in the educational system in Arizona. Such programs, it was held, would serve a dual purpose: to inform Anglo society about the Chicano and the Chicano about himself. The year following the MASO confrontation with the university, a MASO spokesman maintained that not only Chicano studies programs were necessary; there was also a need for the university to consciously and deliberately produce new Chicano teachers and professionals capable of reforming schools and attacking the causes of Chicano poverty. Continuing pressure to bring about institutional change along such lines clearly indicated that Chicano awareness had matured beyond self-conscious posturing to a point of identifying certain fundamental needs and proposing long-range plans to fill those needs.[14]

While student advocates of social change attempted to reach out beyond their academic boundaries, the inner city reflected a growing sensitivity to its own prevailing educational and economic conditions. In Phoenix, residents formed a committee here, joined a coalition there. They supported first one group and then still another in a crazy-quilt pattern of loose-knit cooperation, all for a single, underlying purpose: identify and counteract the negative influences that affected their homes, their schools, their jobs. Inner-city residents who had lent active support to the MASO student group at the university were, in the same period, instrumental in establishing and furthering community-based organizations. In turn, students who were active MASO members also organized or supported community programs. A cursory comparison of rosters shows considerable overlapping of memberships in community organizations, some people being active in two, three or more groups at the same time.[15]

National developmental program monies, United Way funds, and contributions of local volunteers had put the necessary dollars into founding most of the community organizations active in the years 1967 to 1971. GI Forum, LEAP, CEP, OIC, SER, EEOP, MOP, LULAC, Chicanos por la Causa, Valle del Sol Institute, and Barrio Youth Project—each of these was an identifiable organization with its own degree of active support, its own scope of action. The interrelationships between group memberships are demonstrated by the origins and orientations of three sample organizations: Chicanos por la Causa, Valle del Sol Institute, and Barrio Youth Project.

It was when MASO challenged the salary and promotion policies of an inner-city business (the laundry company) that Chicanos por la Causa was founded. Here was a community, rather than an academic, membership that sought to go beyond the single, economic issue MASO had raised. Chicanos por la Causa was designed to attempt broad institutional change in economic conditions related to or proceeding from development in housing, manpower, and business. It is clear there was a direct relationship between MASO and Chicanos por la Causa in terms of mutual support as well as certain shared aims.[16]

"The Junta," a few residents whose close personal, cooperative activities were indicated by their sobriquet, were members or officers of half a dozen community programs. Demonstrating the parallel goals of individual organizations, The Junta joined in an effort to eliminate duplication of services and to unite requests for funds. The result was an organization specifically funded to promote change and provide services in health and education, the Valle del Sol Coalition (later, Valle del Sol Institute.)[17]

The Barrio Youth Project, with a specific goal, reached out to still another group. This organization was child-oriented, and the local parish church (whose pastor had been intimately involved in the MASO protest against the laundry company) provided facilities for a base of operations.[18] The Barrio Youth Project instituted special recreational programs and a hot breakfast program for inner-city school children. The Barrio Youth Project grew from an idea proposed and activated by the same person who had served as MASO spokesman at the university, and it drew heavily for donations and personnel from both the academic and the community spheres of action.[19]

The organizations and their memberships indicate that the Chicano community of inner-city Phoenix was not without organizational structure and individual leadership experience which offered the potential for concerted action to back any effort that had wide community support.

Just such an action did develop, and this time it was the children, black, white and brown, of inner-city residents whose plight created a gut-level reaction that had definite racial elements. This reaction expanded to an emotionally charged attack on the entire structure of an educational institution.

BOYCOTT AT PHOENIX UNION HIGH SCHOOL

Chicano protest flared in the hot September of 1970. Hoodlumism at Phoenix Union (the largest and oldest high school, in the heart of the capital city) struck the spark that flamed up in a crackling series of parents' meetings, "nonnegotiable" demands, a protest march on the capitol, and finally a grueling boycott of classes at the school that lasted from October 9 to November 2. A picket line marched daily. Charges of racism were made and denied. United States Department of Justice officials offered mediation assistance, then withdrew. Parents and students voiced various complaints and offered even more various solutions. An impromptu school was operated as an educational stopgap for boycotting students. A suit was filed in superior court on behalf of the students, citing as defendants the high school principal, the district superintendent, and every member of the board. The story created headlines, feature articles, and editorials for a month. When the boycott ended, all of Maricopa County was aware of the urban Chicano and his dissatisfaction.[20]

Dissatisfaction with Phoenix Union High had been articulated long before Chicano parents, students, and organizations united in the boycott. At the same time that MASO students at ASU were considering their response to Chicano educational needs at the university level, parents were questioning the high school's educational program. In 1968 a loosely organized group of parents set up The Citizens Committee to Discuss Phoenix Union High School Problems. They sought funds to hire consultants who would help develop a program more responsive to the needs of Phoenix Union students, particularly black and Chicano students.[21]

In the 1967/68 school year the curriculum at Phoenix Union prescribed education for students who were 20.22 percent black, 35.05 percent white, and 42.59 percent Mexican-American.[22] Once it was funded, the new Citizens Committee set about structuring a program that they hoped would meet an acknowledged need for remedial training (particularly in reading skills) and would at the same time offer a challenge to more capable students in both vocational and academic areas. In recognition of the tricultural background of students at the school, the Citizens Committee program stressed black- and Hispanic-oriented courses in the humanities to provide balance. The program included recommendations for staffing and implementation, called for special workshop training sessions for teachers prior to implementation, and listed necessary supportive innovations. These included additional tutorial programs and policy-making parental committees.[23] The program was placed before the school board in September 1969. Response was noncommittal, and a series of negotiations with school officials finally led frustrated Chicanos to walk out of a meeting of the school board.[24]

Several weeks later the board acknowledged the recommendations of the Citizens Committee. It also recognized that an outside force was attempting to influence the school's administrative policy and procedure. The board stated its position regarding such influence: "We do take the challenge of educating our minorities seriously, . . . we also take seriously any interruption of that process. We will resist vigorously any attempts to disrupt our schools."[25]

In response to the proposed program, the school system prepared a position paper and forwarded it to the Citizens Committee. The committee had asked immediate implementation of several proposals, particularly in regard to hiring more Mexican-American staff and involving parents in the screening, selection, and hiring process. The position paper pointed to recent increases in Mexican-American staff and pledged to recruit more minority staff, especially Mexican-Americans in the counseling field. Establishment of a special tutoring corps was promised. A campus security problem was acknowledged, and the steps already taken to meet it were listed. Declining enrollment was reflected in the figures given for funds spent, and those pledged, to improve the physical plant at the school.[26]

Certain curriculum suggestions were, in fact, carried out at Phoenix Union in 1969. But while the school system's position paper reiterated the willingness of the administration to consult with parents, at the same time it made quite clear that advice and assistance from the community were not to be confused with final decision-making power. The position paper rejected the plan for a screening and selection committee that could recruit and could approve or reject all teacher, counselor, and teacher-aide applicants. Furthermore, the paper had a word of admonition for those persons involved in developing such a plan: it was not "appropriate for those outside the profession to consider themselves qualified to judge concerning the professional qualifications of applicants or present employees."[27]

Perhaps to reaffirm its own layman "professional qualifications" in the matter, or perhaps with an eye to phasing out what increasingly appeared to be a problem school, the school board proposed to do its own in-depth study of Phoenix Union High with particular attention to projected enrollment through 1980.[28]

This was not the first study designed to plot a future course for the high school. Two years prior, in 1967, a Future Plans Committee, made up of two instructors, two department chairmen, a counselor, a school-community worker, and a former student president at Phoenix Union, submitted findings and projections to the school board.[29] Recommendations were to raze outdated buildings, offer free and reduced-price lunches and a low-cost breakfast program, achieve better representation of minority groups at every level of employment in the school, add courses of study emphasizing Negro and Mexican-American cultural backgrounds and contributions, hold teacher workshop sessions to sensitize faculty to special student and community needs, and improve communications and cooperation between school, parents, and community.[30]

This report also cited as negative conditions the fact that many youngsters were counseled to "setting their sights a little lower" when they made educational and career plans and that many students were often "advised to prepare for a less skilled job."[31] Although in a foreword the report protested such channeling, its curriculum recommendations placed heavy stress on occupational and vocational training and orientation, particularly at the freshman and sophomore levels.[32] It would seem that such a curriculum also constituted setting students' sights a little lower, automatically. The Future Plans Committee, however, did not seem to see any contradiction between their criticisms and their recommendations.

A rationale for the recommendations may be extracted from the superintendent's *Annual Report* which provides a statistical breakdown of student curriculum and enrollment in fast-learner, slow-learner, and retarded-learner programs in all schools in the Phoenix Union High School District. That breakdown, in the light of curriculum recommendations made by the Future Plans Committee, suggests unmistakably that the committee assessed what it presumed to be evidence of the capability and interests of Phoenix Union students and opted in favor of "the greatest good for the greatest number"—manual career training.[33]

In addition, recommendations of the Future Plans Committee were necessarily dictated by their stated belief that the school was not a contributing factor to social and economic conditions. Following a vivid description of the appalling environmental conditions surrounding Phoenix Union High, the report clearly affirmed the committee's thinking on the school system's responsibility in the matter. "These problems are not products of the school, but they are *in* the school. The problems have been created by the community. The school cannot be held accountable for such social injustices as job and housing discrimination."[34]

From such a basis of thought and from its evaluation of the low academic capability and achievement of minorities as designated and tested by the system's standards, it follows that the Future Plans Committee would have chosen to channel students toward manual rather than intellectual development, without consideration of the fact that such a choice produces and perpetuates economic-racial discrimination.

Although the report of the Future Plans Committee incisively identified and described negative conditions and attitudes in the high school and the surrounding area, its patronizing tone in exhorting faculty and administration to sympathize with the problems as outlined made the *Report of Future Plans Committee* a model of starry-eyed liberalism. It was a reflection of the thinking of an era, of a time when the dominant sector of our society grew uncomfortable with its affluence and magnanimously determined to shoulder the responsibility of deciding for the less-fortunate minority sectors how they might share in "the good life." The Phoenix Union High School District had "discovered" poverty, the inner city, the blacks and the Chicanos.

Poverty, the inner city, the blacks, and the Chicanos had, of course, been around for some time in the Phoenix Union High School area. That Phoenix Union High and its surroundings had deteriorated was no surprise to parents and students. They had watched it happen.

Phoenix Union High was founded in 1895. Then, in the early 1950s, the district added to Phoenix Union the aged Phoenix Technical School. That move sufficed for development and improvement while the district directed its attention elsewhere. The reputation Phoenix Union High enjoyed, that of a quality educational institution in all respects, was soon to decline. From 1953 to 1964 the Phoenix Union High School District, in response to new civil rights legislation and a rapidly expanding school population, discontinued its segregated black high school, added seven new secondary schools, and planned to add an eighth by 1971. It appears that in the booming district growth and change no one paid a great deal of attention to Phoenix Union except parents, students, and concerned staff who had to function there.[35]

By the late 1960s the buildings at Phoenix Union showed the scars of time and neglect. The curriculum emphasized vocational training, reflecting the presence of the vocational-technical sister-school. The ethnic composition of Phoenix Union showed a great change, which suggests that at least one part of the student population was fleeing to the new schools in outer areas. There was a steady rise in the percentage of black and Chicano students in attendance and a sharp decline in the percentage of white students. In the three-year period 1967 to 1970 alone, the percentage of white students at Phoenix Union dropped from 35.05 percent to 19.32 percent.[36]

That Phoenix Union High School was in trouble could have been seen long before it was recognized in committee reports. That certain committee reports had generated part of the problem was one contention of increasingly dissatisfied and vocal parents. The majority element in the Phoenix Union High School District system had spent considerable time and effort in committees to assess the situation and determine what was best in the way of education for the minority students who made up the bulk of Phoenix Union's student population. By 1969 parents and students were less and less willing to accept the value or the validity of such a determination. They objected to the physical deterioration of the school, but more significantly they questioned that the educational program in operation was, in fact, the best for the students. Furthermore, if at Phoenix Union education was, indeed, to be designed for "minorities," they wanted minorities to formulate, orient, and execute such education. They demanded at least a voice in determining and conducting education at Phoenix Union.

Such demands stimulated the bureaucracy to new efforts, the peculiar effect of which was more committee reports. While the school board scanned parental recommendations, warned "outsiders" not to judge professionals' qualifications, and jockeyed with several companies to contract for a planning study on the school, everyone got into the act with "concerned" organizational structures designed to *do* something about education[37] All across Maricopa County, all across the state, a welter of discussion, workshop, evaluation, awareness, and planning committees popped up. Any organization with a membership or orientation that might be categorized "minority" was tapped for participation. Just to show how broad-based all this cooperation was going to be, even the American Indian was included.[38]

Winter gave way to spring and spring to summer, and still the committees consulted and compiled. The findings often repeated those detailed years earlier.[39] The only real difference was that this time minorities were not merely consulted; they took an active part in totaling up a large portion of the findings, recommendations, and complaints. This might have gone on indefinitely, drowning demands for action in a sea of paper and procedure.

An example of the kind of procedure that could stymie action on changes proposed for Phoenix Union High appeared in the proposed school budget for 1970/71. Community reaction indicated a mistrust regarding district commitment for improvement. The program and curriculum changes proposed by parents for Phoenix Union High had fallen victim to procedure. Someone noticed that the two-hundred-and-fifty-thousand-dollar price tag put on the Citizens Committee's Freshman Program had turned up in the portion of the school district's annual budget that required voter approval for funding. A new committee, Inner City Parents and Interested Citizens, immediately recommended that the proposed program be shifted to the "lower budget," that portion which did not require voter approval. It was suggested that other spending areas such as athletics, the ROTC program, health education teachers, and a portion of the administration budget be placed in the "upper budget" portion of funding which had to be submitted to the voters. If the voters rejected funding of these areas the Inner City Parents and Interested Citizens obviously considered such curtailment no great loss. Besides, the funding might be approved. The inner-city delegation asked that budget funding procedures be changed to forestall what they believed would be cancellation at the polls of a program that was given high priority only by Phoenix Union High parents and students.[40] Clearly the inner city did not believe middle-class voters in the district would be willing to approve funds to upgrade an inner-city school.

In September, Phoenix Union High opened with a smattering of adaptations from the previous year's Citizens Committee proposals still in operation. It seemed that the proposals had not helped very much. It was still "business as usual," at the school, or perhaps a little worse. The five-thousand-plus student population of 1961 was down to little more than two thousand in the opening days of the 1970/71 school year. Dropouts as a percentage of enrollment had moved steadily upward from 19.7 percent in 1963 to 25.4 percent in 1965, and thereafter it seldom varied by more than a tenth of a percentage point. On the basis of past performance, at least twenty-five of every hundred students who walked through the doors of Phoenix Union High that autumn were doomed to drop out before the school year ended.[41]

Soon after school opened, none of this mattered. The committee reports, the tussles with the school board, the efforts of black, white, and brown parents to work together to gain a voice and a new responsiveness in their children's high school—none of these mattered. Black-Chicano racism took over.

Teen-age strong-arm tactics, purse pilfering, fights, and petty terrorism had intermittently, but increasingly, agitated campus life at Phoenix Union High for several years. Black and Chicano students had a violent confrontation, one that drew city police to the campus in force, only the year before. New security measures designed to ward off repetition of the incident offered daily abrasion to already sensitive relations. Communication between black and Chicano parents had been eroded by the racial undertones that permeated every negative contact between students. Communication with the school administration on the subject stood at an impasse.[42]

One explanation of the attitudes of the blacks was that since Phoenix Union had implemented some of the Citizens Committee recommendations, and since Chicano students outnumbered black students, the school was beginning to respond to Chicano pressure alone. As a corollary "The blacks were becoming defensive. They felt threatened."[43]

Chicano attitudes and emotional responses were mixed. There was the obvious protective concern of parents who felt that their children were being victimized. In addition, among many Chicano parents the campus and street incidents brought to the surface any latent racist reaction toward blacks. Whether or not the Phoenix

Union campus was peaceful did not matter. When it came to blacks, "They didn't want their kids to go to school with them."[44] Whether racist or protective motivations were dominant was irrelevant at the time. The Chicano community saw and reacted to one obvious thing: "Violence was being perpetrated on their kids."[45] Chicano parents and leaders from Chicano organizations, projects, and programs in the inner city united in an action to protect their own.

Weekend meetings of Chicano students and parents produced a list of demands that, following a protest march to Phoenix Union, were presented to the principal. The administration and the school board reviewed the demands and said some would take time, whereas others were impossible. Two days later there was another protest march, this time to the municipal building and the capitol, where protesting parents demanded that the Board of Education meet with them that night. The board refused.[46]

Phoenix Union High administrators added more security measures at the campus, and the situation there was described as calm. Within the week, Chicano parents and leaders attended a regular board meeting, only to walk out. One night the following week, an Ad Hoc Chicano School Board was formed and an ultimatum was issued. By phone and press, notification was given to the district superintendent, the mayor, the state superintendent of public instruction, and all members of the Phoenix Union High School District board to appear at a meeting the next morning. Most of the officials on the list, and some who were not, showed up. They heard the representative of the parents' group plea for the safety of students at Phoenix Union, demand the resignation of the principal, and insist upon the implementation of curriculum reforms proposed earlier. And then the Chicano delegation pulled the plug. The Ad Hoc Chicano School Board called for an immediate boycott of Phoenix Union High School.[47]

That was on a Friday. By Tuesday nearly half of the students at Phoenix Union were absent from classes. Administrators counted the loss in ADA (average daily attendance) funds and spoke of the situation with an emphasis on law and order. The now-functioning Parent-Student Boycott Committee insisted that law and order on the campus was but part of a larger grievance.[48] It is at this point that an effort to bring about a change of direction in the thinking of the Chicano community can be detected.

This was the point at which a readily identifiable situation (terrorism on the campus) generated a strong emotional reaction (parental concern reinforced with a degree of racism) which mobilized the entire inner-city Chicano community. With the united front the community presented at the moment, this was the time to focus attention on long-standing and basic grievances regarding the quality and orientation of education at Phoenix Union High in terms of the kind of society it perpetuated in the inner city. Furthermore, unless the focus of the situation was expanded beyond black-Chicano racism, the boycotting students and enraged parents might well erupt into uncontrollable physical violence and rioting.[49]

Newspaper accounts recorded, day by day and blow by blow, the publicity releases and public statements of the Boycott Committee and the district school board. Editorials insisted that the issue was merely hoodlumism and that only a tiny number of an otherwise peaceful black community was involved. For the most part, the media offered an oversimplified view of the actual sources of community-school conflict, and this view was frequently characterized by a great deal of what can only be called wishful thinking. An examination of correspondence between district officials and the Parent-Student Boycott Committee makes possible a more definitive evaluation of the actual issues around which the boycott action centered and upon which community and school ultimately reached formal agreement.

A parent-student committee had initially presented nine demands to the administration of Phoenix Union High School. These demands were later incorporated into a more specific list of eight presented to the Phoenix Union High district board by the Parent-Student Boycott Committee. These eight demands were the subject of negotiation.

Student security, which had generated the emotion that coalesced in support of the boycott, was seventh on the list of negotiating points, and that is probably an accurate assessment of its considered priority. The second had to do with student security of another type. It was to gain this point that a suit had been filed in superior court on behalf of boycotting students who were being dropped from Phoenix Union High. During negotiations it was proposed, and agreed, that students who had left classes in support of the boycott were to be reinstated, and not reprimanded in any way. For the rest, the Parent-Student Boycott Committee proposed and the board agreed, at least in principle, to attack the broader question of educational responsiveness which the committee had raised.[50] It is clear, therefore, that the issue had grown larger than black-Chicano racism and the immediate problem of student security.

Those who insisted upon seizing the moment of unity generated by racist-tinged violence, and redirecting energies toward a wider, more comprehensive view of the situation, were obviously successful in their efforts. A key factor in their success clearly lies in the interrelationships between members of functioning Chicano organizations in the inner city and members of the Parent-Student Boycott Committee. Three organizations in particular (Valle del Sol Institute, Chicanos por la Causa, and Barrio Youth Project) supplied people from their own key personnel who took up instrumental roles in organizing and directing the boycott operation. Logically, personnel and facilities of these organizations also were employed in boycott activities. (This is particularly true of Barrio Youth Project, where classrooms were operated for boycotting students, and Valle del Sol, where tutoring sessions were conducted after the boycott ended.)

The boycott had the support and involvement of important structures of strongly community-oriented and personally cooperative leadership. The community responded to the leadership. That such leadership chose to play down and redirect racial agitation and aroused parental sympathies is probably the single, satisfactory explanation for the absence of rioting and physical violence in a situation that had all the potential for both.

The publicity and emotion of the Phoenix Union boycott, much like that of the MASO-university confrontation two years prior, wound down abruptly.[51] In both cases some follow-through can be discerned. Public confidence in the leadership involved in each incident can be inferred from the subsequent elections of the MASO demonstration spokesman and of the Parent-Student Boycott Committee chairman to public office as state senator and county supervisor, respectively. Under fire, both the university and the high school implemented programs that, on the surface, appear to be more responsive to the educational needs of Chicanos. (How well these institutions serve the educational needs of other minority students is a question that requires and deserves additional, in-depth evaluation.)

It does not appear likely that the university will see a repetition of the public demonstration of 1968. The inclination and the impetus for that type of action seem to have dissipated. MASO (now MECHA, Movimiento Estudiantil Chicano de Aztlán) remains intact, but its orientation seem to have matured, or at least shifted. The organization is still active in the political arena, but it follows less public, dramatic patterns of action. There is an indication that MECHA, at least on other campuses, is moving toward the literary activism first mentioned in 1968 at ASU.[52]

At Phoenix Union High enrollment has seen no large upswing, and the dropout rate no great downturn. An extensive study made after the boycott, which expanded recommendations for the school, does not seem to have resulted in any thorough pattern of radical or obvious change. The same principal remains at the school and, in the opinion of at least one person involved in the boycott, until there is a change in administration no great change can be expected in the school.[53]

It can be concluded that these two incidents, discussed as examples of emerging Chicano activism, not only reflected but produced a new awareness of self for the Chicano in Maricopa County. In each case the Chicano ultimately moved to challenge the institutions of education in Arizona to recognize his presence and take steps to foster what he perceives as his cultural heritage. Additionally, in both instances there was the insistence that educational institutions acknowledge the powerful effect they have in shaping economic and social conditions in their communities, and insistence that educational institutions reject policies that foster or perpetuate inequities. Thus, perhaps the true fundamental and significant basis for emerging Chicano activism was a growing self-confidence that allowed the urban Chicano in Maricopa County to demand, on his own terms, his own piece of the American economic pie.

That self-confidence, based on consciously developed self-awareness and reinforced by the example of now-successful Chicano individuals and organizations, appears to be expanding in urban Chicano circles where the opportunity for communication and idea exchange is greater. If the majority in our society cannot learn to make room for this newly confident and articulate Chicano element, particularly in coming to terms with educational, housing, and economic conditions of the urban area, the kind of community coalition that made the Phoenix Union boycott possible may again crystallize in anger. Should this occur, as it did in 1970, a similarly rational and cohesive leadership may not be present, or willing, or able, to prevent violence in the inner city a second time.

Notes

1. Valley National Bank, *Arizona Statistical Review* (Phoenix: Valley National Bank, 1972), p. 34; *Arizona Republic–Phoenix Gazette, Inside Phoenix '72* (Phoenix: *Arizona Republic–Phoenix Gazette,* 1972), pp. 13, 14.

2. Valley National Bank, *Statistical Review,* p. 34; *Arizona Republic–Phoenix Gazette, Inside Phoenix '72,* pp. 14, 49; Governor's Office, *Executive Budget, 1973–74,* 2 (Phoenix: Governor's Office, 1973): 658.

3. *State Press,* November 11, 1968.

4. José "Pepe" Martínez (hereinafter, Martínez), in interview at Valle del Sol Institute, April 2, 1973. Gustavo Chávez, "The Laundry Issue: The Birth of

MASO," American Studies Program, Chicano Studies Project–Bibliographer's Office, Arizona State University, 1971, pp. 1–6.

5. *State Press,* November 29, 1968.

6. Chávez, "Laundry Issue," p. 3.

7. *Arizona Republic,* November 21, 1968; *Phoenix Gazette,* November 20, 21, 1968; *State Press,* November 20–22, 1968.

8. *State Press,* November 27, 1968; *Arizona Republic,* article series by Eugene A. Marín, state director, Arizona Economic Opportunity Office, December 9, 1969.

9. Martínez, in interview, April 2, 1973.

10. *State Press,* November 22, 1968, September 24, 1969; Mexican-American-Student-Confederation, San Jose State College chapter, "La Palabra de MASO," San Jose, 1968, mimeographed; see also: Steven Kelman, *Push Comes to Shove—the Escalation of Student Protest* (Boston: Houghton Mifflin, 1970); Kenneth Kenniston, *Young Radicals—Notes on Committed Youth* (New York: Harcourt, 1968.); Martínez, in interview, April 2, 1973.

11. *State Press,* November 26, 1968.

12. Mexican-American-Student-Organization, Arizona State University chapter, "La Disensión," May 4, 31; August 12, 19; September 1, 8; October 1, 2, 5, 12, 14, 16; November 3, 9, 15, 17, 18; December 3, 15, 18, 1970; Chávez, "Laundry Issue," p. 6.

13. *Arizona Republic,* Marín series, December 7, 9, 1969.

14. *State Press,* December 4, 1969, January 9, 1970, January 8, 1971.

15. Listed below are various community organizations in which Mexican-American memberships overlap.

LEAP (Leadership and Education for the Advancement of Phoenix)
CEP (Concentrated Employment Program)
OIC (Opportunities Industrialization Center)
SER (Spanish Education Rehabilitation)
EEOP (Equal Education Opportunities Program)
MOP (Migrant Opportunity Program)
LULAC (League of United Latin-American Citizens)

The following membership list, drawn from those organizations with primarily Chicano or local foundation and orientation, gives a brief indication of group personnel interrelationships involved in the incidents under discussion:

Juan Alvarez. Chicanos por la Causa, Acting Director, 1969; MOP-Phoenix, Peoria.

Henry Arredondo. EEOP, Director; MOP; Minority Group Educational Advisory Commission.

Frank Q. Carillo. LULAC, State Education Director; Minority Group Educational Advisory Commission, Special Subcommittee.

Manuel Domínguez. Valle del Sol Coalition; Valle del Sol Institute, Director; Chicanos por la Causa—member, Board of Directors; Phoenix Urban League; Minority Group Educational Advisory Commission, Special Subcommittee; Parent-Student Boycott Committee, Research Survey, Liaison.

Alfredo Gutierrez. MASO, organizer, officer, spokesman; Barrio Youth Project-organizer, worker; Chicanos por la Causa, Special Projects Assistant; "Boycott School," Director; Parent-Student Boycott Committee, Research Survey, Liaison; State Legislature, Senator, District 23, elected 1972.

Joe Eddie López. Chicanos por la Causa, President, Chairman–Board of Directors; Parents Advisory Committee, PUHS; Freshman Program Curriculum Committee, Chairman; Parent-Student Boycott Committee, Chairman, Spokesman, Author–Research Survey, Liaison; Minority Group Educational Advisory Commission, Special Subcommittee; State Board of Supervisors, Supervisor, Maricopa County, elected 1972.

José "Pepe" Martínez. MASO, organizer, officer; Chicanos por la Causa, Special Projects; Parent-Student Boycott Committee, Research Survey; Valle del Sol Institute, staff.

Earl Wilcox. Barrio Youth Project, Director; Chicanos por la Causa, staff member; Parent-Student Boycott Committee-Research Survey.

Rev. Frank Yoldi. Sacred Heart Parish, Phoenix, Associate Pastor; Santa Rita Community Center (Barrio Youth Project Center); MASO, demonstration guest speaker; Chicanos por la Causa, member, Board of Directors; Parents Advisory Committee, PUHS.

16. Chicanos por la Causa, *Chicanos por la Causa, '69* (Phoenix: Chicanos por la Causa, 1969); Chicanos por la Causa, *Chicanos por la Causa, '71* (Phoenix: Chicanos por la Causa, 1971); and López, in interview, county supervisor's office, April 11, 1973.

17. Manuel Domínguez, in interview, Valle del Sol Institute, April 2, 1973; López, in interview, April 11, 1973.

18. *Arizona Republic,* November 21, 1968; *State Press,* November 27, 1968.

19. Martínez, in interview, April 2, 1973.

20. *Arizona Republic,* October 10, 12–17, 21–24, 26–31, 1970; November 2, 3, 1970; *Phoenix Gazette,* October 12, 14, 17, 21, 23, 24, 26–28, 30, 1970; Belén Servín, "The Phoenix Union High School Boycott," American Studies Program–Director's files, Arizona State University, 1970; Parents Advisory Committee to Phoenix Union High School District Board of Education (hereinafter, PUHS Board), October 15, 1970, Manuel Domínguez personal files (hereinafter, Domínguez File); PUHS Board to Parents-Students Boycott Committee, October 18, 1970, Domínguez File; Trevor G. Browne, president, PUHS Board, to López, chairman, Parents Advisory Committee, October 20, 1970, Domínguez File; Parents-Students Boycott Committee to Browne, October 27, 1970, Domínguez File; Browne to López, October 29, 1970, Domínguez File.

21. López, in interview, April 11, 1973.

22. Phoenix Union High School (hereinafter, PUHS) System, *Pupil Membership Distribution–Minority, Non-Minority Groups* (Phoenix: PUHS System, 1970).

23. Citizens Committee to Discuss PUHS Problems (hereinafter, Committee to Discuss), "Freshman Program: PUHS," mimeographed (Phoenix: Committee to Discuss, 1969).

24. *Arizona Republic,* October 12, 15, 1969.

25. Howard C. Seymour, superintendent, PUHS System, to Committee to Discuss, November 7, 1969, Domínguez File.

26. Seymour to Committee to Discuss, "A Suggested Program of Action, PUHS System for the School Year 1970–71," November 7, 1969, pp. 1, 3, 4, 6, 7, Domínguez File (hereinafter, Position Paper); Dr. Waters, PUHS Board, to Robert Lindberg, director, Pupil Personnel Services, September 25, 1969, Domínguez File; Tony R. Núñez, Pupil Personnel Services, South Mountain High School, to Manuel Domínguez, On-the-Job Training Program, Phoenix Urban League, November 6, 1969, Domínguez File; Ramón M. Baeza to Manuel Domínguez, On-the-Job Training Program, December 4, 1969, Domínguez File.

27. Seymour to Committee to Discuss, November 7, 1969, p. 5, Position Paper; Office of Assistant Superintendent of Instruction, "Summary Report—Meeting of PUHS System Officials with Chicano Students and Chicano Community," September 26, 1969, Domínguez File; Committee to Discuss, "Freshman Program: PUHS," p. 4; *Arizona Republic,* October 16–18, 1969.

28. Seymour to Committee to Discuss, November 7, 1969, p. 7, Position Paper.

29. Future Plans Committee, *Report of Future Plans Committee* (Phoenix: PUHS System, August, 1967).

30. *Ibid.,* pp. 28, 20, 14, 9, 13, 17, in order of listing.

31. *Ibid.,* p. 3.

32. *Ibid.,* pp. 5–8.

33. PUHS System, *Annual Report of the Superintendent of Schools* (Phoenix: PUHS System, 1968), pp. 27–29; PUHS System, *Annual Report of the Superintendent of Schools* (Phoenix: PUHS System, 1966), pp. 19, 20, 77; PUHS and Phoe-

nix College System, *Annual Report of the Superintendent of Schools* (Phoenix: PUHS and Phoenix College System, 1960), pp. 14, 15.

34. *Report of Future Plans Committee*, p. 3.

35. PUHS System, *Annual Report* (1968), p. 1; PUHS District Board, "Agenda," November 14, 1970, Domínguez File.

36. PUHS System, *Annual Report* (1968), pp. 67–68; PUHS System, *Pupil Membership Distribution.*

37. Booz, Allen and Hamilton, Inc., "Proposal for a Planning Study for PUHS," submitted to Howard Seymour, superintendent, PUHS System, January 14, 1970; Parents Advisory Committee, PUHS, "Minutes," February 25, March 4, 1970, Domínguez File.

38. W. P. Shofstall, state superintendent of public instruction, to Manuel Domínguez, December 9, 1969, Domínguez File; E. L. Turner, Jr., State Indian Advisory Committee, to Shofstall, December 15, 1969, Domínquez File; Alice Harper, Minority Educational Advisory Committee, to Shofstall, "Committee Report," December 15, 1969, Domínguez File; J. O. Maynes, Jr., State Department of Public Instruction, to Frank Q. Carillo, López, and Manuel Domínguez, Mexican-American Special Subcommittee members, December 12, 1969, January 27, and March 3, 1970, Domínguez Files; Felizardo Valencia, co-chairman, Mexican-American Advisory Committee to Maynes and Shofstall, "First Draft of Report on Injustices in Education," March 9, 1970, Domínguez File; Arlena E. Seneca, consultant, Human Relations, PUHS System, to Participants in Human Awareness Workshop, March 12, 1970, Domínguez File; Minority Group Educational Advisory Commission, Minority Advisory Committee, "Membership Lists," 1969–70, Domínguez File.

39. Mexican-American Advisory Committee, "Injustices in the Education of Mexican-American Children in Arizona and Recommendations for Change," March 9, 1970, Domínguez File.

40. State of Arizona, Department of Public Instruction, *"Proposed School District Annual Budget, July 1, 1970–June 30, 1971* (Phoenix: State of Arizona, Department of Public Instruction, 1970); Inner City Parents and Interested Citizens, "PUHS Budget Recommendations," May 1, 1970, Domínguez File.

41. PUHS and Phoenix College System, *Annual Report* (1960), p. 5; PUHS System, *Annual Report* (1966), pp. 9, 14; Arizona Tax Research Association, *School Costs—Per Pupil Cost of Operating Public Schools in Arizona* (Phoenix: Arizona Tax Research Association, 1969), p. 5; PUHS System, *Pupil Membership Distribution,* see figures for 1967–68, 1970–71.

42. *Arizona Republic,* October 13, 1969; Seymour to Committee to Discuss, November 7, 1969, pp. 4, 5, Position Paper.

43. López, in interview, April 11, 1973.

44. Manuel Domínguez, in interview, April 2, 1973; López, in interview, April 11, 1973.

45. López, in interview, April 11, 1973.

46. Servín, "The Phoenix Union High School Boycott," pp. 2–6; *Arizona Republic,* October 12, 13, 1970.

47. *Arizona Republic,* October 9, 10, 12, 1970; *Phoenix Gazette,* October 9, 12, 21, 1970.

48. *Arizona Republic,* October 10, 1970.

49. López, in interview, April 11, 1973.

50. "Demands of Chicano Students and Chicano Community Upon the Administration of PUHS," mimeographed, n.d., Domínguez File.

See also: Office of Assistant Superintendent of Instruction, "Summary Report," September 26, 1969, Domínguez File; Parents Advisory Committee to PUHS Board, October 15, 1970, Domínguez File; PUHS Board to Parents-Students Boycott Committee, "We Agree in Principle to the Various Demands," October 18, 1970, Domínguez File; Browne to López, October 20, 1970, Domínguez File; Parents-

Students Boycott Committee to Browne, October 27, 1970, Domínguez File; Browne to López, October 29, 1970, Domínguez File.

51. *Arizona Republic*, November 9, 11, 17, 18, 21, December 2, 1970, January 13, 1971; *Phoenix Gazette*, November 5, 11, 18, December 3, 1970; January 13, 16, February 2, May 21, 16, 1971.

52. *State Press*, March 31, 1971; MECHA Central, Arizona State University chapter, "Minutes of first official meeting and election of officers," March 8, 1971, American Studies Program, Chicano Studies Project–Bibliographer's Office; *Arizona Republic*, April 9, 1973; Martínez, in interview, April 2, 1973; López, in interview, April 11, 1973.

53. López, in interview, April 11, 1973; Michael C. Clark, Robert E. Grinder, and López, Parent-Student Boycott Committee, *Recommendations from a Data Base for Comprehensive Change at PUHS, Research Survey* (Tempe: Bureau of Educational Research and Services, Arizona State University, 1971); PUHS System, *Report to the Board* (Phoenix: PUHS System, February 11, 1971), Domínguez File.

1970 Chicano Moratorium and the Death of Rubén Salazar*

José Angel de la Vara

For a hundred years or more the east side of Los Angeles has been a third-class community inhabited by poor Mexicans, Jews, blacks, Orientals, and their descendants. Today the minority groups dwell in the midst of smoggy foundries, soap factories, chemical plants, railroad switching yards, gas works, sausage factories, warehouses, stockyards, tallow-rendering plants, and junkyards.

Beginning with the close of the war between the United States and Mexico, European-Americans (with the possible exception of Spaniards) have had a very low opinion of minority groups in California, especially of the Mexicans.[1] Up to about fifty years ago, very few members of minority groups lived outside of the barrios or ghettos, even if they could afford to do so.

Although the last lynching of a Mexican in California was in the late 1880s, there has always existed and continues to exist a strong bias against the Mexican people—the bias of the white majority against the brown minority; the bias of overt repression by political forces and law enforcement agencies against powerless, outraged, barrio communities.

Despoliation and exploitation of the Mexican began primarily in 1851 when the Congress passed a bill to settle private land claims in California. The act gave the newly arrived Americano free rein in

---

*José Angel de la Vara, a member of MECHA at Arizona State University, prepared this essay for the course on the Mexican-American Experience.

despoiling the new Chicano of his native lands. The Mexican suffered physical abuse, also. If he reacted normally and did not meekly accept mistreatment, he was likely to be maimed or killed, with almost complete immunity for the wrongdoer. If he retaliated and escaped, he was labeled a bandit and an outlaw.[2]

The plight of Chicanos in the Southwest worsened through the nineteenth century and well into the twentieth. Although they were indigenous, Chicanos were treated as "foreigners"—ostracized socially, politically, and economically. When they were allowed to work, Chicanos were customarily found in the most menial of jobs at wages far below those of Anglo-Americans in comparable employment. Significant educational achievement was virtually nonexistent. Social mobility was carefully restricted as Chicanos were corraled into barrios. There was, however, one area of American society which Chicanos were encouraged to enter: that was, and continues to be, military service.[3]

The problems facing the Southwest's largest minority group—education, housing, jobs, health, and relations with the law—have been studied and restudied, written about and talked about. "But they have festered," said Ed Avila, field deputy to Congressman Edward Roybal, "and issue after issue has been laid to rest with nothing done about them."

East Los Angeles, the nation's largest barrio, is an example par excellence. The unemployment rate is staggering—in some neighborhoods it ranges from 12 percent to as high as 25 percent of the male labor force. Lack of education keeps the Chicano down; he has completed only eight and a half years of schooling—four years less than Anglo-Americans and two years less than blacks. Politically, the Chicano is a eunuch. The community has been so gerrymandered[4] that there are no Chicano state senators, city councilmen, or county supervisors; this lack of representation exists in a city that was founded in 1781 by Mexicans and that today includes more than one million Chicanos.

Whatever many of the more conservative and generally older members of the Chicano community thought of the abrupt appearance of a "Brown Power" movement and such militant groups as the Brown Berets, it was evident in the late 1960s that much of the community was stirred by cries of "Viva La Raza!" and "Chicano Power!" reflecting a growing pride in "things Mexican."

Thus Mexicans manifested their pride in constant protests that Mexicans or persons of Mexican descent have always been portrayed by the dominant society in terms of disdain and ridicule. Chicano organizations hit hard at the reluctance of private industry and government to consider Chicanos as anything but common laborers. There were those who said the spring of 1968 was the beginning of the "Chicano Revolution." These were days of walk-outs, speeches, picketing, and some lawbreaking and arrests.

The young activists who walked out of several East Los Angeles high schools that spring were protesting what they called the in-ability of the educational system to deal with language and cultural differences and the dismal, 50 percent dropout (or is it pushout?) rate at some Chicano schools.

Problems with law enforcement officers became aggravated when Chicanos tried to develop as a people. The Reverend Vahac Mardiro-sian, chairman of the Mexican-American Educational Commission, sadly observed that "The police are not relating meaningfully to the community across the language and cultural barrier. I think they sort of escalate their approach to the Mexican-American youth who is searching for some valid means of expressing his sense of frustra-tion and search for a change."[5]

Of signal concern to the Chicano community has been the dis-proportionate number of Chicanos drafted into military service, and almost invariably shipped off to Southeast Asia to fight in Viet Nam. Chicanos in Viet Nam are, almost to a man, assigned to combat units. Of twenty-seven thousand Chicanos shipped to South-east Asia to fight in this war, more than eight thousand, or about one third, have been killed in action or have died of wounds.[6] This legal sequestration and sacrifice of the young Chicano male popula-tion for dubious Anglo-American "glory" could not go uncontested by the Chicano community. A peaceful moratorium was planned as a protest.

Without a doubt, the Chicano Moratorium ranks as the largest and most successful demonstration by any one community around the interrelated questions of peace and social justice. After a nine-month effort, the youthful Chicano Moratorium Committee suc-ceeded on August 29, 1970, in turning out between twenty thousand and thirty thousand Chicanos, mainly from Los Angeles but with sizeable representation from throughout the country.

The preparations for the demonstration were nothing short of elaborate. It was publicized throughout the Southwest for weeks; Chicanos gathered in East Los Angeles, the greatest *colonia* in the country, to show their opposition to the Asian war that was claiming brown lives in inordinately high numbers. The Congress of Mexican-American Unity had obtained a parade permit from the authorities and conferences were held with the Sheriff's Department to ensure complete coordination. To handle the massive crowds expected, a group of two hundred to three hundred monitors were designated to keep the various groups under control. As another precaution, moratorium leaders had organized a special contingent of lawyers and law students to monitor the parade and provide expert advice on any legal complications. The parade was broken down into units, and a different organization was responsible for each section.[7]

The parade was to follow an arc—east on 3rd Street, southeast on Beverly Boulevard and west on Whittier Boulevard—to the destination, Laguna Park, a one-block square with a sunbaked baseball diamond, tennis court, and swimming pool, in the heart of a commercial section. When it began, the parade was festive and peaceful. Many marchers had been in antiwar protests before, but for many others this was their first exposure to a demonstration. "This was not the usual Berkeley kind of demonstration," noted one veteran protester. "It was not just kids. There were many older, straight people." In a memorandum to the County Human Relations Commission, Executive Director Herbert L. Carter noted that three of his staff had observed or participated in the march and rally. "All agree that the march along east 3rd Street, Atlantic Avenue and Whittier Boulevard was peaceful, festive and nonviolent, except that near the corner of Eastern Avenue at Whittier Boulevard, a young man threw a bottle at a parked patrol car. That young man was immediately reprimanded by parade monitors and was carefully watched throughout the remainder of the parade."[8] In three and a half hours the long, long line covered the two and a half miles to the park. It was a quiet, modest park but well suited for the brothers-in-law, nieces, wives, husbands, and one-year-old babies in their strollers, and for their sodas, candies, balloons, buttons, and picnic lunches.

The marchers filed into Laguna Park. They were weary from the long walk in the eighty-degree weather. Women went around the park asking people whether they wanted water or aspirin, or Band-Aids for blisters. Portable toilets were set up.

A flag of Mexico had been tied high above the baseball field on a light standard. Brightly colored posters were pinned to the fences surrounding a tennis court. The scene was a peaceful one—like one might see on a Sunday afternoon in Chapultepec Park in Mexico City: children playing, young lovers walking around in pairs, men exchanging views, mothers talking about their children and homes. Dr. James S. Koopman, of the UCLA School of Medicine, Department of Pediatrics, agreed that "everyone was assembled peacefully at Laguna Park. My wife and I sat amongst diverse people. Immediately around us were little children playing with a puppy, an older woman with a cane, a pregnant woman with a small baby and a family eating hamburgers and French fries."[9]

The program began and after two speeches a Puerto Rican rhythm group provided entertainment. Lucy E. Mesa, a participant in the parade, recalls that hot Saturday afternoon in August: "Finally, we had reached the park; everyone eager to find a spot on the grass, at last to sit and rest for a while. I was happy because no big hassles had started and I was whispering a silent prayer of thanks that there had been no violence so far. . . . Then I heard sirens."[10]

Apparently, the sirens were those of two Sheriff's Department patrol units answering a "burglary in progress" call at the Green Mill Liquor Store on Whittier Boulevard. The Green Mill was one of the few shops open that Saturday afternoon, and some marchers went into the store thinking its owner, Morris Maroko, was giving away free soft drinks (marchers had been given free refreshments at a number of restaurants and liquor stores along the parade route). A large crowd was in the store buying drinks when others, thinking it was a handout, entered and began helping themselves. The owner became alarmed when the store became overcrowded, and he became apprehensive that some might not pay. Maroko locked the front door, and in the crowding and confusion a silent burglar alarm was touched off. Maroko later said on television that he had not called the police and that there was no looting.

When the sheriff's units arrived on the scene, the few remaining marchers became angry and pelted the deputies with stones. A radio call of "extreme urgency" went out for help, and units from the Special Enforcement Bureau, the specially trained antiriot detail, responded. The deputies, clad in battle gear, began fighting with young and old marchers in the street and soon gained the upper hand.

Rather than isolate the crowd in the street and lead it northward away from the park, however, the deputies began forcing the people toward the peaceful gathering where the rally had been proceeding smoothly for an hour and a half. The trouble at the liquor store happened so fast and so far from the rally proper that most demonstrators did not know what was going on. (The liquor store is not visible from the park.)

Throughout the two and a half miles the parade covered, the marchers were trailed by two large black buses carrying police officers clad in riot gear. Like motorized vultures the buses waited until the demonstrators were assembled in the park. Then the deputies deployed east and west along Whittier Boulevard. The crowd from the liquor store incident was forced into the park as the deputies moved forward in an all-embracing formation, billy clubs in hand. Koopman recalls those confusing initial moments:

> The first sign of any disturbance I saw was when some people in the distance began to stand up. The loudspeaker calmly assured us that nothing was happening and that we should sit down. Seconds later I saw a row of gold helmets marching across the park, forcing everyone toward the high fences. The exit was too small for everyone to leave quickly. I, along with everyone else, panicked. The terrible tragedies of human stampedes in the soccer stadiums of Peru and Argentina were uppermost in my mind.[11]

After the deputies formed their line, skirmishes broke out, then died down. A line of monitors linked arms between the deputies advancing from the north and the body of demonstrators on the south. The bombardment of missiles became intense and then died off. Many demonstrators thought the rally would be allowed to continue. "Get out of here, leave us alone," monitors shouted at the deputies. Then there was a long lull, as monitors and deputies looked at each other across a narrow no-man's land.

But the sheriff's deputies swept the monitors aside and began to throw tear-gas canisters at the unsuspecting crowd. Many of the people were still lying on the grass listening to speeches. Fright and consternation seized them, and most took flight. Tear-gassed children were separated from their parents; many became lost. Shoes, purses, and food baskets were left behind.

As startled demonstrators fled in panic, more aggressive persons in the crowd decided to fight the deputies, subjecting them to some of the fiercest street combat ever encountered. Indiscriminately the deputies struck men and women on the head, shoulders, and stomach. Some of the injured were dragged, semiconscious, to waiting buses.[12] The Los Angeles City Police Department sent reinforcements. More tear gas was used. By now, there was a full-scale melee with fighting spilling over onto Whittier Boulevard. Many store windows were broken, some buildings were set on fire, and some cars were overturned. The militants were reacting to the "animalistic violence" triggered by officers of the law. Sporadic fighting and destruction continued until the early hours of Sunday. When the riot was finally over, three Chicanos had died, sixty-one persons were injured, almost two hundred had been arrested, and over one million dollars in damage had occurred.

Delfino Varela writes in *Regeneración:*

> It is a sharp reflection of racism that when the Anglo-dominated demonstrations were pulled off a few years ago, and the Anglo-dominated efforts of last year [1969] occurred, the newspapers and the media were full of the story. When the police attacked the crowds at Century Plaza the entire city was shaken, and investigations were a dime a dozen. The smallest notice possible was taken of the huge, beautiful, and peaceful march [1970 Chicano Moratorium], until the attack on the crowd.[13]

One person who *was* covering the National Chicano Moratorium Parade with its more than twenty thousand participants was Rubén Salazar, a Chicano newsman. Salazar was news director for the Spanish-language television station, KMEX, in Los Angeles and a columnist for the *Los Angeles Times*. He had covered the war in Viet Nam for the *Times* and was no stranger to frontline hostilities. Often his cables from Saigon reflected his growing distaste for the war. Enrique "Hank" López described him as "our only established newspaper columnist, the most experienced and articulate Chicano in this whole country."

Salazar had, since about eleven o'clock in the morning, spent the day with three men, all of whom would swear they were with him when he died: Guillermo Restrepo, an employee of Salazar, and Gustavo García and Hector Fabio Franco, friends of Restrepo.[14] Salazar and the three men began a walking tour of the disturbance-torn area between three and four o'clock that afternoon, walking east along Whittier Boulevard from Laguna Park. The worst of the rioting had not yet begun, but already small fires flared, looting was in evidence, and unbroken windows were rare.

Between five and five-thirty o'clock, Salazar and Restrepo entered the Silver Dollar Cafe at 4945 Whittier Boulevard to use the restroom. García and Franco followed. Restrepo and Salazar each ordered a beer and were sitting on the two bar stools closest to the front door. At the time, nine other persons were in the cafe. Only a curtain prevented passersby from looking inside the cafe; it was neither closed nor locked.

Before Salazar and Restrepo had ordered their beers, García had gone to the front door to see what was happening in the street. (There are two doors, one that was open onto the street and a second, inner "door," made by two hanging curtains.) García recalls the incident: "When I went out, there was four policemen [later described as sheriff's deputies] right in front of me and one of them . . . he put the gun on my chest and he told me to get in the bar immediately."[15] The officer pushed García with his gun and García returned to the bar. As he entered he met Franco (also on his way to the door to look out), and García told him not to go out because sheriff's deputies were there and about to shoot. Franco went out anyway, saw the deputies with their guns in their hands, and went back inside.

Joe Razo and Raúl Ruiz, co-editors of *La Raza*, an East Los Angeles Spanish-language newspaper, were directly across the street from the Silver Dollar Cafe at that time. The two took more than two hundred photographs of the day's actions including several from in front of the bar. Ruiz and Razo were buying sodas at a small stand when, according to Ruiz, four deputies approached the cafe displaying service revolvers and a shotgun. Razo said that

> Some people were coming out of the front entrance of the cafe but they were stopped by a deputy who pointed his weapon at them . . . chest-level high. The people appeared to be talking to him and attempting to leave [the cafe] . . . but the deputy would not let them move out. He aggressively moved forward and . . . forced those people back into the cafe.[16]

The men who were being forced into the cafe had been standing outside it when deputies moved toward them and ordered them to go inside. One of the men, twenty-one-year-old Jimmy Flores, was told, "get inside the bar or we'll shoot."

Deputies James Lambert and Thomas Wilson and a reserve deputy drove to the Silver Dollar area in response to a Sheriff's Department radioed message that rocks and bottles were being thrown at firemen battling a huge blaze near the cafe. On the deputies' arrival, objects were hurled at them, too, and Wilson fired his tear-gas gun at the crowd to disperse them. Wilson used both "a duster grenade, which shoots out plain tear gas with a small piece of wadding that holds it in the cartridge, and a short-range [tumbler] projectile, which you bounce along the ground into the crowd."[17]

Shortly after the crowd dispersed, Lambert and Wilson were told excitedly, by a deputy and a man in a red vest,[18] that there were men in the cafe with guns. As an acting sergeant that day, Wilson was the officer in charge and made the decision to take the tear-gas gun to the doorway of the cafe. Wilson claimed that he and Deputy Louis Brown—who testified that he did not identify himself as a law officer at any time during the incident—shouted several warnings to evacuate the cafe. The occupants unanimously testified at the subsequent inquest, as did most of the spectators outside the cafe, that no warnings were issued by anyone. (It is difficult to ascertain whether warnings were, in fact, issued. This is a crucial point in interpreting the participants' actions and a determination must be made; the profusion of testimony indicates that none were issued.)

According to Razo and Ruiz, other deputies had approached the area of the cafe while those occupants who were attempting to leave were forced to reenter. One of the deputies, carrying a tear-gas gun, approached the doorway of the cafe. He conferred with other deputies and then aimed the weapon at the doorway and fired a tear-gas shell. About a minute later he fired again, through the cafe entrance. Deputy Wilson then ceased firing for about five minutes, presumably waiting for patrons to come out. No one did.

Again, witnesses noted, there were no orders to come out and no warnings given that a new barrage of tear-gas shells was about to be fired.

Four of the officers then got into a squad car and parked it across the street from the cafe, near Ruiz and Razo and about forty feet from the doorway. Then the deputies got out of their car, and Sergeant Robert Laughlin pointed his tear-gas gun at the cafe. His first shell missed and knocked off a piece of the wall of the cafe. The shell landed near some deputies and apparently gassed them, because they moved away rapidly. The next two shells entered the doorway. *After* these shells were fired, an order was given over a loudspeaker for the people in the cafe to come out. No one did.

The deputies waited about fifteen minutes before giving up, and then began to clear the people from the south side of the street. Lambert and Wilson remained in the area for more than two hours, yet neither deputy made a search of the cafe.

Prior to the first shot being fired into the cafe, all was quiet if not peaceful inside. After seeing the armed deputies outside, Franco ducked back in and began to make for the rear exit, walking down an unoccupied side of the cafe, when the first shot was fired, striking to his right and knocking him to the floor. Apparently, the first object to enter the cafe was a "canister"—a low-velocity missile—and was followed almost immediately by a wall-piercing, high-velocity Federal Flite-Rite projectile labeled "Not for crowd control."

This second projectile, fired into the cafe at close range, penetrated Salazar's head. He died almost instantaneously from a "through-and-through projectile wound of the left temple area causing massive injury to the brain," according to a press release issued jointly by Los Angeles County Coroner Thomas T. Noguchi and the Sheriff's Department after an autopsy.

Immediately after the first two shells were fired at the cafe, Daniel Rivera and his family fled through the rear door of an adjacent bridal shop to escape tear gas that was filtering through a roof from the Silver Dollar Cafe, just a few feet away. Deputies confronted the family a few feet from the rear of the cafe, questioned them, took away a pistol Rivera was carrying, and let them go.

The occupants of the cafe also fled through the rear exit. Franco shouted to Restrepo that Salazar had been killed. Restrepo and García did not believe Salazar was dead; they were certain he was following right behind them. When Salazar did not appear, Restrepo twice tried to reenter the cafe to look for him and twice was repelled by billowing tear gas. Restrepo went up to deputies who were just then approaching the rear of the cafe, showed his press card, and informed them Salazar had been shot. Three different times at three locations deputies pointed their guns at Restrepo, disregarded his press credentials, and said, "Get out of here. Move on." Restrepo's employer finally advised him to return to the television station, while deputies posted guard over the bar.

About seven o'clock in the evening Julián García went to the Silver Dollar Cafe to see what was happening. He went inside but was forced out by tear gas after catching a glimpse of Salazar's body. He approached a deputy, told him he thought a man inside was hurt, and was ordered to go in and investigate. The deputy told García he would be "in violation of some ordinance" if he refused to investigate. García went in and confirmed Salazar's death. Two deputies, testifying later about the incident, said García was ordered to reenter the cafe because they feared his report might be a trap. They also said the tear gas was so thick that one could not have entered without a gas mask, which they did not have. One can only wonder, then, why Julián García was ordered back in to check the body; García had no gas mask, either.

Having waited two hours to ascertain whether someone was in the cafe, the Sheriff's Department proceeded to wait another three hours before verifying Salazar's death. Mrs. Rubén Salazar had to learn about it on a 10:30 P.M. newscast, although officials of KMEX-TV had frantically notified the Sheriff's Department soon after the incident had been reported by Restrepo.

The tragic events left East Los Angeles shocked and paralyzed. "Shocked in disbelief that a peacefully planned demonstration to dramatize the disproportionate number of Spanish-surnamed young men in Viet Nam resulted in destruction of our community. Paralyzed by doubt and concern over the reports of the shooting resulting in the death of our beloved friend and co-worker, Rubén Salazar."[19] Whereas Sheriff Peter Pitchess and Mayor Sam Yorty blamed the entire situation on "outside agitators," outraged Chicano leaders placed the blame directly on the "inefficient, inept, and poorly disciplined" officers of the law. Chicano leaders quite correctly declared that "outsiders are unnecessary to arouse people who have been gassed, kicked, and clubbed."[20]

Already tense, East Los Angeles became more so as the Sheriff's Department increased its manpower in the *colonia*. A coalition of Chicano groups called for an end to the "occupation" of East Los Angeles by policemen who had moved in in the wake of the riot as if to stay. Police surveillance by foot, patrol car, and helicopter became constant. Being stopped and searched was almost a daily routine. The mood of East Los Angeles was alienation, hostility, and tension; and every sign indicated the mood was spreading—throughout the Southwest—from the young to the not so young; from the poor to the middle class; from the dropout to the Ph.D.

To many Chicanos, the behavior of the police was typical of the brutality and harassment that has become "a way of life" in East Los Angeles. Dr. Rodolfo Acuña was arrested when he tried to act as mediator between the police and angry demonstrators. His memory is bitter. "The cops don't want peace. It doesn't matter whether you have a Ph.D. or anything else. You're still a greaser to them. It's suicide to even try to talk to them."[21] Manuel Aragón, former director of the Los Angeles antipoverty program, indicated similar beliefs. "The police have adopted the policy of pre-emptive strike. They see the organization and militancy that's developing in this community and they are determined not to let it get as strong as the black movement has become."[22]

As Chicano leaders decried the Sheriff's Department's intensification of its stop-and-search activities in East Los Angeles, Sheriff's Department spokesmen said that officers were avoiding "incidents of confrontation," and "We have been trying to reduce the tensions, fears and anxieties. The only time an officer makes a search is when a person makes some suspicious act. The ground rules have not changed."[23] The actions of the Sheriff's Department proved its spokesmen to be, if not outright liars, far from truthful.

> Eduardo Zapata Aguirre, head of League of United Citizens to Help Addicts [LUCHA], was stopped by deputies on his way to a TV studio for a taping. Aguirre was arrested on suspicion of not having a driver's license in his possession.
>
> A young volunteer lawyer named Dan Chávez was stopped by deputies as he was leaving a legal services building. Chávez was taken into custody for having an outstanding traffic warrant in Long Beach.
>
> Custody arraignments in the East Los Angeles courthouse usually number about 10 to 15 a day, but were now running 25 to 40.
>
> People were stopped on the street and made to roll up their sleeves while officers checked their arms for needle marks.[24]

The incensed Chicano community demanded "revenge" for Rubén Salazar, insisting that "his murderers be brought to justice." Correctly diagnosing the situation as "extremely explosive," County Coroner Noguchi called for an inquest into Salazar's death, to begin September 10. The proceedings were scheduled to take place in Room 803 of the old Hall of Records. All but seven of the seventy-eight seats in the hearing room were reserved for the Salazar family, various governmental officials, a twenty-eight-member citizens' committee of Chicanos, and representatives of the press. Because of the limited seating space and the widespread interest in the incident, Coroner Noguchi granted a request for live television coverage of the inquest. All seven Los Angeles television stations agreed to take turns in giving live coverage, in color, of the entire coroner's inquest into Salazar's slaying. However, Hearing Officer Norman Pittluck barred television cameras from showing certain witnesses who feared for their lives.[25]

The original inquest panel (or jury) was replaced when several television and newspaper reporters began discussions with the jurors. Panel members were drawn from the superior court jury pool. Attorneys representing the district attorney's office and the Salazar family had no role in the selection process. Finally seated were five men and two women with two women alternates. They were to determine whether Salazar's death was an "accident" or "at the hands of another."

As the sixteen-day inquest took its course, many agreed that the proceedings resembled a trial, with the entire Mexican people indicted for crimes of violence, rather than an objective inquiry into the facts of the death. Many viewers were repeatedly given the impression that three Los Angeles County agencies—the district attorney's office, the coroner's office and the Sheriff's Department—had conspired to portray Chicanos as cowardly, treacherous people who are prone to violence and who would use guerrilla warfare tactics against innocent deputies. However, no facts were ever presented to corroborate these charges.

When Chicano witnesses took the stand to present evidence, questioning took the form of an inquisition. Raúl Ruiz, co-editor of *La Raza,* had photographed many scenes that, according to his interpretation, showed police brutality and overreaction. His entire testimony was closely, minutely examined and implicity rejected. In contrast, the Sheriff's cameraman who showed a videotape of Chicanos throwing rocks and bottles was questioned only briefly and not challenged at all. Another example of the one-sided "trial" approach was seen in the seating of Ralph Mayer, deputy district attorney, at the same table with two sheriff's homicide detectives with whom he consulted continually. (For all practical purposes, only the district attorney's office can take further criminal action after the inquest panel has presented its findings.)

A crucial issue was whether Deputy Wilson was acting within the limits of his orders and the department's training when he shot the projectile into the cafe. The attorney for the Salazar family requested that to clarify the matter the Sheriff's training manual for use of tear-gas equipment be presented as evidence. Inquest Hearing Officer Pittluck refused to subpoena the manual and Sheriff Peter Pitchess refused to hand it over voluntarily. The *Los Angeles Times* editorialized: "As long as Pitchess conceals his department's procedures, public doubts will persist. As long as he evades his obligation to assume responsibility and talk to the people in candor, suspicion will persist."[26]

Chicano observers twice walked out on the opening day of the coroner's inquest into the slaying of Rubén Salazar. The group's two walkouts were punctuated by angry shouts hurled at Hearing Officer Pittluck, who was able to restore order quickly and remain calm. The group, led by Chicano attorney Oscar Acosta, were protesting the testimony of Sheriff's Department Captain Tom W. Pinkston, which did not go into the slaying itself but extensively detailed the clashes, looting, burning, and throwing of objects that occurred the day Salazar was killed.

Acosta was forcibly ejected from the hearing room on the fourth day of the inquest. The incident occurred when Acosta audibly criticized the hearing officer for allegedly letting off Sheriff's Department witnesses with questions gentler than those he put to Raúl Ruiz.[27] Ruiz supported his testimony with dozens of photographs and contended that overreaction by deputies had sparked the riot. At several key points, Ruiz's testimony differed sharply from that of previous witnesses who had been subpoenaed at the request of the Sheriff's Department. As Pittluck began to ask Ruiz questions submitted by Deputy District Attorney Ralph Mayer—such as whether he had seen windows broken, stores looted, rocks hurled—Ruiz protested, "Your line of questioning is prejudicial." The apparent implication of the questions was that Ruiz had selectively photographed scenes of deputies' brutality to citizens.[28]

It was then that Acosta's comments became audible to Pittluck, who quickly ordered Acosta to leave. When Acosta remained seated, Pittluck ordered deputies to remove him from the room. The room erupted into a swirling melee as six deputies tried to get to Acosta, while several men sprang to their feet and rushed to Acosta's aid. An unidentified man was ejected with Acosta as Ruiz remarked bitterly that Acosta, "the only lawyer who wanted to defend us," was "hauled away bodily." (Acosta also led a walkout on the thirteenth day of the inquest; the group was protesting "irrelevant" testimony by sheriff's officers.)

Throughout the duration of the inquest and the Sheriff's Department's investigation of its own actions, the United States Department of Justice declined to launch any federal inquiry into Salazar's death or the East Los Angeles riot. Attorney General John Mitchell had been requested, in a letter signed by twenty-two California legislators, to conduct an impartial Justice Department investigation in order "to reduce the increasing suspicions and atmosphere of distrust surrounding his [Salazar's] death." The letter continued: "It is essential that a fair and impartial investigation of the disturbances be conducted in view of the fact that complete reliance on any local investigatory machinery will only perpetuate instead of reduce the minority community's distrust of their local public officials' commitment to an unbiased investigation of the recent disorders in East Los Angeles."[29] As Los Angeles County supervisors voted unanimously to pay sheriff's deputies for overtime in the riot (one million dollars total), Mayor Sam Yorty, a guest at the opening of the Fiesta Palace Hotel in Mexico City, characterized those who rioted as "agitators, who are as much against Mexico as they are against the United States."

On October 5 the inquiry, by far the longest and costliest such affair in county history, concluded with a verdict that confused many, satisfied few, and meant little. State Assemblyman James A. Hayes, author of the 1969 bill revising the verdict choices for California inquest juries, remarked that only one verdict was available to the jury: death "at the hands of another." Hayes explained that this verdict was substituted in 1969 for three other verdicts from which inquest juries had previously made a choice: "accidental homicide," "justifiable homicide," and "criminal homicide." Hayes said this was done to remove the issue of "intent."

Pittluck, however, misinterpreted "accident" to mean the death was an "unintended result." He misinterpreted "at the hands of another" to mean the death was an "intended result." He so instructed the jurists, who, after a numbing procession of 61 witnesses, 204 exhibits and 2,025 pages of repetitive testimony, came up with two verdicts: death was "at the hands of another person" (four jurors) and death was "by accident" (three jurors).

The majority of the jurors said the verdict on the mode of Salazar's death was meant to reflect strong criticism of the Los Angeles County Sheriff's Department. The four told the *Los Angeles Times* the three other jurors held similarly strong views but felt compelled by Pittluck's instructions to come up with a "weaker" verdict. George Maddox, jury foreman and one of the minority jurors, confirmed this observation. Betty J. Clemente, one of the majority jurors, reflected on the August 29 events:

> The entire jury felt there was definite negligence on the part of the Sheriff's Department and that the deputies did not use discretion or prudence in their acts that day. The main surprise to me was the deputies' lack of organization, their lack of consideration for innocent people. . . . I think if these same officers had been out in Beverly Hills, they would have acted entirely different under similar circumstances.[30]

The majority of the jurors were especially critical of the testimony of the sixty-first and final witness, Sheriff's Deputy Robert Hawkins, a college professor of police science and a training instructor at the Sheriff's Academy. Claiming Hawkins was "trying to pull the wool over people's eyes," George W. Sherard observed that "There were a half-dozen things he said that didn't jibe with a manufacturer's teargas manual he gave to the jury. He was just fabricating mortar to patch up the holes in [Deputy] Wilson's testimony."[31]

The protracted inquest established many of the facts that the public wanted to know. Two weeks of testimony brought out which deputy fired the tear-gas projectile that killed Salazar, his reasons for firing it, and the circumstances surrounding Salazar's death.

But the inquest did not bring out—because the Sheriff's Department resisted bringing out—whether Deputy Thomas Wilson was acting within the limits of his standing orders when he fired the fatal projectile. The inquest did not bring out—because the Sheriff's Department resisted bringing out—what the deputies' standing orders were, and what the department's procedures are, in regard to the use of tear gas, particularly the use of the specialized, and deadly, projectile that killed Salazar.

The *Los Angeles Times* editorialized about the Chicano community's sentiments:

> The district attorney must now decide whether, on the basis of the testimony in the inquest, to charge Wilson with manslaughter. If Sheriff Peter Pitchess continues to cloak the policies and procedures of his Department in secrecy, such a criminal charge may be the only way in which those policies and procedures will be brought to light. A trial of Wilson would establish his own guilt or innocence.[32]

But there was more at stake here than the legal guilt of one deputy. In a larger sense, what was at issue was the authority, the legitimacy, the credibility of the Sheriff's Department in the eyes of the people it serves and protects. The death of Salazar aroused among reasonable men and women serious doubts about the way the department uses weapons and about who decides to use them, when, and why. The editorial further clarified that

> Pitchess' obligation to the people he serves is clearly to assume responsibility for the actions of his men, to discipline them where they are in

error and to uphold them where they are wrongly accused. Above all, he must conduct his Department in such a way that law enforcement is widely accepted as even-handed and fair—particularly in a time of public unrest. . . . It is in his Department's interest, in the community interest, and in the interest of public order, for the Sheriff to reveal what he has hitherto concealed.[33]

District Attorney Evelle Younger, then running for California State Attorney General, decided on October 14 that the facts brought out by the coroner's inquest did not justify criminal charges against Deputy Thomas Wilson. The strange reasoning given by the district attorney by which he arrived at this conclusion neither convinced nor amused the Chicano community which had been waiting to see how the "establishment" would handle the case. Younger stated that since three of the inquest jurors felt Salazar was killed as a result of an accident, he could only conclude that any trial jury would have at least one juror who would feel the same way. He further concluded that, "In the absence of any additional evidence, that case is considered closed." Apparently, over two thousand pages of testimony was not enough. Younger also offered his opinion that no responsible person had suggested that any criminal intent was present on the part of the deputies firing into the cafe.

However, there was some doubt and testimony which directly or indirectly implied that a degree of intent to kill was present in the firing of projectiles and other missiles into the cafe while Salazar, his co-workers, and others were inside. Oscar Acosta charged that deputies, knowing Salazar was inside the cafe and fearing him as an effective voice for the Chicano community, committed "political murder, plain and simple." In Berkeley, City Councilman Ron Dellums called the slaying "an incredible coincidence in that at the time of his death Salazar was working on an exposé of police practices in Los Angeles."

Sheriff Peter Pitchess commented, "There was absolutely no misconduct on the part of the deputies involved or in the procedures they followed."

Meanwhile, in barrios and other Los Angeles ghettos where Chicanos live, there was great hostility, anger, and feelings of alienation. The inquest on Salazar's death made it insultingly clear that there was little chance the Chicano would be accorded justice. Chicano groups predicted that violence was certain to erupt in other cities so long as injustice and insensitivity to the needs of the barrio persisted.

An increasingly greater number of Chicanos—not only militants but many who once were considered "reasonable" or "moderate"—

were reaching the conclusion that burning down the "establishment" would be the only way to achieve some kind of control over one's destiny and community. When there is no justice, what is the alternative?

Notes

1. In 1859 the *San Francisco Herald* referred to the Mexicans of Los Angeles as a degraded race, "many of them exceedingly dark-complexioned, who could not be distinguished from Indians and Negroes."

2. Great celebrations would be held whenever one of the "bandits" was caught and executed. In 1875, for example, when the much-sought "bandit" Tibúrcio Vásquez was apprehended, public schools in Los Angeles closed so that children could go see Vásquez in his cell the day before his hanging.

3. Although encouraged to enter the armed forces, Chicano servicemen are seldom found in the "better" enlisted positions and even less frequently in the officer class. An excellent example of this was the almost total absence of Chicano pilots among returning ex-prisoners of war from Viet Nam in 1973.

4. Joe Razo, "Even if all the women, children and dogs in East Los Angeles voted, we couldn't elect anybody," *New York Times*, September 4, 1970.

5. "Inaction, Growing Militancy Viewed as Causes of Riot," *Los Angeles Times*, August 31, 1970.

6. William J. Drummond, "How East L.A. Protest Turned Into Major Riot," *Los Angeles Times*, September 16, 1970.

7. *Ibid.* Mrs. Jewel Mehlman, an Anglo teacher, recalled, "I marched with such varied peaceniks as UMAS, MAPA, MECHA, LUCHA, the Brown Berets, the Emma Lazarus Jewish Women, the Committee of 100, the Third World, the Peace Action Council, etc.... with people from Chicago, New York, Puerto Rico, Texas, Arizona, and from all over California."

8. *Ibid.*

9. *Ibid.*

10. *Ibid.*

11. *Ibid.*

12. Julián Nava as quoted in *Los Angeles Times*, September 19, 1970: "[I] saw at least two separate incidents where five or six deputies surrounded a single person, struck them down and then beat at them with nightsticks. All you could see was the batons going up and down, up and down, as fast as they could go. . . . Then the prostrate form would be dragged away."

13. *Regeneración* vol. 1, no. 6 (1970).

14. Restrepo said he was with Salazar most of the day and noticed that Salazar, as the day progressed, often looked behind him as they walked. At one point, Restrepo asked Salazar what was wrong and Salazar answered, "I think I'm stupid," but did not explain. Later, Salazar told Restrepo, "Guillermo, I'm getting very scared." Again, Salazar did not explain. "Maybe he thought something was about to happen, or was curious about someone following him—I don't know," said Restrepo. *Los Angeles Times*, September 22, 1970.

15. *Los Angeles Times*, September 2, 1970.

16. *Los Angeles Times*, September 4, 1970.

17. *Los Angeles Times*, September 29, 1970.

18. The busy citizen was Manuel López who, on that hot Saturday afternoon, directed traffic on Whittier Boulevard; diverted cars to side streets by pulling a bus bench across the boulevard; kept bystanders away from a burning carpet store nearby; stood in the boulevard near the Silver Dollar Cafe and directed a group of sheriff's deputies toward the tavern. *Los Angeles Times*, September 12, 1970.

19. *Regeneración* vol. 1, no. 7 (1970).
20. *The Chicanos* (Kingsport, Tenn.: Kingsport Press, 1971), p. 237.
21. *New York Times*, September 4, 1970.
22. *Ibid.*
23. *Los Angeles Times*, September 5, 1970.
24. *Ibid.*
25. *Los Angeles Times*, September 10, 1970.
26. *Los Angeles Times*, October 7, 1970.
27. *Los Angeles Times*, September 16, 1970.
28. *Ibid.*
29. *Los Angeles Times*, September 18, 1970.
30. *Los Angeles Times*, October 8, 1970.
31. *Ibid.*
32. *Los Angeles Times*, October 7, 1970.
33. *Ibid.*

References and Sources

Christian Century 88 (1971).
Interviews with Manuel V. Cisneros, 1970 and 1972, Somerton, Arizona.
Interview with Edmundo Méndez, 1970, Los Angeles.
Interviews with Ramón R. Ruiz, 1970 and 1972, Phoenix.
Los Angeles Times, August 30 through November 15, 1970.
Ed Ludwig and James Santibañez, eds., *The Chicanos: Mexican American Voices* (Kingsport, Tenn.: Kingsport Press, 1971).
New York Times, April 29 through October 15, 1970.
Palo Alto Times, August 31 through October 6, 1970.
Regeneración (Los Angeles), vol. 1, nos. 6, 7, 9 (1970).
Whittier Daily News, August 31 through October 6, 1970.

Dolores Huerta Talks about Republicans, César, Children, and Her Home Town*

Dolores Huerta

INTRODUCTION

The name César Chávez and the struggle to unionize farm labor have become virtually synonymous. People associate few other names with the United Farm Workers union. But Dolores Huerta, the union's fiery vice-president, doesn't seem to mind being overshadowed by Chávez the Personality. She thinks of herself as a "common soldier" in the union's army of workers and volunteers, and shies away from publicity whenever possible.

---

*From "Dolores Huerta Talks about Republicans, César, Children, and Her Home Town," in *La Voz del Pueblo* of November–December, 1972. Reprinted by permission of the publisher.

But her leadership ability is undeniable. Huerta went to the Democratic Convention as a delegate from California and turned this meeting of a political party into what seemed to be a gathering of lettuce boycotters. As one of the union's chief negotiators, she matches the opposition's highly trained and highly paid lawyers with her own self-taught negotiating skills fortified with a strong-minded, inborn stubbornness.

Taking time out from the successful battle against Proposition 22 which [took] her to the [San Francisco] Bay Area, she revealed to *La Voz del Pueblo,* in an unusually candid conversation, little-known facts about her life and her work. Her story follows.

DOLORES HUERTA TALKS

My family goes way back to the 1600s in New Mexico. My father was a migrant worker who used to travel from New Mexico to Wyoming, following the work, living in little shacks. My mother was a very ambitious woman. She got a little lunch counter together, then she got a bigger restaurant, and when the war came she got a hotel. That's how I was able to go to school and how I got a more affluent background than the other kids.

When my dad and my mom divorced, he stayed in New Mexico and she came to California. I would beg my mother to let me go to the fields when I was little, but she would not let me. My brothers used to go pick tomatoes in Stockton, but my mother wasn't going to let *her* daughter go work in any field. So when I was fourteen, I went to work in the packing sheds instead, which were just as bad.

I was a little bit luckier than most Chicanos because I was raised in an integrated neighborhood. All the Chicanos who went to school where I did are all making it. We grew up in Stockton but we weren't in a ghetto. In our school, there was the Mexican, black, white, Indian, Italian; we were all thrown in together. We had all of the old-guard teachers who treated everybody very mean. But they didn't discriminate against one or the other. They treated us all equally mean. So we all hated the teachers, but we didn't hate each other. We didn't have a whole bunch of hang-ups, like hating Anglos, or hating blacks.

When I got into high school, then it was really segregated. There was the real rich and the real poor. We were poor too, and I got hit with a lot of racial discrimination. My four years in high school hit me very hard and it took me a long time to get over it.

When I was in high school I got straight A's in all of my compositions. I can't write any more, but I used to be able to write really nice, poetry and everything. But the teacher told me at the end of the year that she couldn't give me an A because she knew that somebody was writing my papers for me. That really discouraged me, because I used to stay up all night and think, and try to make every paper different, and try to put words in there that I thought were nice. Well, it just kind of crushed me.

I couldn't be active in college though, because it was just too early. I was the only Chicano at Stockton Junior College. At that time, there was just a handful of us that you might call liberals.

I was frustrated. I had a fantastic complex because I seemed to be out of step with everybody and everything. You're trying to go to school and yet you see all of these injustices. It was just such a complex!

Then my mother took me to Mexico City when I was about seventeen. She had never been there either. It was our first trip. But that opened my eyes to the fact that there was nothing wrong with Chicanos. I felt inside that [in the United States] everybody was wrong and I was right. They were wrong in beating the people up in the streets and all of the things they did to people. I felt I had all of these frustrations inside of me, so I started joining different Chicano organizations—El Comité Honorífico, Women's Club, all of these organizations that didn't do anything but give dances and celebrate the Fiestas Patrias.

By the time I was twenty-five years old, I had been married and gotten a divorce. I was still living in Stockton when Fred Ross came into town and he started telling us about forming this organization, the Community Service Organization. And he told us about how in Los Angeles they had sent these policemen to San Quentin and Fred had organized it.

When Fred started telling us that if we got together we could register voters, elect Spanish-speaking representatives, and turn everything around, I just didn't believe it. He showed us how they had gotten these clinics in San Jose and he told us about César Chávez. He showed me all these pictures of big meetings with one hundred to two hundred people together. Well, I thought he was telling me a fairy tale.

I thought he was a Communist, so I went to the FBI and had him checked out. I really did that. I used to work for the Sheriff's Department. See how middle-class I was. In fact, I was a registered Republican at the time. I don't think I was ever a real cop-out, though, because I had always been real close to a lot of the people. My mother even used to tell me all the time that all my friends were either ex-cons or pachucos [zoot-suiters].

But I always thank the day that I met Fred. I always hated injustice and I always wanted to do something to change things. Fred opened a door for me. He changed my whole life. If it weren't for Fred, I'd probably just be in some stupid suburb somewhere.

Anyway, I started my first job getting people to register to vote. Eventually, some of the people started paying attention to us. So then we started fighting the Police Department and we got them to stop searching and harassing people arbitrarily. Then we had a big fight with the County Hospital and we turned that around. But it was just like magic. You start registering people to vote and all of these things start happening.

I was actually in the organization for two years before I got to talk to César [Chávez]. I met him once, but he was very shy. He wouldn't talk to anybody except the people he was organizing. But I heard him speak one time at a board meeting and I was really impressed. Well, after a big voter registration drive in 1960 where we registered one hundred and fifty thousand people, César got this bright idea to send me to Sacramento.

So I went to Sacramento and we got all these bills passed. I headed up the legislative program in 1961 when we fought for the old-age pension for the noncitizens, for *los viejitos* [the little old people]. I lobbied the welfare bill through so that the parents could stay in the home. César and I and the rest of us worked to get the right to register voters door to door, and the right for people to take their driver's license exams in Spanish, and disability insurance for farm workers, and the right for people to get surplus commodities. And, of course, we were the ones who ended the bracero program. I have a lot of experience in legislation, and I guess I've become sort of a trouble-shooter in the union.

I guess because I'm articulate, I came to the forefront. A lot of people who do a lot of hard work in the union are not mentioned anywhere. "Son los soldados razos del movimiento" [We are the common soldiers of the movement]. And that's what I consider myself—just a person working at what I'm supposed to be doing. The fact that I get publicity is sort of a by-product of the union. But there's an awful lot of people who have worked continuously since the union started, a lot of women, for example, who nobody even knows.

There's been no reaction from the farm workers to my role as a woman within the union. They will appreciate anybody who will come in to help them. In terms of the leadership itself I get very little friction from anybody, really. Anyone who can do the job is welcome to come in and share the suffering.

There are a lot of other women in the union besides me and they share some of my problems. But I think it's mostly a personal conflict and it depends how much you let it hang you up in terms of what you're doing. If you let it bug you when people say that you're not being a good mother because you're not with your kids twenty-four hours a day, well then of course it will deter you from what you're doing. In the union, you know, everybody cooperates to take care of your kids.

The idea of the communal family is not new and progressive. It's really kind of old-fashioned. Remember when you were little you always had your uncles, your aunts, your grandmother, and your comrades around. As a child in the Mexican culture you identified with a lot of people, not just your mother and father like they do in the middle-class homes. When people are poor their main interest is family relationships. A baptism or a wedding is a big thing. In middle-class homes you start getting away from that and people become more materialistic. When you have relatives come to visit it's a nuisance instead of a great big occasion.

While I was in jail some of my kids came down to Delano to see me, but my little girl, Angela, didn't come. She wrote me a little note which said, "Dear Mom. I love you very much, but I can't come because the people need me. I've got to go door-knocking this weekend and I can't leave my job." I think that's really great because she puts her priorities on the work she has to do instead of coming down to see me.

The time I spend with my kids is very limited. This year I was in Washington, D.C., for almost two months, then I was in Arizona for another six weeks, then I was in Los Angeles working on the McGovern campaign for another two weeks. So this year I've spent very little time with my children. Since August twenty-seventh I've seen them twice for visits for about an hour.

Sure, it's a hardship for me, but I know that my kids are all working in the union itself. They have to grow up with the responsibility of their work, but they have fun too. Probably the problems they have is like the kind of schools that they go to which are very reactionary.

I think it's important for the children to be fed and clothed, which they are. When I first started working with César I had this problem worrying about whether my kids were going to eat or not, because at the time I started working for the union I was making pretty good money, and I knew I was going to start working without *any* money, and I wondered how I could do it. But the kids have never gone hungry. We've had some rough times, particularly in Delano during the strike, because my kids went without fresh milk for two years. They just had powdered milk we got through donations. It's made them understand what hardship is, and this is good because you can't really relate to suffering unless you've had a little bit of it yourself. But the main thing is that they have their dignity and identity.

My family used to criticize me a lot. They thought that I was a traitor to my Raza, to my family and to everybody else. But I think they finally realized that what I'm doing is important and they're starting to appreciate it now. They thought that I was just neglecting my children and that what I was doing was just for selfish reasons.

The criticism came mostly from my dad and other relatives, but my brothers are very understanding. My mother was a very active woman, and I just followed her. She's dead now, but she always got the prizes for registering the most voters, and she raised us without any hang-ups about things like that.

You could expect that I would get a lot of criticisms from the farm workers themselves, but it mostly comes from middle-class people. They're more hung-up about these things than the poor people are, because the poor people have to haul their kids around from school to school, and the women have to go out and work and they've got to either leave their kids or take them out to the fields with them. So they sympathize a lot more with my problem in terms of my children. Sometimes I think it's bad for people to shelter their kids too much. Giving kids clothes and food is one thing, you know, but it's much more important to teach them that other people besides themselves are important, and that the best thing they can do with their lives is to use it in the service of other people. So my kids know that the way that we live is poor, materially speaking, but it's rich in a lot of other ways. They get to meet a lot of people and their experiences are varied.

I know people who work like fools just to give their kids more material goods. They're depriving their family of themselves, for what? At least my kids know why I'm not home. They know that I'm doing this for something in which we're all working—it makes a whole different thing. My children don't have a lot of material things but they work hard for what they do get, just like everybody else, and that makes them really self-sufficient. They make their own arrangements when they go places. They all have a lot of friends and they don't get all hung-up about having a lot of goodies. I think my kids are very healthy both mentally and physically. All the women in the union have similar problems. They don't have to leave their families for as long as I do. But everybody shares everything, we share the work.

The way we do the work is we do whatever is needed regardless of what we'd really like to do. You have a problem when you develop into a kind of personality like César because that really takes you away from the work that has to be done with the farm workers in education and development of leadership. That's what I'd really like to do. I'd just like to keep working down there with the ranch committees and the farm workers themselves because they have to take over the union. I can put my experience there. César would much rather be organizing than anything. He loves to organize because it's really creative. But he can't do it because right now he has to go around speaking, as I am doing also. I'd rather be working on the strike.

It's hard when you learn how to do something but you have to do something else. But they've kept us on the run. We had been successful in organizing farm workers so in order to try to stop the union they introduced this bill, AB-964. This bill was just exactly like Proposition 22 and they thought they could get it through the legislature. Well, we mobilized and were able to stop it. Thousands of farm workers' supporters went to Sacramento to stop it. That was 1971. They tried it again in 1972 but the bill didn't really go very far. We had been involved with the lettuce negotiation all of last year, after we stopped the boycott. Then they got the bright idea in the Nixon administration to try to take the boycott away from us in the federal courts. What they were using as an argument was that we were covered by the National Labor Relations Law (NLRB) so that we couldn't boycott. They took us to federal court in Fresno saying we were part of the NLRB. Well, this is ridiculous because we've never been part of it. So what this means is that it's strictly a political issue and logic and justice, none of these factors, have anything to do with it.

We went to Washington and started putting heat on the Republican party all over the country. We picketed people like Bañuelos [U.S. Treasurer Romana Bañuelos] and Senators Tower, Percy, and Hatfield. I was in Washington talking to the Republicans and the Democrats trying to stop this thing, kind of coordinating it.

In a way they might win by keeping us on the run but in a way they lose. Arizona is a good example, I was there for about two months before César went out there. They passed a proposition in the legislature similar to Proposition 22 here. So I called César up to ask him to come to a rally. I said "The governor's going to sign the bill but maybe if you come we can at least make a good protest." So we called the governor's office to tell him that César was going to be coming, and would he please give us the courtesy of meeting with us before he signed it. We thought we still might have a chance to stop it. Well, the governor knew that we were having this noon-time rally so he signed the bill at nine o'clock in the morning without even meeting with us. So what's happening now is we're getting everybody registered to vote, we're going to recall the governor and turn the state upside down. We organized the whole state just because the governer signed the stupid bill. So you might say that they win because they make us come out to the cities, but maybe while we're here, we're organizing too. Every time they try to do something against the union it works in our favor.

The main thing they keep us from doing is working with the farm workers. We'd be going after other growers and going to other states but we can't do that right now. But maybe that's the way it's supposed to happen. It's like this letter that this farm worker wrote me. "Dice que parece que estamos siguiendo un mandamiento de Dios" [They say that it seems that we are following a command from God]. We see these things as bad things that are happening to us right now but maybe they're good things and we can't see them that way because God wants us to do them. Every time we had some problem that kept us from ending the grape strike, I'd always tell César it's because God wants us to organize something else before the grape strike is over.

We've been working more and more with the Democratic party, because it's been the more liberal of the two parties. We depended on the Democrats to pass all those bills I told you about. You hardly ever get Republicans to vote for you. We live in a practical world, in a world of survival. And when the Democrats do us dirt, "también los atacamos a ellos" [we'll attack them also], although on an individual basis. So we maintain a certain amount of independence because our first responsibility is to the farm workers.

It's not true that both parties are just as bad for Chicanos, because the few benefits that we have gotten have come through the Democratic party. The only thing I have to say to people who attack the Democrats is that they should attack the Republicans. They should be going after Nixon, after Secretary of Agriculture Butz, after Reagan and all of these Republicans in the valley who vote against us every single time. That's who they should be going after, not after the guys who are trying to help us.

On the other hand, if anybody needs straightening up in the Democratic party, we straighten them up. We went after certain guys, like Alex García who's a Mexican, and we almost got him defeated. He won by two hundred votes, and if it wouldn't have been for the fast in Arizona and our work on the McGovern campaign, we would have beaten Alex García, and Alex knows it.

I think that if people are dissatisfied with the Democratic party they should get involved and take it over. I've told Assemblyman Moretti that he can make a decision either for or against the poor people, and that if he's against us we're going to fight him. But you can't go saying this to Reagan. He won't even meet with us.

There were some problems at the Democratic Convention. It was really unfortunate because there was a little clique that was trying to put down McGovern. The rumor was going around that McGovern wouldn't talk to Chicanos. Well, this was ridiculous because in East Los Angeles McGovern would go to every little place Chicanos wanted him to go, and speak to them. But there were people who were spreading this rumor around. I think they were part of the Nixon sabotage squad! . . .

I know that the farm worker issue is not the only Chicano issue. But in terms of the visibility of the Chicano issues, I think first of all there wasn't an agreement among the Chicanos themselves on what the issues were. Some people talked about bilingual education, other people talked about something else. I don't know, there just wasn't that much of a consensus on what we wanted to make public. So, I talked to Senator McGovern's staff, Frank Mankiewicz and some other people, and I told them that Chicanos wanted more visibility there. Naturally, they turned to me and said they wanted me to make a seconding speech for Eagleton or somebody. And I told them that I didn't want to be in the limelight, that other Chicanos wanted the focus. So that's when they had Mondragón make the speech he made.

I would say the Chicanos were disorganized. They had a platform with a lot of Chicano issues which they wanted to submit. But it was put together kind of fast, I think. You didn't have a kind of cohesiveness. But that's not unusual, you see, because in the black caucus you had the same kind of divisions.

Understanding that Chicanos have to come from all walks of life, from different experiences and different communities, you're not always going to get everybody to think the same. I think the Chicano caucus they had in San Jose is a good idea, where you can get Chicanos to decide the two or three priorities we want for California and get everybody to push together on them. But again, you got too many factions going. Everybody wants their own thing.

We're just now reaching a level where we can get mature political participation. We're going to get it as people get more interested in politics and make it a life-long thing, like Art Flores who ran against Alex García in East Los Angeles. Art really likes politics and he wants to do the right thing and he's not afraid to tell a guy he's an s.o.b. Then there's Peter Chacón, who's an assemblyman, "pero es muy cobarde" [but he is very cowardly]. When people are doing something against Chicanos he's afraid to tell them so, because he says he has to rely on a lot of white votes. So he lets them tell *him* what to do. But if we would have had fifteen Chicanos in California who were really involved in politics, "pero que no fueran miedosos" [but who were not afraid], the whole McGovern campaign would have been run by Chicanos. But we didn't have enough guys who had the political savvy.

But that's all going to change. If you ever get a chance, go down to Parlier. Chicanos turned around the whole city council there. So when the farm workers set up a picket line in Parlier, the cops wouldn't even come near us. There's a whole change in the picture because those people exercised their political power, they participated in democracy.

The worst thing that I see is guys who say, "Man, they don't have no Chicanos up there and they're not doing this or that for Chicanos." But the "vatos" are just criticizing and they're not in there working to make sure that it happens. We criticize and separate ourselves from the process. We've got to jump right in there with both feet.

Most of the people doing the work for us are *gabachillos* [nice Anglos]. When we get Chicano volunteers it's really great. But the Chicanos who come down to work with the farm workers have some hang-ups, especially the guys that come out of college. "En primer lugar, le tienen miedo a la gente" [In the first place, they are afraid of the people]. Unless they come out of the farm worker communities themselves, they get down there and they're afraid of the people. I don't know why it happens, but they're afraid to deal with them. But you have to deal with them like people, not like they were saints. The Chicano guys who come down here have a very tough time adjusting. They don't want to relate to the poor farm workers anymore. They tried so hard to get away from that scene and they don't want to go back to it.

We have a lot of wonderful people working with us. But we need a lot more because we have a whole country to organize. If the people can learn to organize within the union, they can go back to their own communities and organize. We have to organize La Raza in East Los Angeles. We have to do it. We have one thousand farm workers in there right now organizing for the boycott. In the future, we would very much like to organize around an issue that isn't a farm worker issue. But we just can't because we just don't have the time.

Maybe some day we can finish organizing the farm workers, but it's going so slow because of all the fights we have to get into. We'll have a better idea of where we're at once the lettuce boycott is won. See, there's about two hundred to three hundred growers involved in the lettuce boycott. The same growers who grow lettuce grow vegetables like artichokes and broccoli. So if we get that out of the way we'll have about one third of the state of California organized. That's a big chunk. From there, hopefully, we can move on to the citrus and get that out of the way. We have to move into other states, like we did into Arizona.

It would seem that with the Republicans in for another four years, though, we'll have a lot of obstacles. Their strategy was to get Chicanos into the Republican party. But we refuse to meet with, for example, Henry Ramírez [chairman of the President's Cabinet Committee on Opportunities for the Spanish-Speaking]. He went around and said a lot of terrible things about us at the campuses back east. He thought that we didn't have any friends back there. But we do, and they wrote us back and told us that he was saying that the farm workers didn't want the union, that César was a Communist, and just a lot of stupid things. This is supposed to be a responsible man.

Then there is Philip Sánchez [National director of the Office of Economic Opportunity]. I went to his home in Fresno once when a labor contractor shot this farm worker. I was trying to get the D.A.'s office to file a complaint against the labor contractor. So I went to see Philip Sánchez to see if he could help me. But the guy wouldn't help me. Later when the growers got this group of labor contractors together to form a company union against us, Sánchez went and spoke to their meeting. It came out in the paper that he was supporting their organization. As far as I'm concerned, Philip Sánchez has already come out against the farm workers.

It's really funny. Some of the *Puerto Riqueños* who are in the President's Committee for the Spanish-speaking, man, they *tell* the administration what the Puerto Ricans need. "Se pelean con ellos" [They fight with them]. But the Chicanos don't. They're caught. They just become captives.

I spoke to a lot of the guys in Washington who were in these different poverty programs. Some of the Chicanos had been dropped in their positions of leadership. They put [other] guys over [the Chicanos] . . . they put watchdogs on them to make sure that they don't do anything that really helps the farm workers. The guys are really afraid because there's just a few jobs and they can be easily replaced. They're worse off than the farm workers, you see. The farm workers at least have the will to fight. They're not afraid to go out on strike and lose their jobs. But the guy who has a nice fat job and is afraid to go out and fight, well, they've made him a worse slave than the farm worker.

An ex-priest told me one time that César should really be afraid somebody might write a book to expose him. I said, "Don't even kid yourself that César is afraid of anybody because he's not. The only ones who might scare him are God and his wife, Helen. But besides them he's not afraid of anyone.

He's got so much damn courage, "y así come es él" [and he is as he is]. That's the way the farm workers are. They have this incredible strength. I feel like a big phony because I'm over here talking and they're out there in the streets right now, walking around in the rain getting people to vote. "Son tan dispuestos a sufrir" [They are so ready to suffer], and they take whatever they have to take because they have no escape hatch.

Being poor and not having anything just gives an incredible strength to people. The farm workers seem to be able to see around the corner, and César has that quality because he comes out of that environment. César's family were migrant workers. It was kind of the reverse of mine because they started with a farm in Yuma but lost it during the depression. They had to migrate all over the state to earn a living, and they had some really horrible times, worse than anything we ever suffered. So there was a lot more hardship in his background. But his family had a lot of luck. His mom and dad were really together all the time.

César always teases me. He says I'm a liberal. When he wants to get me mad he says, "You're not a Mexican," because he says I have a lot of liberal hang-ups in my head. And I know it's true. I am a logical person. I went to school and you learn that you have to weigh both sides and look at things objectively. But the farm workers know that wrong is wrong. They know that there's evil in the world and that you have to fight evil. They call it like it is.

When I first went to work in the fields after I had met Fred Ross, the first thing that happened was that I was propositioned by a farmer. People who work in the fields have to take this every day of their lives, but I didn't know how to handle it. So I wondered if I should be there at all, because I had gone to college. I had gone to college to get out of hard labor. Then all of a sudden there I was doing it again.

I feel glad now that I was able to do it. It's good my kids have done field work now, too, because they understand what it all means. I feel very humble with the farm workers. I think I've learned more from them than they would ever learn from me.

Raúl Héctor Castro: Poverty to Prominence*

Geoffrey P. Mawn

> "All my life, I've been fighting because people would tell me that I couldn't do this and shouldn't do that because I was a poor Mexican boy."[1]

His remark summarizes the motivating drive behind the achievements of Raúl Castro, a fighter who never sought refuge behind obstacles in striving toward his goal. As a result of his determination and hard work he has excelled; he has risen from poverty to prominence. Accepting the responsibilities of his accomplishments and position, he has contributed significantly not only to his fellow Mexican-Americans and his adopted Arizonans but to all Americans.

Raúl Héctor Castro was born in the mining town of Cananea, Sonora, on June 12, 1916. He was the second-youngest of the fourteen children of Francisco D. and Rosario Acosta Castro.[2] His father was a merchant seaman, diver, and miner in Sonora. Politically active, his father supported the losing side during the revolutionary turmoil instigated by Pancho Villa's terrorist tactics in 1916 and spent six months in prison at Hermosillo as a political prisoner. When amnesty was granted and he was released, Francisco Castro decided to leave Mexico. Seeking a freer and better life across the border, the Castro family immigrated to Pirtleville, the Mexican settlement north of Douglas, Arizona.[3]

But life was not any easier for the Castro family in the United States. As a poor immigrant family with few financial means of support except their own hard work, the Castros found that the United States was not a land of immediate opportunity. Raúl's father worked in the Douglas mines and smelter, and his mother earned small sums and food serving as a midwife in the local community. Raúl and the other children helped contribute to the family economy by sifting earth in a crude sluice box for the small bits of coarse gold. In January 1929, when Raúl was twelve, Francisco Castro died, leaving his widowed wife and children to support themselves during the Great Depression of the 1930s.[4]

"Chopping stepping-stones out of obstacles," Raúl Castro worked his way out of abject poverty. His two methods were employment and education fortified by his aggressive personal drive and assistance from his friends. Mastering English was his hardest problem.

---

*This study, which was assisted by an Arizona State University Graduate Fellowship, was prepared for a graduate course in the History of the American Southwest.

Neither of his parents spoke English and his elementary school teachers often spoke little or no Spanish. Later he recalled being crushed after overhearing a teacher comment, "Those Mexican kids are so dumb you can't teach them anything." School life was a major contact with white Anglo society for the children of Mexican descent in Douglas. But when the school bell rang at the end of the day the Mexican and Mexican-American students went back to their Mexican society.[5]

Realizing the value of a good education, Raúl continued to attend the public schools in Douglas. In 1935 he graduated from Douglas High School acclaimed as an honor student, athlete, and editor of the student newspaper. Desiring to continue his education, he worked his way through Arizona State College at Flagstaff (now Northern Arizona University) by serving as a cook's helper, busboy, and waiter in the dining hall. He supplemented his income by serving as a member of the Arizona National Guard, rising to the rank of sergeant. During his senior year in high school and summer vacations in college, he worked as a laborer in the Douglas copper smelter of the Phelps Dodge Corporation and on the farms and ranches of the area. His competitive nature led him to participate in collegiate football, track, and boxing. Undefeated in four years of intercollegiate boxing competition while at Arizona State College, he was the Border Conference middleweight champion in 1939. That year he earned his bachelor of arts degree and also became a naturalized United States citizen.[6]

After receiving his degree, Castro returned to Douglas where he tried to obtain a job as a high school teacher. His bilingual background and his teacher training fully qualified him for a position in the Douglas school system, but his ambition and desires were thwarted. The local school board informed him that they were no longer hiring Mexican-American teachers for the district. Disgruntled, he hopped a freight train and spent some time touring the United States, working at odd jobs and boxing professionally for his livelihood.[7]

During World War II, he secured a position as a foreign service clerk with the United States Department of State, beginning in 1941. Stationed at the Agua Prieta Consulate across the United States–Mexican border from Douglas, he started work as a stenographer at ninety-two dollars a month. For five years he gradually worked his way up within the Agua Prieta Consulate. But again his advance was checked. Because he was a newly naturalized citizen, State Department regulations stated that he could not compete for higher positions.[8] The late Consul General William P.

Blocker, according to Castro, advised him that he was wasting his time and that he should "find something else. A Mexican-born boy will never get anyplace [*sic*] in the Foreign Service."[9] Unfortunately, Blocker died before changing attitudes made such goals possible.

Castro was disappointed but not defeated. His service in the consular corps stimulated an interest in law which was strengthened by "watching lawyers and judges operate in Mexican courts."[10] After his resignation from the consular service in January 1946, he entered the University of Arizona College of Law. Again lacking financial support for his education, he worked his way through law school by teaching Spanish to day and evening classes at the university.[11]

Having obtained his law degree in 1949, he was admitted to the Arizona bar and opened a law office for general practice. A year later he admitted David K. Wolfe as a junior partner and established the law firm of Castro & Wolfe. This firm specialized in representing small mining operations and farming interests in Mexico. With this specialization, Castro became recognized as an expert on Mexican law and court procedure.[12]

After practicing law for two years, Castro was appointed to the post of deputy county attorney for Pima County by Robert Morrison in January 1951. Reappointed by Morrison's successor, County Attorney Morris K. Udall, Castro served from 1951 to 1954.[13] When Udall made a bid for a superior court judgeship and Morrison ran for state attorney general, Castro announced his candidacy as the Democratic nominee for county attorney. His edge over his Democratic opponent in the primary, Chief Civil Deputy Gordon G. Aldrich, was less than three hundred votes.[14] The Republican nominee in the general election was attorney William K. Richey, a former state representative from Pima County and member of the judiciary committee of the house. Castro outpolled Richey by more than six thousand votes.[15] With his election as county attorney in 1954, he became the first native Mexican to hold this position in Pima County. As chief prosecutor he enhanced his reputation by conducting his office impartially "without either fear or favor."[16] Running for reelection during the Eisenhower landslide election year of 1956, Raúl secured a victory over his hard-running Republican opponent, Richey, by slightly more than one thousand votes following a campaign centered on arguments over the percentages of convictions in felony cases.[17]

Aiming higher, Castro ran for the judgeship in the newly created division five of the superior court. His opponent was Robert O.

Roylston, former assistant United States attorney for five years. The voters agreed that Castro had earned his promotion to the judgeship and elected him by a majority of over two thousand votes, making him the first native Mexican superior court judge in Pima County.[18] Running unopposed for reelection to the superior court bench in 1962, he received a bipartisan vote of confidence of over forty-one thousand votes.[19] In 1960 his fellow judges selected him as the juvenile court judge for Pima County because of his longstanding interest in juvenile affairs. As a superior court judge, Castro served in both the juvenile and adult divisions and handled civil and criminal cases. The Arizona Supreme Court also asked him to sit with them in hearing four cases and to write the opinions in three of the four.[20]

Early on the morning of September 4, 1964, President Lyndon Johnson called Judge Castro to notify him personally that he was going to nominate him as the new ambassador to El Salvador. The nomination was made on the recommendation of United States Senator Carl Hayden of Arizona, then president pro tempore of the Senate, who stated that "Raul Castro's background and understanding about Latin America show he will contribute greatly to the continuation of our good relations with our friends to the south."[21] Lauding Castro's preappointment achievements, President Johnson described him as "especially representative of the Americans who have brought to our society the rich heritage of Mexico."[22]

Castro was eminently qualified for his post. His background as an impoverished immigrant, his Spanish linguistic expertise and cultural affinity, his Roman Catholic religion, and his teaching, legal, and livestock-raising background made him invaluable to poverty-poor El Salvador. He also had been active as chairman of the International Law Committee of the Pima County Bar Association and served as a liaison between the association and visiting foreign barristers. During the previous year he had been sent to Mexico City by Attorney General Robert F. Kennedy as a member of the United States delegation to the Third Interamerican Congress of Attorneys General. From these positions and personal contacts he received a current picture of the problems and possible solutions for the Latin-American republics.[23]

After a brief, routine questioning, the Senate Foreign Relations Committee recommended his nomination by a voice vote. On the following day, October 2, the Senate confirmed the nomination by unanimous voice vote.[24] Thus Castro became the first native Mexican to be appointed an ambassador of the United States. An ironic aspect of this appointment was the substantial difference between his former salary of ninety-two dollars a month with the consulate in Agua Prieta and his new salary of twenty-eight thousand five hundred dollars a year as an ambassador in his return to foreign service.

Ambassador Castro resigned his judgeship and leased his ten-acre El Milagro Ranch with its Shetland pony farm to serve as the United States representative to one of the smallest and most densely populated Central-American republics, with a total population of more than three million. He replaced career diplomat Murat W. Williams who left San Salvador, the capital of El Salvador, after a very successful tour, having succeeded in strengthening the economic and political bonds between the United States and El Salvador.[25]

After his appointment Castro's name was bandied about as an interesting oddity. Continual reference was made to the fact that he was not related to Fidel Castro or Fidel's brother Raúl, who were then governing Cuba. Our Castro cleverly dubbed himself the "Yanqui Castro" and commented that his surname was a common Spanish equivalent of Smith or Jones and not necessarily limited to bearded revolutionaries. His name continued to cause him embarrassment despite his ambassadorial position. Castro encountered problems entering the United States at Miami, Florida, en route to Washington.

> Each time I arrived and presented my passport to the immigration man at Miami airport he took one look at my name, then thumbed through the list of undesirables who were not permitted to enter. Always the name Raúl Castro was there.
>
> It took too much time arguing with these officials that I was really a U.S. ambassador and from Arizona and not the Cuban Raúl Castro. So I switched to flights arriving at Houston or New Orleans.[26]

Other such problems were dispatched with comparable efficiency.

Castro was the antithesis of the "big Yankee imperialist" image. A self-styled "wetback ambassador," he was determined to bridge the international communication gap, assist the less fortunate, and promote greater understanding between the Salvadorans and Americans. As ambassador to El Salvador, Castro was no striped-suit diplomat. Unwilling to remain cooped up in an air-conditioned embassy office and be a theoretician, Castro sought firsthand knowledge of the nation's problems and progress. He continually toured the countryside in his jeep, becoming a familiar figure on the coffee plantations and in the population centers of the small but strategic Central-American nation.

Castro communicated effectively with the Salvadorans from President Fidel Sánchez Hernández down to the common people because of his linguistic competence and his belief that frankness and pride of country were the keynotes of foreign service. As a shirt-sleeve ambassador, his enterprise in administering and implementing projects for the improvement of education, agriculture, and building construction earned him the praise of President Sánchez Hernández as *el envoye que trabaja* (the envoy who works). Since he had developed a close working relationship with the Salvadoran government officials, the problems of his ambassadorship were limited to minor disagreements involving financial aid and technical assistance under programs sponsored by the Agency for International Development (AID).[27]

Two significant events occurred during Castro's stay in El Salvador. The first was the predawn earthquake that struck the country on May 3, 1965, killing more than one hundred and fifty Salvadorans and leaving thirty to forty thousand homeless. Castro personally spearheaded the United States Army's first aid and relief operations and assisted in the rebuilding of the country through the AID programs that financed the construction of more than two hundred schools and several major highways. Long-range plans included the construction of a new four-story, quakeproof United States Embassy, completed in late 1967, to replace the badly battered old one.[28]

A major highlight of Castro's tour of duty was the two-day visit of President Johnson to El Salvador. Johnson journeyed to San Salvador to confer with the presidents of five small Central-American nations, El Salvador, Costa Rica, Honduras, Guatemala, and Nicaragua, and to attend the regional meeting of the seven-year-old Central-American Common Market. The major reason for the visit was to dramatize the United States–supported Central-American Common Market, which the president regarded as an excellent example of regional economic integration, despite its inability to balance import expenditures and export income. The trip also gave the president an opportunity to publicize the efforts of President Sánchez Hernández in guiding one of the most dynamic economies in Central America based on coffee and cotton exports. Castro's own record and the success of the president's Central-American trip, combined with the fortuitous visit of Bolivian President René Barrientos Ortuño to the LBJ Ranch, the day before President Johnson's departure, led to Castro's next diplomatic assignment.[29]

On July 15, 1968, one week after his departure from San Salvador, President Johnson announced the nomination of Raúl Castro as the new ambassador to Bolivia to replace Douglas Henderson who had served in that country since November 1963.[30] This new assignment was a promotion in his diplomatic career. He was moving from the smallest, most densely populated Central-American country to the fifth-largest country in South America. Bolivia, one of the world's largest tin producers, was politically and economically vital to the United States. Its importance previously was shown by the fact that Ernesto "Che" Guevara, Fidel Castro's "director of exported revolutions," chose this South-American nation for his first invasion.

Early in September 1968 Castro presented his credentials as the new United States Ambassador to Bolivia. His ambassadorship to this country was marred by student and leftist demonstrations as well as the continuing terrorism of the remnants of Che Guevara's guerrilla band. On January 10, 1969, a bomb was tossed into the garden of Castro's embassy residence.[31] The death of President René Barrientos Ortuño on April 27, 1969, and the succession of Vice-President Luis Adolfo Siles Salinas further disrupted the faction-torn country. Thousands of well-organized student demonstrators and workers of the opposition National Revolutionary Movement shortened the scheduled twenty-two-hour stop of Governor Nelson A. Rockefeller to two hours. The fact-finding Latin-American tour of Rockefeller in Bolivia was confined to the heavily guarded air terminal at the John F. Kennedy Airport in La Paz, instead of the presidential palace where he had planned to confer with President Siles Salinas.[32] Nor did the political turmoil stop following Rockefeller's departure.

On September 26, 1969, Bolivians experienced their one hundred eighty-fifth coup during the country's one hundred and forty-four years of independence, when General Alfredo Ovando Candia, commander in chief of the armed forces, overthrew the civilian government of Siles Salinas. Bolivia thus became the fifth South American country to fall under a military junta. The new government professed a dual policy of intensified nationalism and agrarian reform, threatened to curtail tin and other mineral exports, and confiscated Bolivian Gulf Oil, a subsidiary of the United States firm Gulf Oil Company. The State Department routinely suspended diplomatic relations.[33]

When the coup occurred, President Richard Nixon was working at Camp David reshaping and formulating a new "low-profile" Latin-American foreign policy. Ignoring the support of the entire Arizona congressional delegation, Nixon accepted Castro's resignation which had been routinely submitted to the new administration early in 1969. The obvious reason for his dismissal was his Democratic affiliation. The State Department noted that Castro was not in La Paz when the coup occurred, because he was in Buenos Aires for several weeks for treatment of a case of viral pneumonia occasioned by the cold, high altitude of the capital. "Washington sources indicated" that Castro had occasioned criticism from Peace Corps volunteers and the Bolivian government, as well as his State Department superiors, because of a talk he gave to the volunteers in La Paz.[34] His personal safety may have been another consideration for his removal because detailed plans of a kidnapping plot were discovered when Bolivian troops killed a local Communist lieutenant of Che Guevara.[35] At the time of his recall, Castro was the last of the Johnson ambassadorial appointees to be removed from a Latin-American post by President Nixon.

Upon his return to Arizona in late 1969, Castro was mentioned as a possible candidate for the 1970 Democratic nomination as the next Arizona governor or United States senator. Instead of campaigning, he resumed his practice of international law, becoming a member of the Tucson law firm of Zipf, Larkin, Lyle and Rogers.[36] In March 1970 Mesa automobile dealer Jack Ross announced his candidacy for governor; in early May, Chandler Mayor George Nader entered the race.[37]

Castro, reluctant to announce his candidacy without political and financial support, did not confirm his intentions until June 18.[38] Then he stated: "I am running, not because my friends want me to, but because I want to be governor of the state of Arizona." The first question reporters wanted answered was whether he thought his Mexican background would be a handicap or an asset. Although admitting that he had waited to make sure Arizonans would support an individual of Mexican descent, Castro quickly noted that voters would judge him on his merit and qualifications for the job and not as a member of a minority group. He felt his background would be an asset rather than a hindrance because "it sounds a chord with every other minority group member, and Americans as a whole have always favored the underdog. And I'm an underdog." Aware that some Mexican-Americans might say he was no longer one of them, since he did not live in the Tucson barrio, he noted his inner-city community involvement and declared that he was a candidate for all Americans and for all Arizonans, running not on the basis of sympathy but on the basis of competency.[39]

Although many political commentators and analysts said he did not have a chance, Castro was willing to take the chance. Indeed, at the outset of his campaign he was unable to find three people to accompany him to the press clubs to make his opening announcements. But by the time of his upset victory in the September Democratic primary, he had the backing of over sixty-three thousand

Democrats. And in the November general election he received the bipartisan support of over two hundred and one thousand voters out of a total of about four hundred and ten thousand, running only slightly over seven thousand four hundred votes behind incumbent Republican Governor Jack Williams.[40]

Political strategy for Castro's spirited but low-key primary and general election campaigns centered around the basic theme of "Let's Keep Raul Castro Working for Arizona."[41] He advertised his impressive record of public service, his versatility, and his positive policies, spiced with his colorful and affable personal appeal. Limited to what he called "a poor man's campaign" on a shoestring budget, Castro nevertheless campaigned at his usual hard-driving, tireless pace, making four to five appearances a day. Well known in Pima County but facing a problem of becoming known in populous Maricopa County, which contains over half of the registered voters of the state, Castro electioneered on sidewalks and in shopping centers of the Phoenix area in an effort to meet Maricopa County voters. Not confining his efforts to the two largest counties, he campaigned actively in the twelve so-called outside counties of the state.

The race for governor was simply a question of contrasting personal styles and personal credentials of civic and government service. Castro called attention to his own varied career and accomplishments as a field hand, smelter worker, teacher, lawyer, prosecutor, judge, and diplomat to support his claim that he was better qualified to understand Arizona's problems and provide dynamic, able leadership in proposing solutions and corrective programs. The basic issues of Castro's campaign were expanded educational opportunities, drug education and rehabilitation of addicts, crime control and law enforcement support, and improvement of the deteriorating relations between Arizona and Sonora. In each area he emphasized his own background and a program of solutions.

Speaking from firsthand experience as a schoolteacher and a member of a disadvantaged minority, he advocated programs such as state-supported kindergartens, bilingual elementary education, and free high school textbooks in order to provide better educational opportunities, not only for minority groups but for all children. He felt his knowledge of students and educators and close work with juveniles would help provide better communication between students and administrators. Overcrowding in schools could be met by using part of an alleged surplus of stabilization and construction funds totaling thirty-three million dollars.

Stressing his early pioneer efforts as a supporter of the first program in the state to combat drug use among juveniles and his work as a prosecutor, juvenile judge, and community worker, he called for a coordinated program of drug education to curb the curiosity of nonusers, physical and psychiatric rehabilitation of addicts, and extended efforts to ferret out and prosecute pushers and peddlers. As a seasoned diplomat with a bilingual background, he pledged his efforts as governor to help improve the economic and political ties and develop strong law enforcement relationships with bordering Sonora and other areas of Latin America. Teamwork with Sonoran officials would help dry up the source of drugs crossing the international boundary. In his previous work as an ambassador and lawyer, he had developed techniques and contacts to achieve this close working relationship. His ambassadorial assignments also showed his executive and administrative abilities.

Pointing to his legal background as a lawyer, county attorney, and judge, Castro criticized the lack of support for law enforcement prevalent in Arizona government and stressed the need for a concentrated campaign against crime, backed by aggressive executive leadership. A governor, he stated, needed a knowledge of law enforcement and court procedures to galvanize public support behind such a program. Upholding the right of everybody to free speech and peaceful demonstration, as a law and order candidate he stated he would deny "the right of anyone—hippie, craftsman, or intellectual—to destroy property, commit violence on any other person, or in any way take the law into his own hands."[42]

But despite his active campaign, his credentials, and his constructive programs, Raúl Castro was the losing candidate in the 1970 Arizona gubernatorial election. Obviously a majority of the Arizona voters were not ready for a change, as incumbents were returned to office in most instances.[43] Political analysts attributed his strong showing against a popular incumbent to the new image he presented in the Democratic party as a moderate liberal with personal appeal, integrity, and a refreshing sense of humor coupled with experience and a program.[44] Castro personally felt the reason for his defeat was his poor organization and underfinancing. One reporter described his Phoenix headquarters as "a study in disorganized, dedicated, enthusiastic activity."[45] Others pointed to the lack of support in the rural counties and in southern Arizona where Democratic Representative Morris Udall polled nearly 70 percent of the vote, about four thousand more votes than Castro.[46] Another, more significant trend was the light turnout among the black Phoenix south side district voters who traditionally vote Democratic. One of the major reasons was the animosity generated within the Mexican-American and black communities by the boycott at the Phoenix Union High

School. Another factor may have been the blacks' reluctance to support another minority group. Even Maricopa's Democratic State Senator Cloves Campbell, the Senate's only black member, thought "there is 'no doubt' that blacks were less than enthusiastic about Castro."[47]

Following the election, Castro returned to his international law practice, but he did not retire from politics. As the chief vote-getter in the election, Castro assumed the role as the titular head of the Arizona Democratic party.[48] As the Democratic opposition leader, Castro attacked the alleged deficiencies of the Williams administration and urged legislation on mandatory auto inspections, voting rights for eighteen-year-olds, bipartisan reapportionment, state-supported kindergartens, and publication of the report on the state's welfare system.[49]

Beginning in June 1972 Castro has come under severe criticism from his fellow Mexican-Americans for not supporting the drive of César Chávez and the United Farm Workers to recall Arizona Governor Jack Williams. Castro has stated publicly that he strongly opposed the 1972 enactment of the controversial Farm Labor Act (Arizona House Bill 2134), which subsequently sparked the initiation of the recall movement. Despite strong pressure from Chicano and Mexican-American groups and the United Farm Workers, he has denounced the recall movement as an improper remedy for this unpopular bill.[50] Obviously, the recall of Governor Williams, even if successful, would not rescind the legislative statute. Castro undoubtedly realizes that the solution to the offensive law lies in a challenge through the judicial process, or through the intiative or referendum procedure. But the heated controversy, resulting from the opposition to the bill and the support for the recall movement, has led some people to criticize and denounce Castro for his refusal to support the recall movement. They emotionally attribute his stance to an indifference toward the inequities among the farm workers and to a break in his continued affinity with his fellow Mexicans and Mexican-Americans. These attackers evidently ignore Castro's background.[51] This background clearly illustrates that he is sensitive to the realistic, rather than the emotive, needs of all people and has fought courageously for legal, political, and economic justice for working men and minority groups. Thus, despite some opposition because of the recall controversy, Raúl Castro is still suggested as a strong potential Democratic candidate for governor in the next regular gubernatorial race in 1974.

Raúl Castro's is a real success story. During his 1970 gubernatorial campaign he told a Yuma audience, "Ever since I was little, I was told, 'Raúl, you haven't got a chance.' . . . Well, I've been lots of places for a guy who didn't have a chance."[52] Moreover, Raúl Castro deserves recognition as one of the Southwest's most illustrious modern Mexican-Americans. He, more than any other contemporary Mexican-American leader, provides a living example of a man who rose from humble beginnings to prominence on the basis of his inherent ability, education, hard work, perseverance, and contributions. Overcoming poverty, language problems, and cultural discrimination, he obtained an education, became a United States citizen, practiced law, was elected county attorney and later superior court judge, and then was appointed ambassador to El Salvador and Bolivia. As the Democratic gubernatorial nominee in 1970, he provided Arizonans with a choice, not of a minority group candidate but of a true leader who aired the public problems and suggested constructive solutions. The career of this distinguished American of Mexican descent is one of achievements. He has proved himself to be a man of energy, persuasiveness, integrity, and knowledge. Raúl Castro has worked his way from poverty to prominence, but he is still a man of and for the people.

Notes

1. *Tucson Daily Citizen*, August 21, 1970.
2. Castro to Hayden (résumé of life), Tucson, August 12, 1963, Arizona State University Library, Hayden Archive, Carl T. Hayden Papers, Appointment Papers, Box 686, Raúl Castro #1.
3. Jim Cook, "From Clerk to Ambassador: Raúl Castro Sees Opportunity in Latin Service," *Arizona Republic*, October 4, 1964; Bernie Wynn, "One Man's Opinion," *Arizona Republic*, October 16, 1970.
4. Cook, "From Clerk to Ambassador."
5. Bernie Wynn, "Castro pinpoints language problem," *Arizona Republic*, October 17, 1970.
6. Castro to Hayden, Tucson, August 12, 1963, Arizona State University Library, Hayden Archive, Carl T. Hayden Papers, Appointment Papers, Box 686, Raúl Castro #1; Cook, "From Clerk to Ambassador." Castro became a citizen in the superior court of Bisbee, Arizona.
7. Cook, "From Clerk to Ambassador."
8. *Ibid.* This statement may be true, but this writer could find no published restrictive regulation of this nature. Perhaps the restriction was a part of the unwritten policy.
9. Raúl Castro, "No Striped Pants Diplomacy," *Arizona*, Sunday magazine supplement to *Arizona Republic*, July 23, 1967; and Harold K. Milks, "Castro leads whirlwind life as campaigner, breadwinner," *Arizona Republic*, September 29, 1970.
10. Castro to Hayden, Tucson, August 12, 1963, Arizona State University Library, Hayden Archive, Carl T. Hayden Papers, Appointment Papers, Box 686, Raúl Castro #1.
11. *Ibid.*
12. *Tucson Daily Citizen*, April 9, 1954; *Arizona Daily Star*, April 9, 1954.
13. *Ibid.*

14. *Arizona Daily Star*, September 9, 1954.

15. *Tucson Daily Citizen*, November 3, 1954, and November 15, 1954. Less than two weeks after his election, Castro married Patricia Steiner Norris, a native of Wisconsin. The Rt. Rev. Daniel J. Gercke, Bishop of Tucson, officiated at the wedding in San Agustín Cathedral on November 13, 1954. See *Tucson Daily Citizen*, November 13, 1954, and *Arizona Daily Star*, November 14, 1954.

16. Clipping (from *Arizona Daily Star* or *Tucson Daily Citizen)*, n.d. [1956], Arizona State University Library, Hayden Archive, Carl T. Hayden Papers, Appointment Papers, Box 686, Raúl Castro #1.

17. *Tucson Daily Citizen*, November 7, 1956; *Arizona Daily Star*, November 8, 1956.

18. *Arizona Daily Star*, November 2, 5, 1958.

19. *Tucson Daily Citizen*, November 7, 1962.

20. Castro to Hayden, Tucson, August 12, 1963, Arizona State University Library, Hayden Archives, Carl T. Hayden Papers, Appointment Papers, Box 686, Raúl Castro #1. As a result of his contributions as an attorney and judge, the Pima County Bar Association chose him as the outstanding naturalized citizen of 1963. *Alianza* (May 1963), p. 14; *Phoenix Gazette*, October 1, 1964.

21. Raúl Castro, "No Striped Pants Diplomacy," *Arizona Republic*, September 5, 1964; *Tucson Daily Citizen*, September 5, 1964; *Phoenix Gazette*, September 5, 1964.

The selection of Castro, a prominent Democrat in Arizona as well as a qualified nominee, was a boost to Johnson's bid for reelection in the upcoming presidential election of 1964. The official announcement of the nomination was made in Arizona by Carl Hayden through Roy L. Elson, his former administrative assistant for ten years. In the announcement, Hayden credited Elson with advising him of the excellent qualifications of Judge Castro for a foreign service assignment. The announcement publicity was a boost for Elson who was one of five Democrats running in the September primary for the party nomination to compete for Barry Goldwater's vacated seat in the United States Senate. The announcement also was made on the day after the opening of Goldwater's campaign as the Republican presidential nominee.

22. *Arizona Daily Star*, October 5, 1964. At a tribute in his honor, Castro received the Americanism Medal of the Daughters of the American Revolution, an award made to naturalized citizens who have distinguished themselves by their contributions. *Tucson Daily Citizen*, October 5, 1964.

23. Castro to Roy L. Elson, Tucson, February 17, 1964, Arizona State University Library, Hayden Archive, Carl T. Hayden Papers, Appointment Papers, Box 686, Raúl Castro #1; *Arizona Daily Star*, February 14, 1964. For the best general study of the Mexican conclave of the attorneys general see Antonio Tinajero-G., "Spanish-Speaking U.S. Delegates Attend Interamerican Congress of Attorneys General," *Alianza* (September 1963), pp. 6–7.

24. *New York Times*, October 2, 3, 1964; telegram, Hayden to Castro, Washington, D.C., October 2, 1964, Arizona State University Library, Hayden Archive, Carl T. Hayden Papers, Yellow Papers 1964, Box 238, C File; *Alianza* (September-December 1964), p. 8.

25. *Arizona Daily Star*, September 5, 1964; *Tucson Daily Citizen*, October 3, 1964. For an interesting piece on the Castros' Shetland ponies and El Milagro Ranch see Barbara Campbell and June Caldwell, "Collectors on a Small Scale," *Arizona Days and Ways*, magazine supplement to *Arizona Republic*, October 5, 1958.

26. *Arizona Republic*, December 19, 1970.

27. Castro, "No Striped Pants Diplomacy"; Harold K. Milks, "Arizona's Shirt-Sleeve Envoy," *Arizona Republic*, November 13, 1967.

28. *Arizona Republic*, November 13, 1967. Also Don Shoemaker, "Real Raul Castro's a Stand-up Guy," *Miami Herald*, October 26, 1966, editorial page; and Jeremiah O'Leary, "U.S.' Own Raul Castro Has Troubles," [Washington?] *Star*,

n.d., both clippings in Arizona State University Library, Hayden Archive, Carl T. Hayden Papers, Appointment Papers, Box 686, Raúl Castro #1.

29. *New York Times,* July 2, 6–8, 1968. The five Central-American presidents were: Fidel Sánchez Hernández of El Salvador, Osvaldo López Arellano of Honduras, Julio César Méndez Montenegro of Guatemala, José Joaquín Tejos of Costa Rica, and Anastasio Somoza Debayle of Nicaragua.

30. *New York Times,* July 16, 1968; *Tucson Daily Citizen,* July 15, 1968; and *Arizona Republic,* July 16, 1968. Castro was succeeded in El Salvador by William G. Bowdler, a career foreign service officer who had served as one of President Johnson's top experts on Central- and Latin-American affairs.

31. *New York Times,* September 4, 1968, and January 11, 1969.

32. *New York Times,* June 1, 1969.

33. *New York Times,* September 27, 28, 1969.

34. John Kamman, "Udall Angrily Denounces GOP for Castro's Ouster," *Tucson Daily Citizen,* September 30, 1969; *Arizona Republic,* September 30, 1969; *Phoenix Gazette,* September 27, 1969; *Arizona Daily Star,* October 1, 1969. One syndicated news service distortedly reported that the reason for Castro's absence was an extensive trip to Buenos Aires and Rio de Janeiro before returning to private life. Castro was replaced by Ernest Victor Siracus, the former deputy chief of mission in Peru, where he had acquired some experience working with military governments.

35. *Arizona Republic,* December 19, 1970. Ambassador and Mrs. Castro were to be offered for imprisoned Regis Debray, a French leftist writer and associate of Guevara.

36. *Arizona Republic,* November 21, 1969; *Arizona Daily Star,* June 13, 1970.

37. *Scottsdale Daily Progress,* May 5, 1970. Jack Williams, the Republican incumbent governor running unopposed, announced his candidacy on April 30. For biographies of Jack Ross see *Arizona Daily Star,* June 14, 1970, and *Mesa Tribune,* August 28, 1970. For a biography of George Nader see *Mesa Tribune,* August 31, 1970.

38. *Tucson Daily Citizen,* June 18, 1970; *Arizona Republic,* June 19, 1970; *Arizona Daily Star,* June 19, 1970. See also *Arizona Republic,* June 12, 1970; and *Arizona Daily Star,* June 12, 13, 1970.

39. *Phoenix Gazette,* June 18, 1970; *Arizona Daily Star,* June 19, 1970; *Tucson Daily Citizen,* June 23, 1970; *Arizona Daily Sun,* June 21, 1970. Newspapers covering the announcement of candidacy even noted his background, using such descriptions as he "tossed his sombrero into the primary election ring." *Arizona Republic,* June 19, 1970.

Castro's active involvement in community affairs began in July 1949, when he was initiated into the Logia Fundadora of the Alianza Hispano-Americana. He immediately assumed control of the organization of the Service Club of the Alianza in Tucson in 1949–50 and served as its first president. The purpose of the Service Club was the investigation of the social and economic problems in the Tucson community and the suggestion and promotion of solutions. *Alianza* (March 1950), pp. 4–5; and (April-May 1956), p. 19. Castro's early interest in juvenile affairs is reflected in an article on juvenile delinquency entitled "Community Responsibilities," in *Alianza* (June-July 1957), p. 9. Castro has served as chairman of the Drop-Out Committee of the Tucson Community Council and the Board of Directors of the Pío Décimo Center. He is a past president of the Pima County Legal Aid Society, the Pima County Tuberculosis and Health Association, and the Arizona County Attorneys and Sheriffs Association. He is also a former member of the Board of Directors of the YMCA, YWCA, Y Camp Board, Boy Scouts of America, Boys' Club of Tucson, and the Girls Living Center in Tucson. His involvement also includes participation in numerous other humanitarian activities, legal associations, and civic projects. *Alianza* (June-July 1958), p. 20; press release, n.d. [*ca.* 1972], in Biographical clipping file, Arizona Collection, Arizona State University Library.

The National Mexican-American Political Association in endorsing Castro noted his universal appeal and qualifications, stating that if elected Castro would be "the most responsive, effective, and sensitive in serving all the people." *Arizona Daily Star*, July 21, 1970.

40. For vote totals see *Phoenix Gazette*, September 9, 1970; *Arizona Republic*, November 5, 1970.

41. Coverage of the 1970 Democratic primary and general election campaigns is based on newspaper items from June through November 1970 in: *Arizona Republic, Phoenix Gazette, Arizona Daily Star, Tucson Daily Citizen, Yuma Daily Sun, Prescott Courier, Arizona Daily Sun, Scottsdale Daily Progress*, and *Mesa Tribune*. Only actual quotations are cited in these notes.

42. *Arizona Daily Star*, June 19, 1970.

43. For two excellent preelection analyses see *Arizona Daily Star*, October 28, 1970; and *Arizona Republic*, October 18, 1970.

44. *Phoenix Gazette*, November 4, 1970.

45. *Arizona Daily Sun*, November 21, 1970; *Phoenix Gazette*, October 29, 1970.

46. *Arizona Daily Star*, November 5, 1970; *Arizona Republic*, November 5, 1970.

47. Roger Timberlake, "Apathy by Black Voters Cited for Castro Defeat," *Tucson Daily Citizen*, November 19, 1970.

48. *Tucson Daily Citizen*, November 26, 1970.

49. *Arizona Republic*, January 15, 1971.

50. *Arizona Daily Star*, June 19, 1972.

51. See note 39.

52. Cathy Richardson, "Raul Castro, Governor Hopeful, Says Being Mexican is Asset," *Yuma Daily Sun*, June 21, 1970.